Mastering Concurrency Programming with Java 9

Second Edition

Fast, reactive and parallel application development

Javier Fernández González

BIRMINGHAM - MUMBAI

Mastering Concurrency Programming with Java 9

Second Edition

First published: February 2016

Second edition: July 2017

Production reference: 1140717

Published by Packt Publishing Ltd.
Livery Place
35 Livery Street
Birmingham
B3 2PB, UK.
ISBN 978-1-78588-794-9

www.packtpub.com

Credits

Author
Javier Fernández González

Reviewer
Miro Wengner

Commissioning Editor
Kunal Parikh

Acquisition Editor
Nitin Dasan

Content Development Editor
Nikhil Borkar

Technical Editor
Subhalaxmi Nadar

Copy Editor
Safis Editing

Project Coordinator
Vaidehi Sawant

Proofreader
Safis Editing

Indexer
Rekha Nair

Graphics
Abhinash Sahu

Production Coordinator
Melwyn Dsa

About the Author

Javier Fernández González is a software architect with almost 15 years of experience working with Java technologies. He has worked as a teacher, researcher, programmer, analyst, writer, and he now works as an architect in all types of projects related to Java, especially J2EE. As a teacher, has taken over 1,000 hours of training sessions in basic Java, J2EE, and the Struts framework. As a researcher, has worked in the field of information retrieval, developing applications for processing large amounts of data in Java, and he has participated in several journal articles and conference presentations as a coauthor. In recent years, has worked on developing J2EE web applications for various clients from different sectors (public administration, insurance, healthcare, transportation, and , many more). Currently, he works as a software architect. He is the author of *Java 7 Concurrency Cookbook*, *Mastering Concurrency Programming with Java 8, First Edition*, and *Java 9 Concurrency Cookbook, Second Edition*.

About the Reviewer

Miro Wengner has been a passionate JVM enthusiast since the moment he joined Sun Microsystems in 2002. He truly believes in distributed system design, concurrency, and parallel computing. One of Miro's biggest hobbies is the development of autonomous systems. He is one of the coauthors of and main contributors to the *Java open-source project Robo4J*. The Robo4J project's goal is to have a fun and outstanding experience in IoT application development.

Miro earns his daily bread by working on distributed web applications in a senior position.

I would like to thank my family and my wife, Tanja, for thier support during the reviewing of this book.

www.PacktPub.com

For support files and downloads related to your book, please visit www.PacktPub.com.

Did you know that Packt offers eBook versions of every book published, with PDF and ePub files available? You can upgrade to the eBook version at www.PacktPub.comand as a print book customer, you are entitled to a discount on the eBook copy. Get in touch with us at service@packtpub.com for more details.

At www.PacktPub.com, you can also read a collection of free technical articles, sign up for a range of free newsletters and receive exclusive discounts and offers on Packt books and eBooks.

https://www.packtpub.com/mapt

Get the most in-demand software skills with Mapt. Mapt gives you full access to all Packt books and video courses, as well as industry-leading tools to help you plan your personal development and advance your career.

Why subscribe?

- Fully searchable across every book published by Packt
- Copy and paste, print, and bookmark content
- On demand and accessible via a web browser

Customer Feedback

Thanks for purchasing this Packt book. At Packt, quality is at the heart of our editorial process. To help us improve, please leave us an honest review on this book's Amazon page at https://www.amazon.com/dp/1785887947.

If you'd like to join our team of regular reviewers, you can e-mail us at customerreviews@packtpub.com. We award our regular reviewers with free eBooks and videos in exchange for their valuable feedback. Help us be relentless in improving our products!

"To Nuria, Paula, and Pelayo, for you infinite love and patience"

Table of Contents

Preface

Nowadays, computer systems (and other related systems, such as tablets or smartphones) allow you to do several tasks at the same time. This is possible because they have concurrent operating systems that control several tasks at the same time. You can also have one application that executes several tasks (read a file, show a message, and read data over a network) if you work with the concurrency API of your favorite programming language. Java includes a very powerful concurrency API that allows you to implement any kind of concurrency applications with very little effort. This API increases the features provided to programmers in every version--now, in Java 8, it has included the Stream API and new methods and classes to facilitate the implementation of concurrent applications. This book covers the most important elements of the Java concurrency API, showing you how to use them in real-world applications. These elements are as follows:

- The Executor framework, to control the execution of a lot of tasks
- The Phaser class, to execute tasks that can be divided into phases
- The fork/join framework, to execute that tasks that solve a problem using the divide and conquer technique
- The Stream API, to process big sources of data, including the new reactive streams
- Concurrent data structures, to store the data in concurrent applications
- Synchronization mechanisms, to organize concurrent tasks

However, the Java concurrency API includes much more--a methodology to design concurrency applications, design patterns, tips and tricks to implement good concurrency applications, the tools and techniques to test concurrency applications, and ways to implement concurrency applications in other languages for the Java Virtual Machine, such as Clojure, Groovy, and Scala.

What this book covers

Chapter 1, *The First Step - Concurrency Design Principles*, covers the design principles of concurrency applications. You will also learn the possible problems of concurrency applications and a methodology to design them, accompanied by some design patterns, tips, and tricks.

Chapter 2, *Working with Basic Elements - Threads and Runnables*, explains how to work with the most basic elements to implement concurrent applications in the Java language: the Runnable interface and the Thread classes. With these elements, you can create a new execution thread that will be executed in parallel with the actual one.

Chapter 3, *Managing Lots of Threads - Executors*, covers the basic principles of the Executor framework. This framework allows you to work with lots of threads without creating or managing them. We will implement the k-nearest neighbors algorithm and a basic client/server application.

Chapter 4, *Getting the Most from Executors*, explores some advanced characteristics of Executors, including the cancellation and scheduling of tasks to execute a task after a delay or every certain period of time. We will implement an advanced client/server application and a news reader.

Chapter 5, *Getting Data from Tasks - The Callable and Future Interfaces*, explains how to work in an Executor with tasks that return a result using the Callable and Future interfaces. We will implement a best-matching algorithm and an application to build an inverted index.

Chapter 6, *Running Tasks Divided into Phases - The Phaser Class*, explains how to use the Phaser class to execute tasks that can be divided into phases in a concurrent way. We will implement a keyword extraction algorithm and a genetic algorithm.

Chapter 7, *Optimizing Divide and Conquer Solutions - The Fork/Join Framework*, explores the use of a special kind of Executor, optimized by those problems that can be resolved using the divide and conquer technique: the fork/join framework and its work-stealing algorithm. We will implement the k-means clustering algorithm, a data filtering algorithm, and the merge-sort algorithm.

Chapter 8, *Processing Massive Datasets with Parallel Streams - The Map and Reduce Model*, explains how to work with streams to process big datasets. In this chapter, you will learn how to implement map and reduce applications using the Stream API, and you will learn many more functions of streams. We will implement a numerical summarization algorithm and an information retrieval search tool.

Chapter 9, *Processing Massive Datasets with Parallel Streams - The Map and Collect Model*, explores how to use the collect method of the Stream API to perform a mutable reduction of a stream of data into a different data structure, including the predefined collectors defined in the Collectors class. We will implement a tool for searching data without indexing, a recommendation system, and an algorithm to calculate the list of common contacts of two persons on a social network.

Chapter 10, *Asynchronous Stream Processing – Reactive Streams*, explains how to implement a concurrent application using reactive streams that defines a standard for asynchronous stream processing with non-blocking back pressure. The basic principles of this kind of streams are defined at `http://www.reactive-streams.org/`, and Java 9 provides the basic interfaces necessary for its implementation.

Chapter 11, *Diving into Concurrent Data Structures and Synchronization Utilities*, covers how to work with the most important concurrent data structures (data structures that can be used in concurrent applications without causing data race conditions) and all the synchronization mechanisms included in the Java concurrency API to organize the execution of tasks.

Chapter 12, *Testing and Monitoring Concurrent Applications*, explains how to obtain information about the status of some of the Java concurrency API elements (Thread, Lock, Executor, and so on). You will also learn how to monitor a concurrent application using the Java VisualVM application and how to test concurrent applications with the MultithreadedTC library and the Java Pathfinder application.

Chapter 13, *Concurrency in JVM – Clojure and Groovy with the Gpars Library and Scala*, explores how to implement concurrent applications in other languages for the Java Virtual Machine. You will learn how to use the concurrent elements provided by the Clojure and Scala programming languages and the GPars library with the Groovy programming language.

What you need for this book

To follow this book, you need basic to medium-level knowledge of the Java programming language. A basic knowledge of concurrency concepts is welcome too.

Who this book is for

If you are a Java developer who knows the basic principles of concurrent programming but wants to become an expert user of the Java concurrency API in order to develop optimized applications that take advantage of all the hardware resources of computers, this book is for you.

Conventions

In this book, you will find a number of text styles that distinguish between different kinds of information. Here are some examples of these styles and an explanation of their meaning. Code words in text, database table names, folder names, filenames, file extensions, pathnames, dummy URLs, user input, and Twitter handles are shown as follows: "The `modify()` method is not atomic and the `Account` class is not thread-safe."

A block of code is set as follows:

```
public void task2() {
    section2_1();
    commonObject2.notify();
    commonObject1.wait();
    section2_2();
}
```

New terms and **important words** are shown in bold. Words that you see on the screen, for example, in menus or dialog boxes, appear in the text like this: "The **Classes** tab shows you information about the class loading"

 Warnings or important notes appear like this.

 Tips and tricks appear like this.

Reader feedback

Feedback from our readers is always welcome. Let us know what you think about this book-what you liked or disliked. Reader feedback is important for us as it helps us develop titles that you will really get the most out of. To send us general feedback, simply e-mail feedback@packtpub.com, and mention the book's title in the subject of your message. If there is a topic that you have expertise in and you are interested in either writing or contributing to a book, see our author guide at www.packtpub.com/authors.

Customer support

Now that you are the proud owner of a Packt book, we have a number of things to help you to get the most from your purchase.

Downloading the example code

You can download the example code files for this book from your account at `http://www.packtpub.com`. If you purchased this book elsewhere, you can visit `http://www.packtpub.com/support` and register to have the files e-mailed directly to you. You can download the code files by following these steps:

1. Log in or register to our website using your e-mail address and password.
2. Hover the mouse pointer on the **SUPPORT** tab at the top.
3. Click on **Code Downloads & Errata**.
4. Enter the name of the book in the **Search** box.
5. Select the book for which you're looking to download the code files.
6. Choose from the drop-down menu where you purchased this book from.
7. Click on **Code Download**.

Once the file is downloaded, please make sure that you unzip or extract the folder using the latest version of:

- WinRAR / 7-Zip for Windows
- Zipeg / iZip / UnRarX for Mac
- 7-Zip / PeaZip for Linux

The code bundle for the book is also hosted on GitHub at `https://github.com/PacktPublishing/Mastering-Concurrency-Programming-with-Java-9-Second-Edition`. We also have other code bundles from our rich catalog of books and videos available at `https://github.com/PacktPublishing/`. Check them out!

Errata

Although we have taken every care to ensure the accuracy of our content, mistakes do happen. If you find a mistake in one of our books-maybe a mistake in the text or the code-we would be grateful if you could report this to us. By doing so, you can save other readers from frustration and help us improve subsequent versions of this book. If you find any errata, please report them by visiting http://www.packtpub.com/submit-errata, selecting your book, clicking on the **Errata Submission Form** link, and entering the details of your errata. Once your errata are verified, your submission will be accepted and the errata will be uploaded to our website or added to any list of existing errata under the Errata section of that title. To view the previously submitted errata, go to https://www.packtpub.com/books/content/support and enter the name of the book in the search field. The required information will appear under the **Errata** section.

Piracy

Piracy of copyrighted material on the Internet is an ongoing problem across all media. At Packt, we take the protection of our copyright and licenses very seriously. If you come across any illegal copies of our works in any form on the Internet, please provide us with the location address or website name immediately so that we can pursue a remedy. Please contact us at copyright@packtpub.com with a link to the suspected pirated material. We appreciate your help in protecting our authors and our ability to bring you valuable content.

Questions

If you have a problem with any aspect of this book, you can contact us at questions@packtpub.com, and we will do our best to address the problem.

1

The First Step - Concurrency Design Principles

Users of computer systems are always looking for better performance of their systems. They want to get higher quality videos, better video games, and faster network speeds. Some years ago, processors gave better performance to users by increasing their speed. But now, processors don't increase their speed. Instead of this, they add more cores so that the operating system can execute more than one task at a time. This is called **concurrency**. Concurrent programming includes all the tools and techniques to have multiple tasks or processes running at the same time in a computer, communicating and synchronizing between them without data loss or inconsistency. In this chapter, we will cover the following topics:

- Basic concurrency concepts
- Possible problems in concurrent applications
- A methodology to design concurrent algorithms
- Java Concurrency API
- Concurrency design patterns
- Tips and tricks to design concurrency algorithms

Basic concurrency concepts

First of all, let's present the basic concepts of concurrency. You must understand these concepts to follow the rest of the book.

Concurrency versus parallelism

Concurrency and parallelism are very similar concepts. Different authors give different definitions for these concepts. The most accepted definition talks about concurrency as being when you have more than one task in a single processor with a single core. In this case, the operating system's task scheduler quickly switches from one task to another, so it seems that all the tasks run simultaneously. The same definition talks about parallelism as being when you have more than one task running simultaneously on different computers, processors, or cores inside a processor.

Another definition talks about concurrency being when you have more than one task (different tasks) that run simultaneously on your system. Yet another definition discusses parallelism as being when you have different instances of the same task that run simultaneously over different parts of a dataset.

The last definition talks about parallelism being when you have more than one task that runs simultaneously in your system and talks about concurrency as a way to explain the different techniques and mechanisms the programmer has to synchronize with the tasks and their access to shared resources.

As you can see, both concepts are very similar, and this similarity has increased with the development of multicore processors.

Synchronization

In concurrency, we can define **synchronization** as the coordination of two or more tasks to get the desired results. We have two kinds of synchronization:

- **Control synchronization**: When, for example, one task depends on the end of another task, the second task can't start before the first has finished
- **Data access synchronization**: When two or more tasks have access to a shared variable and only one of the tasks can access the variable

A concept closely related to synchronization is **critical section**. A critical section is a piece of code that can be only executed by one task at a time because of its access to a shared resource. **Mutual exclusion** is the mechanism used to guarantee this requirement and can be implemented in different ways.

Keep in mind that synchronization helps you avoid some errors you might have with concurrent tasks (they will be described later in this chapter), but it introduces some overhead to your algorithm. You have to calculate the number of tasks very carefully, which can be performed independently without intercommunication you will have in your parallel algorithm. It's the **granularity** of your concurrent algorithm. If you have a **coarse-grained granularity** (big tasks with low intercommunication), the overhead due to synchronization will be low. However, maybe you won't benefit from all the cores of your system. If you have a **fine-grained granularity** (small tasks with high intercommunication), the overhead due to synchronization will be high, and perhaps the throughput of your algorithm won't be good.

There are different mechanisms to get synchronization in a concurrent system. The most popular mechanisms from a theoretical point of view are:

- **Semaphore**: A semaphore is a mechanism that can be used to control the access to one or more units of a resource. It has a variable that stores the number of resources that can be used and two atomic operations to manage the value of the variable. A **mutex** (short for **mutual exclusion**) is a special kind of semaphore that can take only two values (*resource is free* and *resource is busy*), and only the process that sets the mutex to *busy* can release it. A mutex can help you to avoid race conditions by protecting a critical section.
- **Monitor**: A monitor is a mechanism to get mutual exclusion over a shared resource. It has a mutex, a condition variable, and two operations to wait for the condition and signal the condition. Once you signal the condition, only one of the tasks that are waiting for it continues with its execution.

The last concept related to synchronization you're going to learn in this chapter is **thread safety**. A piece of code (or a method or an object) is **thread-safe** if all the users of shared data are protected by synchronization mechanisms. A non-blocking, **compare-and-swap (CAS)** primitive of the data is immutable, so you can use that code in a concurrent application without any problems.

Immutable object

An **immutable object** is an object with a very special characteristic. You can't modify its visible state (the value of its attributes) after its initialization. If you want to modify an immutable object, you have to create a new one.

Its main advantage is that it is thread-safe. You can use it in concurrent applications without any problem.

An example of an immutable object is the `String` class in Java. When you assign a new value to a `String` object, you are creating a new one.

Atomic operations and variables

An **atomic operation** is a kind of operation that appears to occur instantaneously to the rest of the tasks of the program. In a concurrent application, you can implement an atomic operation with a critical section to the whole operation using a synchronization mechanism.

An **atomic variable** is a kind of variable that has atomic operations to set and get its value. You can implement an atomic variable using a synchronization mechanism or in a lock-free manner using CAS that doesn't need synchronization.

Shared memory versus message passing

Tasks can use two different methods to communicate with each other. The first one is **shared memory** and, normally, it is used when the tasks are running on the same computer. The tasks use the same memory area where they write and read values. To avoid problems, the access to this shared memory has to be in a critical section protected by a synchronization mechanism.

The other synchronization mechanism is **message passing** and, normally, it is used when the tasks are running on different computers. When tasks needs to communicate with another, it sends a message that follows a predefined protocol. This communication can be synchronous if the sender keeps it blocked waiting for a response or asynchronous if the sender continues with their execution after sending the message.

Possible problems in concurrent applications

Programming a concurrent application is not an easy job. Incorrect use of the synchronization mechanisms can create different problems with the tasks in your application. In this section, we describe some of these problems.

Data race

You can have a **data race** (also named **race condition**) in your application when you have two or more tasks writing a shared variable outside a critical section, that's to say, without using any synchronization mechanisms.

Under these circumstances, the final result of your application may depend on the order or execution of the tasks. Look at the following example:

```
package com.packt.java.concurrency;

public class Account {

  private float balance;

  public void modify (float difference) {

    float value=this.balance;
    this.balance=value+difference;
  }

}
```

Imagine that two different tasks execute the modify() method in the same Account object. Depending on the order of execution of the sentences in the tasks, the final result can vary. Suppose that the initial balance is 1000 and the two tasks call the modify() method with 1000 as a parameter. The final result should be 3000, but if both tasks execute the first sentence at the same time and then the second sentence at the same time, the final result will be 2000. As you can see, the modify() method is not atomic and the Account class is not thread-safe.

Deadlock

There is a **deadlock** in your concurrent application when there are two or more tasks waiting for a shared resource that must be free from another thread that is waiting for another shared resource that must be free by one of the first ones. It happens when four conditions happen simultaneously in the system. They are the **Coffman conditions**, which are as follows:

- **Mutual exclusion**: The resources involved in the deadlock must be nonshareable. Only one task can use the resource at a time.
- **Hold and wait condition**: A task has the mutual exclusion for a resource and it's requesting the mutual exclusion for another resource. While it's waiting, it doesn't release any resources.
- **No pre-emption**: The resources can only be released by the tasks that hold them.
- **Circular wait**: There is a circular waiting where *Task 1* is waiting for a resource that is being held by *Task 2*, which is waiting for a resource being held by *Task 3*, and so on until we have *Task n* that is waiting for a resource being held by *Task 1*.

Some mechanisms exist that you can use to avoid deadlocks:

- **Ignore them**: This is the most commonly used mechanism. You suppose that a deadlock will never occur on your system, and if it occurs, you can see the consequences of stopping your application and having to re-execute it.
- **Detection**: The system has a special task that analyzes the state of the system to detect whether a deadlock has occurred. If it detects a deadlock, it can take action to remedy the problem. For example, finishing one task or forcing the liberation of a resource.
- **Prevention**: If you want to prevent deadlocks in your system, you have to prevent one or more of the Coffman conditions.
- **Avoidance**: Deadlocks can be avoided if you have information about the resources that are used by a task before it begins its execution. When a task wants to start its execution, you can analyze the resources that are free in the system and the resources that the task needs so it is able to decide whether it can start its execution or not.

Livelock

A **livelock** occurs when you have two tasks in your system that are always changing their states due to the actions of the other. Consequently, they are in a loop of state changes and unable to continue.

For example, you have two tasks - *Task 1* and *Task 2*, and both need two resources - *Resource 1* and *Resource 2*. Suppose that *Task 1* has a lock on *Resource 1*, and *Task 2* has a lock on *Resource 2*. As they are unable to gain access to the resource they need, they free their resources and begin the cycle again. This situation can continue indefinitely, so the tasks will never end their execution.

Resource starvation

Resource starvation occurs when you have a task in your system that never gets a resource that it needs to continue with its execution. When there is more than one task waiting for a resource and the resource is released, the system has to choose the next task that can use it. If your system doesn't have a good algorithm, it can have threads that are waiting for a long time for the resource.

Fairness is the solution to this problem. All the tasks that are waiting for a resource must have the resource in a given period of time. An option is to implement an algorithm that takes into account the time that a task has been waiting for a resource when it chooses the next task that will hold a resource. However, fair implementation of locks requires additional overhead, which may lower your program throughput.

Priority inversion

Priority inversion occurs when a low priority task holds a resource that is needed by a high priority task, so the low priority task finishes its execution before the high priority task.

A methodology to design concurrent algorithms

In this section, we're going to propose a five-step methodology to get a concurrent version of a sequential algorithm. It's based on the one presented by Intel in their *Threading Methodology: Principles and Practices* document.

The starting point - a sequential version of the algorithm

Our starting point to implement a concurrent algorithm will be a sequential version of the algorithm. Of course, we could design a concurrent algorithm from scratch, but I think that a sequential version of the algorithm will give us two advantages:

- We can use the sequential algorithm to test whether our concurrent algorithm generates correct results. Both algorithms must generate the same output when they receive the same input, so we can detect some problems in the concurrent version, such as data races or similar conditions.
- We can measure the throughput of both algorithms to see if the use of concurrency gives us a real improvement in the response time or in the amount of data the algorithm can process in a time.

Step 1 - analysis

In this step, we are going to analyze the sequential version of the algorithm to look for the parts of its code that can be executed in a parallel way. We should pay special attention to those parts that are executed most of the time or that execute more code because, by implementing a concurrent version of those parts, we're going to get a greater performance improvement.

Good candidates for this process are loops, where one step is independent of the other steps, or portions of code are independent of other parts of the code (for example, an algorithm to initialize an application that opens the connections with the database, loads the configuration files, and initializes some objects; all these tasks are independent of each other).

Step 2 - design

Once you know what parts of the code you are going to parallelize, you have to decide how to do that parallelization.

The changes in the code will affect two main parts of the application:

- The structure of the code
- The organization of the data structures

You can take two different approaches to accomplish this task:

- **Task decomposition**: You do task decomposition when you split the code into two or more independent tasks that can be executed at once. Maybe some of these tasks have to be executed in a given order or have to wait at the same point. You must use synchronization mechanisms to get this behavior.
- **Data decomposition**: You do data decomposition when you have multiple instances of the same task that work with a subset of the dataset. This dataset will be a shared resource, so if the tasks need to modify the data, you have to protect access to it, implementing a critical section.

Another important point to keep in mind is the granularity of your solution. The objective of implementing a parallel version of an algorithm is to achieve improved performance, so you should use all the available processors or cores. On the other hand, when you use a synchronization mechanism, you introduce some extra instructions that must be executed. If you split the algorithm into a lot of small tasks (fine-grained granularity), the extra code introduced by the synchronization can provoke performance degradation. If you split the algorithm into fewer tasks than cores (coarse-grained granularity), you are not taking advantage of all resources. Also, you must take into account the work every thread must do, especially if you implement a fine-grained granularity. If you have a task longer than the rest, that task will determine the execution time of the application. You have to find the equilibrium between these two points.

Step 3 - implementation

The next step is to implement the parallel algorithm using a programming language and, if it's necessary, a thread library. In the examples of this book, you are going to use Java to implement all the algorithms.

Step 4 - testing

After finishing the implementation, you should test the parallel algorithm. If you have a sequential version of the algorithm, you can compare the results of both algorithms to verify that your parallel implementation is correct.

Testing and debugging a parallel implementation are difficult tasks because the order of execution of the different tasks of the application is not guaranteed. In Chapter 12, *Testing and Monitoring Concurrent Applications*, you will learn tips, tricks, and tools to do these tasks efficiently.

Step 5 - tuning

The last step is to compare the throughput of the parallel and the sequential algorithms. If the results are not as expected, you must review the algorithm, looking for the cause of the bad performance of the parallel algorithm.

You can also test different parameters of the algorithm (for example, granularity, or number of tasks) to find the best configuration.

There are different metrics to measure the possible performance improvement you can obtain parallelizing an algorithm. The three most popular metrics are:

- **Speedup**: This is a metric for relative performance improvements between the parallel and the sequential versions of the algorithm:

$$Speedup = \frac{T_{sequential}}{T_{concurrent}}$$

  Here, $T_{sequential}$ is the execution time of the sequential version of the algorithm and $T_{concurrent}$ is the execution time of the parallel version.

- **Amdahl's law**: Used to calculate the maximum expected improvement obtained with the parallelization of an algorithm:

$$Speedup \leq \frac{1}{(1-p)+\dfrac{P}{N}}$$

  Here, P is the percentage of code that can be parallelized and N is the number of cores of the computer where you're going to execute the algorithm.

  For example, if you can parallelize 75% of the code and you have four cores, the maximum speedup will be given by the following formula:

$$Speedup \leq \frac{1}{(1-0.75)+\left(\dfrac{0.75}{4}\right)} \leq \frac{1}{0.44} \leq 2.29$$

- **Gustafson-Barsis' law**: Amdahl's law has a limitation. It supposes that you have the same input dataset when you increase the number of cores, but normally, when you have more cores, you want to process more data. Gustafson's law proposes that when you have more cores available, bigger problems can be solved at the same time using the following formula:

$$Speedup = P - \alpha * (P - 1)$$

Here, N is the number of cores and P is the percentage of parallelizable code.

If we use the same example as before, the scaled speedup calculated by the Gustafson law is:

$$Speedup = 4 - 0.25 * (3) = 3.25$$

Conclusion

In this section, you learned some important issues you have to take into account when you want to parallelize a sequential algorithm.

First of all, not every algorithm can be parallelized. For example, if you have to execute a loop where the result of iteration depends on the result of the previous iteration, you can't parallelize that loop. Recurrent algorithms are another example of algorithms that can be parallelized for a similar reason.

Another important thing you have to keep in mind is that the sequential version with better performance of an algorithm can be a bad starting point to parallelize it. If you start parallelizing an algorithm and you find yourself in trouble because you cannot easily find independent portions of the code, you have to look for other versions of the algorithm and verify that the version can be parallelized in an easier way.

Finally, when you implement a concurrent application (from scratch or based on a sequential algorithm), you must take into account the following points:

- **Efficiency**: The parallel algorithm must end in less time than the sequential algorithm. The first goal of parallelizing an algorithm is that its running time is less than the sequential one, or it can process more data in the same time.

- **Simplicity**: When you implement an algorithm (parallel or not), you must keep it as simple as possible. It will be easier to implement, test, debug, and maintain, and it will have less errors.
- **Portability**: Your parallel algorithm should be executed on different platforms with minimum changes. As in this book you will use Java, this point will be very easy. With Java, you can execute your programs on every operating system without any changes (if you implement the program as you must).
- **Scalability**: What happens to your algorithm if you increase the number of cores? As mentioned before, you should use every available core so your algorithm is ready to take advantage of all available resources.

Java Concurrency API

The Java programming language has a very rich concurrency API. It contains classes to manage the basic elements of concurrency, such as `Thread`, `Lock`, and `Semaphore`, and classes that implement very high-level synchronization mechanisms, such as the **executor** framework or the new parallel `Stream` API.

In this section, we will cover the basic classes that form the concurrency API.

Basic concurrency classes

The basic classes of the Concurrency API are:

- **The Thread class**: This class represents all the threads that execute a concurrent Java application
- **The Runnable interface**: This is another way to create concurrent applications in Java
- **The ThreadLocal class**: This is a class to store variables locally to a thread
- **The ThreadFactory interface**: This is the base of the `Factory` design pattern, that you can use to create customized threads

Synchronization mechanisms

The Java Concurrency API includes different synchronization mechanisms that allow you to:

- Define a critical section to access a shared resource
- Synchronize different tasks at a common point

The following mechanisms are the most important synchronization mechanisms:

- **The synchronized keyword**: The `synchronized` keyword allows you to define a critical section in a block of code or in an entire method.
- **The Lock interface**: `Lock` provides a more flexible synchronization operation than the `synchronized` keyword. There are different kinds of Locks: `ReentrantLock`, to implement a Lock that can be associated with a condition; `ReentrantReadWriteLock` that separates the read and write operations; and `StampedLock`, a new feature of Java 8 that includes three modes for controlling read/write access.
- **The Semaphore class**: The class that implements the classical semaphore to implement the synchronization. Java supports binary and general semaphores.
- **The CountDownLatch class**: A class that allows a task to wait for the finalization of multiple operations.
- **The CyclicBarrier class**: A class that allows the synchronization of multiple threads at a common point.
- **The Phaser class**: A class that allows you to control the execution of tasks divided into phases. None of the tasks advance to the next phase until all of the tasks have finished the current phase.

Executors

The executor framework is a mechanism that allows you to separate thread creation and management for the implementation of concurrent tasks. You don't have to worry about the creation and management of threads, only to create tasks and send them to the executor. The main classes involved in this framework are:

- **The Executor and ExecutorService interface**: This includes the `execute()` method common to all executors
- **ThreadPoolExecutor**: This is a class that allows you to get an executor with a pool of threads and, optionally, define a maximum number of parallel tasks

- **ScheduledThreadPoolExecutor**: This is a special kind of executor to allow you to execute tasks after a delay or periodically
- **Executors**: This is a class that facilitates the creation of executors
- **The Callable interface**: This is an alternative to the `Runnable` interface - a separate task that can return a value
- **The Future interface**: This is an interface that includes the methods to obtain the value returned by a `Callable` interface and to control its status

The fork/join framework

The **fork/join** framework defines a special kind of executor specialized in the resolution of problems with the divide and conquer technique. It includes a mechanism to optimize the execution of the concurrent tasks that solve these kinds of problems. Fork/Join is specially tailored for fine-grained parallelism, as it has very low overhead in order to place the new tasks into the queue and take queued tasks for execution. The main classes and interfaces involved in this framework are:

- `ForkJoinPool`: This is a class that implements the executor that is going to run the tasks
- `ForkJoinTask`: This is a task that can be executed in the `ForkJoinPool` class
- `ForkJoinWorkerThread`: This is a thread that is going to execute tasks in the `ForkJoinPool` class

Parallel streams

Streams and **lambda expressions** were the two most important new features of the Java 8 version. Streams have been added as a method in the `Collection` interface and other data sources and allow the processing of all elements of a data structure generating new structures, filtering data, and implementing algorithms using the map and reduce technique.

A special kind of stream is a parallel stream that realizes its operations in a parallel way. The most important elements involved in the use of parallel streams are:

- **The Stream interface**: This is an interface that defines all the operations that you can perform on a stream.
- **Optional**: This is a container object that may or may not contain a non-null value.

- **Collectors**: This is a class that implements reduction operations that can be used as part of a stream sequence of operations.
- **Lambda expressions**: Streams have been thought of to work with Lambda expressions. Most of stream methods accept a lambda expression as a parameter. This allows you to implement a more compact version of operations.

Concurrent data structures

Normal data structures of the Java API (`ArrayList`, `Hashtable`, and so on) are not ready to work in a concurrent application unless you use an external synchronization mechanism. If you use it, you will be adding a lot of extra computing time to your application. If you don't use it, it's probable that you will add race conditions to your application. If you modify them from several threads and race conditions occur, you may experience various exceptions (such as, `ConcurrentModificationException` and `ArrayIndexOutOfBoundsException`), silent data loss, or your program may even get stuck in an endless loop.

The Java Concurrency API includes a lot of data structures that can be used in concurrent applications without risk. We can classify them into two groups:

- **Blocking data structures**: These include methods that block the calling task when, for example, the data structure is empty and you want to get a value.
- **Non-blocking data structures:** If the operation can be made immediately, it won't block the calling tasks. It returns a null value or throws an exception.

These are some of the data structures:

- `ConcurrentLinkedDeque`: This is a non-blocking list
- `ConcurrentLinkedQueue`: This is a non-blocking queue
- `LinkedBlockingDeque`: This is a blocking list
- `LinkedBlockingQueue`: This is a blocking queue
- `PriorityBlockingQueue`: This is a blocking queue that orders its elements based on their priority
- `ConcurrentSkipListMap`: This is a non-blocking navigable map
- `ConcurrentHashMap`: This is a non-blocking hash map
- `AtomicBoolean`, `AtomicInteger`, `AtomicLong`, and `AtomicReference`: These are atomic implementations of the basic Java data types

Concurrency design patterns

In software engineering, a **design pattern** is a solution to a common problem. This solution has been used many times, and it has proved to be an optimal solution to the problem. You can use them to avoid 'reinventing the wheel' every time you have to solve one of these problems. **Singleton** or **Factory** are examples of common design patterns used in almost every application.

Concurrency also has its own design patterns. In this section, we describe some of the most useful concurrency design patterns and their implementation in the Java language.

Signaling

This design pattern explains how to implement the situation where a task has to notify an event to another task. The easiest way to implement this pattern is with a semaphore or a mutex, using the `ReentrantLock` or `Semaphore` classes of the Java language or even the `wait()` and `notify()` methods included in the `Object` class.

See the following example:

```
public void task1() {
   section1();
   commonObject.notify();
}

public void task2() {
   commonObject.wait();
   section2();
}
```

Under these circumstances, the `section2()` method will always be executed after the `section1()` method.

Rendezvous

This design pattern is a generalization of the **Signaling** pattern. In this case, the first task waits for an event of the second task and the second task waits for an event of the first task. The solution is similar to that of Signaling, but in this case, you must use two objects instead of one.

See the following example:

```
public void task1() {
  section1_1();
  commonObject1.notify();
  commonObject2.wait();
  section1_2();
}
public void task2() {
  section2_1();
  commonObject2.notify();
  commonObject1.wait();
  section2_2();
}
```

Under these circumstances, section2_2() will always be executed after section1_1() and section1_2() after section2_1(). Take into account that if you put the call to the wait() method before the call to the notify() method, you will have a deadlock.

Mutex

A mutex is a mechanism that you can use to implement a critical section, ensuring the mutual exclusion. That is to say, only one task can execute the portion of code protected by the mutex at once. In Java, you can implement a critical section using the synchronized keyword (that allows you to protect a portion of code or a full method), the ReentrantLock class, or the Semaphore class.

Look at the following example:

```
public void task() {
  preCriticalSection();
  try {
    lockObject.lock() // The critical section begins
    criticalSection();
  } catch (Exception e) {

  } finally {
    lockObject.unlock(); // The critical section ends
     postCriticalSection();
  }
}
```

Multiplex

The **Multiplex design pattern** is a generalization of the Mutex. In this case, a determined number of tasks can execute the critical section at once. It is useful, for example, when you have multiple copies of a resource. The easiest way to implement this design pattern in Java is using the `Semaphore` class initialized to the number of tasks that can execute the critical section at once.

Look at the following example:

```
public void task() {
  preCriticalSection();
  semaphoreObject.acquire();
  criticalSection();
  semaphoreObject.release();
  postCriticalSection();
}
```

Barrier

This design pattern explains how to implement the situation where you need to synchronize some tasks at a common point. None of the tasks can continue with their execution until all the tasks have arrived at the synchronization point. Java Concurrency API provides the `CyclicBarrier` class, which is an implementation of this design pattern.

Look at the following example:

```
public void task() {
  preSyncPoint();
  barrierObject.await();
  postSyncPoint();
}
```

Double-checked locking

This design pattern provides a solution to the problem that occurs when you acquire a lock and then check for a condition. If the condition is false, you have the overhead of acquiring the lock ideally. An example of this situation is the lazy initialization of objects. If you have a class implementing the `Singleton` design pattern, you may have some code like this:

```
public class Singleton{
  private static Singleton reference;
  private static final Lock lock=new ReentrantLock();
```

```
  public static Singleton getReference() {
    try {
      lock.lock();
      if (reference==null) {
        reference=new Object();
      }
    } catch (Exception e) {
        System.out.println(e);
    } finally {
        lock.unlock();
    }
    return reference;
  }
}
```

A possible solution could be to include the lock inside the conditions:

```
public class Singleton{
  private Object reference;
  private Lock lock=new ReentrantLock();
  public Object getReference() {
    if (reference==null) {
      lock.lock();
      if (reference == null) {
        reference=new Object();
      }
      lock.unlock();
    }
    return reference;
  }
}
```

This solution still has problems. If two tasks check the condition at once, you will create two objects. The best solution to this problem doesn't use any explicit synchronization mechanisms:

```
public class Singleton {

  private static class LazySingleton {
    private static final Singleton INSTANCE = new Singleton();
  }

  public static Singleton getSingleton() {
    return LazySingleton.INSTANCE;
  }

}
```

Read-write lock

When you protect access to a shared variable with a lock, only one task can access that variable, independently of the operation you are going to perform on it. Sometimes, you will have variables that you modify a few times but you read many times. In this circumstance, a lock provides poor performance because all the read operations can be made concurrently without any problem. To solve this problem, we can use the read-write lock design pattern. This pattern defines a special kind of lock with two internal locks: one for read operations and another for write operations. The behavior of this lock is as follows:

- If one task is doing a read operation and another task wants to do another read operation, it can do it
- If one task is doing a read operation and another task wants to do a write operation, it's blocked until all the readers finish
- If one task is doing a write operation and another task wants to do an operation (read or write), it's blocked until the writer finishes

The Java Concurrency API includes the class ReentrantReadWriteLock that implements this design pattern. If you want to implement this pattern from scratch, you have to be very careful with the priority between read-tasks and write-tasks. If too many read-tasks exist, write-tasks can be waiting too long.

Thread pool

This design pattern tries to remove the overhead introduced by creating a thread per task you want to execute. It's formed by a set of threads and a queue of tasks you want to execute. The set of threads usually has a fixed size. When a thread finishes the execution of a task, it doesn't finish its execution. It looks for another task in the queue. If there is another task, it executes it. If not, the thread waits until a task is inserted in the queue, but it's not destroyed.

The Java Concurrency API includes some classes that implement the ExecutorService interface that internally uses a pool of threads.

Thread local storage

This design pattern defines how to use global or static variables locally to tasks. When you have a static attribute in a class, all the objects of a class access the same occurrences of the attribute. If you use thread local storage, each thread accesses a different instance of the variable.

The Java Concurrency API includes the `ThreadLocal` class to implement this design pattern.

Tips and tricks for designing concurrent algorithms

In this section, we have compiled some tips and tricks you have to keep in mind to design good concurrent applications.

Identifying the correct independent tasks

You can only execute concurrent tasks that are independent of each other. If you have two or more tasks with an order dependency between them, maybe it doesn't interest you to try to execute them concurrently and include a synchronization mechanism to guarantee the execution order. The tasks will execute in a sequential way, and you will have to overcome the synchronization mechanism. A different situation is when you have a task with some prerequisites, but these prerequisites are independent of each other. In this case, you can execute the prerequisites concurrently and then use a synchronization class to control the execution of the task after you finish all the prerequisites.

Another situation where you can't use concurrency is when you have a loop, and all the steps use data generated in the step before, or there is some status information that goes from one step to the next step.

Implementing concurrency at the highest possible level

Rich threading APIs, such as the Java Concurrency API, offer you different classes to implement concurrency in your applications. In the case of Java, you can control the creation and synchronization of threads using the `Thread` or `Lock` classes, but it also offers you high-level concurrency objects, such as executors or the fork/join framework, that allow you to execute concurrent tasks. This high-level mechanism offers you the following benefits:

- You don't have to worry about the creation and management of threads. You only create tasks and send it to execute. The Java Concurrency API controls the creation and management of threads for you.
- They are optimized to give better performance than using threads directly. For example, they use a pool of threads to reuse and avoid thread creation for every task. You can implement these mechanisms from scratch, but it will take you a lot of time, and it will be a complex task.
- They include advanced features that make the API more powerful. For example, with executors in Java, you can execute tasks that return a result in the form of a Future object. Again, you can implement these mechanisms from scratch, but it's not advisable.
- Your application will be migrated more easily from one operating system to another, and it will be more scalable.
- Your application might become faster in future Java versions. Java developers constantly improve the internals, and JVM optimizations will be likely more tailored for JDK APIs.

In summary, for performance and development time reasons, analyze the high-level mechanisms your thread API offers you before implementing your concurrent algorithm.

Taking scalability into account

One of the main objectives, when you implement a concurrent algorithm, is to take advantage of all the resources of your computer, especially the number of processors or cores. But this number may change over time. Hardware is constantly evolving and its cost becomes lower each year.

When you design a concurrent algorithm using data decomposition, don't presuppose the number of cores or processors that your application will execute on. Get the information of the system dynamically (for example, in Java, you can get it with the method `Runtime.getRuntime().availableProcessors()`) and make your algorithm use that information to calculate the number of tasks it's going to execute. This process will have an overhead over the execution time of your algorithm, but your algorithm will be more scalable.

If you design a concurrent algorithm using task decomposition, the situation can be more difficult. You depend on the number of independent tasks you have in the algorithm and forcing a greater number of tasks will increment the overhead introduced by synchronization mechanisms and the global performance of the application can be even worse. Analyze in detail the algorithm to determine whether you can have a dynamic number of tasks or not.

Using thread-safe APIs

If you need to use a Java library in a concurrent application, read its documentation first to know whether it's thread-safe or not. If it's thread-safe, you can use it in your application without any problem. If it's not, you have the following two options:

- If a thread-safe alternative exists, you should use it
- If a thread-safe alternative doesn't exist, you should add the necessary synchronization to avoid all possible problematic situations, especially data race conditions

For example, if you need a List in a concurrent application, you should not use the `ArrayList` class if you are going to update it from several threads, because it's not thread-safe. In this case, you can use a thread-safe class such as `ConcurrentLinkedDeque`, `CopyOnWriteArrayList`, or `LinkedBlockingDeque`. If the class you want to use is not thread-safe, first you must look for the thread-safe alternative. It will probably be more optimized to work with concurrency than any alternative that you can implement.

Never assume an execution order

The execution of tasks in a concurrent application when you don't use any synchronization mechanisms is nondeterministic. The order of execution of the tasks and the time each task is in execution is determined by the scheduler of the operating system. It doesn't care if you observe that the execution order is the same in a number of executions. The next one could be different.

The result of this assumption used to be a data race problem. The final result of your algorithm depends on the execution order of the tasks. Sometimes, the result can be correct, but at other times, it can be incorrect. It can be very difficult to detect the cause of data race conditions, so you must be careful not to forget all the necessary synchronization elements.

Preferring local thread variables over static and shared when possible

Thread local variables are a special kind of variables. Every task will have an independent value for this variable, so you don't need any synchronization mechanisms to protect the access to this variable.

This can sound a little strange. Every object has its own copy of the attributes of the class, so why do we need the thread local variables? Consider this situation. You create a `Runnable` task and you want to execute multiple instances of that task. You can create a `Runnable` object per thread you want to execute, but another option is to create a `Runnable` object and use that object to create all the threads. In the last case, all the threads will have access to the same copy of the attributes of the class, except if you use the `ThreadLocal` class. The `ThreadLocal` class guarantees you that every thread will access its own instance of the variable without the use of a Lock, a semaphore, or a similar class.

Another situation when you can take advantage of the `Thread` local variables is with static attributes. All instances of a class share static attributes, except you declare them with the `ThreadLocal` class. In this case, every thread will have access to its own copy.

Another option you have is to use something like `ConcurrentHashMap<Thread, MyType>` and use it like `var.get(Thread.currentThread())` or `var.put(Thread.currentThread(), newValue)`. Usually, this approach is significantly slower than `ThreadLocal` because of possible contention (`ThreadLocal` has no contention at all). It has an advantage though: you can clear the map completely and the value will disappear for every thread, thus, sometimes it's useful to use such an approach.

Finding the easier parallelizable version of the algorithm

We can define an algorithm as a sequence of steps to solve a problem. There are different ways to solve the same problem. Some are faster, some use less resources, and others fit better with special characteristics of the input data. For example, if you want to order a set of numbers, you can use one of the multiple sorting algorithms that have been implemented.

In a previous section of this chapter, we recommended you use a sequential algorithm as the starting point to implement a concurrent algorithm. There are two main advantages to this approach:

- You can easily test the correctness of the results of your parallel algorithm
- You can measure the improvement in performance obtained with the use of concurrency

But not every algorithm can be parallelized, at least not so easily. You might think that the best starting point would be the sequential algorithm with best performance solving the problem you want to parallelize, but this can be an incorrect assumption. You should look for an algorithm than can be easily parallelized. Then, you can compare the concurrent algorithm with the sequential one with best performance to see which of those offers the best throughput.

Using immutable objects when possible

One of the main problems you can have in a concurrent application is a data race condition. As we explained before, this happens when two or more tasks can modify the data stored in a shared variable and the access to that variable is not implemented inside a critical section.

For example, when you work with an object-oriented language such as Java, you implement your application as a collection of objects. Each object has a number of attributes and some methods to read and change the values of the attributes. If some tasks share an object and call to a method to change a value of an attribute of that object and that method is not protected by a synchronization mechanism, you will probably have data inconsistency problems.

There are special kinds of objects, called immutable objects. Its main characteristic is that you can't modify any of its attributes after its initialization. If you want to modify the value of an attribute, you must create another object. The `String` class in Java is the best example of immutable objects. When you use an operator (for example, = or +=) that we might think changes the value of a String, you are really creating a new object.

The use of immutable objects in a concurrent application has two very important advantages:

- You don't need any synchronization mechanisms to protect the methods of these classes. If two tasks want to modify the same object, they will create new objects, so two tasks modifying the same object at a time will never occur.
- You won't have any data inconsistency problems, as a conclusion of the first point.

There is a drawback with immutable objects. You can create too many objects, and this may affect the throughput and the use of memory of the application. If you have a simple object without internal data structures, it's usually not a problem to make it immutable. However, making complex objects, which incorporate collections of other objects, immutable usually leads to serious performance problems.

Avoiding deadlocks by ordering the locks

One of the best mechanisms to avoid a deadlock situation in a concurrent application is to force tasks to always, get shared resources in the same order. An easy way to do this is to assign a number to every resource. When a task needs more than one resource, it has to request them in order.

For example, if you have two tasks, T1 and T2, and both need two resources, R1 and R2, you can force both to request the R1 resource first, and then the R2 resource. You will never have a deadlock.

On the other hand, if T1 first requests R1 and then R2, and T2 first requests R2 and then R1, you can have a deadlock.

For example, a bad use of this tip is as follows. You have two tasks that need to get two `Lock` objects. They try to get the locks in a different order:

```
public void operation1() {
  lock1.lock();
  lock2.lock();
    .
}
public void operation2() {
  lock2.lock();
  lock1.lock();
}
```

It's possible that `operation1()` executes its first sentence and `operation2()` its first sentence too, so they will be waiting for the other `Lock` and you will have a deadlock.

You can avoid this simply by getting the locks in the same order. If you change `operation2()`, you will never have a deadlock, as follows:

```
public void operation2() {
  lock1.lock();
  lock2.lock();
}
```

Using atomic variables instead of synchronization

When you have to share data between two or more tasks, you have to use a synchronization mechanism to protect access to that data and avoid any data inconsistency problems.

Under some circumstances, you can use the `volatile` keyword and not use a synchronization mechanism. If only one of the tasks modifies the data and the rest of the tasks read it, you can use the volatile keyword without any synchronization or data inconsistency problems. In other scenarios, you need to use a lock, the synchronized keyword, or any other synchronization method.

In Java 5, the concurrency API included a new kind of variables, denominated atomic variables. These variables are classes that support atomic operations on single variables. They include a method, denominated by `compareAndSet(oldValue, newValue)` that includes a mechanism to detect, if the assignment of the new value to the variable is done in one step. If the value of the variable is equal to `oldValue`, it changes it to `newValue` and returns `true`. Else, it returns `false`. There are more methods that work in a similar way, such as `getAndIncrement()` or `getAndDecrement()`. These methods are also atomic.

This solution is lock-free; that is to say, it doesn't use locks or any synchronization mechanisms, so its performance is better than any synchronized solution.

The most important atomic variables that you can use in Java are:

- AtomicInteger
- AtomicLong
- AtomicReference
- AtomicBoolean
- LongAdder
- DoubleAdder

Holding locks for as short a time as possible

Locks, like any other synchronization mechanism, allow you to define a critical section that only one task can execute at a time. While a task is executing the critical section, the other tasks that want to execute it are blocked and have to wait for the liberation of the critical section. The application is working in a sequential way.

You have to pay special attention to the instructions you include in your critical sections because you can degrade the performance of your application without realizing it. You must make your critical section as small as possible, and it must include only the instructions that work on shared data with other tasks, so the time that the application is executing in a sequential way would be minimal.

Avoid executing the code you don't control inside the critical section. For example, you are writing a library that accepts a user-defined Callable, which you need to launch sometimes. You don't know exactly what will be in that Callable. Maybe it blocks input/output, acquires some locks, calls other methods of your library, or just works for a very long time. Thus, whenever possible, try to execute it when your library does not hold any locks. If it's impossible for your algorithm, specify this behavior in your library documentation and possibly specify the limitations to the user-supplied code (for example, it should not take any locks). A good example of such documentation can be found in the `compute()` method of the `ConcurrentHashMap` class.

Taking precautions using lazy initialization

Lazy initialization is a mechanism that delays object creation until they are used in the application for the first time. It has the main advantage of minimizing the use of memory because you only create the objects that are really needed, but it can be a problem in concurrent applications.

If you have a method that initializes an object and this method is called by two different tasks at once, you can initialize two different objects. This, for example, can be a problem with singleton classes, because you only want to create one object of those classes.

An elegant solution to this problem has been an implemented by the initialization-on-demand holder idiom (https://en.wikipedia.org/wiki/Initialization-on-demand_holder_idiom).

Avoiding the use of blocking operations inside a critical section

Blocking operations are those operations that block the tasks that call them until an event occurs. For example, when you read data from a file or write data to the console, the task that calls these operations must wait until they finish.

If you include one of these operations in a critical section, you are degrading the performance of your application because none of the tasks that want to execute that critical section can execute it. The one that is inside the critical section is waiting for the finalization of an I/O operation, and the others are waiting for the critical section.

Unless it is imperative, don't include blocking operations inside a critical section.

Summary

Concurrent programming includes all the tools and techniques to have multiple tasks or processes running at the same time in a computer, communicating and synchronizing between them without data loss or inconsistency.

We started this chapter by introducing the basic concepts of concurrency. You must know and understand terms like concurrency, parallelism, and synchronization to fully understand the examples in this book. However, concurrency can generate some problems, such as data race conditions, deadlocks, livelocks, and others. You must also know the potential problems of a concurrent application. It will help you identify and solve these problems.

We also explained a simple methodology of five steps introduced by Intel to convert a sequential algorithm into a concurrent one and showed you some concurrency design patterns implemented in the Java language and some tips to take into account when you implement a concurrent application.

Finally, we explained briefly the components of the Java Concurrency API. It's a very rich API with low and very high-level mechanisms that allow you to implement powerful concurrency applications easily. We also described the Java memory model, which determines how concurrent applications manage the memory and the execution order of instructions internally.

In the next chapter, you will learn how to use the basic elements of concurrent applications in Java - the `Thread` class and the `Runnable` interface.

2
Working with Basic Elements - Threads and Runnables

Execution threads are the core of concurrent applications. When you implement a concurrent application, no matter the language, you have to create different execution threads that run in parallel in a non-deterministic order unless you use a synchronization element (such as a semaphore). In Java you can create execution threads in two ways:

- Extending the `Thread` class
- Implementing the `Runnable` interface

In this chapter, you will learn how to use these elements to implement concurrent applications in Java. We will cover the following topics:

- Threads in Java: characteristics and states
- The `Thread` class and the `Runnable` interface
- First example: matrix multiplication
- Second example: file search

Threads in Java

Nowadays, computer users (and mobile and tablet users too) use different applications at the same time when they work with their computers. They can be writing a document with a word processor while they're reading the news or posting in a social network and listening to music. They can do all these things at the same time because modern operating systems support multiprocessing.

They can execute different tasks at the same time. But inside an application, you can also do different things at the same time. For example, if you're working with your word processor, you can save the file while you're adding text with bold style. You can do this because the modern programming languages used to write those applications allow programmers to create multiple execution threads inside an application. Each execution thread executes a different task so you can do different things at the same time.

Java implements execution threads using the `Thread` class. You can create an execution thread in your application using the following mechanisms:

- You can extend the `Thread` class and override the `run()` method
- You can implement the `Runnable` interface and pass an object of that class to the constructor of a `Thread` object

In both cases, you will have a `Thread` object, but the second approach is recommended over the first one. Its main advantages are:

- `Runnable` is an interface: You can implement other interfaces and extend other classes. With the `Thread` class you can only extend that class.
- `Runnable` objects can be executed with threads, but also in other Java concurrency objects as executors. This gives you more flexibility to change your concurrent applications.
- You can use the same `Runnable` object with different threads.

Once you have a `Thread` object, you must use the `start()` method to create a new execution thread and execute the `run()` method of the `Thread`. If you call the `run()` method directly, you will be calling a normal Java method and no new execution thread will be created. Let's see the most important characteristics of threads in the Java programming language.

Threads in Java - characteristics and states

The first thing we have to say about threads in Java is that all Java programs, concurrent or not, have one `Thread` called the main thread. As you may know, a Java SE program starts its execution with the `main()` method. When you execute that program, the **Java Virtual Machine (JVM)** creates a new `Thread` and executes the `main()` method in that thread. This is a unique thread in non-concurrent applications and the first one in the concurrent ones.

In Java, as with other programming languages, threads share all the resources of the application, including memory and open files. This is a powerful tool because they can share information in a fast and easy way, but as we explain in Chapter 1, *The First Step - Concurrency Design Principles*, it must be done using adequate synchronization elements to avoid data race conditions.

All threads in Java have a priority, an integer value that can be between the values Thread.MIN_PRIORITY and Thread.MAX_PRIORITY. (Actually, their values are 1 and 10.) By default, all threads are created with the priority Thread.NORM_PRIORITY (actually, its value is 5). You can use the method setPriority() to change the priority of a Thread (it can throw a SecurityException exception if you are not allowed to do that operation) and the getPriority() method to get the priority of a Thread. This priority is a hint to the Java Virtual Machine and to the underlying operating system about which threads are preferred, but it's not a contract. There's no guarantee about the order of execution of the threads. Normally, threads with a higher priority will be executed before threads with a lower priority but, as I told you before, there's no guarantee of this.

You can create two kinds of threads in Java:

- Daemon threads
- Non-daemon threads

The difference between them is in how they affect the end of a program. A Java program ends its execution when one of the following circumstances occurs:

- The program executes the exit() method of the Runtime class and the user has authorization to execute that method
- All the non-daemon threads of the application have ended its execution, no matter if there are daemon threads running or not

With these characteristics, daemon threads are usually used to execute auxiliary tasks in the applications as garbage collectors or cache managers. You can use the isDaemon() method to check if a thread is a daemon thread or not and the setDaemon() method to establish a thread as a daemon one. Take into account that you must call this method before the thread starts its execution with the start() method.

Finally, threads can pass through different states depending on the situation. All the possible states are defined in the `Thread.States` class and you can use the `getState()` method to get the status of a `Thread`. Obviously, you can change the status of the thread directly. These are the possible statuses of a thread:

- `NEW`: The `Thread` has been created but it hasn't started its execution yet
- `RUNNABLE`: The `Thread` is running in the Java Virtual Machine
- `BLOCKED`: The `Thread` is waiting for a lock
- `WAITING`: The `Thread` is waiting for the action of another thread
- `TIME_WAITING`: The `Thread` is waiting for the action of another thread but has a time limit
- `THREAD`: The `Thread` has finished its execution

Threads can only be in one state at a given time. These states do not map to OS thread states, they are states used by the JVM. Now that we know the most important characteristics of threads in the Java programming language, let's see the most important methods of the `Runnable` interface and the `Thread` class.

The Thread class and the Runnable interface

As we mentioned before, you can create new execution threads using one of the following two mechanisms:

- Extending the `Thread` class and override its `run()` method
- Implementing the `Runnable` interface and passing an instance of that object to the constructor of a `Thread` object

Java good practices recommend using the second approach over the first one and that will be the approach we will use in this chapter and in the whole book.

The `Runnable` interface only defines one method: the `run()` method. This is the main method of every thread. When you start a new executing the `start()` method, it will call the `run()` method (of the `Thread` class or of the `Runnable` object passed as parameter in the constructor of the `Thread` class).

The `Thread` class, in contrast, has a lot of different methods. It has a `run()` method that you must override if you implement your thread, extending the `Thread` class and the `start()` method that you must call to create a new execution thread. These are other interesting methods of the `Thread` class:

- Methods to get and set information for a `Thread`:
    - `getId()`: This method returns the identifier of the `Thread`. It is a positive integer number assigned when it's created. It is unique during its entire life and it can't be changed.
    - `getName()`/`setName()`: This method allows you to get or set the name of the `Thread`. This name is a `String` that can also be established in the constructor of the `Thread` class.
    - `getPriority()`/`setPriority()`: You can use these methods to obtain and establish the priority of the `Thread`. We explained before in this chapter how Java manages the priority of its threads.
    - `isDaemon()`/`setDaemon()`: This method allows you to obtain or establish the condition of the daemon of the `Thread`. We explained how this condition works before.
    - `getState()`: This method returns the state of the `Thread`. We explained all the possible states of a `Thread` earlier.

- `interrupt()`/`interrupted()`/`isInterrupted()`: The first method is used to indicate to a `Thread` that you're requesting the end of its execution. The other two methods can be used to check the interrupt status. The main difference between those methods is that the `interrupted()` method clears the value of the interrupted flag when it's called and the `isInterrupted()` method does not. A call to the `interrupt()` method doesn't end the execution of a `Thread`. It is the responsibility of the `Thread` to check the status of that flag and respond accordingly.
- `sleep()`: This method allows you to suspend the execution of the thread for a period of time. It receives a long value that is the number of milliseconds for which you want to suspend the execution of the `Thread`.
- `join()`: This method suspends the execution of the thread that makes the call until the end of the execution of the thread used to call the method. You can use this method to wait for the finalization of another `Thread`.

- `setUncaughtExceptionHandler()`: This method is used to establish the controller of unchecked exceptions that can occur while you're executing the threads.
- `currentThread()`: This is a static method of the `Thread` class that returns the `Thread` object that is actually executing this code.

Throughout the following sections, you will learn how to use these methods to implement two examples:

- An application to multiply matrices
- An application to search for a file in the operating system

First example: matrix multiplication

Matrix multiplication is one of the basic operations that you can do with matrices and a classic problem used in concurrent and parallel programming courses. If you have a matrix *A* with *m* rows and *n* columns and another matrix *B* with *n* columns and *p* columns, you can multiply both matrices and obtain a matrix *C* with *m* rows and *p* columns. You can check `https://en.wikipedia.org/wiki/Matrix_multiplication` to find a detailed description about this operation.

In this section, we will implement a serial version of an algorithm to multiply two matrices and three different concurrent versions. Then, we will compare the four solutions to see when concurrency gives us a better performance.

Common classes

To implement this example we have used a class named `MatrixGenerator`. We use it to generate random matrices to multiply. This class has a method named `generate()` that receives the number of rows and columns you want in your matrix as parameters and generates a matrix with those dimensions with random double numbers. This is the source code of the class:

```
public class MatrixGenerator {

  public static double[][] generate (int rows, int columns) {
    double[][] ret=new double[rows][columns];
    Random random=new Random();
    for (int i=0; i<rows; i++) {
      for (int j=0; j<columns; j++) {
```

```
            ret[i][j]=random.nextDouble()*10;
        }
    }
    return ret;
    }
}
```

Serial version

We have implemented the serial version of the algorithm in the SerialMultiplier class. This class only has one static method named multiply() that receives three double matrices as parameters: the two we're going to multiply and the one to store the result.

We don't check the dimensions of the matrices. We will guarantee that they are correct. We use a triple nested loop to calculate the result matrix. This is the source code of the SerialMultiplier class:

```
public class SerialMultiplier {

    public static void multiply (double[][] matrix1, double[][] matrix2,
                                 double[][] result) {
        int rows1=matrix1.length;
        int columns1=matrix1[0].length;

        int columns2=matrix2[0].length;

        for (int i=0; i<rows1; i++) {
            for (int j=0; j<columns2; j++) {
                result[i][j]=0;
                for (int k=0; k<columns1; k++) {
                    result[i][j]+=matrix1[i][k]*matrix2[k][j];
                }
            }
        }
    }
}
```

We have also implemented a main class to test the serial multiplier algorithm named `SerialMain` class. In the `main()` method, we generate two random matrices with `2000` rows and `2000` columns and calculate the multiplication of both matrices using the `SerialMultiplier` class. We measure the execution time of the algorithm in milliseconds, as follows:

```
public class SerialMain {

  public static void main(String[] args) {

    double matrix1[][] = MatrixGenerator.generate(2000, 2000);
    double matrix2[][] = MatrixGenerator.generate(2000, 2000);
    double resultSerial[][]= new double[matrix1.length]
                                       [matrix2[0].length];

    Date start=new Date();
    SerialMultiplier.multiply(matrix1, matrix2, resultSerial);
    Date end=new Date();
    System.out.printf("Serial: %d%n",end.getTime()-start.getTime());
  }
}
```

Parallel versions

We have implemented three different concurrent algorithms to implement these examples with different granularity:

- One thread per element in the result matrix
- One thread per row in the result matrix
- As many threads as available processors or cores in the JVM

Let's see the source code of these three versions.

First concurrent version - a thread per element

In this version, we will create a new execution thread per element in the result matrix. For example, if you multiply two matrices with 2,000 rows and 2,000 columns, the resulting matrix will have 4,000,000 elements, so we will create 4,000,000 `Thread` objects. If we start all the threads at the same time we will probably overload the system, so we will launch the threads in groups of 10 threads.

After we've started 10 threads, we wait for their finalization using the `join()` method, and once they have finished, we start another 10. We follow this process until all the necessary threads have been launched. There's no reason to select 10 as the number of threads. You can opt to change that number and see the effects it has over the performance of the algorithm.

We will implement the `IndividualMultiplierTask` and the `ParallelIndividualMultiplier` classes. The `IndividualMultiplierTask` class will implement each `Thread`. It implements the `Runnable` interface and will use five internal attributes: the two matrices to multiply, the matrix with the result, and the row and the column of the element we want to calculate. We will use the constructor of the class to initialize all those attributes:

```
public class IndividualMultiplierTask implements Runnable {

    private final double[][] result;
    private final double[][] matrix1;
    private final double[][] matrix2;

    private final int row;
    private final int column;

    public IndividualMultiplierTask(double[][] result, double[][]
                                    matrix1, double[][] matrix2,
                                    int i, int j) {
      this.result = result;
      this.matrix1 = matrix1;
      this.matrix2 = matrix2;
      this.row = i;
      this.column = j;
    }
```

The `run()` method will calculate the value of the element determined by the `row` and `column` attributes. The following piece of code shows you how to implement that behavior:

```
    @Override
    public void run() {
      result[row][column] = 0;
      for (int k = 0; k < matrix1[row].length; k++) {
        result[row][column] += matrix1[row][k] * matrix2[k][column];
      }

    }
}
```

The `ParallelIndividualMultiplier` will create all the execution threads necessary to calculate the result matrix. It has a method called `multiply()` that receives the two matrices we're going to multiply and a third one to store the result as parameters. It will process all the elements of the result matrix and creates an `IndividualMultiplierTask` to calculate each one. As we mentioned before, we launch the threads in groups of 10. After we have started 10 threads, we use the auxiliary method `waitForThreads()` to wait for the finalization of those 10 threads using the `join()` method. The following block of code shows you the implementation of this class:

```
public class ParallelIndividualMultiplier {

  public static void multiply(double[][] matrix1, double[][] matrix2,
                              double[][] result) {

    List<Thread> threads=new ArrayList<>();

    int rows1=matrix1.length;

    int rows2=matrix2.length;

    for (int i=0; i<rows1; i++) {
      for (int j=0; j<columns2; j++) {
        IndividualMultiplierTask task=new IndividualMultiplierTask
                                 (result, matrix1, matrix2, i, j);
        Thread thread=new Thread(task);
        thread.start();
        threads.add(thread);

        if (threads.size() % 10 == 0) {
          waitForThreads(threads);
        }
      }
    }

  }

  private static void waitForThreads(List<Thread> threads){
    for (Thread thread: threads) {
      try {
        thread.join();
      } catch (InterruptedException e) {
        e.printStackTrace();
      }
    }

    threads.clear();
```

```
    }

}
```

As with other examples, we have created a main class to test this example. It's very similar to the `SerialMain` class but in this case we have called it `ParallelIndividualMain` class. We don't include the source code of this class here.

Second concurrent version - a thread per row

In this version, we're going to create a new executing thread per row in the result matrix. For example, if we multiply two matrices with 2000 rows and 2000 columns, we're going to create 2000 threads. As we did in the previous example, we will launch the threads in groups of 10 threads and then we wait for their finalization before we start new threads.

We're going to implement the `RowMultiplierTask` and the `ParallelRowMultiplier` classes to implement this version. The `RowMultiplierTask` will implement each `Thread`. It implements the `Runnable` interface and will use five internal attributes: the two matrices to multiply, the matrix with the result, and the row of the result matrix we want to calculate. We will use the constructor of the class to initialize all those attributes, as follows:

```java
public class RowMultiplierTask implements Runnable {

    private final double[][] result;
    private final double[][] matrix1;
    private final double[][] matrix2;

    private final int row;

    public RowMultiplierTask(double[][] result, double[][] matrix1,
                             double[][] matrix2, int i) {
        this.result = result;
        this.matrix1 = matrix1;
        this.matrix2 = matrix2;
        this.row = i;
    }
```

The `run()` method will have two loops. The first one will process all the elements of the `row` of the result matrix it will calculate and the second one will calculate the result value of each element.

```java
@Override
public void run() {
    for (int j = 0; j < matrix2[0].length; j++) {
        result[row][j] = 0;
```

```
            for (int k = 0; k < matrix1[row].length; k++) {
              result[row][j] += matrix1[row][k] * matrix2[k][j];
            }
          }
        }
      }
```

The `ParallelRowMultiplier` will create all the execution threads necessary to calculate the result matrix. It has a method called `multiply()` that receives the two matrices we're going to multiply and a third one to store the result as parameters. It will process all the rows of the result matrix and create a `RowMultiplierTask` to process each one. As we mentioned earlier, we launch the threads in groups of 10. After we have started 10 threads, we use the auxiliary method `waitForThreads()` to wait for the finalization of those 10 threads using the `join()` method. The following block of code shows you how to implement that class:

```
public class ParallelRowMultiplier {

  public static void multiply(double[][] matrix1, double[][]
                              matrix2, double[][] result) {

    List<Thread> threads = new ArrayList<>();

    int rows1 = matrix1.length;

    for (int i = 0; i < rows1; i++) {
      RowMultiplierTask task = new RowMultiplierTask(result,
                                    matrix1, matrix2, i);
      Thread thread = new Thread(task);
      thread.start();
      threads.add(thread);

      if (threads.size() % 10 == 0) {
        waitForThreads(threads);
      }
    }
  }

  private static void waitForThreads(List<Thread> threads){
    for (Thread thread : threads) {
      try {
        thread.join();
      } catch (InterruptedException e) {
        e.printStackTrace();
      }
    }
```

```
        threads.clear();
    }

}
```

As with other examples, we have created a main class to test this example. It's very similar to the `SerialMain` class, but in this case, we have called it the `ParallelRowMain` class. We don't include the source code of this class here.

Third concurrent version - the number of threads is determined by the processors

Finally, in the last version, we only create as many threads as there are cores or processors available to the JVM. We use the `availableProcessors()` method of the `Runtime` class to calculate that number.

We implement this version in the `GroupMultiplierTask` and `ParallelGroupMultiplier` classes. The `GroupMultiplierTask` implements the threads we're going to create. It implements the `Runnable` interface and uses five internal attributes: the two matrices to multiply, the matrix with the result, and the initial and final rows of the result matrix this task is going to calculate. We will use the constructor of the class to initialize all those attributes. The following block of code shows you how to implement the first part of the class:

```
public class GroupMultiplierTask implements Runnable {

  private final double[][] result;
  private final double[][] matrix1;
  private final double[][] matrix2;

  private final int startIndex;
  private final int endIndex;

  public GroupMultiplierTask(double[][] result, double[][]
                             matrix1, double[][] matrix2,
                             int startIndex, int endIndex) {
    this.result = result;
    this.matrix1 = matrix1;
    this.matrix2 = matrix2;
    this.startIndex = startIndex;
    this.endIndex = endIndex;
  }
```

The `run()` method will use three loops to implement their calculations. The first one will go over the rows of the result matrix this task is going to calculate, the second one will process all the elements of each row, and the last one will calculate the value of each element:

```
@Override
public void run() {
   for (int i = startIndex; i < endIndex; i++) {
      for (int j = 0; j < matrix2[0].length; j++) {
         result[i][j] = 0;
         for (int k = 0; k < matrix1[i].length; k++) {
            result[i][j] += matrix1[i][k] * matrix2[k][j];
         }
      }
   }
}
```

The `ParallelGroupMutiplier` class is going to create the threads to calculate the result matrix. It has a method called `multiply()` that receives the two matrices we're going to multiply and a third one to store the result as parameters. First, it gets the number of available processors using the `availableProcessors()` method of the `Runtime` class. Then, it calculates the rows that each task has to process and creates and starts those threads. Finally, we wait for the finalization of the threads using the `join()` method:

```
public class ParallelGroupMultiplier {

   public static void multiply(double[][] matrix1, double[][] matrix2,
                               double[][] result) {
      List<Thread> threads=new ArrayList<>();

      int rows1=matrix1.length;

      int numThreads=Runtime.getRuntime().availableProcessors();
      int startIndex, endIndex, step;
      step=rows1 / numThreads;
      startIndex=0;
      endIndex=step;

      for (int i=0; i<numThreads; i++) {
         GroupMultiplierTask task=new GroupMultiplierTask
                    (result, matrix1, matrix2, startIndex, endIndex);
         Thread thread=new Thread(task);
         thread.start();
         threads.add(thread);
         startIndex=endIndex;
         endIndex= i==numThreads-2?rows1:endIndex+step;
      }
```

```
for (Thread thread: threads) {
  try {
    thread.join();
  } catch (InterruptedException e) {
    e.printStackTrace();
  }
}

}

}
```

As with other examples, we have created a main class to test this example. It's very similar to the `SerialMain` class but in this case we have called it the `ParallelGroupMain` class. We don't include the source code of this class here.

Comparing the solutions

Let's compare the different solutions (serial and concurrent) of the four versions of the multiplier algorithm we have implemented in this section. To test the algorithm, we have executed the examples using the **JMH framework** (`http://openjdk.java.net/projects/code-tools/jmh/`), which allows you to implement micro benchmarks in Java. Using a framework for benchmarking is a better solution that simply measures time using methods such as `currentTimeMillis()` or `nanoTime()`. We have executed them 10 times in two different architectures:

- A computer with an Intel Core i5-5300 CPU with Windows 7 and 16 GB of RAM. This processor has two cores and each core can execute two threads, so we will have four parallel threads.
- A computer with an AMD A8-640 APU with Windows 10 and 8 GB of RAM. This processor has four cores.

We have tested our algorithms with three different sizes of random matrices:

- 500x500
- 1000x1000
- 2000x2000

The medium execution times and their standard deviation in milliseconds are discussed in the following table:

Algorithm	Size	AMD	Intel
Serial	500	1821.729 ± 366.885	447.920 ± 49.864
	1000	27661.481 ± 796.670	5474.942 ± 164.447
	2000	315457.940 ± 32961.165	70968.563 ± 4056.883
Parallel Individual	500	43512.382 ± 813.131	17152.883 ± 170.408
	1000	164968.834 ± 1034.453	72858.419 ± 381.258
	2000	774681.287 ± 17380.02	316466.479 ± 5033.577
Parallel Row	500	685.465 ± 72.474	229.228 ± 61.497
	1000	8565 ± 437.611	3710.613 ± 411.490
	2000	92923.685 ± 11595.433	42655.081 ± 1370.940
Parallel Group	500	515.743 ± 51.106	133.530 ± 12.271
	1000	7466.880 ± 409.136	3862.635 ± 368.427
	2000	86639.811 ± 2834.1	43353.603 ± 1857.568

We can draw the following conclusions:

- There's a big difference between both architectures, but you have to take into account that they have different processors, operating systems, memory, and hard disks.
- But the results are equivalent in both architectures. We get the best results with the Parallel Group and Parallel Row architectures. The Parallel Individual architecture gets the worst results.

This example shows us that we have to be careful when we develop a concurrent application. If we don't choose a good solution, we will obtain poor performance.

We can compare the best concurrent version method with the serial version using the speed-up for the 500x500 matrix to see how concurrency improves the performance of our algorithm:

$$S_{AMD} = \frac{T_{serial}}{T_{concurrent}} = \frac{1821.729}{515.743} = 3.53$$

$$S_{Intel} = \frac{T_{serial}}{T_{concurrent}} = \frac{447.920}{133.530} = 3.35$$

Second example - file search

All operating systems include the option to search for files that verify some conditions in your file system (for example, the name or part of the name, the date of modification, and so on). In our case, we're going to implement an algorithm that looks for a file with a predetermined name. Our algorithms will take the initial path to start the search and the file we're going to look for as input. The JDK provides the ability to walk a directory tree structure, so there should be no need to implement your own in the real world.

Common classes

Both versions of the algorithm will share a common class to store the results of our search. We will call this class `Result` and it will have two attributes: a `Boolean` value named `found` that determines if we have found the file we were looking for and a `String` value named `path` with the full path of the file if we have found it.

The code for this class is very simple so it won't be included here.

Serial version

The serial version of this algorithm is very simple. We take the initial path of the search, get the files and the directories' contents, and process them. For files, we compare their name with the name we're looking for. If both names are equal, we fill the `Result` object and finish the execution of the algorithm. For directories, we made a recursive call to the operation to search the file inside those directories.

We are going to implement this operation in the `searchFiles()` method of the `SerialFileSearch` class. This is the source code of the `SerialFileSearch` class:

```
public class SerialFileSearch {

  public static void searchFiles(File file, String fileName,
                                 Result result) {

    File[] contents;
    contents=file.listFiles();

    if ((contents==null) || (contents.length==0)) {
      return;
    }

    for (File content : contents) {
      if (content.isDirectory()) {
        searchFiles(content,fileName, result);
      } else {
        if (content.getName().equals(fileName)) {
          result.setPath(content.getAbsolutePath());
          result.setFound(true);
          System.out.printf("Serial Search: Path: %s%n",
                            result.getPath());
          return;
        }
      }
      if (result.isFound()) {
        return;
      }
    }
  }
}
```

Concurrent version

There are different ways to parallelize this algorithm. For example:

- You can create an execution thread per directory we want to process.
- You can divide the directory tree into groups and create an execution thread per group. The number of groups you create will determine the number of execution threads your application will use.
- You can use as many threads as cores that are available to the JVM.

In this case, we have to take into account that our algorithm will use intensive I/O operations. Only one thread can read the disk at a time, so not all solutions will increase the performance of the serial version of the algorithm.

We will use the last option to implement our concurrent version. We will store the directories included in the initial path in a ConcurrentLinkedQueue (an implementation of a Queue interface that can be used in concurrent applications) and create as many threads as processors that are available to the JVM. Each thread will take a path from the queue and process this directory and all its subdirectories and files. When it has processed all the files and directories in that directory, it takes another from the queue.

If one of the threads finds the file we were looking for, it ends its execution immediately. In that case, we finish the execution of the other threads using the interrupt() method.

We have implemented this version of the algorithm in the ParallelGroupFileTask and ParallelGroupFileSearch classes. The ParallelGroupFileTask class implements all the threads we're going to use to find the file. It implements the Runnable interface and uses four internal attributes: a String attribute named fileName that stores the name of the file we're looking for, the ConcurrentLinkedQueue of File objects named directories that stores the list of directories we're going to process, a Result object named parallelResult to store the result of our search, and a Boolean attribute named found to mark if we find the file we were looking for. We're going to use the constructor of the class to initialize all the attributes:

```
public class ParallelGroupFileTask implements Runnable {

    private final String fileName;
    private final ConcurrentLinkedQueue<File> directories;
    private final Result parallelResult;
    private boolean found;

    public ParallelGroupFileTask(String fileName, Result parallelResult,
                        ConcurrentLinkedQueue<File>directories) {
      this.fileName = fileName;
      this.parallelResult = parallelResult;
      this.directories = directories;
      this.found = false;
    }
```

The `run()` method has a loop that will be executed while there are elements in the queue and we haven't found the file. It takes the next directory to process using the `poll()` method of the `ConcurrentLinkedQueue` class and calls to the auxiliary method `processDirectory()`. If we have found the file (the found attribute is true), we end the execution of the thread with the return instruction:

```
@Override
public void run() {
  while (directories.size() > 0) {
    File file = directories.poll();
    try {
      processDirectory(file, fileName, parallelResult);
      if (found) {
        System.out.printf("%s has found the file%n",
                          Thread.currentThread().getName());
        System.out.printf("Parallel Search: Path: %s%n",
                          parallelResult.getPath());
        return;
      }
    } catch (InterruptedException e) {
      System.out.printf("%s has been interrupted%n",
                        Thread.currentThread().getName());
    }
  }
}
```

The `processDirectory()` method will receive the `File` object that stores the directory to process, the name of the file we're looking for, and the `Result` object to store the result if we found it as parameters. It obtains the contents of the `File` using the `listFiles()` method that returns an array of `File` objects and processes that array. For directories, it makes a recursive call to this method with the new object. For files, it calls the auxiliary `processFile()` method:

```
private void processDirectory(File file, String fileName,
                              Result parallelResult) throws
            InterruptedException {
  File[] contents;
  contents = file.listFiles();

  if ((contents == null) || (contents.length == 0)) {
    return;
  }

  for (File content : contents) {
    if (content.isDirectory()) {
      processDirectory(content, fileName, parallelResult);
```

```
            if (Thread.currentThread().isInterrupted()) {
              throw new InterruptedException();
            }
            if (found) {
              return;
            }
        } else {
          processFile(content, fileName, parallelResult);
          if (Thread.currentThread().isInterrupted()) {
            throw new InterruptedException();
          }
          if (found) {
            return;
          }
        }
      }
    }
```

We also check, after we have processed every directory and every file, if the thread has been interrupted. We use the `currentThread()` method of the `Thread` class to get the `Thread` object that is executing this task and then the `isInterrupted()` method to verify if the thread has been interrupted or not. If the thread has been interrupted, we throw a new `InterruptedExeption` exception that we catch in the `run()` method to end the execution of the thread. This mechanism allows us to finish our search when we have found the file.

We also check if the found attribute is true or not. If is true, we return immediately to finish the execution of the thread.

The `processFile()` method receives the `File` object that stores the file we have to process, the name of the file we're looking for, and a `Result` object to store the result of the operation if we have found the file as parameters. We compare the name of the `File` we're processing with the name of the file we're looking for. If both names are equal, we fill the `Result` object and establish the found attribute as true:

```
    private void processFile(File content, String fileName,
                             Result parallelResult) {
      if (content.getName().equals(fileName)) {
        parallelResult.setPath(content.getAbsolutePath());
        this.found = true;
      }
    }

    public boolean getFound() {
      return found;
    }
  }
```

The `ParallelGroupFileSearch` class implements the whole algorithm using the auxiliary tasks. It's going to implement the static `searchFiles()` method. It receives a `File` object that points to the base path of the search, a `String` named `fileName` that stores the name of the file we're looking for, and a `Result` object to store the result of the operation as parameters.

First, it creates the `ConcurrentLinkedQueue` object and stores in it all the directories included in the base path:

```
public class ParallelGroupFileSearch {

  public static void searchFiles(File file, String fileName,
                              Result parallelResult) {

    ConcurrentLinkedQueue<File> directories = new
                                ConcurrentLinkedQueue<>();
    File[] contents = file.listFiles();

    for (File content : contents) {
      if (content.isDirectory()) {
        directories.add(content);
      }
    }
```

Then, we obtain the number of threads available to the JVM using the `availableProcessors()` method of the `Runtime` class and create a `ParallelFileGroupTask` and a `Thread` per processor.

```
int numThreads = Runtime.getRuntime().availableProcessors();
Thread[] threads = new Thread[numThreads];
ParallelGroupFileTask[] tasks = new ParallelGroupFileTask
                                          [numThreads];

for (int i = 0; i < numThreads; i++) {
  tasks[i] = new ParallelGroupFileTask(fileName, parallelResult,
                                  directories);
  threads[i] = new Thread(tasks[i]);
  threads[i].start();
}
```

Finally, we wait until one thread finds the file or all the threads have finished their execution. In the first case, we cancel the execution of the other threads using the `interrupt()` method and the mechanism explained before. We use the `getState()` method of the `Thread` class to check if the threads have finished their execution:

```
boolean finish = false;
int numFinished = 0;

while (!finish) {
  numFinished = 0;
  for (int i = 0; i < threads.length; i++) {
    if (threads[i].getState() == State.TERMINATED) {
      numFinished++;
      if (tasks[i].getFound()) {
        finish = true;
      }
    }
  }
  if (numFinished == threads.length) {
    finish = true;
  }
}
if (numFinished != threads.length) {
  for (Thread thread : threads) {
    thread.interrupt();
  }
}
}
```

Comparing the solutions

Let's compare the different solutions (serial and concurrent) of the four versions of the multiplier algorithm we have implemented in this section. To test the algorithm, we have executed the examples using the **JMH framework** (`http://openjdk.java.net/projects/code-tools/jmh/`), which allows you to implement micro benchmarks in Java. Using a framework for benchmarking is a better solution and simply measures time using methods such as `currentTimeMillis()` or `nanoTime()`. We have executed them 10 times in two different architectures:

- A computer with an Intel Core i5-5300 CPU with Windows 7 and 16 GB of RAM. This processor has two cores and each core can execute two threads, so we will have four parallel threads.
- A computer with an AMD A8-640 APU with Windows 10 and 8 GB of RAM. This processor has four cores.

We have tested our algorithms with two different file names in the Windows directory:

- `hosts`
- `yyy.yyy`

We have tested our algorithm on a Windows operating system. The first file exists and the second one doesn't. If you use another operating system, change the names of the files accordingly. The median execution times and their standard deviation in milliseconds are discussed in the following table:

Algorithm	Size	AMD	Intel
Serial	hosts	5869.019 ± 124.548	2955.535 ± 69.252
	yyy.yyy	26474.179 ± 785.680	14508.276 ± 195.725
Parallel	hosts	2792.313 ± 100.885	1972.248 ± 193.386
	yyy.yyy	21337.288 ± 954.344	12742.856 ± 361.681

We can draw the following conclusions:

- There's a difference between the performance in both architectures, but you have to take into account that they have different processors, operating systems, memory and hard disks.
- But the results are equivalent in both architectures. The parallel algorithm has a better performance than the serial one. The difference is larger with the hosts file than with the file that doesn't exist.

We can compare the best concurrent version method with the serial version using the speed-up for the hosts file to see how concurrency improves the performance of our algorithm:

$$S_{AMD} = \frac{T_{serial}}{T_{concurrent}} = \frac{5869.019}{2792.313} = 2.10$$

$$S_{Intel} = \frac{T_{serial}}{T_{concurrent}} = \frac{2955.535}{1972.248} = 1.5$$

Summary

In this chapter, we have presented the most basic elements to create execution threads in Java: the `Runnable` interface and the `Thread` class. We can create threads in Java in two different ways:

- Extending the `Thread` class and overriding the `run()` method
- Implementing the `Runnable` interface and passing an object of that class to the constructor of the `Thread` class

The second mechanism is preferred over the first one because they give us more flexibility.

We also learned how the `Thread` class has different methods that allow us to get information about the thread, change its priority, or wait for its finalization. We have used all these methods in two examples, one to multiply matrices and the other to search files in a directory. In both cases, concurrency gives us better performance but we also have learned that we have to be careful when implementing a concurrent version of an algorithm. A bad selection for how we use concurrency can give us bad performance.

In the next chapter, we will introduce the Executor framework, which will allow us to create concurrency applications without worrying about thread creation and management.

3
Managing Lots of Threads - Executors

When you implement a simple concurrent application, you create and execute a thread per concurrent task. This approach can have some important issues. Since Java version 5, the Java concurrency API has included the Executor framework to improve the performance of concurrent applications with a lot of concurrent tasks. In this chapter, we will cover the following:

- An introduction to executors
- The first example - the k-nearest neighbors algorithm
- The second example - concurrency in a client/server environment

An introduction to executors

As we explain in `Chapter 2`, *Working with Basic Elements - Threads and Runnables*, the basic mechanism to implement a concurrent application in Java is:

- **A class that implements the Runnable interface**: This is the code you want to implement in a concurrent way
- **An instance of the Thread class**: This is the thread that is going to execute the code in a concurrent way

With this approach, you're responsible for creating and manning the thread objects and implementing the mechanisms of synchronization between the threads. However, it can create some problems, especially with those applications with a lot of concurrent tasks. If you create too many threads, you can degrade the performance of your application or even hang the entire system.

Java version 5 included the Executor framework to solve these problems and provide an efficient solution that is easier to use for programmers than the traditional concurrency mechanisms.

In this chapter, we will introduce the basic characteristics of the Executor framework by implementing the following two examples using that framework:

- **The k-nearest neighbors algorithm**: This is a basic machine learning algorithm used in classification. It determines the tag of a test example based on the tag of the k most similar examples in the train dataset.
- **Concurrency in a client/server environment**: Applications that serve information to thousands or millions of clients are critical nowadays. It is essential to implement the server side of the system in an optimal way.

In Chapter 4, *Getting the Most from Executors*, and Chapter 5, *Getting Data from Tasks - The Callable and Future Interfaces*, we will introduce more advanced aspects of executors.

Basic characteristics of executors

The main characteristics of executors are:

- You don't need to create any Thread objects. If you want to execute a concurrent task, you only create an instance of the task (for example, a class that implements the Runnable interface) and send it to the executor. It will manage the thread that will execute the task.
- Executors reduce the overhead introduced by thread creation reusing the threads. Internally, it manages a pool of threads named **worker-threads**. If you send a task to the executor and a worker-thread is idle, the executor uses that thread to execute the task.

- It's easy to control the resources used by the executor. You can limit the maximum number of worker-threads of your executor. If you send more tasks than worker-threads, the executor stores them in a queue. When a worker-thread finishes the execution of a task, they take another from the queue.

- You have to finish the execution of an executor explicitly. You have to indicate to the executor that it has to finish its execution and kill the created threads. If you don't do this, it won't finish its execution and your application won't end.

Executors have more interesting characteristics that make them very powerful and flexible.

Basic components of the Executor framework

The Executor framework has various interfaces and classes that implement all the functionality provided by executors. The basic components of the framework are:

- **The Executor interface**: This is the basic interface of the `Executor` framework. It only defines a method that allows the programmer to send a `Runnable` object to an executor.

- **The ExecutorService interface**: This interface extends the `Executor` interface and includes more methods to increase the functionality of the framework, such as the following:
  - Execute tasks that return a result: The `run()` method provided by the `Runnable` interface doesn't return a result, but with executors, you can have tasks that return a result
  - Execute a list of tasks with a single method call
  - Finish the execution of an executor and wait for its termination

- **The ThreadPoolExecutor class**: This class implements the `Executor` and `ExecutorService` interfaces. In addition, it includes some additional methods to get the status of the executor (the number of worker-threads, number of executed tasks, and so on), methods to establish the parameters of the executor (minimum and maximum number of worker-threads, time that idle threads will wait for new tasks, and so on), and methods that allow programmers to extend and adapt functionality.

- **The Executors class**: This class provides utility methods to create `Executor` objects and other related classes.

First example - the k-nearest neighbors algorithm

The k-nearest neighbors algorithm is a simple machine learning algorithm used for supervised classification. The main components of this algorithm are:

- **A train dataset**: This dataset is formed by instances with one or more attributes that define every instance and a special attribute that determines the label of the instance
- **A distance metric**: This metric is used to determine the distance (or similarity) between the instances of the train dataset and the new instances you want to classify
- **A test dataset**: This dataset is used to measure the behavior of the algorithm

When it has to classify an instance, it calculates the distance against this instance and all the instances of the train dataset. Then, it takes the k-nearest instances and looks at the tag of those instances. The tag with most instances is the tag assigned to the input instance.

In this chapter, we are going to work with the **Bank Marketing** dataset of the **UCI Machine Learning Repository**, which you can download from `http://archive.ics.uci.edu/ml/datasets/Bank+Marketing`. To measure the distance between instances, we are going to use the **Euclidean** distance. With this metric, all the attributes of instances must have numerical values. Some of the attributes of the Bank Marketing dataset are categorical (that is to say, they can take one or more predefined values), so we can't use the Euclidean distance directly with this dataset. It's possible to assign ordinal numbers to each categorical value, for example, for marital status, 0 would be *single*, 1 would be *married*, and 2 would be *divorced*. However, this would imply that the *divorced* person is closer to *married* than to *single*, which is disputable. To make all the categorical values equally distant, we create separate attributes such as *married*, *single*, and *divorced*, which have only two values: 0 (*no*) and 1 (*yes*).

Our dataset has 66 attributes and two possible tags: *yes* and *no*. We also divided the data into two subsets:

- **The train dataset**: With 39,129 instances
- **The test dataset**: With 2,059 instances

As we explained in `Chapter 1`, *The First Step - Concurrency Design Principles*, we first implemented a serial version of the algorithm. Then, we looked for the parts of the algorithm that could be parallelized, and we used the Executor framework to execute the concurrent tasks. In the following sections, we explain the serial implementation of the k-nearest neighbors algorithm and two different concurrent versions. The first one has a concurrency with very fine-grained granularity, whereas the second one has coarse-grained granularity.

k-nearest neighbors - serial version

We have implemented the serial version of the algorithm in the `KnnClassifier` class. Internally, this class stores the train dataset and the number `k` (the number of examples that we will use to determine the tag of an instance):

```
public class KnnClassifier {

  private final List <? extends Sample>dataSet;
  private int k;

  public KnnClassifier(List <? extends Sample>dataSet, int k) {
    this.dataSet=dataSet;
    this.k=k;
  }
```

The `KnnClassifier` class only implements a method named `classify` that receives a `Sample` object with the instance we want to classify, and it returns a string with the tag assigned to that instance:

```
public String classify (Sample example) {
```

This method has three main parts; first, we calculate the distances between the input example and all the examples of the train dataset:

```
Distance[] distances=new Distance[dataSet.size()];
int index=0;

for (Sample localExample : dataSet) {
  distances[index]=new Distance();
  distances[index].setIndex(index);
  distances[index].setDistance(EuclideanDistanceCalculator
                        .calculate(localExample, example));
  index++;
}
```

Then, we sort the examples from the lower to the higher distance, using the `Arrays.sort()` method:

```
Arrays.sort(distances);
```

Finally, we count the tag with most instances in the k-nearest examples:

```
Map<String, Integer> results = new HashMap<>();
for (int i = 0; i < k; i++) {
  Sample localExample = dataSet.get(distances[i].getIndex());
  String tag = localExample.getTag();
  results.merge(tag, 1, (a, b) ->a+b);
}
return Collections.max(results.entrySet(),
                    Map.Entry.comparingByValue()).getKey();
}
```

To calculate the distance between two examples, we can use the Euclidean distance implemented in an auxiliary class. This is the code of that class:

```
public class EuclideanDistanceCalculator {
  public static double calculate (Sample example1, Sample example2) {
    double ret=0.0d;

    double[] data1=example1.getExample();
    double[] data2=example2.getExample();

    if (data1.length!=data2.length) {
      throw new IllegalArgumentException ("Vector doesn't have
                                        the same length");
    }

    for (int i=0; i<data1.length; i++) {
      ret+=Math.pow(data1[i]-data2[i], 2);
    }
    return Math.sqrt(ret);
  }

}
```

We have also used the `Distance` class to store the distance between the `Sample` input and an instance of the train dataset. It only has two attributes: the index of the example of the train dataset and the distance to the input example. In addition, it implements the `Comparable` interface to use the `Arrays.sort()` method. Finally, the `Sample` class stores an instance. It only has an array of doubles and a string with the tag of that instance.

K-nearest neighbors - a fine-grained concurrent version

If you analyze the serial version of the k-nearest neighbors algorithm, you can find the following two points where you can parallelize the algorithm:

- **The computation of the distances**: Every loop iteration that calculates the distance between the input example and one of the examples of the train dataset is independent of the others
- **The sort of the distances**: Java 8 included the `parallelSort()` method in the `Array` class to sort arrays in a concurrent way

In the first concurrent version of the algorithm, we are going to create a task per distance between examples that we're going to calculate. We are also going to give the possibility to make a concurrent sort of arrays of distances. We have implemented this version of the algorithm in a class named `KnnClassifierParrallelIndividual`. It stores the train dataset, the k parameter, the `ThreadPoolExecutor` object to execute the parallel tasks, an attribute to store the number of worker-threads we want to have in the executor, and an attribute to store if we want to make a parallel sort.

We are going to create an executor with a fixed number of threads so that we can control the resources of the system that this executor is going to use. This number will be the number of processors available in the system that we obtain with the `availableProcessors()` method of the `Runtime` class multiplied by the value of a parameter of the constructor named `factor`. Its value will be the number of threads you will have from the processor. We will always use the value 1, but you can test with other values and compare the results. This is the constructor of the classification:

```
public class KnnClassifierParallelIndividual {

   private final List<? extends Sample>dataSet;
   private final int k;
   private final ThreadPoolExecutor executor;
   private final int numThreads;
   private final boolean parallelSort;

   public KnnClassifierParallelIndividual(List<? extends Sample>dataSet,
                                   int k, int factor,
                                   booleanparallelSort) {
      this.dataSet=dataSet;
      this.k=k;
      numThreads=factor* (Runtime.getRuntime().availableProcessors());
      executor=(ThreadPoolExecutor)Executors
```

```
                              .newFixedThreadPool(numThreads);
        this.parallelSort=parallelSort;
    }
```

To create the executor, we have used the `Executors` utility class and its `newFixedThreadPool()` method. This method receives the number of worker-threads you want to have in the executor. The executor will never have more worker-threads than the number you specified in the constructor. This method returns an `ExecutorService` object, but we cast it to a `ThreadPoolExecutor` object to have access to methods provided by the class and not included in the interface.

This class also implements the `classify()` method that receives an example and returns a string.

First, we create a task for every distance we need to calculate and send them to the executor. Then, the main thread has to wait for the end of the execution of those tasks. To control that finalization, we used a synchronization mechanism provided by the Java concurrency API: the `CountDownLatch` class. This class allows a thread to wait until other threads have arrived at a determined point in their code. It's initialized with the number of threads you want to wait for. It implements two methods:

- `getDown()`: This method decreases the number of threads you have to wait for
- `await()`: This method suspends the thread that calls it until the counter reaches zero

In this case, we initialize the `CountDownLatch` class with the number of tasks we are going to execute in the executor. The main thread calls the `await()` method and every task, when it finishes its calculation, calls the `getDown()` method:

```
public String classify (Sample example) throws Exception {

  Distance[] distances=new Distance[dataSet.size()];
  CountDownLatchendController=new CountDownLatch(dataSet.size());

  int index=0;
  for (Sample localExample : dataSet) {
    IndividualDistanceTask task=new IndividualDistanceTask(distances,
                      index, localExample, example, endController);
    executor.execute(task);
    index++;
  }
  endController.await();
```

Then, depending on the value of the `parallelSort` attribute, we call the `Arrays.sort()` or `Arrays.parallelSort()` method.

```
if (parallelSort) {
  Arrays.parallelSort(distances);
} else {
  Arrays.sort(distances);
}
```

Finally, we calculate the tag assigned to the input examples. This code is the same as in the serial version.

The `KnnClassifierParallelIndividual` class also includes a method to shut down the executor calling its `shutdown()` method. It you don't call this method, your application will never end because threads created by the executor are still alive and waiting for new tasks to do. Previously submitted tasks are executed, and newly submitted tasks are rejected. The method doesn't wait for the finalization of the executor and returns immediately:

```
public void destroy() {
  executor.shutdown();
}
```

A critical part of this example is the `IndividualDistanceTask` class. This is the class that calculates the distance between the input example and an example of the train dataset as a concurrent task. It stores the full array of distances (we are going to establish the value of one of its positions only), the index of the example of the train dataset, both examples, and the `CountDownLatch` object used to control the end of the tasks. It implements the `Runnable` interface, so it can be executed in the executor. This is the constructor of the class:

```
public class IndividualDistanceTask implements Runnable {

  private final Distance[] distances;
  private final int index;
  private final Sample localExample;
  private final Sample example;
  private final CountDownLatchendController;

  public IndividualDistanceTask(Distance[] distances, int index, Sample
                                localExample,Sample example,
                                CountDownLatchendController) {
    this.distances=distances;
    this.index=index;
    this.localExample=localExample;
    this.example=example;
    this.endController=endController;
  }
```

The run() method calculates the distance between the two examples using the EuclideanDistanceCalculator class explained before and stores the result in the corresponding position of the distances:

```
@Override
public void run() {
  distances[index] = new Distance();
  distances[index].setIndex(index);
  distances[index].setDistance(EuclideanDistanceCalculator
                        .calculate(localExample, example));
  endController.countDown();
}
```

 Note that although all the tasks share the array of distances, we don't need to use any synchronization mechanisms because each task will modify a different position of the array.

k-nearest neighbors - a coarse-grained concurrent version

The concurrent solution presented in the previous section may have a problem. You are executing too many tasks. If you stop to think, in this case, we have more than 29,000 train examples, so you're going to launch 29,000 tasks per example you want to classify. On the other hand, we have created an executor with a maximum of numThreads worker-threads, so another option is to launch only numThreads tasks and split the train dataset in numThreads groups. For example, if we execute the examples with a quad-core processor, each task will calculate the distances between the input example and approximately 7,000 train examples.

We have implemented this solution in the KnnClassifierParallelGroup class. It's very similar to the KnnClassifierParallelIndividual class with two main differences: firstly, the initial part of the classify() method. Now, we will only have numThreads tasks and we have to split the train dataset into numThreads subsets:

```
public String classify(Sample example) throws Exception {

  Distance distances[] = new Distance[dataSet.size()];
  CountDownLatchendController = new CountDownLatch(numThreads);

  int length = dataSet.size() / numThreads;
  intstartIndex = 0, endIndex = length;
```

```
for (int i = 0; i <numThreads; i++) {
  GroupDistanceTask task = new GroupDistanceTask(distances, startIndex,
                          endIndex, dataSet, example, endController);
  startIndex = endIndex;
  if (i <numThreads - 2) {
    endIndex = endIndex + length;
  } else {
    endIndex = dataSet.size();
  }
  executor.execute(task);

}
endController.await();
```

We calculate the number of samples per task in the length variable. Then, we assign to each thread the start and end indexes of the samples they have to process. For all the threads except the last one, we add the length value to the start index to calculate the end index. For the last one, the last index is the size of the dataset.

Second, this class uses `GroupDistanceTask` instead of `IndividualDistanceTask`. The main difference between those classes is that the first one processes a subset of the train dataset, so it stores the full train dataset and the first and last positions of the dataset it has to process:

```
public class GroupDistanceTask implements Runnable {
  private final Distance[] distances;
  private final intstartIndex, endIndex;
  private final Example example;
  private final List<? extends Example>dataSet;
  private final CountDownLatchendController;

  public GroupDistanceTask(Distance[] distances, intstartIndex,
                  intendIndex, List<? extends Example>dataSet,
                  Example example, CountDownLatchendController) {
    this.distances = distances;
    this.startIndex = startIndex;
    this.endIndex = endIndex;
    this.example = example;
    this.dataSet = dataSet;
    this.endController = endController;
  }
```

The `run()` method processes a set of examples instead of only one example:

```
public void run() {
   for (int index = startIndex; index <endIndex; index++) {
      Sample localExample=dataSet.get(index);
      distances[index] = new Distance();
      distances[index].setIndex(index);
      distances[index].setDistance(EuclideanDistanceCalculator
                                  .calculate(localExample, example));
   }
   endController.countDown();
}
```

Comparing the solutions

Let's compare the different versions of the k-nearest neighbors algorithms we have implemented. We have the following five different versions:

- The serial version
- The fine-grained concurrent version with serial sorting
- The fine-grained concurrent version with concurrent sorting
- The coarse-grained concurrent version with serial sorting
- The coarse-grained concurrent version with concurrent sorting

To test the algorithm, we have used 2,059 test instances that we take from the Bank Marketing dataset. We have classified all those examples using the five versions of the algorithm using the values of k as 10, 30, and 50 and measuring their execution time.

We have executed the examples using the **JMH framework** (`http://openjdk.java.net/projects/code-tools/jmh/`), which allows you to implement micro benchmarks in Java. Using a framework for benchmarking is a better solution that simply measures time using methods such as `currentTimeMillis()` or `nanoTime()`. We have executed them 10 times in two different architectures

- A computer with an Intel Core i5-5300 CPU with Windows 7 and 16 GB of RAM. This processor has two cores and each core can execute two threads, so we will have four parallel threads.
- A computer with an AMD A8-640 APU with Windows 10 and 8 GB of RAM. This processor has four cores.

These are the executions times in seconds:

Algorithm	K	AMD	Intel
Serial	10	309.99	126.26
	30	310.22	125.65
	50	309.59	126.48
Fine-grained serial sort	10	153.19	89.97
	30	152.85	90.61
	50	155.01	89.97
Fine-grained concurrent sort	10	120.10	76.81
	30	122.00	76.69
	50	125.61	73.33
Coarse-grained serial sort	10	138.28	77,99
	30	137.54	78,69
	50	137.85	78,25
Coarse-grained concurrent sort	10	107.62	66,48
	30	107.36	65,93
	50	106.61	66,22

We can draw the following conclusions:

- The selected values of the K parameter (10, 30, and 50) don't affect the execution time of the algorithm. The five versions present similar results for the three values in both architectures.
- As was expected, the use of the concurrent sort with the `Arrays.parallelSort()` method gives a great improvement in performance in the fine-grained and the coarse-grained concurrent versions of the algorithms.
- Both concurrent versions increment the performance of the application, but the coarse-grained version offers a great improvement in performance, with serial or parallel sorting.

So, the best version of the algorithm is the coarse-grained solution using parallel sorting, if we compare it with the serial version calculating the speedup.

$$S = \frac{T_{serial}}{T_{concurrent}} = \frac{99.218}{53.255} = 1.86$$

This example shows how a good selection of a concurrent solution can give us a great improvement and a bad selection can give us a bad performance.

Second example - concurrency in a client/server environment

The client/server model is a software architecture where applications are split into two parts: the server part that provides resources (data, operations, printer, storage, and so on) and the client part that uses the resources provided by the server. Traditionally, this architecture was used in the enterprise world but, with the boom in the internet, is still an actual topic. You can see a web application as a client/server application where the server part is the backend part of the application that is executed on a web server and the web navigator executes the client part of the application. SOA (short for Service-Oriented Architecture) is another example of a client/server architecture where the web services exposed are the server part and the different clients that consume them are the client part.

In a client/server environment, we usually have one server and a lot of clients that use the services provided by the server, so the performance of the server is a critical aspect when you have to design one of these systems.

In this section, we will implement a simple client/server application. It will make a search of data over the **World Development Indicators** of the **World Bank** that you can download from here: http://data.worldbank.org/data-catalog/world-development-indicators. This data contains the values of different indicators over all the countries in the world from 1960 to 2014.

The main characteristics of our server will be:

- The client and the server will connect using sockets
- The client will send its queries in a string, and the server will respond with results in another string

- The server can respond to three different queries:
    - **Query**: The format of this query is
      `q;codCountry;codIndicator;year` where `codCountry` is the
      code of the country, `codIndicator` is the code of the indicator,
      and `year` is an optional parameter with the year you want to
      query. The server will respond with the information in a single
      string.
    - **Report**: The format of this query is `r;codIndicator` where
      `codIndicator` is the code of the indicator you want to report. The
      server will respond with the mean value of that indicator for all
      countries over the years in a single string.
    - **Stop**: The format of this query is `z;`. The server stops its execution
      when it receives this command.
- In other cases, the server returns an error message.

As in the previous example, we will show you how to implement a serial version of this
client/server application. Then, we will show you how to implement a concurrent version
using an executor. Finally, we will compare the two solutions to view the advantages of the
use of concurrency in this case.

Client/server - serial version

The serial version of our server application has three main parts:

- The **DAO** (short for **Data Access Object**) part, responsible for access to the data
  and obtaining the results of the query
- The command part, formed by a command for each kind of query
- The server part, which receives the queries, calls the corresponding command,
  and returns the results to the client

Let's see each of these parts in detail.

The DAO part

As we mentioned before, the server will make a search of data over the world development
indicators of the World Bank. This data is in a CSV file. The DAO component in the
application loads the entire file into a `List` object in memory. It implements a method per
query it will attend that goes over the list looking for the data.

We don't include the code of this class here because it's simple to implement and it's not the main purpose of this book.

The command part

The command part is an intermediary between the DAO and the server parts. We have implemented a base abstract `Command` class to be the base class of all the commands:

```
public abstract class Command {

  protected final String[] command;

  public Command (String [] command) {
    this.command=command;
  }

  public abstract String execute ();

}
```

Then, we have implemented a command for each query. The query is implemented in the `QueryCommand` class. The `execute()` method is as follows:

```
public String execute() {
  WDIDAOdao=WDIDAO.getDAO();

  if (command.length==3) {
    return dao.query(command[1], command[2]);
  } else if (command.length==4) {
  try {
    return dao.query(command[1], command[2],
                     Short.parseShort(command[3]));
  } catch (Exception e) {
    return "ERROR;Bad Command";
  }
  } else {
    return "ERROR;Bad Command";
  }
}
```

The report is implemented in `ReportCommand`. The `execute()` method is as follows:

```
@Override
public String execute() {

  WDIDAOdao=WDIDAO.getDAO();
```

```
    return dao.report(command[1]);
  }
```

The stop query is implemented in the `StopCommand` class. Its `execute()` method is as follows:

```
@Override
public String execute() {
  return "Server stopped";
}
```

Finally, the error situations are processed by the `ErrorCommand` class. Its `execute()` method is as follows:

```
@Override
public String execute() {
  return "Unknown command: "+command[0];
}
```

The server part

Finally, the server part is implemented in the `SerialServer` class. First of all, it initializes the DAO calling the `getDAO()` method. The main objective is that the DAO loads all the data:

```
public class SerialServer {

  public static void main(String[] args) throws IOException {
    WDIDAOdao = WDIDAO.getDAO();
    booleanstopServer = false;
    System.out.println("Initialization completed.");

    try (ServerSocketserverSocket = new ServerSocket(Constants
                                        .SERIAL_PORT)) {
```

After this, we have a loop that will be executed until the server receives a stop query. This loop performs the following four steps:

- Receives a query for a client
- Parses and splits the elements of the query
- Calls the corresponding command
- Returns the results to the client

These four steps are shown in the following code snippet:

```
do {
  try (Socket clientSocket = serverSocket.accept();
    PrintWriter out = new PrintWriter(clientSocket.getOutputStream(),
                                      true);
    BufferedReader in = new BufferedReader(new InputStreamReader
                                 (clientSocket.getInputStream())));) {
    String line = in.readLine();
    Command command;

    String[] commandData = line.split(";");
    System.out.println("Command: " + commandData[0]);
    switch (commandData[0]) {
      case "q":
        System.out.println("Query");
        command = new QueryCommand(commandData);
        break;
      case "r":
        System.out.println("Report");
        command = new ReportCommand(commandData);
        break;
      case "z":
        System.out.println("Stop");
        command = new StopCommand(commandData);
        stopServer = true;
        break;
      default:
        System.out.println("Error");
        command = new ErrorCommand(commandData);
    }
    String response = command.execute();
    System.out.println(response);
  } catch (IOException e) {
    e.printStackTrace();
  }
} while (!stopServer);
```

Client/version - parallel version

The serial version of the server has a very important limitation. While it is processing one query, it can't attend to other queries. If the server needs an important amount of time to respond to every request, or to certain requests, the performance of the server will be very low.

We can obtain a better performance using concurrency. If the server creates a thread when it receives a request, it can delegate all the processes of the query to the thread and it can attend new requests. This approach can also have some problems. If we receive a high number of queries, we can saturate the system, creating too many threads. But if we use an executor with a fixed number of threads, we can control the resources used by our server and obtain a better performance than the serial version.

To convert our serial server to a concurrent one using an executor, we have to modify the server part. The DAO part is the same, and we have changed the names of the classes that implement the command part, but their implementation is almost the same. Only the stop query changes because now it has more responsibilities. Let's see the details of the implementation of the concurrent server part.

The server part

The concurrent server part is implemented in the `ConcurrentServer` part. We have added two elements not included in the serial server: a cache system, implemented in the `ParallelCache` class, and a log system, implemented in the `Logger` class. First of all, it initializes the DAO part calling the `getDAO()` method. The main objective is that the DAO loads all the data and creates a `ThreadPoolExecutor` object using the `newFixedThreadPool()` method of the `Executors` class. This method receives the maximum number of worker-threads we want in our server. The executor will never have more than those worker-threads. To get the number of worker-threads, we get the number of cores of our system using the `availableProcessors()` method of the `Runtime` class:

```
public class ConcurrentServer {

    private static ThreadPoolExecutor executor;
    private static ParallelCache cache;
    private static ServerSocketserverSocket;
    private static volatileboolean stopped=false;
    public static void main(String[] args) {
        serverSocket=null;
        WDIDAOdao=WDIDAO.getDAO();
        executor=(ThreadPoolExecutor) Executors.newFixedThreadPool
                        (Runtime.getRuntime().availableProcessors());
        cache=new ParallelCache();
        Logger.initializeLog();

        System.out.println("Initialization completed.");
```

The `stopped` Boolean variable is declared as volatile because it will be changed from another thread. The `volatile` keyword ensures that when the `stopped` variable is set to `true` by another thread, this change will be visible in the main method. Without the `volatile` keyword, the change cannot be visible due to CPU caching or compiler optimizations. Then, we initialize `ServerSocket` to listen for the requests:

```
serverSocket = new ServerSocket(Constants.CONCURRENT_PORT);
```

We can't use a try-with-resources statement to manage the server socket. When we receive a `stop` command, we need to shut down the server, but the server is waiting in the `accept()` method of the `serverSocket` object. To force the server to leave that method, we need to explicitly close the server (we'll do that in the `shutdown()` method), so we can't let the try-with-resources statement close the socket for us.

After this, we have a loop that will be executed until the server receives a stop query. This loop performs three steps as follows:

- Receives a query for a client
- Creates a task to process that query
- Sends the task to the executor

These three steps are shown in the following code snippet:

```
do {
  try {
    Socket clientSocket = serverSocket.accept();
    RequestTask task = new RequestTask(clientSocket);
    executor.execute(task);
  } catch (IOException e) {
    e.printStackTrace();
  }
} while (!stopped);
```

Finally, once the server has finished its execution (leaving the loop), we have to wait for the finalization of the executor using the `awaitTermination()` method. This method will block the main thread until the executor has finished its `execution()` method. Then, we shut down the cache system and wait for a message to indicate the end of the execution of the server as follows:

```
executor.awaitTermination(1, TimeUnit.DAYS);
System.out.println("Shutting down cache");
cache.shutdown();
System.out.println("Cache ok");

System.out.println("Main server thread ended");
```

We have added two additional methods: the `getExecutor()` method , which returns the `ThreadPoolExecutor` object that is used to execute the concurrent tasks and the `shutdown()` method, which is used to finish the executor of the server in an ordered way. It calls the `shutdown()` method of the executor and closes `ServerSocket`:

```
public static void shutdown() {
  stopped = true;
  System.out.println("Shutting down the server...");
  System.out.println("Shutting down executor");
  executor.shutdown();
  System.out.println("Executor ok");
  System.out.println("Closing socket");
  try {
    serverSocket.close();
    System.out.println("Socket ok");
  } catch (IOException e) {
    e.printStackTrace();
  }
  System.out.println("Shutting down logger");
  Logger.sendMessage("Shutting down the logger");
  Logger.shutdown();
  System.out.println("Logger ok");
}
```

In the concurrent server, there is an essential part: the `RequestTask` class that processes every request of the client. This class implements the `Runnable` interface, so it can be executed in an executor in a concurrent way. Its constructor receives the `Socket` parameter that will be used to communicate to the client:

```
public class RequestTask implements Runnable {

  private final Socket clientSocket;

  public RequestTask(Socket clientSocket) {
    this.clientSocket = clientSocket;
  }
```

The `run()` method does everything the serial server does to respond to every request:

- Receives a query for a client
- Parses and splits the elements of the query
- Calls the corresponding command
- Returns the results to the client

The following is its code snippet:

```
public void run() {

  try (PrintWriter out = new  PrintWriter(clientSocket
                                      .getOutputStream(), true);
  BufferedReader in = new BufferedReader(new InputStreamReader
                              (clientSocket.getInputStream()));) {

    String line = in.readLine();
    Logger.sendMessage(line);
    ParallelCache cache = ConcurrentServer.getCache();
    String ret = cache.get(line);

    if (ret == null) {
      Command command;
      String[] commandData = line.split(";");
      System.out.println("Command: " + commandData[0]);
      switch (commandData[0]) {
        case "q":
          System.err.println("Query");
          command = new ConcurrentQueryCommand(commandData);
          break;
        case "r":
          System.err.println("Report");
          command = new ConcurrentReportCommand(commandData);
          break;
        case "s":
          System.err.println("Status");
          command = new ConcurrentStatusCommand(commandData);
          break;
        case "z":
          System.err.println("Stop");
          command = new ConcurrentStopCommand(commandData);
          break;
        default:
          System.err.println("Error");
          command = new ConcurrentErrorCommand(commandData);
          break;
      }
      ret = command.execute();
      if (command.isCacheable()) {
        cache.put(line, ret);
      }
    } else {
      Logger.sendMessage("Command "+line+" was found in the cache");
    }
```

```
    System.out.println(ret);
  } catch (Exception e) {
    e.printStackTrace();
  } finally {
    try {
      clientSocket.close();
    } catch (IOException e) {
      e.printStackTrace();
    }
  }
}
```

The command part

In the command part, we have renamed all the classes as you can see in the previous fragment of code. The implementation is the same except in the `ConcurrentStopCommand` class. Now, it calls the `shutdown()` method of the `ConcurrentServer` class to terminate the execution of the server in an ordered way. The following is the source code of the `execute()` method:

```
@Override
public String execute() {
  ConcurrentServer.shutdown();
  return "Server stopped";
}
```

Also, now the `Command` class contains a new `isCacheable()` Boolean method that returns `true` if the command result is stored in the cache and `false` otherwise.

Extra components of the concurrent server

We have implemented some extra components in the concurrent server: a new command to return information about the status of the server, a cache system to store the results of the commands, time-saving when a request is repeated, and a log system to write error and debug information. The following sections describe each of these components.

The status command

First of all, we have a new possible query. It has the formats and is processed by the
ConcurrentStatusCommand class. It gets ThreadPoolExecutor used by the server and
obtains information about the status of the executor:

```
public class ConcurrentStatusCommand extends Command {
  public ConcurrentStatusCommand (String[] command) {
    super(command);
    setCacheable(false);
  }
  @Override
  public String execute() {
    StringBuildersb=new StringBuilder();
    ThreadPoolExecutor executor=ConcurrentServer.getExecutor();
    Logger.sendMessage(sb.toString());
    return sb.toString();
  }
}
```

The information we can obtain from the server is:

- getActiveCount(): This returns the approximate number of tasks that execute
  our concurrent tasks. There could be more threads in the pool, but they could be
  idle.
- getMaximumPoolSize(): This returns the maximum number of worker-threads
  the executor can have.
- getCorePoolSize(): This returns the core number of worker-threads the
  executor will have. This number determines the minimum number of threads the
  pool will have.
- getPoolSize(): This returns the current number of threads in the pool.
- getLargestPoolSize(): This returns the maximum number of threads of the
  pool during its execution.
- getCompletedTaskCount(): This returns the number of tasks the executor has
  executed.
- getTaskCount(): This returns the approximate number of tasks that have ever
  been scheduled for execution.
- getQueue().size(): This returns the number of tasks that are waiting in the
  queue of tasks.

As we have created our executor using the `newFixedThreadPool()` method of the `Executor` class, our executor will have the same maximum and core worker-threads.

The cache system

We have included a cache system in our parallel server to avoid the search of data that have been recently been made. Our cache system has three elements:

- **The CacheItem class**: This class represents every element stored in the cache. It has four attributes:
    - The command stored in the cache. We will store the `query` and `report` commands in the cache.
    - The response generated by that command.
    - The creation date of the item in the cache.
    - The last time this item was accessed in the cache.

- **The CleanCacheTask class**: If we store all the commands in the cache but never delete the elements stored in it, the cache will increase its size indefinitely. To avoid this situation, we can have a task that deletes elements in the cache. We are going to implement this task as a `Thread` object. There are two options:
    - You can have the maximum size in the cache. If the cache has more elements than the maximum size, you can delete the elements that have been accessed less recently.
    - You can delete the elements that haven't been accessed for a predefined period of time from the cache. We are going to use this approach.

- **The ParallelCache class**: This class implements the operations to store and retrieve elements in the cache. To store the data in the cache, we have used a `ConcurrentHashMap` data structure. As the cache will be shared between all the tasks of the server, we have to use a synchronization mechanism to protect the access to the cache, avoiding data race conditions. We have three options:
    - We can use a non-synchronized data structure (for example, a `HashMap`) and add the necessary code to synchronize accesses to this data structure, for example, with a lock. You can also convert a `HashMap` into a synchronized structure using the `synchronizedMap()` method of the `Collections` class.
    - Use a synchronized data structure, for example, `Hashtable`. In this case, we don't have data race conditions, but the performance can be better.

- Use a concurrent data structure, for example, a ConcurrentHashMap class, which eliminates the possibility of data race conditions and it's optimized to work in a high concurrent environment. This is the option we're going to implement using an object of the ConcurrentHashMap class.

The code of the CleanCacheTask class is as follows:

```java
public class CleanCacheTask implements Runnable {

  private final ParallelCache cache;

  public CleanCacheTask(ParallelCache cache) {
    this.cache = cache;
  }

  @Override
  public void run() {
    try {
      while (!Thread.currentThread().interrupted()) {
        TimeUnit.SECONDS.sleep(10);
        cache.cleanCache();
      }
    } catch (InterruptedException e) {

    }
  }

}
```

The class has a ParallelCache object. Every 10 seconds, it executes the cleanCache() method of the ParallelCache instance.

The ParallelCache class has five different methods. First, the constructor of the class that initializes the elements of the cache. It creates the ConcurrentHashMap object and starts a thread that will execute the CleanCacheTask class:

```java
public class ParallelCache {

  private final ConcurrentHashMap<String, CacheItem> cache;
  private final CleanCacheTask task;
  private final Thread thread;
  public static intMAX_LIVING_TIME_MILLIS = 600_000;
```

```
public ParallelCache() {
  cache=new ConcurrentHashMap<>();
  task=new CleanCacheTask(this);
  thread=new Thread(task);
  thread.start();
}
```

Then, there are two methods to store and retrieve an element in the cache. We use the put() method to insert the element in the HashMap and the get() method to retrieve the element from the HashMap:

```
public void put(String command, String response) {
  CacheItem item = new CacheItem(command, response);
  cache.put(command, item);
}

public String get (String command) {
  CacheItem item=cache.get(command);
  if (item==null) {
    return null;
  }
  item.setAccessDate(new Date());
  return item.getResponse();
}
```

Then, the method to clean the cache used by the CleanCacheTask class is:

```
public void cleanCache() {
  Date revisionDate = new Date();
  Iterator<CacheItem> iterator = cache.values().iterator();

  while (iterator.hasNext()) {
    CacheItem item = iterator.next();
    if (revisionDate.getTime() - item.getAccessDate().getTime()
        >MAX_LIVING_TIME_MILLIS) {
      iterator.remove();
    }
  }
}
```

Finally, the method to shut down the cache that interrupts the thread executing the CleanCacheTask class and the method that returns the number of elements stored in the cache are:

```
public void shutdown() {
  thread.interrupt();
}
```

```
public intgetItemCount() {
  return cache.size();
}
```

The log system

In all the examples in this chapter, we write information in the console using the `System.out.println()` method. When you implement an enterprise application that is going to execute in a production environment, it's a better idea to use a log system to write debug and error information. In Java, `log4j` is the most popular log system. In this example, we are going to implement our own log system implementing the producer/consumer concurrency design pattern. The tasks that will use our log system will be the producers and a special task (executed as a thread), which will write the log information into a file, will be the consumer. The components of this log system are:

- **LogTask**: This class implements the log consumer that after every 10 seconds reads the log messages stored in the queue and writes them to a file. It will be executed by a `Thread` object.
- **Logger**: This is the main class of our log system. It has a queue where the producers will store the information and the consumer will read it. It also includes the methods to add a message into the queue and a method to get all the messages stored in the queue and writes them to disk.

To implement the queue, as happens with the cache system, we need a concurrent data structure to avoid any data inconsistency errors. We have two options:

- Use a **blocking data structure**, which blocks the thread when the queue is full (in our case, it will never be full) or empty.
- Use a **non-blocking data structure**, which returns a special value if the queue is full or empty.

We have chosen a non-blocking data structure, the `ConcurrentLinkedQueue` class, which implements the `Queue` interface. We use the `offer()` method to insert elements in the queue and the `poll()` method to get elements from it.

The `LogTask` class code is very simple:

```
public class LogTask implements Runnable {

  @Override
  public void run() {
    try {
```

```
        while (Thread.currentThread().interrupted()) {
          TimeUnit.SECONDS.sleep(10);
          Logger.writeLogs();
        }
      } catch (InterruptedException e) {
    }
    Logger.writeLogs();
  }
}
```

The class implements the `Runnable` interface and, in the `run()` method, calls the `writeLogs()` method of the `Logger` class every 10 seconds.

The `Logger` class has five different static methods. First of all is a static block of code that initializes and starts a thread that executes the `LogTask` and creates the `ConcurrentLinkedQueue` class used to store the log data:

```
public class Logger {

  private static ConcurrentLinkedQueue<String>logQueue = new
                          ConcurrentLinkedQueue<String>();

  private static Thread thread;

  private static final String LOG_FILE = Paths.get("output",
                          "server.log").toString();

  static {
    LogTask task = new LogTask();
    thread = new Thread(task);
  }
```

Then, there is a `sendMessage()` method that receives a string as parameter and stores that message in the queue. To store the message, it uses the `offer()` method:

```
public static void sendMessage(String message) {
  logQueue.offer(new Date()+": "+message);
}
```

A critical method of this class is the `writeLogs()` class. It obtains and deletes all the log messages stored in the queue using the `poll()` method of the `ConcurrentLinkedQueue` class and writes them to a file:

```
public static void writeLogs() {
  String message;
  Path path = Paths.get(LOG_FILE);
  try (BufferedWriterfileWriter = Files.newBufferedWriter(path,
```

```
                                    StandardOpenOption.CREATE,
                                    StandardOpenOption.APPEND)) {
    while ((message = logQueue.poll()) != null) {
      fileWriter.write(new Date()+": "+message);
      fileWriter.newLine();
    }
  } catch (IOException e) {
    e.printStackTrace();
  }
}
```

Finally, two methods: one to truncate the log file and the other to finish the executor of the log system, which interrupts the thread that is executing `LogTask`:

```
public static void initializeLog() {
  Path path = Paths.get(LOG_FILE);
  if (Files.exists(path)) {
    try (OutputStream out = Files.newOutputStream(path,
                            StandardOpenOption.TRUNCATE_EXISTING)) {

    } catch (IOException e) {
      e.printStackTrace();
    }
  }
  thread.start();
}
public static void shutdown() {
  thread.interrupt();
}
```

Comparing the two solutions

Now it's time to test the serial and concurrent server and see which has a better performance. We have automated the tests by implementing four classes that make queries to the servers. These classes are:

- `SerialClient`: This implements a possible client of the serial server. It makes nine requests using the query message and a query using the report message. It repeats the process 10 times, so it requests 90 queries and 10 reports.
- `MultipleSerialClients`: This class simulates the existence of several clients at the same time. For this, we create a thread for each `SerialClient` and execute them at the same time to see the performance of the server. We have tested from one to five concurrent clients.

- `ConcurrentClient`: This is analogous to the `SerialClient` class, but it calls the concurrent server instead of the serial one.
- `MultipleConcurrentClients`: This is analogous to the `MultipleSerialClients` class, but it calls the concurrent server instead of the serial one.

To test the serial server, you can follow these steps:

1. Launch the serial server and wait for its initialization.
2. Launch the `MultipleSerialClients` class, which launches one, then two, three, four, and, finally, five `SerialClient` classes.

You can follow a similar process with the concurrent server:

1. Launch the concurrent server and wait for its initialization.
2. Launch the `MultipleConcurrentClients` class, which launches one, two, three, four, and, finally, five `ConcurrentClient` classes.

To compare the execution times of both versions, we have implemented a microbenchmark using the JMH framework (`http://openjdk.java.net/projects/code-tools/jmh/`) that allows you to implement microbenchmarks in Java. Using a framework for benchmarking is a better solution that simply measures time using methods such as `currentTimeMillis()` or `nanoTime()`. We have executed them 10 times in two different architectures:

- A computer with an Intel Core i5-5300 CPU with Windows 7 and 16 GB of RAM. This processor has two cores and each core can execute two threads, so we will have four parallel threads.
- A computer with an AMD A8-640 APU with Windows 10 and 8 GB of RAM. This processor has four cores.

These are the results of all these executions:

Clients	AMD			Intel		
	Serial	Concurrent	Speedup	Serial	Concurrent	Speedup
1	4.970	4.391	1.13	1.090	0.914	1.19
2	9.713	5.154	1.88	1.981	1.312	1.51
3	14.565	6.244	2.33	2.903	1.644	1.77
4	19.751	7.676	2.57	3.878	1.988	1.95
5	24.212	8.434	2.87	4.775	2.346	2.04

The contents of the cells are the mean time of each client in seconds. We can draw the following conclusions:

- Execution times in both architectures are very different. Take into account that there are more elements, such as the hard disk, the memory, or the operating system, that can affect the performance. In both cases, speedup is very similar.
- The performance of both kinds of servers is affected by the number of concurrent clients that send requests to our server.
- In all cases, the execution times of the concurrent version are much lower than the execution times of the serial one.

Other methods of interest

Throughout the pages of this chapter, we have used some classes of the Java concurrency API to implement basic functionalities of the Executor framework. These classes also have other interesting methods. In this section, we explain some of them.

The `Executors` class provides other methods to create `ThreadPoolExecutor` objects. These methods are:

- `newCachedThreadPool()`: This method creates a `ThreadPoolExecutor` object that reuses a worker-thread if it's idle, but it creates a new one if it's necessary. There is no maximum number of worker-threads.
- `newSingleThreadExecutor()`: This method creates a `ThreadPoolExecutor` object that uses only a single worker-thread. The tasks you send to the executor are stored in a queue until the worker-thread can execute them.
- The `CountDownLatch` class provides the following additional methods:
    - `await(long timeout, TimeUnit unit)`: It waits till the internal counter arrives at zero to pass the time specified in the parameters. If the time passes, the method returns the `false` value.
    - `getCount()`: This method returns the actual value of the internal counter.

There are two types of concurrent data structures in Java:

- **Blocking data structures**: When you call a method and the library can't do that operation (for example, you try to obtain an element, and the data structure is empty), they block the thread until the operation can be done.
- **Non-blocking data structures**: When you call a method and the library can't do that operation (because the structure is empty or full), the method returns a special value or throws an exception.

There are data structures that implement both behaviors and data structures that implement only one. Usually, blocking data structures also implement the methods with non-blocking behavior, and non-blocking data structures don't implement the blocking methods.

The methods that implement the blocking operations are:

- `put()`, `putFirst()`, `putLast()`: These insert an element in the data structure. If it's full, it blocks the thread until there is space.
- `take()`, `takeFirst()`, `takeLast()`: These return and remove an element of the data structure. If it's empty, it blocks the thread until there is an element in it.

The methods that implement the non-blocking operations are:

- `add()`, `addFirst()`, `addLast()`: These insert an element in the data structure. If it's full, the method throws an `IllegalStateException` exception.
- `remove()`, `removeFirst()`, `removeLast()`: These return and remove an element from the data structure. If it's empty, the method throws an `IllegalStateException` exception.
- `element()`, `getFirst()`, `getLast()`: These return but don't remove an element from the data structure. If it's empty, the method throws an `IllegalStateException` exception.
- `offer()`, `offerFirst()`, `offerLast()`: These insert an element value in the data structure. If it's full, they return the `false` Boolean value.
- `poll()`, `pollFirst()`, `pollLast()`: These return and remove an element from the data structure. If it's empty, they return the null value.
- `peek()`, `peekFirst()`, `peekLast()`: These return but don't remove an element from the data structure. If it's empty, they return the null value.

In `Chapter 11`, *Diving into Concurrent Data Structures and Synchronization Utilities*, we will describe concurrent data structures in more detail.

Summary

In simple concurrent applications, we execute concurrent tasks using the `Runnable` interface and the `Thread` class. We create and manage the threads and control their execution. We can't follow this approach in big concurrent applications because it can create many problems. For these cases, the Java concurrency API has introduced the Executor framework. In this chapter, we presented the basic characteristics and components that form this framework. First of all, we explored the `Executor` interface, which defines the basic method to send a `Runnable` task to an executor. This interface has a subinterface, the `ExecutorService` interface, which includes methods to send to the executor tasks that return a result (these tasks implement the `Callable` interface, as we will see in `Chapter 5`, *Getting Data from Tasks - Callable and Future Interfaces*), and a list of tasks.

The `ThreadPoolExecutor` class is the basic implementation of both interfaces: adding additional methods to get information about the status of the executor and the number of threads or tasks that it is executing. The easiest way to create an object of this class is using the `Executors` utility class, which includes methods to create different kinds of executors.

We showed you how to use executors and convert serial algorithms to concurrent ones using executors implementing two real-world examples. The first example is the k-nearest neighbors algorithm, which we applied to the Bank Marketing dataset of the UCI machine learning repository. The second example is a client/server application to make queries over the World Development Indicators of the World Bank.

In both cases, the use of executors gave us a great improvement in performance.

In the next chapter, we will describe how to implement advanced techniques with executors. We are going to complete our client/server application by adding the possibility to cancel and execute tasks with a higher priority that will be executed before the tasks with a lower priority. We also will show you how to implement tasks that will execute periodically, implementing an RSS news reader.

4
Getting the Most from Executors

In Chapter 3, *Managing Lots of Threads - Executors*, we introduced the basic characteristics of executors as a way to improve the performance of concurrent applications that execute lots of concurrent tasks. In this chapter, we go a step further and explain advanced characteristics of executors that make them a powerful tool for your concurrent application. In this chapter, we will cover the following:

- Advanced characteristics of executors
- First example - an advanced server application
- Second example - executing periodic tasks
- Additional information about executors

Advanced characteristics of executors

An executor is a class that allows programmers to execute concurrent tasks without being worried about the creation and management of threads. Programmers create Runnable objects and send them to the executor that creates and manages the necessary threads to execute those tasks. In Chapter 3, *Managing Lots of Threads - Executors*, we introduced the basic characteristics of the executor framework:

- How to create an executor and the different options we have when we create one
- How to send a concurrent task to an executor
- How to control the resources used by the executor
- How the executor, internally, uses a pool of threads to optimize the performance of the application

However, executors can give you many more options to make them a powerful mechanism for your concurrent application.

Cancellation of tasks

You can cancel the execution of a task after you send it to an executor. When you send a Runnable object to an executor using the submit() method, it returns an implementation of the Future interface. This class allows you to control the execution of the task. It has the cancel() method that attempts to cancel the execution of the task. It receives a Boolean value as a parameter. If it takes the true value and the executor is executing this task, the thread executing the task will be interrupted.

These are the situations when the task you want to cancel can't be canceled:

- The task has already been canceled
- The task has finished its execution
- The task is running and you supplied false as a parameter to the cancel() method
- Other reasons not specified in the API documentation

The cancel() method returns a Boolean value to indicate whether the task has been canceled or not.

Scheduling the execution of tasks

The ThreadPoolExecutor class is a basic implementation of the Executor and ExecutorService interfaces. But the Java concurrency API provides an extension of this class to allow the execution of scheduled tasks. This is the ScheduledThreadPoolExeuctor class, and you can:

- Execute a task after a delay
- Execute a task periodically; this includes the execution of tasks at a fixed rate or with a fixed delay

Overriding the executor methods

The executor framework is a very flexible mechanism. You can implement your own executor extending one of the existing classes (`ThreadPoolExecutor` or `ScheduledThreadPoolExecutor`) to get the desired behavior. These classes include methods that make it easy to change how the executor works. If you override `ThreadPoolExecutor`, you can override the following methods:

- `beforeExecute()`: This method is invoked before the execution of concurrent tasks in an executor. It receives the `Runnable` object that is going to be executed and the `Thread` object that will execute it. The `Runnable` object that this method receives is an instance of the `FutureTask` class and not the `Runnable` object you sent to the executor using the `submit()` method.
- `afterExecute()`: This method is invoked after the execution of a concurrent task in the executor. It receives the `Runnable` object that has been executed and a `Throwable` object that stores a possible exception thrown inside the task. As in the `beforeExecute()` method, the `Runnable` object is an instance of the `FutureTask` class.
- `newTaskFor()`: This method creates the task that is going to execute the `Runnable` object you sent using the `submit()` method. It must return an implementation of the `RunnableFuture` interface. By default, Open JDK 9 and Oracle JDK 9 returns an instance of the `FutureTask` class, but this might change in future implementations.

If you extend the `ScheduledThreadPoolExecutor` class, you can override the `decorateTask()` method. This method is like the `newTaskFor()` method for scheduled tasks. It allows you to override the tasks executed by the executor.

Changing some initialization parameters

You can also change the behavior of an executor by changing some parameters when it's created. The most useful ones are as follows:

- `BlockingQueue<Runnable>`: Every executor uses an internal `BlockingQueue` to store the tasks that are waiting for its execution. You can pass any implementation of this interface as a parameter. For example, you can change the default order used by the executor to execute the tasks.

- `ThreadFactory`: You can specify an implementation of the `ThreadFactory` interface, and the executor will use that factory to create the threads that will execute the tasks. For example, you can use a `ThreadFactory` interface to create an extension of the `Thread` class that saves log information about the execution times of the tasks.

- `RejectedExecutionHandler`: After you call the `shutdown()` or the `shutdownNow()` method, all the tasks that are sent to the executor will be rejected. You can specify an implementation of the `RejectedExecutionHandler` interface to manage this situation.

First example - an advanced server application

In `Chapter 3`, *Managing Lots of Threads - Executors*, we present an example of a client/server application. We implemented a server to search data over the **World Development Indicators** of the World Bank and a client that makes multiple calls to that server to test the performance of the executor.

In this section, we will extend that example to add to it the following characteristics:

- You can cancel the execution of queries in the server, using a new cancellation query.
- You can control the order of execution of queries using a priority parameter. Tasks with a higher priority will be executed first.
- The server will calculate the number of tasks and the total execution time used by the different users that use the server.

To implement these new characteristics, we have made the following changes to the server:

- We have added two parameters to every query. The first one is the name of the user that sends the query, and the other is the priority of the query. The new format of the queries is:
  - **Query:**
    `q;username;priority;codCountry;codIndicator;year`
    where `username` is the name of the user, `priority` is the priority of the query, `codCountry` is the code of the country, `codIndicator` is the code of the indicator, and `year` is an optional parameter with the year you want to query.

- **Report**: `r;username;priority;codIndicator` where `username` is the name of the user, `priority` is the priority of the query, and `codIndicator` is the code of the indicator you want to report.
  - **Status**: `s;username;priority` where `username` is the name of the user and `priority` is the priority of the query.
  - **Stop**: `z;username;priority` where username is the name of the user, and priority is the priority of the query.
- We have implemented a new query:
  - **Cancel**: `c;username;priority` where `username` is the name of the user, and `priority` is the priority of the query.
- We have implemented our own executor to:
  - Calculate the server use per user.
  - Execute the tasks by priority
  - Control the rejection of tasks
  - We have adapted `ConcurrentServer` and `RequestTask` to take into account the new elements of the server

The other elements of the server (the cache system, the log system, and the `DAO` class) are the same, so they won't be described again.

The ServerExecutor class

As we mentioned earlier, we have implemented our own executor to execute the tasks of the server. We also have implemented some additional but necessary classes to provide all the functionality. Let's describe these classes.

The statistics object

Our server will calculate the number of tasks that every user executes on it and the total execution time these tasks use. To store this data, we have implemented the `ExecutorStatistics` class. It has two attributes to store the information:

```
public class ExecutorStatistics {
    private AtomicLong executionTime = new AtomicLong(0L);
    private AtomicInteger numTasks = new AtomicInteger(0);
```

These attributes are `AtomicVariables` that support atomic operations on single variables. This allows you to use those variables in different threads without using any synchronization mechanisms. Then, it has two methods to increment the number of tasks and the execution time:

```
public void addExecutionTime(long time) {
  executionTime.addAndGet(time);
}
public void addTask() {
  numTasks.incrementAndGet();
}
```

Finally, we have added methods to get the value of both attributes, and we have overridden the `toString()` method to get the information in a readable way:

```
@Override
public String toString() {
  return "Executed Tasks: "+ getNumTasks()+". Execution Time: "+
          getExecutionTime();
}
```

The rejected task controller

When you create an executor, you can specify a class to manage its rejected tasks. A task is rejected by the executor when you submit it after the `shutdown()` or `shutdownNow()` method has been invoked in the executor.

To control this circumstance, we have implemented the `RejectedTaskController` class. This class implements the `RejectedExecutionHandler` interface and implements the `rejectedExecution()` method:

```
public class RejectedTaskController implements
                        RejectedExecutionHandler {

  @Override
  public void rejectedExecution(Runnable task, ThreadPoolExecutor
                                executor) {
    ConcurrentCommand command=(ConcurrentCommand)task;

    try (Socket clientSocket=command.getSocket();
      PrintWriter out = new PrintWriter(clientSocket
                                  .getOutputStream(),true);
    ) {
      String message="The server is shutting down."+
                  " Your request can not be served."+
```

```
                        " Shutting Down: "+
        String.valueOf(executor.isShutdown()) + ". Terminated: "+
        String.valueOf(executor.isTerminated())+ ". Terminating: "+
        String.valueOf(executor.isTerminating());
    System.out.println(message);
  } catch (IOException e) {
    e.printStackTrace();
  }
}
```

The `rejectedExecution()` method is called once per task that is rejected and receives the task that has been rejected, and the executor that has rejected the task, as parameters.

The executor tasks

When you submit a `Runnable` object to an executor, it doesn't execute that `Runnable` object directly. It creates a new object, an instance of the `FutureTask` class, and it's this task that is executed by the worker thread of the executor.

In our case, to measure the execution time of the tasks, we have implemented our own `FutureTask` implementation in the `ServerTask` class. It extends the `FutureTask` class and implements the `Comparable` interface as follows:

```
public class ServerTask<V> extends FutureTask<V> implements
  Comparable<ServerTask<V>>{
```

Internally, it stores the query that is going to execute as a `ConcurrentCommand` object:

```
private ConcurrentCommand command;
```

In the constructor, it uses the constructor of the `FutureTask` class and stores the `ConcurrentCommand` object:

```
public ServerTask(ConcurrentCommand command) {
  super(command, null);
  this.command=command;
}

public ConcurrentCommand getCommand() {
  return command;
}

public void setCommand(ConcurrentCommand command) {
  this.command = command;
}
```

Finally, it implements the `compareTo()` operation comparing the commands stored by the two `ServerTask` instances:

```
@Override
  public int compareTo(ServerTask<V> other) {
   return command.compareTo(other.getCommand());
  }
```

The executor

Now that we have the auxiliary classes of the executor, we have to implement the executor itself. We have implemented the `ServerExecutor` class for this purpose. It extends the `ThreadPoolExecutor` class and has some internal attributes, as follows:

- `startTimes`: This is a `ConcurrentHashMap` to store the start date of every task. The key of the class will be the `ServerTask` object (a `Runnable` object), and the value will be a `Date` object.
- `executionStatistics`: This is a `ConcurrentHashMap` to store the statistics of use per user. The key will be the username and the value will be an `ExecutorStatistics` object.
- `CORE_POOL_SIZE`, `MAXIMUM_POOL_SIZE`, and `KEEP_ALIVE_TIME`: These are constants to define the characteristics of the executor.
- `REJECTED_TASK_CONTROLLER`: This is a `RejectedTaskController` class attribute to control tasks rejected by the executor.

This can be explained from the following code:

```
public class ServerExecutor extends ThreadPoolExecutor {
  private ConcurrentHashMap<Runnable, Date> startTimes;
  private ConcurrentHashMap<String, ExecutorStatistics>
                         executionStatistics;
  private static int CORE_POOL_SIZE = Runtime.getRuntime()
                                  .availableProcessors();
  private static int MAXIMUM_POOL_SIZE = Runtime.getRuntime()
                                    .availableProcessors();
  private static long KEEP_ALIVE_TIME = 10;

  private static RejectedTaskController REJECTED_TASK_CONTROLLER
                       = new RejectedTaskController();

  public ServerExecutor() {
    super(CORE_POOL_SIZE, MAXIMUM_POOL_SIZE, KEEP_ALIVE_TIME,
         TimeUnit.SECONDS, new PriorityBlockingQueue<>(),
```

```
                REJECTED_TASK_CONTROLLER);

     startTimes = new ConcurrentHashMap<>();
     executionStatistics = new ConcurrentHashMap<>();
  }
```

The constructor of the class calls to the parent constructor, creating a
`PriorityBlockingQueue` class to store the tasks that will be executed in the executor. This
class orders the elements according to the result of the execution of the `compareTo()`
method (so the elements stored in it have to implement the `Comparable` interface). The
utilization of this class will allow us to execute our tasks by priority.

Then, we have overridden some methods of the `ThreadPoolExecutor` class. First is the
`beforeExecute()` method. This method is executed before the execution of every task. It
receives the `ServerTask` object and the thread that is going to execute the task as
parameters. In our case, we store the actual date in the `ConcurrentHashMap` with the start
dates of every task as follows:

```
protected void beforeExecute(Thread t, Runnable r) {
   super.beforeExecute(t, r);
   startTimes.put(r, new Date());
}
```

The next method is the `afterExecute()` method. This method is executed after the
execution of every task in the executor and receives the `ServerTask` object that has been
executed as parameter and a `Throwable` object. This last parameter will have a value only
when an exception is thrown during the execution of the task. In our case, we will use this
method to:

1. Calculate the execution time of the task.
2. Update the statistics of the user in the following manner:

```
@Override
protected void afterExecute(Runnable r, Throwable t) {
   super.afterExecute(r, t);
   ServerTask<?> task=(ServerTask<?>)r;
   ConcurrentCommand command=task.getCommand();

   if (t==null) {
     if (!task.isCancelled()) {
       Date startDate = startTimes.remove(r);
       Date endDate=new Date();
       long executionTime= endDate.getTime() -
                           startDate.getTime();
       ExecutorStatistics statistics = executionStatistics
```

```
                              .computeIfAbsent (command.getUsername (),
                          n -> new ExecutorStatistics ());
            statistics.addExecutionTime(executionTime);
            statistics.addTask();
            ConcurrentServer.finishTask (command.getUsername (),
                                  command);
        }
        else {
          String message="The task" + command.hashCode () + "of
                          user" + command.getUsername () + "has
                          been cancelled.";
          Logger.sendMessage(message);
        }

      } else {
        String message="The exception "+t.getMessage ()+" has
                        been thrown.";
        Logger.sendMessage(message);
      }
    }
  }
```

Finally, we have overridden the `newTaskFor()` method. This method will be executed to convert the `Runnable` object we send to the executor using the `submit()` method in the instance of `FutureTask` that will be executed by the executor. In our case, we replace the default `FutureTask` by our `ServerTask` object:

```
@Override
protected <T> RunnableFuture<T> newTaskFor(Runnable runnable, T
                                           value) {
    return new ServerTask<T>(runnable);
}
```

We have included an additional method in the executor to write all the statistics stored in the executor in the log system. This method will be called at the end of the execution of the server, as you will see later. We have the following code:

```
public void writeStatistics() {

    for(Entry<String, ExecutorStatistics> entry: executionStatistics
          .entrySet()) {
      String user = entry.getKey();
      ExecutorStatistics stats = entry.getValue();
      Logger.sendMessage(user+":"+stats);
    }
}
```

The command classes

The command classes execute the different queries you can send to the server. You can send five different queries to your server:

- **Query**: This is to get information about a country, an indicator, and optionally a year. It's implemented by the `ConcurrentQueryCommand` class.
- **Report**: This is to get information about an indicator. It's implemented by the `ConcurrentReportCommand` class.
- **Status**: This is to get information about the status of a server. It's implemented by the `ConcurrentStatusCommand` class.
- **Cancel**: This is to cancel a user's tasks of a user. It's implemented by the `ConcurrentCancelCommand` class.
- **Stop**: To stop the execution of the server. It's implemented by the `ConcurrentStopCommand` class.

We also have the `ConcurrentErrorCommand` class, which manages the situation when an unknown command arrives at the server, and the `ConcurrentCommand` class, which is the base class of all the commands.

The ConcurrentCommand class

This is the base class of every command. It includes all the common behaviors of all the commands, including the following:

- Calling the method that implements the specific logic of every command
- Writing the results to the client
- Closing all the resources used in the communication

The class extends the `Command` class and implements the `Comparable` and `Runnable` interfaces. In the example in `Chapter 3`, *Managing Lots of Threads - Executors*, the commands were simple classes, but in this example, the concurrent commands are `Runnable` objects that will be sent to the executor.

```
public abstract class ConcurrentCommand extends Command implements
        Comparable<ConcurrentCommand>, Runnable{
```

It has three attributes:

- `username`: This is to store the name of the user that sends the query.
- `priority`: This is to store the priority of the query. It will determine the order of execution of the query.
- `socket`: This is the socket used in the communication to the client.

The constructor of the class initializes these attributes:

```
private String username;
private byte priority;
private Socket socket;

public ConcurrentCommand(Socket socket, String[] command) {
  super(command);
  username=command[1];
  priority=Byte.parseByte(command[2]);
  this.socket=socket;

}
```

The main functionality of this class is in the abstract `execute()` method, which will be implemented by every concrete command to calculate and return the results of the query, and in the `run()` method. The `run()` method calls the `execute()` method, stores the result in the cache, writes the result in the socket, and closes all the resources used in the communication. We have the following:

```
@Override
public abstract String execute();

@Override
public void run() {

  String message="Running a Task: Username: "+username+";
                  Priority: "+priority;
  Logger.sendMessage(message);

  String ret=execute();

  ParallelCache cache = ConcurrentServer.getCache();

  if (isCacheable()) {
    cache.put(String.join(";",command), ret);
  }

  try (PrintWriter out = new PrintWriter(socket.getOutputStream(),
```

```
                                                  true);) {

    System.out.println(ret);

  } catch (IOException e) {
    e.printStackTrace();
  }
  System.out.println(ret);
}
```

Finally, the `compareTo()` method uses the priority attribute to determine the order of the tasks. This will be used by the `PriorityBlockingQueue` class to order the tasks, so the tasks with a higher priority will be executed before. Take into account that a task has a higher priority depending on whether the `getPriority()` method returns a lower value. If the `getPriority()` of a task returns 1, that task will have a higher priority than a task where the `getPriority()` method returns 2:

```
@Override
public int compareTo(ConcurrentCommand o) {
  return Byte.compare(o.getPriority(), this.getPriority());
}
```

The concrete commands

We have made minor changes in the classes that implement the different commands, and we added a new one implemented by the `ConcurrentCancelCommand` class. The main logic of these classes is included in the `execute()` method that calculates the response to the query and returns it as a string.

The `execute()` method of the new `ConcurrentCancelCommand` makes a call to the `cancelTasks()` method of the `ConcurrentServer` class. This method will stop the execution of all the pending tasks associated with the user passed as a parameter:

```
@Override
public String execute() {
  ConcurrentServer.cancelTasks(getUsername());

  String message = "Tasks of user "+getUsername()+
                   " has been cancelled.";
  Logger.sendMessage(message);
  return message;
}
```

The execute() method of the ConcurrentQueryCommand uses the query() method of the WDIDAO class to get the data requested by the user. In Chapter 3, *Managing Lots of Threads - Executor*, you can find the implementation of this method. The implementation is almost the same. The only difference is the command array indices as follows:

```
@Override
public String execute() {

  WDIDAO dao=WDIDAO.getDAO();

  if (command.length==5) {
    return dao.query(command[3], command[4]);
  } else if (command.length==6) {
    try {
      return dao.query(command[3], command[4],
                       Short.parseShort(command[5]));
    } catch (NumberFormatException e) {
      return "ERROR;Bad Command";
    }
  } else {
    return "ERROR;Bad Command";
  }
}
```

The execute() method of the ConcurrentReportCommand uses the report() method of the WDIDAO class to get the data. In Chapter 3, *Managing Lots of Threads - Executors*, you also can find the implementation of this method. The implementation here is almost the same. The only difference is the command array index:

```
@Override
public String execute() {

  WDIDAO dao=WDIDAO.getDAO();
  return dao.report(command[3]);
}
```

The ConcurrentStatusCommand has an additional parameter in its constructor: the Executor object that will execute the commands. This command uses this object to obtain information about the executor and send it as a response to the user. The implementation is almost the same as in Chapter 3, *Managing Lots of Threads - Executors*. We have used the same methods to get the status of the Executor object.

ConcurrentStopCommand and ConcurrentErrorCommand are also the same as in Chapter 3, *Managing Lots of Threads - Executors*, so we don't include their source code.

The server part

The server part receives the queries from the clients of the server, creates the command classes that execute those queries, and sends them to the executor. It is implemented by two classes:

- **The ConcurrentServer class**: It includes the `main()` method of the server and additional methods to cancel tasks and finish the execution of the system
- **The RequestTask class**: This class creates the commands and sends them to the executor

The main difference from the example in `Chapter 3`, *Managing Lots of Threads - Executors* is the role of the `RequestTask` class. In the `SimpleServer` example, the `ConcurrentServer` class creates a `RequestTask` object per query and sends them to the executor. In this example, we will only have an instance of the `RequestTask` that will be executed as a thread. When the `ConcurrentSever` receives a connection, it stores the socket to communicate with the client in a concurrent list of pending connections. The `RequestTask` thread reads that socket, processes the data sent by the client, creates the corresponding command, and sends the command to the executor.

The main reason for this change is to leave only the code for the queries in the tasks executed by the executor and leave the preprocessed code outside the executor.

The ConcurrentServer class

The `ConcurrentServer` class needs some internal attributes to work properly:

- A `ParallelCache` instance to use the cache system.
- A `ServerSocket` instance to get connections from the clients.
- A `Boolean` value to know when it has to stop its execution.
- A `LinkedBlockingQueue` instance to store the sockets of the clients that send a message to the server. These sockets will be processed by the `RequestTask` class.
- A `ConcurrentHashMap` to store the `Future` objects associated with every task executed in the executor. The key will be the username of the users that sends the queries, and the values will be another `Map` whose key will be the `ConcurrenCommand` objects and the value will be the `Future` instance associated with that task. We use these `Future` instances to cancel the execution of tasks.
- A `RequestTask` instance to create the commands and send them to the executor.
- A `Thread` object to execute the `RequestTask` object.

The code for this is as follows:

```
public class ConcurrentServer {
  private static ParallelCache cache;
  private static volatile boolean stopped=false;
  private static LinkedBlockingQueue<Socket> pendingConnections;
  private static ConcurrentMap<String, ConcurrentMap
                   <ConcurrentCommand, ServerTask<?>>>
                   taskController;
  private static Thread requestThread;
  private static RequestTask task;
```

The `main()` method of this class initializes these objects and opens the `ServerSocket` instance to listen to the connections from the clients. In addition, it creates the `RequestTask` object and executes it as a thread. It will be in a loop until the `shutdown()` method changes the value of the stopped attribute. After this, it waits for the finalization of the `Executor` object, using the `endTermination()` method of the `RequestTask` object, and shuts down the `Logger` system and the `RequestTask` object with the `finishServer()` method:

```
public static void main(String[] args) {

  WDIDAO dao=WDIDAO.getDAO();
  cache=new ParallelCache();
  Logger.initializeLog();
  pendingConnections = new LinkedBlockingQueue<Socket>();
  taskController = new ConcurrentHashMap<String,
                    ConcurrentHashMap<Integer, Future<?>>>();
  task=new RequestTask(pendingConnections, taskController);
  requestThread=new Thread(task);
  requestThread.start();

  System.out.println("Initialization completed.");

  serverSocket= new ServerSocket(Constants.CONCURRENT_PORT);
  do {
    try {
      Socket clientSocket = serverSocket.accept();
      pendingConnections.put(clientSocket);
    } catch (Exception e) {
      e.printStackTrace();
    }
  } while (!stopped);
  finishServer();
  System.out.println("Shutting down cache");
```

```
   cache.shutdown();
   System.out.println("Cache ok" + new Date());

 }
```

It includes two methods to shut down the executor of the server. The `shutdown()` method changes the value of the stopped variable and closes the `serverSocket` instance. The `finishServer()` method stops the executor, interrupts the thread that executes the `RequestTask` object, and shuts downs the `Logger` system. We divided this process into two parts to use the `Logger` system until the last instruction of the server:

```
public static void shutdown() {
  stopped=true;
  try {
    serverSocket.close();
  } catch (IOException e) {
    e.printStackTrace();
  }
}

private static void finishServer() {
  System.out.println("Shutting down the server...");
  task.shutdown();
  System.out.println("Shutting down Request task");
  requestThread.interrupt();
  System.out.println("Request task ok");
  System.out.println("Closing socket");
  System.out.println("Shutting down logger");
  Logger.sendMessage("Shutting down the logger");
  Logger.shutdown();
  System.out.println("Logger ok");
  System.out.println("Main server thread ended");
}
```

The server includes the method that cancels the tasks associated with a user. As we mentioned before, the `Server` class uses a nested `ConcurrentHashMap` to store all the tasks associated with a user. First, we obtain the `Map` with all the tasks of a user and then we process all the `Future` objects of those tasks calling to the `cancel()` method of the `Future` objects. We pass the value `true` as a parameter, so if the executor is running a task from that user, it will be interrupted. We have included the necessary code to avoid the cancellation of the one `ConcurrentCancelCommand`:

```
public static void cancelTasks(String username) {

  ConcurrentMap<ConcurrentCommand, ServerTask<?>> userTasks =
                           taskController.get(username);
```

```
    if (userTasks == null) {
      return;
    }
    int taskNumber = 0;

    Iterator<ServerTask<?>> it = userTasks.values().iterator();
    while(it.hasNext()) {
      ServerTask<?> task = it.next();
      ConcurrentCommand command = task.getCommand();
      if(!(command instanceof ConcurrentCancelCommand) &&
          task.cancel(true)) {
        taskNumber++;
        Logger.sendMessage("Task with code "+command.hashCode()+
                           "cancelled: "+ command.getClass()
                           .getSimpleName());
        it.remove();
      }
    }
    String message=taskNumber+" tasks has been cancelled.";
    Logger.sendMessage(message);
  }
```

Finally, we have included a method to eliminate the Future object associated with tasks from our nested map of ServerTask objects when that task finishes its execution normally. It's the finishTask() method:

```
public static void finishTask(String username, ConcurrentCommand
                              command) {

  ConcurrentMap<ConcurrentCommand, ServerTask<?>> userTasks =
                          taskController.get(username);
  userTasks.remove(command);
  String message = "Task with code "+command.hashCode()+
                   " has finished";
  Logger.sendMessage(message);

}
```

The RequestTask class

The RequestTask class is the intermediary between the ConcurrentServer class, which connects to the clients, and the Executor class, which executes concurrent tasks. It opens the socket with the client, reads the query data, creates the adequate command, and sends it to the executor.

It uses some internal attributes:

- A `LinkedBlockingQueue` where the `ConcurrentServer` class stores the client sockets
- A `ServerExecutor` to execute the commands as concurrent tasks
- A `ConcurrentHashMap` to store the `Future` objects associated with the tasks

The constructor of the class initializes all these objects.

```
public class RequestTask implements Runnable {
    private LinkedBlockingQueue<Socket> pendingConnections;
    private ServerExecutor executor = new ServerExecutor();
    private ConcurrentMap<String, ConcurrentMap<ConcurrentCommand,
                    ServerTask<?>>> taskController;
    public RequestTask(LinkedBlockingQueue<Socket>
                    pendingConnections, ConcurrentHashMap<String,
                        ConcurrentHashMap<Integer, Future<?>>>
                    taskController) {
        this.pendingConnections = pendingConnections;
        this.taskController = taskController;
    }
```

The main method of this class is the `run()` method. It executes a loop until the thread is interrupted processing the sockets stored in the `pendingConnections` object. In this object, the `ConcurrentServer` class stores sockets to communicate with the different clients that sends a query to the server. It opens the socket, reads the data, and creates the corresponding command. This also sends the command to the executor and stores the `Future` object in the double `ConcurrentHashMap` associated with the `hashCode` of the task and with the user that sent the query:

```
public void run() {
    try {
        while (!Thread.currentThread().interrupted()) {
            try {
                Socket clientSocket = pendingConnections.take();
                BufferedReader in = new BufferedReader(new
                        InputStreamReader (clientSocket.getInputStream()));
                String line = in.readLine();

                Logger.sendMessage(line);
                ConcurrentCommand command;

                ParallelCache cache = ConcurrentServer.getCache();
                String ret = cache.get(line);
                if (ret == null) {
                    String[] commandData = line.split(";");
```

```
        System.out.println("Command: " + commandData[0]);
        switch (commandData[0]) {
          case "q":
            System.out.println("Query");
            command = new ConcurrentQueryCommand(clientSocket,
                                                 commandData);
            break;
          case "r":
            System.out.println("Report");
            command = new ConcurrentReportCommand (clientSocket,
                                                   commandData);
            break;
          case "s":
            System.out.println("Status");
            command = new ConcurrentStatusCommand(executor,
                                                  clientSocket,
                                                  commandData);
            break;
          case "z":
            System.out.println("Stop");
            command = new ConcurrentStopCommand(clientSocket,
                                                commandData);
            break;
          case "c":
            System.out.println("Cancel");
            command = new ConcurrentCancelCommand (clientSocket,
                                                   commandData);
            break;
          default:
            System.out.println("Error");
            command = new ConcurrentErrorCommand(clientSocket,
                                                 commandData);
            break;
        }

        ServerTask<?> controller = (ServerTask<?>)executor
                                        .submit(command);
        storeContoller(command.getUsername(), controller, command);
      } else {
        PrintWriter out = new PrintWriter (clientSocket
                                    .getOutputStream(), true);
        System.out.println(ret);
        clientSocket.close();
      }

    } catch (IOException e) {
      e.printStackTrace();
    }
```

```
      }
    } catch (InterruptedException e) {
    // No Action Required
  }
}
```

The `storeController()` method is the one that stores the `Future` object in the double `ConcurrentHashMap`:

```
private void storeContoller(String userName, ServerTask<?>
                          controller, ConcurrentCommand command) {
taskController.computeIfAbsent(userName, k -> new
                 ConcurrentHashMap<>()).put(command,
controller);taskController.computeIfAbsent(userName, k -> new
                 ConcurrentHashMap<>()).put(command, controller);
}
```

Finally, we have included two methods to manage the execution of the `Executor` class: one to call the `shutdown()` method for the executor and another to wait for its finalization. Remember that you must explicitly call the `shutdown()` or the `shutdownNow()` methods to end the execution of an executor. If not, the program won't terminate. Look at the following:

```
public void shutdown() {

  String message="Request Task: "+pendingConnections.size()+"
                  pending connections.";
  Logger.sendMessage(message);
  executor.shutdown();
}

public void terminate() {
  try {
    executor.awaitTermination(1,TimeUnit.DAYS);
    executor.writeStatistics();
  } catch (InterruptedException e) {
    e.printStackTrace();
  }

}
```

The client part

Now it's time to test our server. In this case, we don't worry much about the execution time. The main objective of our test is to check whether the new features work well.

We have split the client part into the following two classes:

- **The ConcurrentClient class**: This implements an individual client of the server. Each instance of this class has a different username. It makes 100 queries, 90 of type query, and 10 of type report. The query queries have a priority of 5, and the report queries have a lower priority (10).
- **The MultipleConcurrentClient class**: This measures the behavior of multiple concurrent clients in parallel. We have tested the server with one to five concurrent clients. This class also tests the cancellation and stop commands.

We have included an executor to execute concurrent requests to the server to increase the level of concurrency of the client.

In the following screenshot, you can see the results of the cancellation of tasks:

```
2295 3 01:13:39 CET 2016: Fri Dec 23 01:13:34 CET 2016: Task with code 195713384cancelled: ConcurrentQueryCommand
2296 3 01:13:39 CET 2016: Fri Dec 23 01:13:34 CET 2016: Task with code 1547932103cancelled: ConcurrentReportCommand
2297 3 01:13:39 CET 2016: Fri Dec 23 01:13:34 CET 2016: Task with code 1917877449cancelled: ConcurrentQueryCommand
2298 3 01:13:39 CET 2016: Fri Dec 23 01:13:34 CET 2016: Task with code 158306644cancelled: ConcurrentQueryCommand
2299 3 01:13:39 CET 2016: Fri Dec 23 01:13:34 CET 2016: Task with code 336552833cancelled: ConcurrentQueryCommand
2300 3 01:13:39 CET 2016: Fri Dec 23 01:13:34 CET 2016: 5 tasks has been cancelled.
2301 3 01:13:39 CET 2016: Fri Dec 23 01:13:34 CET 2016: Tasks of user USER_2 has been cancelled.
```

In this case, four tasks of the USER_2 user have been canceled.

The following screenshot shows the final statistics about the number of tasks and execution time of every user:

```
4509 Fri Dec 23 00:46:00 CET 2016: Fri Dec 23 00:46:00 CET 2016: Task with code 938223162 has finished
4510 Fri Dec 23 00:46:00 CET 2016: Fri Dec 23 00:46:00 CET 2016: USER_2:Executed Tasks: 400. Execution Time: 10574
4511 Fri Dec 23 00:46:00 CET 2016: Fri Dec 23 00:46:00 CET 2016: USER_3:Executed Tasks: 300. Execution Time: 7074
4512 Fri Dec 23 00:46:00 CET 2016: Fri Dec 23 00:46:00 CET 2016: USER_1:Executed Tasks: 500. Execution Time: 14454
4513 Fri Dec 23 00:46:00 CET 2016: Fri Dec 23 00:46:00 CET 2016: admin:Executed Tasks: 1. Execution Time: 1
4514 Fri Dec 23 00:46:00 CET 2016: Fri Dec 23 00:46:00 CET 2016: USER_4:Executed Tasks: 200. Execution Time: 5381
4515 Fri Dec 23 00:46:00 CET 2016: Fri Dec 23 00:46:00 CET 2016: USER_5:Executed Tasks: 100. Execution Time: 2443
4516 Fri Dec 23 00:46:00 CET 2016: Fri Dec 23 00:46:00 CET 2016: Shuttingdown the logger
```

Second example - executing periodic tasks

In the previous examples with executors, the tasks were executed once, and they were executed as soon as possible. The executor framework includes another executor implementation that gives us more flexibility about the execution time of the tasks. It's the `ScheduledThreadPoolExecutor` class that allows us to execute tasks periodically and to execute tasks after a delay.

In this section, you will learn how to execute periodic tasks implementing an **RSS** feed reader. This is a simple case where you need to make the same task (reading the news of an RSS feed) at a certain time. Our example will have the following characteristics:

- Store the RSS sources in a file. We have chosen news about the world from some important newspapers such as The New York Times, the Daily News, or The Guardian.
- We sent a `Runnable` object to the executor per RSS source. Every time the executor runs each one, it parses the RSS source and converts them to a list of `CommonInformationItem` objects with the content of the RSS.
- We use the `Producer/Consumer` design pattern to write the RSS news onto disk. The producers will be the tasks of the executor that write every `CommonInformationItem` into a buffer. Only the new items will be stored in the buffer. The consumer will be an independent thread that reads the news from the buffer and writes it to a disk.

The time between the finalization of the execution of a task and its next execution will be one minute.

We also have implemented an advanced version of the example where the time between two executions of a task can vary.

The common parts

As we mentioned earlier, we read an RSS feed and convert it to a list of objects. To parse the RSS file, we treat it as an XML file, and we have implemented a **SAX** (short for **Simple API for XML**) parser in the `RSSDataCapturer` class. It parses the file and creates a list of `CommonInformationItem`. This class stores the following information about every RSS item:

- **Title**: Title of the RSS item
- **Date**: Date of the RSS item
- **Link**: Link to the RSS item
- **Description**: The text of the RSS item
- **ID**: The ID of the RSS item. If the item doesn't include an ID, we calculate it
- **Source**: The name of the RSS source

We store the news onto a disk using the Producer/Consumer design pattern, so we need a buffer to store the news and a `Consumer` class that, in this case, reads the news from the buffer and stores it onto the disk.

We implemented the buffer in the `NewsBuffer` class. It has two internal attributes:

- **A LinkedBlockingQueue**: This is a concurrent data structure with blocking operations. If we want to obtain an item from the list and it's empty, the thread of the calling method will be blocked until there are elements in the list. We will use this structure to store `CommonInformationItems`.
- **A ConcurrentHashMap**: This is a concurrent implementation of a `HashMap`. We will use it to store the IDs of the news item stored in the buffer before.

We will only insert the news that wasn't inserted before in the buffer:

```
public class NewsBuffer {
  private LinkedBlockingQueue<CommonInformationItem> buffer;
  private ConcurrentHashMap<String, String> storedItems;

  public NewsBuffer() {
    buffer=new LinkedBlockingQueue<>();
    storedItems=new ConcurrentHashMap<String, String>();
  }
```

We have two methods in the `NewsBuffer` class, one to store an item into the buffer that previously checks in the item that has been inserted before and another to obtain the next item from the buffer. We use the `compute()` method to insert elements in the `ConcurrentHashMap`. This method receives a lambda expression as a parameter with the key and the actual value associated with this key (null if the key has no associated value). In our case, we add the item to the buffer it has not processed before. We use the `add()` and `take()` methods to insert and to obtain and delete elements from the queue.

```
public void add (CommonInformationItem item) {
  storedItems.compute(item.getId(), (id, oldSource) -> {
    if(oldSource == null) {
      buffer.add(item);
      return item.getSource();
    } else {
      System.out.println("Item "+item.getId()+" has been processed
                          before");
      return oldSource;
    }
  });
}

public CommonInformationItem get() throws InterruptedException {
  return buffer.take();
}
```

The items of the buffer will be written onto disk by the `NewsWriter` class that will be executed as an independent thread. It only has an internal attribute that points to the `NewsBuffer` class used in the application:

```
public class NewsWriter implements Runnable {
  private NewsBuffer buffer;
  public NewsWriter(NewsBuffer buffer) {
    this.buffer=buffer;
  }
```

The `run()` method of this `Runnable` object takes `CommonInformationItem` instances from the buffer and saves them to a disk. As we use the blocking method, if the buffer is empty, this thread will be blocked until there are elements in the buffer:

```
public void run() {
  try {
    while (!Thread.currentThread().interrupted()) {
      CommonInformationItem item=buffer.get();
      Path path=Paths.get ("output\\"+item.getFileName());

      try (BufferedWriter fileWriter = Files.newBufferedWriter
                          (path, StandardOpenOption.CREATE)) {
        fileWriter.write(item.toString());
      } catch (IOException e) {
        e.printStackTrace();
      }

    }
  } catch (InterruptedException e) {
    //Normal execution
  }
}
```

The basic reader

The basic reader will use a standard `ScheduledThreadPoolExecutor` class to execute the tasks periodically. We will execute a task per RSS source, and there will be one minute between the termination of one execution of a task and the commencement of the next execution. These concurrent tasks are implemented in the `NewsTask` class. It has three internal attributes to store the name of the RSS feed, its URL, and the `NewsBuffer` class to store the news:

```
public class NewsTask implements Runnable {
  private String name;
  private String url;
```

```
private NewsBuffer buffer;

public NewsTask (String name, String url, NewsBuffer buffer) {
  this.name=name;
  this.url=url;
  this.buffer=buffer;
}
```

The `run()` method of this `Runnable` object simply parses the RSS feed, getting a list of `CommonItemInterface` instances and storing them into the buffer. This method will be executed in a periodic way. In every execution, the `run()` method will be executed from the beginning to the end:

```
@Override
public void run() {
  System.out.println(name + " : Running. " + new Date());
  RSSDataCapturer capturer = new RSSDataCapturer(name);
  List<CommonInformationItem> items=capturer.load(url);

  for (CommonInformationItem item: items) {
    buffer.add(item);
  }
}
```

In this example, we have also implemented another thread to implement the initialization of the executor and the tasks and then wait for the finalization of the execution. We have named this class `NewsSystem`. It has three internal attributes to store the path to the file with the RSS sources, the buffer to store the news, and a `CountDownLatch` object to control the end of its execution. The `CountDownLatch` class is a synchronization mechanism that allows you have a thread wait for an event. We will detail the utilization of this class in Chapter 11, *Diving into Concurrent Data Structures and Synchronization Utilities*. We have the following:

```
public class NewsSystem implements Runnable {
  private String route;
  private ScheduledThreadPoolExecutor executor;
  private NewsBuffer buffer;
  private CountDownLatch latch=new CountDownLatch(1);

  public NewsSystem(String route) {
    this.route = route;
    executor = new ScheduledThreadPoolExecutor
                   (Runtime.getRuntime().availableProcessors());
    buffer=new NewsBuffer();
  }
```

In the `run()` method, we read all the RSS sources, create a `NewsTask` class for each one, and send them to our `ScheduledThreadPool` executor. We have created the executor using the `newScheduledThreadPool()` method of the `Executors` class, and we send the tasks to it using the `scheduleAtFixedDelay()` method. We also start the `NewsWriter` instance as a thread. The `run()` method waits for someone to tell it to finish its execution using the `await()` method of the `CountDownLatch` class and ends the execution of the `NewsWriter` task and `ScheduledExecutor`.

```
@Override
public void run() {
  Path file = Paths.get(route);
  NewsWriter newsWriter=new NewsWriter(buffer);
  Thread t=new Thread(newsWriter);
  t.start();

  try (InputStream in = Files.newInputStream(file);
  BufferedReader reader = new BufferedReader(new
                          InputStreamReader(in))) {
    String line = null;
    while ((line = reader.readLine()) != null) {
      String data[] = line.split(";");

      NewsTask task = new NewsTask(data[0], data[1], buffer);
      System.out.println("Task "+task.getName());
      executor.scheduleWithFixedDelay(task,0, 1,
                                TimeUnit.MINUTES);
    }
  }  catch (Exception e) {
    e.printStackTrace();
  }

  synchronized (this) {
  try {
    latch.await();
  } catch (InterruptedException e) {
    e.printStackTrace();
  }
  }

  System.out.println("Shutting down the executor.");
  executor.shutdown();
  t.interrupt();
  System.out.println("The system has finished.");

}
```

We have also implemented the `shutdown()` method. This method will notify the `NewsSystem` class that it must end its execution using the `countDown()` method of the `CountDownLatch` class. This method will wake up the `run()` method, so it will shut down the executor that is running the `NewsTask` objects.

```
public void shutdown() {
   latch.countDown();
}
```

The last class of this example is the `Main` class, which implements the `main()` method of the example. It starts a `NewsSystem` instance as a thread, waits 10 minutes, notifies its finalization to the thread, and consequently finishes the execution of the system as follows:

```
public class Main {

  public static void main(String[] args) {

    // Creates the System an execute it as a Thread
    NewsSystem system=new NewsSystem("data\\sources.txt");

    Thread t=new Thread(system);

    t.start();

    // Waits 10 minutes
    try {
      TimeUnit.MINUTES.sleep(10);
    } catch (InterruptedException e) {
      e.printStackTrace();
    }

    // Notifies the finalization of the System

    system.shutdown();
  }
}
```

When you execute this example, you see how the different tasks are executed in a periodic way and how the news items are written to disk, as shown in the following screenshot:

```
Task The New York Times
Task Daily News
Task Washington Post
Task Los Angeles Times
Task Wall Street Journal
Task Denver Post
Task New York Post
Task Newsday
Task BBC
Task Financial Times
The New York Times: Running. Fri Dec 23 12:05:38 CET 2016
Daily News: Running. Fri Dec 23 12:05:38 CET 2016
Washington Post: Running. Fri Dec 23 12:05:38 CET 2016
Los Angeles Times: Running. Fri Dec 23 12:05:38 CET 2016
Wall Street Journal: Running. Fri Dec 23 12:05:39 CET 2016
Denver Post: Running. Fri Dec 23 12:05:39 CET 2016
Item https://www.washingtonpost.com/world/the_americas/explosi
New York Post: Running. Fri Dec 23 12:05:39 CET 2016
Newsday: Running. Fri Dec 23 12:05:39 CET 2016
BBC: Running. Fri Dec 23 12:05:39 CET 2016
Financial Times: Running. Fri Dec 23 12:05:39 CET 2016
```

The advanced reader

The basic news reader is an example of the utilization of a
`ScheduledThreadPoolExecutor` class, but we can go a step further. As occurs with
`ThreadPoolExecutor`, we can implement our own `ScheduledThreadPoolExecutor` to
obtain a particular behavior. In our case, we want the delay time of our periodic task
changes to depend on the moment of the day. In this part, you will learn how to implement
this behavior.

The first step is to implement a class that tells us the delay between two executions of a
periodic task. We named this the `Timer` class. It only has a static method named
`getPeriod()` that returns the number of milliseconds between the end of one execution
and the start of the next one. This is our implementation, but you can make your own:

```java
public class Timer {
  public static long getPeriod() {
    Calendar calendar = Calendar.getInstance();
    int hour = calendar.get(Calendar.HOUR_OF_DAY);

    if ((hour >= 6) && (hour <= 8)) {
      return TimeUnit.MILLISECONDS.convert(1, TimeUnit.MINUTES);
    }

    if ((hour >= 13) && (hour <= 14)) {
```

```
        return TimeUnit.MILLISECONDS.convert(1, TimeUnit.MINUTES);
    }

    if ((hour >= 20) && (hour <= 22)) {
        return TimeUnit.MILLISECONDS.convert(1, TimeUnit.MINUTES);
    }
    return TimeUnit.MILLISECONDS.convert(2, TimeUnit.MINUTES);
    }
}
```

Next, we have to implement the internal tasks of our executor. When you send a Runnable object to an executor, externally, you see that object as the concurrent task but the executor converts this object into another task, an instance of the `FutureTask` class, that includes the `run()` method to execute the task, and the methods of the `Future` interface to manage the execution of the task. To implement this example, we have to implement a class that extends the `FutureTask` class, and, as we will execute these tasks into a `scheduled` executor, it has to implement the `RunnableScheduledFuture` interface. This interface provides the `getDelay()` method that returns the time remaining till the next execution of a task. We have implemented these internal tasks in the `ExecutorTask` class. It has four internal attributes:

- The original `RunnableScheduledFuture` internal task created by the `ScheduledThreadPoolExecutor` class
- The scheduled executor that will execute the task
- The start date of the next execution of the task
- The name of the RSS feed

The code for this is as follows:

```
public class ExecutorTask<V> extends FutureTask<V> implements
                                RunnableScheduledFuture<V> {
    private RunnableScheduledFuture<V> task;

    private NewsExecutor executor;

    private long startDate;

    private String name;

    public ExecutorTask(Runnable runnable, V result,
                    RunnableScheduledFuture<V> task,
                    NewsExecutor executor) {
        super(runnable, result);
        this.task = task;
        this.executor = executor;
```

```
      this.name=((NewsTask)runnable).getName();
      this.startDate=new Date().getTime();
  }
```

We have overridden or implemented different methods in this class. The first one is the `getDelay()` method, which as we told you before, returns the time remaining till the next execution of a task in the given unit of time:

```
@Override
public long getDelay(TimeUnit unit) {
  long delay;
  if (!isPeriodic()) {
    delay = task.getDelay(unit);
  } else {
    if (startDate == 0) {
      delay = task.getDelay(unit);
    } else {
      Date now = new Date();
      delay = startDate - now.getTime();
      delay = unit.convert(delay, TimeUnit.MILLISECONDS);
    }

  }

  return delay;
}
```

The next one is the `compareTo()` method that compares two tasks taking into account the start date of the next execution of the tasks:

```
@Override
public int compareTo(Delayed object) {
  return Long.compare(this.getStartDate(),
                    ((ExecutorTask<V>)object).getStartDate());
}
```

Then the `isPeriodic()` method returns `true` if the task is periodic or `false` if not:

```
@Override
public boolean isPeriodic() {
  return task.isPeriodic();
}
```

Finally, the `run()` method implements the most important part of this example. First, we call the `runAndReset()` method of the `FutureTask` class. This method executes the task and resets its status, so it can be executed again. Then, we calculate the start date of the next execution using the `Timer` class, and finally, we have to insert the task again in the queue of the `ScheduledThreadPoolExecutor` class. If we don't do this final step, the task won't be executed again as follows:

```
@Override
public void run() {
  if (isPeriodic() && (!executor.isShutdown())) {
    super.runAndReset();
    Date now=new Date();
    startDate=now.getTime()+Timer.getPeriod();
    executor.getQueue().add(this);
    System.out.println("Start Date: "+new Date(startDate));
  }
}
```

Once we have the tasks for the executor, we have to implement the executor. We have implemented the `NewsExecutor` class that extends the `ScheduledThreadPoolExecutor` class. We have overridden the `decorateTask()` method. With this method, you can replace the internal task used by the scheduled executor. By default, it returns a default implementation of the `RunnableScheduledFuture` interface, but in our case, it will return an instance of the `ExecutorClass` instance:

```
public class NewsExecutor extends ScheduledThreadPoolExecutor {

  public NewsExecutor(int corePoolSize) {
    super(corePoolSize);
  }

  @Override
  protected <V> RunnableScheduledFuture<V> decorateTask(Runnable
                    runnable, RunnableScheduledFuture<V> task) {
    ExecutorTask<V> myTask = new ExecutorTask<>(runnable, null,
                                                task, this);
    return myTask;
  }
}
```

We have to implement other versions of the `NewsSystem` and the `Main` classes to use the `NewsExecutor`. We have implemented `NewsAdvancedSystem` and `AdvancedMain` for this purpose.

Now you can run the advanced news system to see how the delay time between executions changes.

Additional information about executors

In this chapter, we have extended `ThreadPoolExecutor` and the `ScheduledThreadPoolExecutor` class, and overridden some of their methods. But you can override more methods if you want a more specific behavior. These are some methods you can override:

- `shutdown()`: You must explicitly call this method to end the execution of the executor. You can override it to add some code to free additional resources used by your own executor.
- `shutdownNow()`: The difference between `shutdown()` and `shutdownNow()` is that the `shutdown()` method waits for the finalization of all the tasks that are waiting in the executor.
- `submit()`, `invokeall()`, or `invokeany()`: You call these methods to send concurrent tasks to the executor. You can override them if you need to do some actions before or after a task is inserted in the task queue of the executor. Note that adding a custom action before or after the task is enqueued is different from adding a custom action before or after it's executed, which we did when overriding `beforeExecute()` and `afterExecute()` methods.

In the news reader example, we use the `scheduleWithFixedDelay()` method to send tasks to the executor. But the `ScheduledThreadPoolExecutor` class has other methods to execute periodic tasks or tasks after a delay:

- `schedule()`: This method executes a task after the given delay. The task is executed only once.
- `scheduleAtFixedRate()`: This method executes a periodic task with the given period. The difference with the `ScheduleWithFixedDelay()` method is that in the last one, the delay between two executions goes from the end of the first one to the start of the second one, and in the first one, the delay between two executions goes between the start of both.

Summary

In this chapter, we presented two examples that explored the advanced characteristics of executors. In the first example, we continued with the client/server example of Chapter 3, *Managing Lots of Threads - Executors*. We have implemented our own executor extending the ThreadPoolExecutor class to execute tasks by priority and to measure the executing time of tasks per user. We also included a new command to allow the cancellation of tasks.

In the second example, we explained how to use the ScheduledThreadPoolExecutor class to execute periodic tasks. We implemented two versions of a news reader. The first one showed how to use the basic functionality of the ScheduledExecutorService, and the second one showed how to override the behavior of the ScheduledExecutorService class to, for example, change the delay time between the two executions of a task.

In the next chapter, you will learn how to execute Executor tasks that return a result. If you extend the Thread class or implement the Runnable interface, the run() method doesn't return any results, but the executor framework includes the Callable interface allows you to implement tasks that return a result.

5
Getting Data from Tasks - The Callable and Future Interfaces

In Chapter 3, *Managing Lots of Threads - Executors*, and Chapter 4, *Getting the Most from Executors*, we introduced the Executor framework to improve the performance of concurrent applications and showed you how to implement advanced characteristics to adapt this framework to your needs. In these chapters, all the tasks executed by the executor were based on the Runnable interface and its run() method that doesn't return a value. However, the Executor framework allows us to execute other kinds of tasks that return a result based on the Callable and Future interfaces. Callable is a functional interface which defines the method call(). The method call() may throw a checked Exception which is different to the Runnable interface. The result of a Callable interface process is wrapped by the Future interface. The Future represents the result of asynchronous computation. In this chapter, we will cover the following topics:

- An introduction to the Callable and Future interfaces
- First example - a best-matching algorithm for words
- Second example - building an inverted index of a collection of documents

Introducing the Callable and Future interfaces

The Executor framework allows programmers to execute concurrent tasks without creating and managing threads. You create tasks and send them to the executor. It creates and manages the necessary threads.

In an executor, you can execute two kinds of tasks:

- **Tasks based on the Runnable interface**: These tasks implement the run() method that doesn't return any results.
- **Tasks based on the Callable interface**: These tasks implement the call() interface that returns an object as a result. The concrete type that will be returned by the call() method is specified by a generic type parameter of the Callable interface. To get the result returned by the task, the executor will return an implementation of the Future interface for every task.

In previous chapters, you learned how to create executors, send tasks based on the Runnable interface to it, and personalize the executor to adapt it to your needs. In this chapter, you will learn how to work with tasks based on the Callable and Future interfaces.

The Callable interface

The Callable interface is very similar to the Runnable interface. The main characteristics of this interface are:

- It's a generic interface. It has a single type parameter that corresponds to the return type of the call() method.
- It declares the call() method. This method will be executed by the executor when it runs the task. It must return an object of the type specified in the declaration.
- The call() method can throw any checked exception. You can process the exceptions implementing your own executor and overriding the afterExecute() method.

The Future interface

When you send a Callable task to an executor, it will return an implementation of the Future interface that allows you to control the execution and the status of the task and to get the result. The main characteristics of this interface are:

- You can cancel the execution of the task using the cancel() method. This method has a Boolean parameter to specify whether you want to interrupt the task whether it's running or not.

- You can check whether the task has been cancelled (with the `isCancelled()` method) or has finished (with the `isDone()` method).
- You can get the value returned by the task using the `get()` method. There are two variants of this method. The first one doesn't have parameters and returns the value returned by the task if it has finished its execution. If the task hasn't finished its execution, it suspends the execution thread until the tasks finish. The second variant admits two parameters: a period of time and `TimeUnit` of that period. The main difference with the first one is that the thread waits for the period of time passed as a parameter. If the period ends and the task hasn't finished its execution, the method throws a `TimeoutException` exception.

First example - a best-matching algorithm for words

The main objective of a **best-matching algorithm** for words is to find the words most similar to a string passed as a parameter. To implement one of these algorithms, you need the following:

- **A list of words**: In our case, we have used the **UK Advanced Cryptics Dictionary (UKACD)**, which is a word list compiled for the crossword community. It has 250,353 words and idioms. It can be downloaded for free from `http://www.crosswordman.com/wordlist.html`.
- **A metric to measure the similarity between two words**: We have used the **Levenshtein** distance that is used to measure the difference between two sequences of characters. The Levenshtein distance is the minimal number of insertions, deletions, or substitutions that is necessary to transform the first string into the second string. You can find a brief description of this metric at `https://en.wikipedia.org/wiki/Levenshtein_distance`.

In our example, you will implement two operations:

- The first operation returns a list of the most similar words to a character sequence using the Levenshtein distance.
- The second operation determines whether a character sequence exists in our dictionary using the Levenshtein distance. It would be faster if we used the `equals()` method, but our version is a more interesting option for the objectives of the book.

You will implement serial and concurrent versions of these operations to verify that concurrency can help us in this case.

The common classes

In all the tasks implemented in this example, you will use the following three basic classes:

- The `WordsLoader` class that loads the list of words into a list of string objects.
- The `LevenshteinDistance` class that calculates the Levenshtein distance between two strings.
- The `BestMatchingData` class that stores the results of the best-matching algorithms. It stores a list of words and the distance of these words with the input string.

The UKACD is in a file with a word per line, so the `WordsLoader` class implements the `load()` static method that receives the path of the file that contains the list of words and returns a list of string objects with the 250,353 words.

The `LevenshteinDistance` class implements the `calculate()` method that receives two string objects as parameters and returns an `int` value with the distance between these two words. This is the code for this classification:

```
public class LevenshteinDistance {

  public static int calculate (String string1, String string2) {
    int[][] distances=new
    int[string1.length()+1][string2.length()+1];

    for (int i=1; i<=string1.length();i++) {
      distances[i][0]=i;
    }

    for (int j=1; j<=string2.length(); j++) {
      distances[0][j]=j;
    }

    for(int i=1; i<=string1.length(); i++) {
      for (int j=1; j<=string2.length(); j++) {
        if (string1.charAt(i-1)==string2.charAt(j-1)) {
          distances[i][j]=distances[i-1][j-1];
        } else {
          distances[i][j]=minimum(distances[i-1][j],
                    distances[i][j-1],distances[i-1][j-1])+1;
        }
      }
```

```
      }
    }

    return distances[string1.length()][string2.length()];
  }

  private static int minimum(int i, int j, int k) {
    return Math.min(i,Math.min(j, k));
  }
}
```

The `BestMatchingData` class has only two attributes: a list of strings to store a list of words, and an integer attribute named `distance` to store the distance of these words with the input string.

A best-matching algorithm - the serial version

First, we are going to implement the serial version of the best-matching algorithm. We are going to use this version as the starting point for the concurrent one and then we will compare the execution times of both versions to verify that concurrency helps us to achieve better performance.

We have implemented the serial version of the best-matching algorithm in the following two classes:

- The `BestMatchingSerialCalculation` class that calculates the list of the most similar words to the input string
- The `BestMatchingSerialMain` that includes the `main()` method, which executes the algorithm, measures the execution time, and shows the results in the console

Let's analyze the source code of both classes.

The BestMatchingSerialCalculation class

This class has only one method, named `getBestMatchingWords()` that receives two parameters: a string with the sequence we take as reference and the list of strings with all the words of the dictionary. It returns a `BestMatchingData` object with the results of the algorithm:

```
public class BestMatchingSerialCalculation {

    public static BestMatchingData getBestMatchingWords(String
                word, List<String> dictionary) {
        List<String> results=new ArrayList<String>();
        int minDistance=Integer.MAX_VALUE;
        int distance;
```

After the initialization of the internal variables, the algorithm processes all the words in the dictionary, calculating the Levenshtein distance between these words and the string of reference. If the calculated distance for a word is less than the actual minimum distance, we clear the list of results and store the actual word in the list. If the calculated distance for a word is equal to the actual minimum distance, we add that word to the list of results:

```
for (String str: dictionary) {
    distance=LevenshteinDistance.calculate(word,str);
    if (distance<minDistance) {
        results.clear();
        minDistance=distance;
        results.add(str);
    } else if (distance==minDistance) {
        results.add(str);
    }
}
```

Finally, we create the `BestMatchingData` object to return the results of the algorithm:

```
        BestMatchingData result=new BestMatchingData();
        result.setWords(results);
        result.setDistance(minDistance);
        return result;
    }

}
```

The BestMachingSerialMain class

This is the main class of the example. It loads the UKACD file, calls
`getBestMatchingWords()` with the string received as a parameter, and shows the results
in the console, including the execution time of the algorithm. Refer to the following code:

```
public class BestMatchingSerialMain {

  public static void main(String[] args) {

    Date startTime, endTime;
    List<String> dictionary=WordsLoader.load("data/UK Advanced
                                 Cryptics Dictionary.txt");

    System.out.println("Dictionary Size: "+dictionary.size());

    startTime=new Date();
    BestMatchingData result= BestMatchingSerialCalculation
                          .getBestMatchingWords
                          (args[0], dictionary);
    List<String> results=result.getWords();
    endTime=new Date();
    System.out.println("Word: "+args[0]);
    System.out.println("Minimum distance: " +result.getDistance());
    System.out.println("List of best matching words: "
                       +results.size());
    results.forEach(System.out::println);
    System.out.println("Execution Time: "+(endTime.getTime()-
                       startTime.getTime()));
  }

}
```

Here, we used a new Java 8 language construct, named method reference, and a new
`List.forEach()` method to output the result. The `forEach()` method is a terminal
operation which performs a side effect on all elements.

A best-matching algorithm - the first concurrent version

We have implemented two different concurrent versions of the best-matching algorithm.
The first one is based on the `Callable` interface and the `submit()` method defined in the
`AbstractExecutorService` interface.

We have implemented this version of the algorithm using the following three classes:

- The `BestMatchingBasicTask` class that implements the tasks that implement the `Callable` interface and will be executed in the executor
- The `BestMatchingBasicConcurrentCalculation` class that creates the executor and necessary tasks and sends them to the executor
- The `BestMatchingConcurrentMain` class that implements the `main()` method to execute the algorithm and show the results in the console

Let's see the source code of these classes.

The BestMatchingBasicTask class

As we mentioned before, this class will implement the tasks that will obtain the list of best-matching words. This task will implement the `Callable` interface parameterized with the `BestMatchingData` class. This means that this class will implement the `call()` method, and this method will return a `BestMatchingData` object.

Each task will process a part of the dictionary and will return the results obtained for that part. We have used four internal attributes, as follows:

- The first position (inclusive) of the dictionary it will analyze
- The last position (exclusive) of the dictionary it will analyze
- The dictionary as a list of strings
- The reference input string

The code for this is the following:

```
public class BestMatchingBasicTask implements Callable
                            <BestMatchingData > {

    private int startIndex;
    private int endIndex;
    private List < String > dictionary;
    private String word;

    public BestMatchingBasicTask(int startIndex, int endIndex,
                    List < String > dictionary, String word) {
        this.startIndex = startIndex;
        this.endIndex = endIndex;
        this.dictionary = dictionary;
        this.word = word;
    }
```

The `call()` method processes all the words between the `startIndex` and `endIndex` attributes and calculates the Levenshtein distance between those words and the input string. It will return only the nearest words to the input string. If during the process, it finds a word nearer than the previous ones, it clears the result list and adds the new word to that list. If it finds a word that is at the same distance than the results found up until then, it adds the word to the result list as follows:

```
@Override
  public BestMatchingData call() throws Exception {
    List<String> results=new ArrayList<String>();
    int minDistance=Integer.MAX_VALUE;
    int distance;
    for (int i=startIndex; i<endIndex; i++) {
      distance = LevenshteinDistance.calculate(word,dictionary.get(i));
      if (distance<minDistance) {
        results.clear();
        minDistance=distance;
        results.add(dictionary.get(i));
      } else if (distance==minDistance) {
        results.add(dictionary.get(i));
      }
    }
```

At the end, we create a `BestMatchingData` object with the list of words we have found and their distance to the input string, and return that object as follows:

```
    BestMatchingData result=new BestMatchingData();
    result.setWords(results);
    result.setDistance(minDistance);
    return result;
    }
}
```

The main difference between the tasks based on the `Runnable` interface is the return sentence included in the last line of the method. The `run()` method doesn't return a value, so those tasks cannot return a result. The `call()` method, on the other hand, returns an object (the class of that object is defined in the implements sentence), so this kind of task can return a result.

The BestMatchingBasicConcurrentCalculation class

This class is responsible for the creation of the necessary tasks to process the complete dictionary, the executor to execute those tasks, and to control the execution of the tasks in the executor.

It only has one method, `getBestMatchingWords()`, that receives two input parameters--
the dictionary with the complete list of words and the reference string. It returns a
`BestMatchingData` object with the results of the algorithm. First, we have created and
initialized the executor. We have used the number of cores of the machine as the maximum
number of threads we want to use on it. Take a look at the following code block:

```
public class BestMatchingBasicConcurrentCalculation {

    public static BestMatchingData getBestMatchingWords(String
            word, List<String> dictionary) throws InterruptedException,
            ExecutionException {

        int numCores = Runtime.getRuntime().availableProcessors();
        ThreadPoolExecutor executor = (ThreadPoolExecutor)
                    Executors.newFixedThreadPool(numCores);
```

Then, we calculate the size of the parts of the dictionary each task will process and create a
list of `Future` objects to store the results of the tasks. When you send a task based on the
`Callable` interface to an executor, you will get an implementation of the `Future` interface.
You can use that object to:

- Know whether the task has been executed
- Get the result of the execution of the task (the object returned by the `call()`
  method)
- Cancel the execution of the tasks

The code for this is as follows:

```
int size = dictionary.size();
int step = size / numCores;
int startIndex, endIndex;
List<Future<BestMatchingData>> results = new ArrayList<>();
```

Then, we create the tasks, send them to the executor using the `submit()` method, and add
the `Future` object that method returns to the list of `Future` objects. The `submit()` method
returns immediately. It doesn't wait until the task is executed. We have the following code:

```
for (int i = 0; i < numCores; i++) {
  startIndex = i * step;
  if (i == numCores - 1) {
    endIndex = dictionary.size();
  } else {
    endIndex = (i + 1) * step;
  }
  BestMatchingBasicTask task = new BestMatchingBasicTask(startIndex,
```

```
                                    endIndex, dictionary, word);
    Future<BestMatchingData> future = executor.submit(task);
    results.add(future);
}
```

Once we have sent the tasks to the executor, we call the `shutdown()` method of the executor to finish its execution and iterate over the list of `Future` objects to get the results of each task. We have used the `get()` method without any parameters. This method returns the object returned by the `call()` method if the task has finished its execution. If the task is not finished, the method puts the calling thread to sleep until the task has finished and the results are available.

We compose a results list with the results of the tasks, so we will only return the list with the words nearest to the reference string, as follows:

```
executor.shutdown();
List<String> words=new ArrayList<String>();
int minDistance=Integer.MAX_VALUE;
for (Future<BestMatchingData> future: results) {
  BestMatchingData data=future.get();
if (data.getDistance()<minDistance) {
  words.clear();
  minDistance=data.getDistance();
  words.addAll(data.getWords());
} else if (data.getDistance()==minDistance) {
  words.addAll(data.getWords());
}

}
```

Finally, we create and return a `BestMatchingData` object with the results of the algorithm:

```
BestMatchingData result=new BestMatchingData();
result.setDistance(minDistance);
result.setWords(words);
return result;
}
}
```

The BestMatchingConcurrentMain class is very similar to BestMatchingSerialMain presented before. The only difference is the class used (BestMatchingBasicConcurrentCalculation instead of BestMatchingSerialCalculation), so we don't include the source code here. Note that we used neither thread-safe data structures nor synchronization, as our concurrent tasks worked on independent pieces of data, and the final results were merged in a sequential manner after the concurrent tasks were terminated.

A best-matching algorithm - the second concurrent version

We have implemented the second version of the best-matching algorithm using the invokeAll() method of the AbstractExecutorService (implemented in the ThreadPoolExecutorClass). In the previous version, we used the submit() method that receives a Callable object and returns a Future object. The invokeAll() method receives a List of Callable objects as a parameter and returns a List of Future ones. The first Future is associated with the first Callable, and so on. There is another important difference between these two methods. Although the submit() method returns immediately, the invokeAll() method returns when all the Callable tasks have ended their execution. This means that all the Future objects returned will return true if you call their isDone() method.

To implement this version, we have used the BestMatchingBasicTask class implemented in the previous example and have implemented the BestMatchingAdvancedConcurrentCalculation class. The differences with the BestMatchingBasicConcurrentTask class are in the creation of the tasks and in the process of the results. In the creation of tasks, now we create a list and store it on the tasks we want to execute:

```
for (int i = 0; i < numCores; i++) {
  startIndex = i * step;
  if (i == numCores - 1) {
    endIndex = dictionary.size();
  } else {
    endIndex = (i + 1) * step;
  }
  BestMatchingBasicTask task = new BestMatchingBasicTask(startIndex,
                                    endIndex, dictionary, word);
  tasks.add(task);
}
```

To process the results, we call the `invokeAll()` method and then go over the list of `Future` objects returned:

```
results = executor.invokeAll(tasks);
executor.shutdown();
List<String> words = new ArrayList<String>();
int minDistance = Integer.MAX_VALUE;
for (Future<BestMatchingData> future : results) {
BestMatchingData data = future.get();
if (data.getDistance() < minDistance) {
  words.clear();
  minDistance = data.getDistance();
  words.addAll(data.getWords());
} else if (data.getDistance()== minDistance) {
  words.addAll(data.getWords());
}
}
BestMatchingData result = new BestMatchingData();
result.setDistance(minDistance);
result.setWords(words);
return result;
}
```

To execute this version, we have implemented `BestMatchingConcurrentAdvancedMain`. Its source code is very similar to the previous ones, so it's not included.

Word exists algorithm - a serial version

As part of this example, we have implemented another operation to check whether a `String` exists in our lists of words. To check whether the word exists or not, we use the Levenshtein distance again. We consider that a word exists if it has a distance of 0 with a word of the list. It would be faster if we make the comparison using the `equals()` or `equalsIgnoreCase()` methods or reading the input words into a `HashSet` and using the `contains()` method (much more efficient than our version), but we consider that our version will be more useful for the purposes of the book.

As in previous examples, first, we have implemented the serial version of the operation to use it as a base to implement the concurrent one and compare the execution times of both versions.

To implement the serial version, we have used two classes:

- The `ExistSerialCalculation` class, which implements the `existWord()` method that compares the input string with all the words in the dictionary until it finds it
- The `ExistSerialMain` class, which launches the examples and measures the execution time

Let's analyze the source code of both classes.

The ExistSerialCalculation class

This class has only one method, that is, the `existWord()` method. It receives two parameters--the word we are looking for and the complete list of words. It goes over the full list, which calculates the Levenshtein distance between the input word and the words in the list until it finds the word (the distance is 0), in which case it returns the true value, or it finishes the list of words without finding the word, in which case it returns the false value. Refer to the following code block:

```
public class ExistSerialCalculation {

  public static boolean existWord(String word, List<String>
                                  dictionary) {
    for (String str: dictionary) {
      if (LevenshteinDistance.calculate(word, str) == 0) {
        return true;
      }
    }
    return false;
  }
}
```

The ExistSerialMain class

This class implements the `main()` method to call the `exist()` method. It gets the first parameter of the main method as the word we want to look for and calls that method. It measures its execution time and shows the results in the console. We have the following code:

```
public class ExistSerialMain {

  public static void main(String[] args) {
```

```
    Date startTime, endTime;
    List<String> dictionary=WordsLoader.load("data/UK Advanced
                                      Cryptics Dictionary.txt");

    System.out.println("Dictionary Size: "+dictionary.size());

    startTime=new Date();
    boolean result=ExistSerialCalculation.existWord(args[0],
                                        dictionary);
    endTime=new Date();

    System.out.println("Word: "+args[0]);
    System.out.println("Exists: "+result);
    System.out.println("Execution Time: "+(endTime.getTime()-
                    startTime.getTime()));
  }
}
```

Word exists algorithm - the concurrent version

To implement the concurrent version of this operation, we have to take into account its most important characteristic. We don't need to process the whole list of words. When we find the word, we can finish the process of the list and return the result. This operation, which does not process the whole input data and stops when a condition is fulfilled, is called **short-circuit operation**.

The AbstractExecutorService interface defines an operation (implemented in the ThreadPoolExecutor class) that fits perfectly with this idea. It's the invokeAny() method. This method sends the list of Callable tasks that it receives as a parameter to the executor and returns the result of the first task that has finished its execution without throwing an exception. If all the tasks throw an exception, this method throws an ExecutionException exception.

As in previous examples, we have implemented different classes to implement this version of the algorithm:

- The ExistBasicTask class that implements the tasks we are going to execute in the executor
- The ExistBasicConcurrentCalculation class that creates the executor and the tasks, and sends the tasks to the executor
- The ExistBasicConcurrentMain class that executes the examples, measuring their running time

The ExistBasicTasks class

This class implements the tasks that are going to search for the word. It implements the `Callable` interface parameterized with the Boolean class. The `call()` method will return the true value if the task finds the word. It uses four internal attributes:

- The complete list of words
- The first word (included) in the list the task will process
- The last word (excluded) in the list the task will process
- The word the task will look for

We have the following code:

```
public class ExistBasicTask implements Callable<Boolean> {

    private int startIndex;
    private int endIndex;
    private List<String> dictionary;
    private String word;

    public ExistBasicTask(int startIndex, int endIndex,
                        List<String> dictionary, String word) {
      this.startIndex=startIndex;
      this.endIndex=endIndex;
      this.dictionary=dictionary;
      this.word=word;
    }
```

The `call` method will traverse the part of the list assigned to this task. It calculates the Levenshtein distance between the input word and the words of the list. If it finds the word, it will return the true value.

If the task processes all of its words and it doesn't find the word, it will throw an exception to adapt to the behavior of the `invokeAny()` method. If the task returns the false value in this case, the `invokeAny()` method will return the `false` value without waiting for the rest of the tasks. Maybe other tasks will find the word.

We have the following code:

```
@Override
public Boolean call() throws Exception {
  for (int i=startIndex; i<endIndex; i++) {
    if (LevenshteinDistance.calculate(word, dictionary.get(i))==0) {
      return true;
    }
  }
  if (Thread.interrupted()) {
    return false;
  }
  throw new NoSuchElementException("The word "+word+"
                                  doesn't exists.");
}
```

The ExistBasicConcurrentCalculation class

This class will execute the search of the input word in the full list of words, creating and executing the necessary tasks. It only implements one method, named existWord(). It receives two parameters, the input string and the complete list of words, and returns a Boolean value indicating whether the word exists or not.

First, we create the executor to execute the tasks. We use the Executor class and create a ThreadPoolExecutor class with a maximum of threads determined by the number of available hardware threads of the machine, as follows:

```
public class ExistBasicConcurrentCalculation {

  public static boolean existWord(String word, List<String> dictionary)
                    throws InterruptedException, ExecutionException{
    int numCores = Runtime.getRuntime().availableProcessors();
    ThreadPoolExecutor executor = (ThreadPoolExecutor)
                    Executors.newFixedThreadPool(numCores);
```

Then, we create the same number of tasks as the threads are running in the executor. Each task will process an equal part of the list of words. We create the tasks and store them in a list:

```
int size = dictionary.size();
int step = size / numCores;
int startIndex, endIndex;
List<ExistBasicTask> tasks = new ArrayList<>();

for (int i = 0; i < numCores; i++) {
  startIndex = i * step;
```

```
if (i == numCores - 1) {
  endIndex = dictionary.size();
} else {
  endIndex = (i + 1) * step;
}
ExistBasicTask task = new ExistBasicTask(startIndex, endIndex,
                                         dictionary, word);
tasks.add(task);
}
```

Then, we use the `invokeAny()` method to execute the tasks in the executor. If the methods return a Boolean value, the word exists. We return that value. If the method throws an exception, the word doesn't exist. We print the exception in the console and return the `false` value. In both cases, we call the `shutdown()` method of the executor to terminate its execution, as follows:

```
try {
  Boolean result=executor.invokeAny(tasks);
  return result;
} catch (ExecutionException e) {
  if (e.getCause() instanceof NoSuchElementException)
    return false;
    throw e;
  } finally {
    executor.shutdown();
  }
}
}
```

Instead of using the `shutdown()` method, we can use the `shutdownNow()` method. The main difference between the methods is that the `shutdown()` method executes all pending tasks before terminating the execution of the `Executor`, while the `shutdownNow()` method doesn't execute pending tasks.

The ExistBasicConcurrentMain class

This class implements the `main()` method of this example. It's equal to the `ExistSerialMain` class with one difference, it uses the `ExistBasicConcurrentCalculation` class instead of the `ExistSerialCalculation`, so its source code is not included.

Comparing the solutions

Let's compare the different solutions (serial and concurrent) of the two operations we have implemented in this section. We have executed the examples using the **JMH framework** (`http://openjdk.java.net/projects/code-tools/jmh/`) that allows you to implement micro benchmarks in Java. Using a framework for benchmarking is a better solution which simply measures time using such methods as `currentTimeMillis()` or `nanoTime()`. We have executed them 10 times in two different architectures:

- A computer with an Intel Core i5-5300 CPU with Windows 7 and 16 GB of RAM. This processor has two cores and each core can execute two threads, so we will have four parallel threads.
- A computer with an AMD A8-640 APU with Windows 10 and 8 GB of RAM. This processor has four cores.

Best-matching algorithms

In this case, we have implemented three versions of the algorithm:

- The serial version
- The concurrent version, sending a task one at a time
- The concurrent version, using the `invokeAll()` method

To test the algorithms, we have used three different strings that don't exist in the list of words:

- `Stitter`
- `Abicus`
- `Lonx`

These are the words returned by the best-matching algorithm for each word:

- `Stitter`: `sitter`, `skitter`, `slitter`, `spitter`, `stilter`, `stinter`, `stotter`, `stutter`, and `titter`
- `Abicus`: `abacus` and `amicus`
- `Lonx`: `lanx`, `lone`, `long`, `lox`, and `lynx`

The median execution times in milliseconds are discussed in the following table:

Algorithm	Intel Architecture			Amd Architecture		
	Stitter	Abicus	Lonx	Stitter	Abicus	Lonx
Serial	414.56	376.34	296.81	708.98	633.61	467.03
Concurrent: submit() method	229.56	217.76	173.89	361.97	299.26	233.22
Concurrent: invokeAll() method	257.31	225.82	171.98	333.93	324.08	250.06

We can draw the following conclusions:

- The concurrent versions of the algorithm achieve a better performance than the serial one in both architectures.
- The concurrent versions of the algorithm obtain similar results between them. We can compare the concurrent version method with the serial version using the speed-up for the word Lonx to see how concurrency improves the performance of our algorithm:

$$S_{AMD} = \frac{T_{serial}}{T_{concurrent}} = \frac{467.03}{232.22} = 2.01$$

$$S_{Intel} = \frac{T_{serial}}{T_{concurrent}} = \frac{296.81}{171.98} = 1.72$$

Exist algorithms

In this case, we have implemented two versions of the algorithms:

- The serial version
- The concurrent version, using the `invokeAny()` method

To test the algorithm, we have used some strings:

- The string xyzt that doesn't exist in the list of words
- The string stutter that exists in the list of words near the end of the list
- The string abacus that exists in the list of words very close to the start of the list
- The string lynx that exists in the list of words just after the second half of the list

The median execution times in milliseconds are shown in the following diagram:

Algorithm	Intel Architecture		AMD Architecture	
	Word	Execution time (milliseconds)	Word	Execution time (milliseconds)
Serial	abacus	69.79	abacus	94.59
	lynx	148.46	lynx	292.86
	stutter	336.61	stutter	592.102
	xyzt	280.93	xyzt	452.53
Concurrent	abacus	73.28	abacus	76.27
	lynx	100.51	lynx	110.51
	stutter	154.63	stutter	186.28
	xyzt	178.33	xyzt	270.37

We can draw the following conclusions:

- In general, the concurrent version of the algorithm provides better performance than the serial one.
- The position of a word in the list is a critical factor. With the word abacus, which appears at the beginning of the list, both algorithms give a similar execution time; but with the word stutter, the difference is very large.

If we compare the concurrent version with the serial one for the word `lynx` using the speed-up, the result is:

$$S_{AMD} = \frac{T_{serial}}{T_{concurrent}} = \frac{292.86}{110.51} = 2.65$$

$$S_{Intel} = \frac{T_{serial}}{T_{concurrent}} = \frac{148.46}{100.51} = 1.48$$

The second example - creating an inverted index for a collection of documents

In the *information retrieval* world, an *inverted index* is a common data structure used to speed up the searches of text in a collection of documents. It stores all the words of the document collection and a list of the documents that contain that word.

To construct the index, we have to parse all the documents of the collection and construct the index in an incremental way. For every document, we extract the significant words of that document (deleting the most common words, also called **stop words**, and maybe applying a stemming algorithm) and then add those words to the index. If a word exists in the index, we add the document to the list of documents associated with that word. If a word doesn't exist, add the word to the list of words of the index and associate the document to that word. You can add parameters to the association as the term frequency of the word in the document that provides you more information.

When you make a search of a word or a list of words in the document collection, you use the inverted index to obtain the list of documents associated with each word and create a unique list with the results of the search.

In this section, you will learn how to use Java concurrency utilities to construct an inverted index file for a collection of documents. As document collection, we have taken the Wikipedia pages with information about movies to construct a set of 100,673 documents. We have converted each Wikipedia page into a text file. You can download this document collection with the code of this book.

To construct the inverted index, we don't delete any words and don't use any stemming algorithms either. We want to keep the algorithm as simple as possible to focus attention on the concurrency utilities.

The same principles explained here can be used to obtain other information about a document collection, for example, a vector representation of every document that can be used as an input for a **clustering algorithm**, as you will learn in Chapter 7, *Optimizing Divide and Conquer Solutions - The Fork/Join Framework*.

As with other examples, you will implement serial and concurrent versions of these operations to verify that concurrency can help us in this case.

Common classes

Both versions, serial and concurrent, have in common the classes to load the document collection into a Java object. We have used the following two classes:

- The Document class that stores the list of words contained in the document
- The DocumentParse class that converts a document stored in a file in a document object

Let's analyze the source code of both classes.

The Document class

The Document class is very simple. It has only two attributes and the methods to get and set the values of those attributes. These attributes are:

- The name of the file, as a string.
- The vocabulary (that is, the list of words used in the document) as a HashMap. The *key* is the *words*, and the values are the number of times the word appears in the document.

The DocumentParser class

As we mentioned earlier, this class converts a document stored in a file in a document into a `Document` object. It splits this word into three methods. The first one is the `parse()` method that receives the path to the file as a parameter and returns a `HashMap` with the vocabulary of that document. This method reads all the lines of the file using the `readAllLines()` method of the `Files` class and uses the `parseLine()` method to convert each line into a list of words and add them to the vocabulary, as follows:

```
public class DocumentParser {

  public Map<String, Integer>  parse(String route) {
    Map<String, Integer> ret=new HashMap<String,Integer>();
    Path file=Paths.get(route);
    try {
      List<String> lines = Files.readAllLines(file);
      for (String line : lines) {
        parseLine(line,ret);
      }
    } catch (IOException e) {
      e.printStackTrace();
    }
    return ret;

  }
```

The `parseLine()` method processes the line, extracting its words. We consider that a word is a sequence of alphabetical characters to continue with the simplicity of this example. We have used the `Pattern` class to extract the words and the `Normalizer` class to convert the words to lowercase and delete the accents of the vowel, as follows:

```
private static final Pattern PATTERN = Pattern.compile
                                   ("\\P{IsAlphabetic}+");

  private void parseLine(String line, Map<String, Integer> ret) {
    for(String word: PATTERN.split(line)) {
      if(!word.isEmpty())
        ret.merge(Normalizer.normalize(word, Normalizer.Form.NFKD)
                      .toLowerCase(), 1, (a, b) -> a+b);
    }
  }
}
```

The serial version

The serial version of this example is implemented in the `SerialIndexing` class. This class has the `main()` method that reads all the documents, gets their vocabulary, and constructs the inverted index in an incremental way.

First, we initialize the necessary variables. The collection of documents is stored in the `data` directory, so we store all the documents in an array of `File` objects. We also initialize the `invertedIndex` object. We use a `HashMap`, where the keys are the words and the values are a list of strings with the name of the files that contain the word, as follows:

```
public class SerialIndexing {

  public static void main(String[] args) {

    Date start, end;
    File source = new File("data");
    File[] files = source.listFiles();
    Map<String, List<String>> invertedIndex=new
                        HashMap<String,List<String>> ();
```

Then, we parse all the documents using the `DocumentParse` class and use the `updateInvertedIndex()` method to add the vocabulary obtained from each document into the inverted index. We measure the execution time of all the processes. We have the following code:

```
start=new Date();
for (File file : files) {

  DocumentParser parser = new DocumentParser();

  if (file.getName().endsWith(".txt")) {
    Map<String, Integer> voc = parser.parse(file.getAbsolutePath());
    updateInvertedIndex(voc,invertedIndex, file.getName());
  }
}
end=new Date();
```

Finally, we show the results of the execution in the console:

```
System.out.println("Execution Time: "+(end.getTime()-
                    start.getTime()));
System.out.println("invertedIndex: "+invertedIndex.size());
}
```

The `updateInvertedIndex()` method adds the vocabulary of a document into the inverted index structure. It processes all the words that form the vocabulary. If the word exists in the inverted index, we add the name of the document to the list of documents associated with that word. If the word doesn't exist, we add the word and associate the document with that word, as follows:

```
private static void updateInvertedIndex(Map<String, Integer> voc,
        Map<String, List<String>> invertedIndex, String fileName) {
  for (String word : voc.keySet()) {
    if (word.length() >= 3) {
      invertedIndex.computeIfAbsent(word, k -> new
          ArrayList<>()).add(fileName);
    }
  }
}
```

The first concurrent version - a task per document

Now it's time to implement the concurrent version of the text indexing algorithm. Clearly, we can parallelize the process of every document. This includes reading the document from the file and processing every line to get the vocabulary of the document. The tasks can return that vocabulary as their result, so we can implement tasks based in the `Callable` interface.

In the previous example, we used three methods to send `Callable` tasks to the executor:

- `submit()`
- `invokeAll()`
- `invokeAny()`

We have to process all the documents, so we have to discard the `invokeAny()` method. The other two methods are inconvenient. If we use the `submit()` method, we have to decide when we process the results of the task. If we send a task per document, we can process the results:

- After sending every task, this is nonviable
- After the finalization of all the tasks, we have to store a lot of `Future` objects
- After sending a group of tasks, we have to include code to synchronize both operations

All these approaches have a problem--we process the results of the tasks in a sequential way. If we use the `invokeAll()` method, we are in a situation similar to point 2. We have to wait for the finalization of all the tasks.

One possible option is to create other tasks to process the `Future` objects associated with every task, and the Java concurrency API provides us with an elegant mechanism to implement this solution with the `CompletionService` interface and its implementation, the `ExecutorCompletionService` class.

A `CompletionService` object is a mechanism that has an executor and allows you to decouple the production of tasks and the consumption of the results of those tasks. You can send tasks to the executor using the `submit()` method and get the results of the tasks when they finish using the `poll()` or `take()` methods. So, for our solution, we are going to implement the following elements:

- A `CompletionService` object to execute the tasks.
- A task per document to parse the document and generate its vocabulary. This task will be executed by the `CompletionService` object. These tasks are implemented in the `IndexingTask` class.
- Two threads to process the results of the tasks and construct the inverted index. These threads are implemented in the `InvertedIndexTask` class.
- A `main()` method to create and execute all the elements. This `main()` method is implemented in the `ConcurrentIndexingMain` class.

Let's analyze the source code of these classes.

The IndexingTask class

This class implements the tasks that will parse a document to obtain its vocabulary. It implements the `Callable` interface parameterized with the `Document` class. It has an internal attribute to store the `File` object that represents the document it has to parse. Take a look at the following code:

```
public class IndexingTask implements Callable<Document> {
    private File file;
    public IndexingTask(File file) {
        this.file=file;
    }
```

In the `call()` method, it simply uses the `parse()` method of the `DocumentParser` class to parse the document and obtain the vocabulary and create and return the `Document` object with the data obtained:

```
@Override
public Document call() throws Exception {
  DocumentParser parser = new DocumentParser();

  Map<String, Integer> voc = parser.parse(file.getAbsolutePath());

  Document document=new Document();
  document.setFileName(file.getName());
  document.setVoc(voc);
  return document;
  }
}
```

The InvertedIndexTask class

This class implements the tasks that get the `Document` objects generated by the `IndexingTask` objects and construct the inverted index. These tasks will be executed as `Thread` objects (we don't use an executor in this case), so they are based in the `Runnable` interface.

The `InvertedIndexTask` class uses three internal attributes:

- A `CompletionService` object parameterized with the `Document` class to get access to the objects returned by the `IndexingTask` objects.
- A `ConcurrentHashMap` to store the inverted index. The keys are the words and the values are `ConcurrentLinkedDeque` of `String` with the names of the files. In this case, we have to use concurrent data structures, and the ones used in the serial version are not synchronized.
- A Boolean value to indicate to the task that it can finish its work.

The code for this is as follows:

```
public class InvertedIndexTask implements Runnable {

  private CompletionService<Document> completionService;
  private ConcurrentHashMap<String,
          ConcurrentLinkedDeque<String>> invertedIndex;
  public InvertedIndexTask(CompletionService<Document>
          completionService, ConcurrentHashMap<String,
          ConcurrentLinkedDeque<String>> invertedIndex) {
```

```
      this.completionService = completionService;
      this.invertedIndex = invertedIndex;


   }
```

The `run()` method uses the method `take()` from `CompletionService` to obtain the `Future` object associated with a task. We implement a loop that will be running until the thread is interrupted. Once the thread has been interrupted, it processes all the pending `Future` objects using the `poll()` method. We update the inverted index using the `updateInvertedIndex()` method with the object returned by the `take()` method. We have the following method:

```
public void run() {
  try {
    while (!Thread.interrupted()) {
      try {
        Document document = completionService.take().get();
        updateInvertedIndex(document.getVoc(), invertedIndex,
                            document.getFileName());
      } catch (InterruptedException e) {
        break;
      }
    }
    while (true) {
      Future<Document> future = completionService.poll();
      if (future == null)
        break;
      Document document = future.get();
      updateInvertedIndex(document.getVoc(), invertedIndex,
                          document.getFileName());
    }
  } catch (InterruptedException | ExecutionException e) {
    e.printStackTrace();
  }
}
```

Finally, the `updateInvertedIndex` method receives the vocabulary obtained from a document, the inverted index, and the name of the file that has been processed as parameters. It processes all the words from the vocabulary. We use the `computeIfAbsent()` method to add the word to `invertedIndex` if it's not present:

```
private void updateInvertedIndex(Map<String, Integer> voc,
      ConcurrentHashMap<String, ConcurrentLinkedDeque<String>>
      invertedIndex, String fileName) {
  for (String word : voc.keySet()) {
    if (word.length() >= 3) {
      invertedIndex.computeIfAbsent(word, k -> new
```

```
                              ConcurrentLinkedDeque<>()).add(fileName);
        }
    }
}
```

The ConcurrentIndexing class

This is the main class in the example. It creates and launches all the components, waits for its finalization, and prints the final execution time in the console.

First, it creates and initializes all the variables needed for its execution:

- An executor to run the `InvertedTask` tasks. As with the previous examples, we use the number of cores of the machine as the maximum number of work threads in the executor, but in this case, we leave one core to execute the independent threads.
- A `CompletionService` object to run the tasks. We use the executor created before to initialize this object.
- A `ConcurrentHashMap` to store the inverted index.
- An array of `File` objects with all the documents we have to process.

We have the following method:

```
public class ConcurrentIndexing {

  public static void main(String[] args) {

    int numCores=Runtime.getRuntime().availableProcessors();
    ThreadPoolExecutor executor=(ThreadPoolExecutor)
          Executors.newFixedThreadPool(Math.max(numCores-1, 1));
    ExecutorCompletionService<Document> completionService=new
                  ExecutorCompletionService<>(executor);
    ConcurrentHashMap<String, ConcurrentLinkedDeque<String>>
                  invertedIndex=new ConcurrentHashMap
                  <String,ConcurrentLinkedDeque<String>> ();

    Date start, end;

    File source = new File("data");
    File[] files = source.listFiles();
```

Then, we process all the files of the array. For every file, we create an `InvertedTask` object and send it to the `CompletionService` class using the `submit()` method. We have introduced a mechanism to avoid the overload of the `Executor`. We check the size of the queue of pending tasks and if it has a size bigger than 1000, we sleep the thread so we don't send more tasks while that size isn't decreasing:

```
start=new Date();
for (File file : files) {
  IndexingTask task=new IndexingTask(file);
  completionService.submit(task);
  if (executor.getQueue().size()>1000) {
    do {
      try {
        TimeUnit.MILLISECONDS.sleep(50);
      } catch (InterruptedException e) {
        e.printStackTrace();
      }
    } while (executor.getQueue().size()>1000);
  }
}
```

Then, we create two `InvertedIndexTask` objects to process the results returned by the `InvertedTask` tasks and execute them as normal `Thread` objects:

```
InvertedIndexTask invertedIndexTask=new InvertedIndexTask
                              (completionService,invertedIndex);
Thread thread1=new Thread(invertedIndexTask);
thread1.start();
InvertedIndexTask invertedIndexTask2=new InvertedIndexTask
                              (completionService,invertedIndex);
Thread thread2=new Thread(invertedIndexTask2);
thread2.start();
```

Once we have launched all the elements, we wait for the finalization of the executor using the `shutdown()` and the `awaitTermination()` methods. The `awaitTermination()` method will return when all the `InvertedTask` tasks have finished its execution, so we can finish the threads that execute the `InvertedIndexTask` tasks. To do this, we interrupt these threads (see my comment about `InvertedIndexTask`), as shown in the following code snippet:

```
executor.shutdown();
try {
  executor.awaitTermination(1, TimeUnit.DAYS);
  thread1.interrupt();
  thread2.interrupt();
  thread1.join();
```

```
    thread2.join();
} catch (InterruptedException e) {
    e.printStackTrace();
}
```

Finally, we write the size of the inverted index and the execution time of all the processes in the console:

```
end=new Date();
System.out.println("Execution Time: "+(end.getTime()-
                    start.getTime()));
System.out.println("invertedIndex: "+invertedIndex.size());
}


}
```

The second concurrent version - multiple documents per task

We have implemented a second concurrent version of this example. The basic principles are the same as the first version, but in this case, each task will process more than one document instead of only one. The number of documents processed by each task will be an input parameter of the main method. We have tested the results with 100, 1000, and 5000 documents per task.

To implement this new approach, we are going to implement three new classes:

- The MultipleIndexingTask class, which is equivalent to the IndexingTask class, but it will process a list of documents instead of only one
- The MultipleInvertedIndexTask class, which is equivalent to the InvertedIndexTask class, but now the tasks will retrieve a list of Document objects instead of only one
- The MultipleConcurrentIndexing class, which is equivalent to the ConcurrentIndexing class but using the new classes

As much of the source code is similar to the previous version, we only show the differences.

The MultipleIndexingTask class

As we mentioned earlier, this class is similar to the `IndexingTask` class presented before. The main difference is that it uses a list of `File` objects instead of only one file:

```
public class MultipleIndexingTask implements Callable<List<Document>> {

  private List<File> files;

  public MultipleIndexingTask(List<File> files) {
    this.files = files;
  }
```

The `call()` method returns a list of `Document` objects instead of only one:

```
@Override
public List<Document> call() throws Exception {
  List<Document> documents = new ArrayList<Document>();
  for (File file : files) {
    DocumentParser parser = new DocumentParser();

    Hashtable<String, Integer> voc = parser.parse
                                    (file.getAbsolutePath());

    Document document = new Document();
    document.setFileName(file.getName());
    document.setVoc(voc);

    documents.add(document);
  }

  return documents;
}
}
```

The MultipleInvertedIndexTask class

As we mentioned before, this class is similar to `InvertedIndexClass` presented earlier. The main difference is in the `run()` method. The `Future` object returned by the `poll()` method returns a list of `Document` objects, so we have to process the whole list. Take a look at the following code snippet:

```
@Override
  public void run() {
    try {
      while (!Thread.interrupted()) {
```

```
        try {
          List<Document> documents = completionService.take().get();
          for (Document document : documents) {
            updateInvertedIndex(document.getVoc(), invertedIndex,
                                  document.getFileName());
          }
        } catch (InterruptedException e) {
          break;
        }
      }
      while (true) {
        Future<List<Document>> future = completionService.poll();
        if (future == null)
          break;
          List<Document> documents = future.get();
          for (Document document : documents) {
            updateInvertedIndex(document.getVoc(), invertedIndex,
                                  document.getFileName());
          }
        }
      } catch (InterruptedException | ExecutionException e) {
        e.printStackTrace();
      }
    }
```

The MultipleConcurrentIndexing class

As we mentioned earlier, this class is similar to the `ConcurrentIndexing` class. The only difference is the utilization of the new classes and the use of the first parameter to determine the number of documents processed per task. We have the following method:

```
start=new Date();
List<File> taskFiles=new ArrayList<>();
for (File file : files) {
  taskFiles.add(file);
  if (taskFiles.size()==NUMBER_OF_TASKS) {
    MultipleIndexingTask task=new MultipleIndexingTask(taskFiles);
    completionService.submit(task);
    taskFiles=new ArrayList<>();
    if (executor.getQueue().size()>10) {
      do {
        try {
          TimeUnit.MILLISECONDS.sleep(50);
        } catch (InterruptedException e) {
          e.printStackTrace();
        }
      } while (executor.getQueue().size()>10);
```

```
    }
  }
}
if (taskFiles.size()>0) {
  MultipleIndexingTask task=new MultipleIndexingTask(taskFiles);
  completionService.submit(task);
}

MultipleInvertedIndexTask invertedIndexTask=new
            MultipleInvertedIndexTask(completionService,invertedIndex);
Thread thread1=new Thread(invertedIndexTask);
thread1.start();
MultipleInvertedIndexTask invertedIndexTask2=new
            MultipleInvertedIndexTask (completionService,invertedIndex);
Thread thread2=new Thread(invertedIndexTask2);
thread2.start();
```

Comparing the solutions

Let's compare the solutions of the three versions of the example we have implemented. As we mentioned earlier, as document collection, we have taken the Wikipedia pages with information about movies to construct a set of 100,673 documents. We have converted each Wikipedia page into a text file. You can download this document collection with all the information about the book.

We have executed five different versions of the solutions:

- The serial version
- The concurrent version with one task per document
- The concurrent version with multiple tasks per document, with 100, 1,000, and 5,000 documents per task

We have executed the examples using the **JMH framework** (http://openjdk.java.net/projects/code-tools/jmh/) that allows you to implement micro benchmarks in Java. Using a framework for benchmarking is a better solution that simply measures time using methods such as currentTimeMillis() or nanoTime(). We have executed them 10 times in two different architectures:

- A computer with an Intel Core i5-5300 CPU with Windows 7 and 16 GB of RAM. This processor has two cores and each core can execute two threads, so we will have four parallel threads.
- A computer with an AMD A8-640 APU with Windows 10 and 8 GB of RAM. This processor has four cores.

The following table shows the execution time of the five versions:

Algorithm	Intel	Amd
	Execution time (milliseconds)	**Execution time (milliseconds)**
Serial	29,305.63	137,519.75
Concurrent: one document per task	13,704.17	75,593.93
Concurrent: 100 documents per task	26,579.30	195,928.209
Concurrent: 1000 documents per task	25,126.47	133,080.655
Concurrent: 5000 documents per task	23,454.38	118,789.394

We can draw the following conclusions:

- Concurrent versions almost always obtain better performance than the serial one
- For the concurrent versions, if we increase the number of documents per task, we obtain better results

In this example, there's a big difference between the two architectures, but take into account the fact that other factors, such as the hard disk, the memory space, and speed have a very big influence on the results of this example, as it reads more than 100,000 files and uses memory intensively.

If we compare the concurrent version with the serial one using the speed-up, the results are:

$$S_{AMD} = \frac{T_{serial}}{T_{concurrent}} = \frac{137,519.75}{75,593.93} = 1.82$$

$$S_{Intel} = \frac{T_{serial}}{T_{concurrent}} = \frac{29,305.63}{13,704.17} = 2.13$$

Other methods of interest

In this chapter, we have used some methods of the `AbstractExecutorService` interface (implemented in the `ThreadPoolExecutor` class) and `CompletionService` interfaces (implemented in the `ExecutorCompletionService`) to manage the results of `Callable` tasks. However, there are other versions of the methods we have used and other methods we want to mention here.

Let's discuss the following methods about the `AbstractExecutorService` interface:

- `invokeAll (Collection<? extends Callable<T>> tasks, long timeout, TimeUnit unit)`: This method returns a list of `Future` objects associated with the list of `Callable` tasks passed as parameters when all the tasks have finished their execution or the timeout specified by the second and third parameters expires.
- `invokeAny (Collection<? Extends Callable<T>> tasks, long timeout, TimeUnit unit)`: This method returns the result of the first task of the list of `Callable` tasks passed as a parameter that finishes their execution without throwing an exception if they finish before the timeout specified by the second and third parameters expires. If the timeout expires, the method throws a `TimeoutException` exception.

Let's discuss the following methods about the `Compl0065tionService` interface:

- The `poll()` method: We have used a version of this method with two parameters, but there is also a version without parameters. From the internal data structures, this version retrieves and removes the `Future` object of the next task that has finished since the last call to the `poll()` or `take()` methods. If no tasks have finished, its execution returns a null value.
- The `take()` method: This method is similar to the previous one, but if no tasks have finished, it sleeps the thread until one task finishes its execution.

Summary

In this chapter, you learned the different mechanisms that you can use to work with tasks that return a result. These tasks are based on the `Callable` interface, which declares the `call()` method. This is a parameterized interface with the class returned by the call method.

When you execute a `Callable` task in an executor, you will always obtain an implementation of the `Future` interface. You can use this object to cancel the execution of the task, know if the task has finished its execution, or get the result returned by the `call()` method.

You send `Callable` tasks to the executor using three different methods. With the `submit()` method, you send one task, and you will immediately get a `Future` object associated with this task. With the `invokeAll()` method, you send a list of tasks and will get a list of `Future` objects when all the tasks have finished their execution. With the `invokeAny()` method, you send a list of tasks, and you will receive the result (not a `Future` object) of the first task that finishes without throwing an exception. The rest of the tasks are canceled.

The Java concurrency API provides another mechanism to work with these kinds of tasks. This mechanism is defined in the `CompletionService` interface and implemented in the `ExecutorCompletionService` class. This mechanism allows you to decouple the execution of tasks and the processing of their results. The `CompletionService` interface works internally with an executor and provides the `submit()` method to send tasks to the `CompletionService` interface, and the `poll()` and `take()` methods to get the results of the tasks. These results are provided in the same order in which tasks finish their execution.

You also learned to implement these concepts with two real-world examples. First, a best-matching algorithm using the UKACD dataset and, second, an inverted index constructor using a dataset with more than 100,000 documents with information about movies extracted from Wikipedia.

In the next chapter, you will learn how to execute algorithms in a concurrent way that can be divided into phases. The main characteristic of these phases is that you must finish one completely before you can start the next one. Java concurrency API provides the `Phaser` class to facilitate the concurrent implementation of these algorithms. It allows you to synchronize all the tasks involved in it at the end of a phase, so none of them will start the next one until all have finished the current one.

6
Running Tasks Divided into Phases - The Phaser Class

The most important element in a concurrent API is the synchronization mechanism it offers to the programmer. **Synchronization** is the coordination of two or more tasks to get the desired result. You can synchronize the execution of two or more tasks, when they have to be executed in a predefined order, or synchronize the access to a shared resource, when only one thread at a time can execute a fragment of code or modify a block of memory. The Java 9 concurrency API provides a lot of synchronization mechanisms, from the basic synchronized keyword and the Lock interface and their implementations, to protect a critical section, to the more advanced CyclicBarrier or CountDownLatch classes, which allow you to synchronize the order of execution of different tasks. In Java 7, the concurrency API introduces the Phaser class. This class provides a powerful mechanism (**phaser**) to execute tasks divided into phases. The task can ask the Phaser class to wait until all other participants finish the phase. In this chapter, we will cover the following topics:

- An introduction to the Phaser class
- First example - a keyword extraction algorithm
- Second example - a genetic algorithm

An introduction to the Phaser class

The `Phaser` class is a synchronization mechanism designed to control the execution of algorithms that can be divided into phases in a concurrent way. If you have a process with clearly defined steps, so you have to finish the first one before you can start the second one, and so on, you can use this class to make a concurrent version of your process. The main characteristics of the `Phaser` class are:

- The phaser must know the number of tasks it has to control. Java refers to this as the registration of the participants. A participant can register in a phaser any time.
- The tasks must inform the phaser when they finish a phase. The phaser will make that task sleep until all the participants have finished that phase.
- Internally, the phaser saves an integer number that stores the number of phase changes the phase has made.
- A participant can leave the control of the phaser any time. Java refers to this as deregistering the participants.
- You can execute custom code when the phaser makes a phase change.
- You can control the termination of the phaser. If a phaser is terminated, no new participants will be accepted and no synchronization between tasks will be made.
- You can use some methods to know the status and the number of participants of a phaser.

Registration and deregistration of participants

As we mentioned before, a phaser must know the number of tasks it has to control. It has to know how many different threads are executing the phase-divided algorithm to control the simultaneous phase change in a correct way.

Java refers to this process as the registration of participants. The normal situation is that participants are registered at the beginning of the execution, but a participant can be registered any time.

You can register a participant using different methods:

- When you create the `Phaser` object: The `Phaser` class provides four different constructors. Two of them are commonly used:
  - `phaser()`: This constructor creates a phaser with zero participants
  - `phaser(int parties)`: This constructor creates a phaser with the given number of participants
- Explicitly, using one of these methods:
  - `bulkRegister(int parties)`: Register the given number of new participants at the same time
  - `register()`: Register one new participant

When one of the tasks controlled by the phaser finishes its execution, it must deregister from the phaser. If you don't do this, the phaser will wait endlessly for it in the next phase change. To deregister a participant, you can use this `arriveAndDeregister()` method. You use this method to indicate to the phaser that this task has finished the current phase and it won't participate in the next phases.

Synchronizing phase change

The main purpose of the phaser is to allow the implementation of algorithms that are clearly divided into phases in a concurrent way. None of the tasks can advance to the next phase until all the tasks have finished the previous phase. The `Phaser` class provides three methods to signal that the task has finished the phase: `arrive()`, `arriveAndDeregister()`, and `arriveAndAwaitAdvance()`. If one of the tasks doesn't call one of these methods, the rest of the participant tasks will be blocked by the phaser indefinitely. To advance to the next phase, the following methods are used:

- `arriveAndAwaitAdvance()`: A task uses this method to indicate to the phaser that it has finished the current phase and wants to continue with the next one. The phaser will block the tasks until all the participant tasks have called one of the synchronization methods.
- `awaitAdvance(int phase)`: A task uses this method to indicate to the phaser that it wants to wait for the finalization of the current phase if the number we pass as a parameter and the actual phase of the phaser are equal. If they aren't equal, this method returns immediately.

Other functionalities

When all the participant tasks have finished the execution of a phase and before they continue with the next one, the `Phaser` class executes the `onAdvance()` method. This method receives the following two parameters:

- `phase`: This is the number of the phase that has finished. The first phase is the number zero.
- `registeredParties`: This indicates the number of participant tasks.

If you want to execute some code between two phases, for example, to sort or to transform some data, you can implement your own phaser, extending the `Phaser` class and overriding this method.

A phaser can be in two states:

- **Active**: The phaser enters into this state when it's created and new participants are registered and continues on it until its termination. When it's in this state, it accepts new participants and works as explained before.
- **Termination**: The phaser enters into this state when the `onAdvance()` method returns the `true` value. By default, it returns the `true` value when all the participants have been deregistered.

 When a phaser is in the termination state, the registration of new participants has no effect and synchronization methods return immediately.

Finally, the `Phaser` class provides some methods to get information about the status and participants in the phaser:

- `getRegisteredParties()`: This method returns the number of participants in the phaser
- `getPhase()`: This method returns the number of the current phase
- `getArrivedParties()`: This method returns the number of participants that have finished the current phase
- `getUnarrivedParties()`: This method returns the number of participants that haven't finished the current phase
- `isTerminated()`: This method returns the true value if the phaser is in the `Termination` state and false otherwise

First example - a keyword extraction algorithm

In this section, you are going to use a phaser to implement a **keyword extraction algorithm**. The main purpose of these kinds of algorithms is to extract the words from a text document or a collection of documents, which define the document or the document inside the collection, better. These terms can be used to summarize the documents, cluster them, or to improve the information search process.

The most basic algorithm to extract the keywords of the documents in a collection (but it's still commonly used nowadays) is based on the **TF-IDF** measure where:

- **Term Frequency (TF)** is the number of times that a d appears in a document.
- **Document Frequency (DF)** is the number of documents that contain a word. The **Inverse Document Frequency (IDF)** measures the information that word provides to distinguish a document from others. If a word is very common, its IDF will be low, but if the word appears in only a few documents, its IDF will be high.

The *TF-IDF* of the word *t* in the document *d* can be calculated using the following formula:

$$TF - IDF = TF \times IDF = F_{t,d} * \log\left(\frac{N}{n_t}\right)$$

The attributes used in the preceding formula can be explained as follows:

- $F_{t,d}$ is the number of appearances of the word *t* in the document *d*
- N is the number of documents in the collection
- n_t is the number of documents that contain the word *t*

To obtain the keywords of a document, you can select the words with higher values for its *TF-IDF*.

The algorithm you are going to implement will calculate the best keywords in a document collection executing the following phases:

- **Phase 1**: Parse all the documents and extract the *DF* of all the words. Note that you will only have the exact values once you have parsed all the documents.
- **Phase 2**: Calculate the *TF-IDF* for all the words in all the documents. Select 10 keywords per document (the 10 words with a higher value of the *TF-IDF* measure).
- **Phase 3**: Obtain a list of the best keywords. We consider that those are the words, which are a keyword in a higher number of documents.

To test the algorithm, we will use the Wikipedia pages with information about movies as our document collection. We used the same collection in Chapter 5, *Getting Data from Tasks - The Callable and Future Interfaces*. This collection is formed of 100,673 documents. We have converted each Wikipedia page into a text file. You can download this document collection with all the information about the book.

You are going to implement two different versions of the algorithm: a basic serial one and a concurrent one using the Phaser class. After this, we will compare the execution time of both versions to verify that concurrency provides us with better performance.

Common classes

Both versions of the algorithm share some common functionality to parse the documents and to store information about documents, keywords, and words. The common classes are:

- The Document class, which stores the name of the file that contains the document and the words that form it
- The Word class, which stores the string with the word and the measures of that word (*TF*, *DF*, and *TF-IDF*)
- The Keyword class, which stores the string with the word and the number of documents in which the word is a keyword
- The DocumentParser class, which extracts the words for a document

Let's look at these classes in more detail.

The Word class

The `Word` class stores information about a word. This information includes the whole word and the measures that affect it, that is to say, its *TF* in a document, its global *DF*, and the resultant *TF-IDF*.

This class implements the `Comparable` interface because we're going to sort an array of words in order to obtain the ones with a higher *TF-IDF*. Refer to the following code:

```
public class Word implements Comparable<Word> {
```

Then, we declare the attributes of the class and implement the getters and setters (these ones are not included):

```
private String word;
private int tf;
private int df;
private double tfIdf;
```

We have implemented other methods of interest, as follows:

- The constructor of the class, which initializes the word (with the word received as parameter) and the `df` attribute (with a value of 1).
- The `addTf()` method, which increments the `tf` attribute.
- The `merge()` method, which receives a `Word` object and merges the same word from two different documents. It sums the `tf` and `df` attributes of both objects.

Then, we implement a special version of the `setDf()` method. It receives the value of the `df` attribute as a parameter and the total number of documents in the collection, and it calculates the `tfIdf` attribute:

```
public void setDf(int df, int N) {
  this.df = df;
  tfIdf = tf * Math.log(Double.valueOf(N) / df);
}
```

Finally, we implement the `compareTo()` method. We want the words ordered from higher to lower `tfIdf` attribute:

```
@Override
  public int compareTo(Word o) {
    return Double.compare(o.getTfIdf(), this.getTfIdf());
  }
}
```

The Keyword class

The Keyword class stores information about a keyword. This information includes the whole word and the number of documents in which this word is a keyword.

As with the word class, it implements the Comparable interface because we're going to sort an array of keywords to obtain the best keywords:

```
public class Keyword implements Comparable<Keyword> {
```

Then, we declare the attributes of the class and implement the methods to establish and return its values (these ones are not included here):

```
private String word;
private int df;
```

Finally, we implement the compareTo() method. We want the keywords ordered from higher to lower number of documents:

```
@Override
public int compareTo(Keyword o) {

  return Integer.compare(o.getDf(), this.getDf());
  }
}
```

The Document class

The Document class stores the information about a document in the collection (remember that our collection has 100,673 documents), which includes the name of the file and the set of words that forms the document. That set of words, usually named the vocabulary of the document, is implemented as a HashMap using the whole word as a string as the key and a Word object as the value:

```
public class Document {
   private String fileName;
   private HashMap <String, Word> voc;
```

We have implemented a constructor that creates the HashMap and methods to get and set the name of the file and to return the vocabulary of the document (these methods are not included). We have also implemented a method to add a word in the vocabulary. If the word doesn't exist in it, we add it.

If the word exists in the vocabulary, we increment the `tf` attribute of the word. We have used the `computeIfAbsent()` method of the `voc` object. This method inserts the word in the `HashMap` if it doesn't exist and then increments the `tf` using the `addTf()` method:

```
public void addWord(String string) {
  voc.computeIfAbsent(string, k -> new Word(k)).addTf();
  }
}
```

The `HashMap` class is not synchronized, but we can use it in our concurrent application because it will not be shared between different tasks. A `Document` object will be generated only by one task, so we won't have race conditions in our concurrent version derived by the utilization of the `HashMap` class.

The DocumentParser class

The `DocumentParser` class reads the content of a text file and converts it into a `Document` object. It splits the text into words and stores them in the `Document` object to generate the vocabulary of the class. This class has two static methods. The first one is the `parse()` method that receives a string with the path of the file and returns a `Document` object. It opens the file and reads it line by line, using the `parseLine()` method to convert each line into a sequence of words, and stores them in the `Document` class:

```
public class DocumentParser {

  public static Document parse(String path) {
    Document ret = new Document();
    Path file = Paths.get(path);
    ret.setFileName(file.toString());

    try (BufferedReader reader =
         Files.newBufferedReader(file)) {
      for(String line : Files.readAllLines(file)) {
        parseLine(line, ret);
      }
    } catch (IOException x) {
      x.printStackTrace();
    }
    return ret;

  }
```

The `parseLine()` method receives the line to parse and the `Document` object to store the words as parameters.

First, it deletes the accents of the line using the `Normalizer` class and converts it into lowercase:

```
private static void parseLine(String line, Document ret) {

    line = Normalizer.normalize(line, Normalizer.Form.NFKD);
    line = line.replaceAll("[^\\p{ASCII}]", "");
    line = line.toLowerCase();
```

Then, we split the line into words using the `StringTokenizer` class and add those words to the `Document` object:

```
private static void parseLine(String line, Document ret) {

    // Clean string
    line = Normalizer.normalize(line, Normalizer.Form.NFKD);
    line = line.replaceAll("[^\\p{ASCII}]", "");
    line = line.toLowerCase();

    // Tokenizer

    for(String w: line.split("\\W+")) {
        ret.addWord(w);
    }
}

}
```

The serial version

We have implemented the serial version of our keyword algorithm in the `SerialKeywordExtraction` class. It defines the `main()` method you are going to execute to test the algorithm.

The first step is to declare the following necessary internal variables to execute the algorithm:

- Two `Date` objects to measure the execution time
- A string to store the name of the directory that contains the document collection
- An array of `File` objects to store the files with the document collection
- A `HashMap` to store the global vocabulary of the document collection

- A `HashMap` to store the keywords
- Two `int` values to measure statistic data about the execution

The following includes the declaration of these variables:

```
public class SerialKeywordExtraction {

  public static void main(String[] args) {

    Date start, end;

    File source = new File("data");
    File[] files = source.listFiles();
    HashMap<String, Word> globalVoc = new HashMap<>();
    HashMap<String, Integer> globalKeywords = new HashMap<>();
    int totalCalls = 0;
    int numDocuments = 0;

    start = new Date();
```

Then, we have included the first phase of the algorithm. We parse all the documents using the `parse()` method of the `DocumentParser` class. This method returns a `Document` object, which contains the vocabulary of that document. We add the document vocabulary to the global vocabulary using the `merge()` method of the `HashMap` class. If a word doesn't exist, it inserts it in the `HashMap`. If the word exists, two word objects are merged together, summing the `Tf` and `Df` attributes:

```
if(files == null) {
  System.err.println("Unable to read the 'data' folder");
  return;
}
for (File file : files) {

  if (file.getName().endsWith(".txt")) {
    Document doc = DocumentParser.parse (file.getAbsolutePath());
    for (Word word : doc.getVoc().values()) {
      globalVoc.merge(word.getWord(), word, Word::merge);
    }
    numDocuments++;
  }
}
System.out.println("Corpus: " + numDocuments + " documents.");
```

After this phase, the `globalVocHashMap` class contains all the words of the document collection with their global `TF` (the total number of appearances of the word in the collection) and their `DF`.

Then, we have included the second phase of the algorithm. We are going to calculate the keywords of each document using the *TF-IDF* measure, as we explained before. We have to parse each document again to generate its vocabulary. We have to do this because we can't store the vocabularies of the 100,673 documents that form our document collection in memory. If you work with a smaller document collection, you can try to parse the documents only once and store the vocabularies of all the documents in memory, but in our case, it's impossible. So, we parse all the documents again, and, for each word, we update the df attribute using the values stored in the globalVoc. We also construct an array with all the words in the document:

```
for (File file : files) {
  if (file.getName().endsWith(".txt")) {
    Document doc = DocumentParser.parse(file.getAbsolutePath());
    List<Word> keywords = new ArrayList<>( doc.getVoc().values());

    int index = 0;
    for (Word word : keywords) {
      Word globalWord = globalVoc.get(word.getWord());
      word.setDf(globalWord.getDf(), numDocuments);
    }
```

Now, we have the list of keywords with all the words in the document with their *TF-IDF* calculated. We use the sort() method of the Collections class to sort the list, getting the words with a higher value of *TF-IDF* in the first position. Then we get the first 10 words of that list to store them in the globalKeywordsHashMap using the addKeyword() method.

There is no special reason to choose the first 10 words. You can try other options, as a percentage of the words or a minimum value of the TF-IDF measure, and see their behavior:

```
    Collections.sort(keywords);

    int counter = 0;

    for (Word word : keywords) {
      addKeyword(globalKeywords, word.getWord());
      totalCalls++;
    }
  }
}
```

Finally, we have included the third phase of our algorithm. We convert the globalKeywordsHashMap into a list of Keyword objects, use the sort() method of the Collections class to sort that array, getting the keywords with a higher DF value in the first positions of the list, and write the first 100 words in the console.

Refer to the following code:

```
List<Keyword> orderedGlobalKeywords = new ArrayList<>();
for (Entry<String, Integer> entry : globalKeywords.entrySet()) {
  Keyword keyword = new Keyword();
  keyword.setWord(entry.getKey());
  keyword.setDf(entry.getValue());
  orderedGlobalKeywords.add(keyword);
}

Collections.sort(orderedGlobalKeywords);

if (orderedGlobalKeywords.size() > 100) {
  orderedGlobalKeywords = orderedGlobalKeywords.subList(0, 100);
}
for (Keyword keyword : orderedGlobalKeywords) {
  System.out.println(keyword.getWord() + ": " + keyword.getDf());
}
```

As in the second phase, there is no special reason to choose the first 100 words. You can try other options if you want.

To finish the main method, we write the execution time and other statistic data in the console:

```
end = new Date();
System.out.println("Execution Time: " + (end.getTime() -
                   start.getTime()));
System.out.println("Vocabulary Size: " + globalVoc.size());
 System.out.println("Keyword Size: " + globalKeywords.size());
System.out.println("Number of Documents: " + numDocuments);
System.out.println("Total calls: " + totalCalls);

}
```

The `SerialKeywyordExtraction` class also includes the `addKeyword()` method, which updates the information of a keyword in the `globalKeywordsHashMap` class. If the word exists, the class updates its DF, and if the word doesn't exist, it inserts it. Refer to the following code:

```
private static void addKeyword(Map<String, Integer>
                   globalKeywords, String word) {
  globalKeywords.merge(word, 1, Integer::sum);
}

}
```

The concurrent version

To implement the concurrent version of this example, we have used two different classes, as follows:

- The KeywordExtractionTasks class, which implements the tasks that are going to calculate the keywords in a concurrent way. We are going to execute the tasks as Thread objects, so this class implements the Runnable interface.
- The ConcurrentKeywordExtraction class, which provides the main() method to execute the algorithm and creates, starts, and waits for the finish of the tasks.

Let's look at these classes in detail.

The KeywordExtractionTask class

As we mentioned before, this class implements the tasks that are going to calculate the final keyword list. It implements the Runnable interface, so we can execute them as a Thread, and internally uses some attributes, most of which are shared between all the tasks:

- **Two ConcurrentHashMap objects to store the global vocabulary and the global keywords**: We use the ConcurrentHashMap because these objects are going to be updated by all the tasks, so we have to use a concurrent data structure to avoid race conditions.
- **Two ConcurrentLinkedDeque of File objects, to store the list of files that forms the document collection**: We use the ConcurrentLinkedDeque class because all the tasks are going to extract (get and delete) elements of the list simultaneously, so we have to use a concurrent data structure to avoid race conditions. If we use a normal List, the same File can be parsed twice by different tasks. We have two ConcurrentLinkedDeque because we have to parse the collection of documents twice. As we mentioned before, we parse the document collection, extracting the File objects from the data structures, so, when we have parsed the collection, the data structure will be empty.
- **A Phaser object to control the execution of the tasks**: As we explained before, our keyword extraction algorithm is executed in three phases. None of the tasks advance to the next phase until all the tasks have finished the previous one. We use the Phaser object to control this. If we don't control this, we will obtain inconsistent results.

- **The final step has to be executed by only one thread**: We are going to distinguish one main task from the others using a Boolean value. These main tasks will execute that final phase.
- **The total number of documents in the collection**: We need this value to calculate the *TF-IDF* measure.

We have included a constructor to initialize all these attributes:

```
public class KeywordExtractionTask implements Runnable {

  private ConcurrentHashMap<String, Word> globalVoc;
  private ConcurrentHashMap<String, Integer> globalKeywords;

  private ConcurrentLinkedDeque<File> concurrentFileListPhase1;
  private ConcurrentLinkedDeque<File> concurrentFileListPhase2;

  private Phaser phaser;

  private String name;
  private boolean main;

  private int parsedDocuments;
  private int numDocuments;

  public KeywordExtractionTask(
          ConcurrentLinkedDeque<File> concurrentFileListPhase1,
          ConcurrentLinkedDeque<File> concurrentFileListPhase2,
          Phaser phaser, ConcurrentHashMap<String, Word>
            globalVoc,
          ConcurrentHashMap<String, Integer> globalKeywords,
            int numDocuments, String name, boolean main) {
    this.concurrentFileListPhase1 = concurrentFileListPhase1;
    this.concurrentFileListPhase2 = concurrentFileListPhase2;
    this.globalVoc = globalVoc;
    this.globalKeywords = globalKeywords;
    this.phaser = phaser;
    this.main = main;
    this.name = name;
    this.numDocuments = numDocuments;
  }
```

The `run()` method implements the algorithm with its three phases. First, we call the `arriveAndAwaitAdvance()` method of the phaser to wait for the creation of the other tasks. All the tasks will start their execution at the same moment. Then, as we explained in the serial version of the algorithm, we parse all the documents and build the `globalVocConcurrentHashMap` class with all the words and their global `TF` and `DF` values. To complete phase one, we again call the `arriveAndAwaitAdvance()` method to wait for the finalization of the other tasks before the execution of the second phase:

```
@Override
public void run() {
  File file;

  // Phase 1
  phaser.arriveAndAwaitAdvance();
  System.out.println(name + ": Phase 1");
  while ((file = concurrentFileListPhase1.poll()) != null) {
    Document doc = DocumentParser.parse(file.getAbsolutePath());
      for (Word word : doc.getVoc().values()) {
        globalVoc.merge(word.getWord(), word, Word::merge);
      }
      parsedDocuments++;
  }

    System.out.println(name + ": " + parsedDocuments +
                         " parsed.");
  phaser.arriveAndAwaitAdvance();
```

As you can see, to get the `File` objects to process, we use the `poll()` method of the `ConcurrentLinkedDeque` class. This method retrieves and removes the first element of `Deque`, so the next task will obtain a different file to parse, and no file will be parsed twice.

The second phase calculates the `globalKeywords` structure, as we explained in the serial version of the algorithm. First, calculate the best 10 keywords of every document and then insert them in the `ConcurrentHashMap` class. The code is the same as in the serial version, changing the serial data structures for the concurrent ones:

```
// Phase 2
System.out.println(name + ": Phase 2");
while ((file = concurrentFileListPhase2.poll()) != null) {

  Document doc = DocumentParser.parse(file.getAbsolutePath());
  List<Word> keywords = new ArrayList<>(doc.getVoc().values());

  for (Word word : keywords) {
    Word globalWord = globalVoc.get(word.getWord());
    word.setDf(globalWord.getDf(), numDocuments);
```

```
    }
    Collections.sort(keywords);

    if(keywords.size() > 10) keywords = keywords.subList(0, 10);
        for (Word word : keywords) {
            addKeyword(globalKeywords, word.getWord());
        }
    }
    System.out.println(name + ": " + parsedDocuments +
                        " parsed.");
```

The final phase will be different for the main task and for the others. The main task uses the `arriveAndAwaitAdvance()` method of the `Phaser` class to wait for the finalization of the second phase of all the tasks before writing the best 100 keywords of the whole collection in the console. Finally, it uses the `arriveAndDeregister()` method to deregister from the phaser.

The rest of the tasks use the `arriveAndDeregister()` method to mark the finalization of the second phase, deregister from the phaser, and finish their execution.

When all the tasks have finished their work, all of them deregister themselves from the phaser. The phaser will have zero parties, and it will enter the termination state:

```
    if (main) {
        phaser.arriveAndAwaitAdvance();

        Iterator<Entry<String, Integer>> iterator =
                        globalKeywords.entrySet().iterator();     Keyword
    orderedGlobalKeywords[] = new
                        Keyword[globalKeywords.size()];
        int index = 0;
        while (iterator.hasNext()) {
            Entry<String, AtomicInteger> entry = iterator.next();
            Keyword keyword = new Keyword();
            keyword.setWord(entry.getKey());
            keyword.setDf(entry.getValue().get());
            orderedGlobalKeywords[index] = keyword;
            index++;
        }

        System.out.println("Keyword Size: " +
                        orderedGlobalKeywords.length);

        Arrays.parallelSort(orderedGlobalKeywords);
        int counter = 0;
        for (int i = 0; i < orderedGlobalKeywords.length; i++){
```

```
        Keyword keyword = orderedGlobalKeywords[i];
        System.out.println(keyword.getWord() + ": " +
                           keyword.getDf());
        counter++;
        if (counter == 100) {
          break;
        }
      }
    }
    phaser.arriveAndDeregister();

    System.out.println("Thread " + name + " has finished.");
  }
```

The ConcurrentKeywordExtraction class

The ConcurrentKeywordExtraction class initializes the shared objects, creates the tasks, executes them, and waits for its finalization. It implements the main() method, which can receive an optional parameter. By default, we are doing the number of tasks determined by the availableProcessors() method of the Runtime class, which returns the number of hardware threads available to the **Java Virtual Machine (JVM)**. If we receive a parameter, we convert it into an integer and use it as a multiplier of the number of available processors to determine the number of tasks we are going to create.

First, we initialize all the necessary data structures and parameters. To fill the two ConcurrentLinkedDeque structures, we use the listFiles() method of the File class to get an array of File objects with the files that end with the txt suffix.

We also create the Phaser object using the constructor without parameters, so all the tasks must register themselves in the phaser explicitly. Refer to the following code:

```
public class ConcurrentKeywordExtraction {

  public static void main(String[] args) {

    Date start, end;

    ConcurrentHashMap<String, Word> globalVoc = new
                              ConcurrentHashMap<>();
    ConcurrentHashMap<String, Integer> globalKeywords = new
                              ConcurrentHashMap<>();

    start = new Date();
    File source = new File("data");
```

```
File[] files = source.listFiles(f ->
                        f.getName().endsWith(".txt"));
if (files == null) {
  System.err.println("The 'data' folder not found!");
  return;
}
ConcurrentLinkedDeque<File> concurrentFileListPhase1 = new
        ConcurrentLinkedDeque<>(Arrays.asList(files));
ConcurrentLinkedDeque<File> concurrentFileListPhase2 = new
        ConcurrentLinkedDeque<>(Arrays.asList(files));

int numDocuments = files.length();
int factor = 1;
if (args.length > 0) {
  factor = Integer.valueOf(args[0]);
}

int numTasks = factor *
        Runtime.getRuntime().availableProcessors();
Phaser phaser = new Phaser();

Thread[] threads = new Thread[numTasks];
KeywordExtractionTask[] tasks = new
                KeywordExtractionTask[numTasks];
```

Then, we create the first task with the main parameter set to true, and the rest with the main parameter set to false. After the creation of each task, we use the register() method of the Phaser class to register a new participant in the phaser, as follows:

```
for (int i = 0; i < numTasks; i++) {
  tasks[i] = new KeywordExtractionTask(concurrentFileListPhase1,
              concurrentFileListPhase2, phaser, globalVoc,
              globalKeywords, concurrentFileListPhase1.size(),
              "Task" + i, i==0);
  phaser.register();
  System.out.println(phaser.getRegisteredParties() + "
                tasks arrived to the Phaser.");
}
```

Then, we create and start the thread objects that run the tasks and wait for its finalization:

```
for (int i = 0; i < numTasks; i++) {
  threads[i] = new Thread(tasks[i]);
  threads[i].start();
}

for (int i = 0; i < numTasks; i++) {
  try {
```

```
        threads[i].join();
    } catch (InterruptedException e) {
        e.printStackTrace();
    }
}
```

Finally, we write some statistic information about the execution in the console, including the execution time:

```
    System.out.println("Is Terminated: " + phaser.isTerminated());

    end = new Date();
    System.out.println("Execution Time: " + (end.getTime() -
                        start.getTime()));
    System.out.println("Vocabulary Size: " + globalVoc.size());
    System.out.println("Number of Documents: " + numDocuments);

    }

}
```

Comparing the two solutions

Let's compare the serial and concurrent versions of our keyword extraction algorithm. To test the algorithm, we used our document collection with 100,673 documents.

We executed the examples using the **JMH framework** (http://openjdk.java.net/projects/code-tools/jmh/), which allows you to implement micro benchmarks in Java. Using a framework for benchmarking is a better solution, which simply measures time using methods such as currentTimeMillis() or nanoTime(). We executed them 10 times in two different architectures:

- A computer with an Intel Core i5-5300 CPU with Windows 7 and 16 GB of RAM - this processor has two cores and each core can execute two threads, so we will have four parallel threads
- A computer with an AMD A8-640 APU with Windows 10 and 8 GB of RAM - this processor has four cores

Algorithm	Intel		AMD	
	Factor	Execution Time (seconds)	Factor	Execution Time (seconds)
Serial	N/A	76.252	N/A	168.816
Concurrent	1	35.092	1	60.740
	2	34.495	2	60.806
	3	34.518	3	58.752

We can draw the following conclusions:

- The concurrent version of the algorithm increases the performance of the serial version in both architectures.
- If we use more tasks than the number of the available hardware threads, we don't get a better result. There's a slight difference, but it's not significant.

We compare the concurrent and serial versions of the algorithm, calculating the speed-up using the following formula:

$$S_{AMD} = \frac{T_{serial}}{T_{concurrent}} = \frac{168.816}{58.752} = 2{,}87$$

$$S_{Intel} = \frac{T_{serial}}{T_{concurrent}} = \frac{76.252}{34.518} = 2.21$$

The second example - a genetic algorithm

Genetic algorithms are adaptive heuristic search algorithms based on the natural selection principles used to generate good solutions to optimization and search problems. They work with possible solutions to a problem, named individuals, or phenotypes. Each individual has a representation formed of a set of properties named chromosomes. Normally, the individuals are represented by a sequence of bits, but you can choose the representation that better fits your problem.

You also need a function to determine whether a solution is good or bad, named the **fitness function**. The main objective of the genetic algorithm is to find a solution that maximizes or minimizes that function.

The genetic algorithm starts with a set of possible solutions to the problem. This set of possible solutions is called the population. You can generate this initial set randomly or use some kind of heuristic function to obtain better initial solutions.

Once you have the initial population, you begin an iterative process with three phases. Each step of that iterative process is called a generation. The phases of each generation are:

- **Selection**: You select the better individuals of your population. These are the individuals with a better value in the fitness function.
- **Crossover**: You cross the individuals selected in the previous step to generate the new individuals that form the new generation. This operation takes two individuals and generates two new individuals. The implementation of this operation depends on the problem you want to solve and the representation of the individuals you have chosen.
- **Mutation**: You can apply a mutation operator to alter the values of an individual. Normally, you will apply that operation to a very low number of individuals. While mutation is a very important operation to find a good solution, we don't apply it to simplify our example.

You repeat these three operations until you meet your finish criteria. These finish criteria can be:

- A fixed number of generations
- A predefined value of the fitness function
- A solution that meets the predefined criteria is found
- A time limit
- A manual stop

Normally, you will store the best individual you have found across the process outside of the population. This individual will be the solution proposed by the algorithm, and normally, it's going to be a better solution, as we generate new generations.

In this section, we are going to implement a genetic algorithm to solve the well-known **Traveling Salesman Problem (TSP)**. In this problem, you have a set of cities and the distances between them, and you want to find the optimal route to go through all the cities, minimizing the total distance of travel. As with other examples, we have implemented a serial version and a concurrent one using the `Phaser` class. The main characteristics of a genetic algorithm applied to the TSP problems are:

- **Individuals**: An individual represents the traversal order of the cities.
- **Crossover**: You have to create valid solutions after the crossover operation. You must visit each city only once.
- **Fitness function**: The main objective of the algorithm is to minimize the total distance to travel between the cities.
- **Finish criteria**: We are going to execute the algorithm for a predefined number of generations.

For example, you could have a distance matrix with four cities, as shown in the following table:

	City 1	City 2	City 3	City 4
City 1	0	11	6	9
City 2	7	0	8	2
City 3	7	3	0	3
City 4	10	9	4	0

This means that the distance between **City 2** and **City 1** is **7**, but the distance between **City 1** and **City 2** is **11**. An individual could be (2,4,3,1) and its fitness function is the sum of the distances between 2 and 4, 4 and 3, 3 and 1, and 1 and 2, that is, 2+4+7+11=24.

If you want to make the crossover between the individuals (1,2,3,4) and (1,3,2,4), you can't generate the individual (1,2,2,4) because you are visiting City 2 twice. You could generate the individuals (1,2,4,3) and (1,3,4,2).

To test the algorithm, we have used two examples of the **City Distance Datasets** (`http://people.sc.fsu.edu/~jburkardt/datasets/cities/cities.html`) with 15 (`lau15_dist`) and 57 (`kn57_dist`) cities, respectively.

Common classes

Both versions use the following three common classes:

- The `DataLoader` class, which loads the distance matrix from a file. We don't include the code of this class here. It has a static method that receives the name of the file and returns an `int[][]` matrix with the distances between the cities. The distances are stored in a CSV file (we have made a slight transformation to the original format), so it's easy to make the conversion.
- The Individual class stores the information of an individual of the population (a possible solution to the problem). To represent each individual, we have chosen an array of integer values that stores the order in which you visit the different cities.
- The `GeneticOperators` class implements the crossover, selection, and evaluation of the population or an individual.

Let's see the details of the `Individual` and `GeneticOperators` classes.

The Individual class

This class stores each possible solution to our TSP problem. We call each possible solution an individual, and its representation, chromosomes. In our case, we represent each possible solution as an array of integers. That array contains the order in which our salesman will go through the cities. This class also has an integer value to store the result of the fitness function. We have the following code:

```
public class Individual implements Comparable<Individual> {
  private Integer[] chromosomes;
  private int value;
```

We have included two constructors. The first one receives the number of cities you must visit, and we create an empty array. The other receives an `Individual` object and copies its chromosomes, as follows:

```
public Individual(int size) {
  chromosomes=new Integer[size];
}

public Individual(Individual other) {
  chromosomes = other.getChromosomes().clone();

}
```

We have also implemented the `compareTo()` method to compare two individuals using the result of the `fitness` function:

```
@Override
public int compareTo(Individual o) {
  return Integer.compare(this.getValue(), o.getValue());
}
```

Finally, we have included methods to get and set the values of the attributes.

The GeneticOperators class

This is a complex class because it implements the internal logic of the genetic algorithm. It provides methods to make the initialization, selection, crossover, and evaluation operations, introduced at the beginning of this section. We are going to describe only the methods provided by this class, but not how they are implemented, to avoid unnecessary complexity. You can get the source code of the example to analyze the implementation of the methods.

The methods provided by this class are:

- `initialize(int numberOfIndividuals, int size)`: This creates a new population. The number of individuals of that population will be determined by the `numberOfIndividuals` parameter. The number of chromosomes (cities in our case) will be determined by the size parameter. It returns an array of `Individual` objects. It uses the method `initialize(Integer[])` to initialize each individual.
- `initialize(Integer[] chromosomes)`: This initializes the chromosomes of an individual in a random way. It generates valid individuals (you have to visit each city only once).
- `selection(Individual[] population)`: This method implements the selection operation to get the best individuals of a population. It returns those individuals in an array. The size of that array will be half of the population size. You can test other criteria to determine the number of the selected individuals. We select the individuals with the best fit function.

- `crossover(Individual[] selected, int numberOfIndividuals, int size)`: This method receives the selected individuals of a generation as a parameter and generates the population of the next generation using the crossover operation. The number of individuals of the next generation will be determined by the parameter of the same name. The number of chromosomes of each individual will be determined by the size parameter. It uses the method `crossover(Individual, Individual, Individual, Individual)` to generate two new individuals from the two selected ones.
- `crossover(Individual parent1, Individual parent2, Individual individual1, Individual individual2)`: This method performs the crossover operation, taking the `parent1` and `parent2` individuals to generate the `individual1` and `individual2` individuals of the next generation.
- `evaluate(Individual[] population, int [][] distanceMatrix)`: This applies the `fitness` function to all the individuals of the population, using the distance matrix it receives as a parameter. Finally, it sorts the population from the best to worst solution. It uses the method `evaluate(Individual, int[][])` to evaluate each individual.
- `evaluate(Individual individual, int[][] distanceMatrix)`: This applies the `fitness` function to one individual.

With this class and its methods, you have all you need to implement a genetic algorithm to solve the TSP problem.

The serial version

We have implemented the serial version of the algorithm with the following two classes:

- The `SerialGeneticAlgorithm` class, which implements the algorithm
- The `SerialMain` class, which executes the algorithm with the input parameters and measures the execution time

Let's analyze both classes in detail.

The SerialGeneticAlgorithm class

This class implements the serial version of our genetic algorithm. Internally, it uses the following four attributes:

- The distance matrix with the distances between all the cities
- The number of generations
- The number of individuals in the population
- The number of chromosomes in each individual

The class also has a constructor to initialize all the attributes:

```
private int[][] distanceMatrix;

private int numberOfGenerations;
private int numberOfIndividuals;

private int size;

public SerialGeneticAlgorithm(int[][] distanceMatrix,
            int numberOfGenerations, int numberOfIndividuals) {
  this.distanceMatrix = distanceMatrix;
  this.numberOfGenerations = numberOfGenerations;
  this.numberOfIndividuals = numberOfIndividuals;
  size = distanceMatrix.length;
}
```

The main method of the class is the `calculate()` method. First, use the `initialize()` method to create the initial population. Then, evaluate the initial population and get its best individual as the first solution of the algorithm:

```
public Individual calculate() {
  Individual best;

  Individual[] population = GeneticOperators.initialize(
                    numberOfIndividuals, size);
  GeneticOperators.evaluate(population, distanceMatrix);

  best = population[0];
```

Then, it executes a loop determined by the `numberOfGenerations` attribute. In each cycle, it uses the `selection()` method to obtain the selected individuals, uses the `crossover()` method to calculate the next generation, evaluates this new generation, and if the best solution of the new generation is better than the best individual up until now, replaces it. When the loop finishes, we return the best individual as the solution proposed by the algorithm:

```
for (int i = 1; i <= numberOfGenerations; i++) {
  Individual[] selected =
                    GeneticOperators.selection(population);
  population = GeneticOperators.crossover(selected,
                            numberOfIndividuals, size);
  GeneticOperators.evaluate(population, distanceMatrix);
  if (population[0].getValue() < best.getValue()) {
    best = population[0];
  }

}

  return best;
}
```

The SerialMain class

This class executes the genetic algorithm for the two datasets used in this section: the `lau15` with 15 cities and the `kn57` with 57 cities.

The `main()` method must receive two parameters. The first one is the number of generations we want to create, and the second parameter is the number of individuals we want to have in each generation:

```
public class SerialMain {

  public static void main(String[] args) {

    Date start, end;

    int generations = Integer.valueOf(args[0]);
    int individuals = Integer.valueOf(args[1]);
```

For each example, we load the distance matrix using the `load()` method of the `DataLoader` class, create the `SerialGeneticAlgorith` object, execute the `calculate()` method measuring the execution time, and write the execution time and the result in the console:

```
for (String name : new String[] { "lau15_dist", "kn57_dist" }) {
   int[][] distanceMatrix = DataLoader.load(Paths.get("data",
                                            name + ".txt"));
   SerialGeneticAlgorithm serialGeneticAlgorithm = new
           SerialGeneticAlgorithm(distanceMatrix, generations,
           individuals);
   start = new Date();
   Individual result = serialGeneticAlgorithm.calculate();
   end = new Date();
   System.out.println ("=======================================");
   System.out.println("Example:"+name);
   System.out.println("Generations: " + generations);
   System.out.println("Population: " + individuals);
   System.out.println("Execution Time: " + (end.getTime() -
                        start.getTime()));
   System.out.println("Best Individual: " + result);
   System.out.println("Total Distance: " + result.getValue());
   System.out.println ("=======================================");
}
```

The concurrent version

We have implemented the concurrent version of the genetic algorithms different classes:

- The `SharedData` class stores all the objects that will be shared between the tasks
- The `GeneticPhaser` class extends the `Phaser` class and overrides its `onAdvance()` method to execute code when all the tasks finish a phase
- The `ConcurrentGeneticTask` class implements the tasks that will implement the phases of the genetic algorithm
- The `ConcurrentGeneticAlgorithm` class will implement the concurrent version of the genetic algorithm using the previous classes
- The `ConcurrentMain` class will test the concurrent version of the genetic algorithm in our two datasets

Internally, the `ConcurrentGeneticTask` class will execute three phases. The first one is the selection phase and will only be executed by one task. The second one is the crossover phase, where all the tasks will construct the new generation using the selected individuals, and the last phase is the evaluation phase, where all the tasks will evaluate the individuals of the new generation.

Let's look at each of those classes in detail.

The SharedData class

As we mentioned before, this class contains all the objects shared by the tasks. This includes the following:

- The population array with all the individuals of a generation.
- The selected array with the selected individuals.
- An atomic integer, called index. This is the only thread-safe object used to know the index of the individual a task has to generate or process.
- The best individual of all the generations, which will be returned as the solution of the algorithm.
- The distance matrix, with the distances between the cities.

All these objects will be shared by all the threads, but we only need to use one concurrent data structure. This is the only attribute that will be effectively shared by all the tasks. The rest of the objects will be only read (the distance matrix), or each task will access a different part of the object (the population and selected arrays), so we don't need to use concurrent data structures or synchronization mechanisms to avoid race conditions:

```
public class SharedData {

    private Individual[] population;
    private Individual selected[];
    private AtomicInteger index;
    private Individual best;
    private int[][] distanceMatrix;
}
```

This class also includes the getters and setters to get and establish the values of these attributes.

The GeneticPhaser class

We need to execute code on the phase changes of our tasks, so we have to implement our own phaser and override the `onAdvance()` method, which is executed after all the parties have finished a phase and before they begin the execution of the next one. The `GeneticPhaser` class implements this phaser. It stores the `SharedData` object to work with it and receives it as a parameter to the constructor:

```
public class GeneticPhaser extends Phaser {

  private SharedData data;

  public GeneticPhaser(int parties, SharedData data) {
    super(parties);
    this.data=data;
  }
```

The `onAdvance()` method will receive the number of the phase to the phaser and the number of registered parties as parameters. The phaser internally stores the number of phases as an integer that grows sequentially with every change of phase. On the contrary, our algorithm has only three phases, which will be executed a lot of times. We have to convert the phaser phase number to the genetic algorithm phase number to know if the tasks are going to execute the selection, crossover, or evaluation phases. To do this, we calculate the remainder between the phase number of the phaser and three, as follows:

```
protected boolean onAdvance(int phase, int registeredParties) {
  int realPhase=phase%3;
  if (registeredParties>0) {
    switch (realPhase) {
      case 0:
      case 1:
        data.getIndex().set(0);
        break;
      case 2:
        Arrays.sort(data.getPopulation());
        if (data.getPopulation()[0].getValue() <
            data.getBest().getValue()) {
          data.setBest(data.getPopulation()[0]);
        }
        break;
    }
    return false;
  }
  return true;
}
```

If the remainder is zero, the tasks have finished the selection phase and are going to execute the crossover phase. We initialize the index object with the value zero.

If the remainder is one, the tasks have finished the crossover phase and are going to execute the evaluation phase. We initialize the index object with the value zero.

Finally, if the remainder is two, the tasks have finished the evaluation phase and are going to start again with the selection phase. We sort the population based on the fitness function and update, if necessary, the best individual.

Take into account that this method will only be executed by one thread independently of the tasks. It will be executed in the thread of the task, which was the last to finish the previous phase (inside `arriveAndAwaitAdvance()` call). The rest of the tasks will be sleeping and waiting for the phaser.

The ConcurrentGeneticTask class

This class implements the tasks that collaborate to execute the genetic algorithm. They execute the three phases (selection, crossover, and evaluation) of the algorithm. The selection phase will be executed by only one task (we call it the main task), while the rest of the phases will be executed by all the tasks.

Internally, it uses four attributes:

- A `GeneticPhaser` object to synchronize the tasks at the end of each phase
- A `SharedData` object to access the shared data
- The number of generations it has to calculate
- The `Boolean` flag, which indicates whether it is the main task or not

All these attributes are initialized in the constructor of the class:

```
public class ConcurrentGeneticTask implements Runnable {
  private GeneticPhaser phaser;
  private SharedData data;
  private int numberOfGenerations;
  private boolean main;

  public ConcurrentGeneticTask(GeneticPhaser phaser, int
                     numberOfGenerations, boolean main) {
    this.phaser = phaser;
    this.numberOfGenerations = numberOfGenerations;
    this.main = main;
    this.data = phaser.getData();
  }
```

The `run()` method implements the logic of the genetic algorithm. It has a loop to generate the specified generations. As we mentioned before, only the main task will execute the selection phase. The rest of the tasks will use the `arriveAndAwaitAdvance()` method to wait for the finalization of this phase. Refer to the following code:

```
@Override
public void run() {

  Random rm = new Random(System.nanoTime());
  for (int i = 0; i < numberOfGenerations; i++) {
    if (main) {
      data.setSelected(GeneticOperators.selection(data
                       .getPopulation()));
    }
    phaser.arriveAndAwaitAdvance();
```

The second phase is the crossover phase. We use the `AtomicInteger` variable index stored in the `SharedData` class to get the next position in the population array each task will calculate. As we mentioned before, the crossover operation generates two new individuals, so each task first reserves two positions in the population array. For this purpose, we use the `getAndAdd(2)` method, which returns the actual value of the variable and increments its value by two units. It's an atomic variable, so we don't have to use any synchronization mechanism - it's inherent to the atomic variables. Refer to the following code:

```
// Crossover
int individualIndex;
do {
  individualIndex = data.getIndex().getAndAdd(2);
  if (individualIndex < data.getPopulation().length) {
    int secondIndividual = individualIndex++;

    int p1Index = rm.nextInt (data.getSelected().length);
    int p2Index;
    do {
      p2Index = rm.nextInt (data.getSelected().length);
    } while (p1Index == p2Index);

    Individual parent1 = data.getSelected() [p1Index];
    Individual parent2 = data.getSelected() [p2Index];
    Individual individual1 = data.getPopulation()
                      [individualIndex];
    Individual individual2 = data.getPopulation()
                      [secondIndividual];
    GeneticOperators.crossover(parent1, parent2,
                      individual1, individual2);
  }
```

```
  } while (individualIndex < data.getPopulation().length);
  phaser.arriveAndAwaitAdvance();
```

When all the individuals of the new population have been generated, the tasks use the `arriveAndAwaitAdvance()` method to synchronize the end of the phase.

The last phase is the evaluation phase. We use the `AtomicInteger` index again. Each task gets the actual value of the variable, which represents the position of an individual in the population, and increments its value using the `getAndIncrement()` value. Once all the individuals have been evaluated, we use the `arriveAndAwaitAdvance()` method to synchronize the end of this phase. Remember that, when all the tasks have finished this phase, the `GeneticPhaser` class will execute the code that sorts the population array and updates, if necessary, the best individual variable as follows:

```
    // Evaluation
    do {
      individualIndex = data.getIndex().getAndIncrement();
      if (individualIndex < data.getPopulation().length) {
        GeneticOperators.evaluate(data.getPopulation()
                    [individualIndex], data.getDistanceMatrix());
      }
    } while (individualIndex < data.getPopulation().length);
    phaser.arriveAndAwaitAdvance();

  }

  phaser.arriveAndDeregister();
}
```

Finally, when all the generations have been calculated, the tasks use the `arriveAndDeregister()` method to indicate the end of its execution, so the phaser will enter its finalization state.

The ConcurrentGeneticAlgorithm class

This class is the external interface of the genetic algorithm. Internally, it creates, starts, and waits for the finalization of the tasks that calculate the different generations. It uses four attributes: the number of generations, the number of individuals in each generation, the number of chromosomes of each individual, and the distance matrix, as follows:

```
public class ConcurrentGeneticAlgorithm {

  private int numberOfGenerations;
  private int numberOfIndividuals;
  private int[][] distanceMatrix;
```

```
   private int size;

   public ConcurrentGeneticAlgorithm(int[][] distanceMatrix, int
               numberOfGenerations, int numberOfIndividuals) {
      this.distanceMatrix=distanceMatrix;
      this.numberOfGenerations=numberOfGenerations;
      this.numberOfIndividuals=numberOfIndividuals;
      size=distanceMatrix.length;
   }
```

The `calculate()` method executes the genetic algorithm and returns the best individual.
First, it creates the initial population using the `initialize()` method, evaluates that
population, and creates and initializes a `SharedData` object with all the necessary data, as
follows:

```
public Individual calculate() {

   Individual[] population=
            GeneticOperators.initialize(numberOfIndividuals,size);
   GeneticOperators.evaluate(population,distanceMatrix);

   SharedData data=new SharedData();
   data.setPopulation(population);
   data.setDistanceMatrix(distanceMatrix);
   data.setBest(population[0]);
```

Then, it creates the tasks. We use the number of available hardware threads of the
computer, returned by the method `availableProcessors()` of the `Runtime` class, as the
number of tasks we are going to create. We also create a `GeneticPhaser` object to
synchronize the execution of those tasks, as follows:

```
   int numTasks=Runtime.getRuntime().availableProcessors();
   GeneticPhaser phaser=new GeneticPhaser(numTasks,data);

   ConcurrentGeneticTask[] tasks=new ConcurrentGeneticTask[numTasks];
   Thread[] threads=new Thread[numTasks];

   tasks[0]=new ConcurrentGeneticTask(phaser, numberOfGenerations,
                                   true);
   for (int i=1; i< numTasks; i++) {
      tasks[i]=new ConcurrentGeneticTask(phaser, numberOfGenerations,
                                   false);
   }
```

Then, we create the `Thread` objects to execute the tasks, start them, and wait for its finalization. Finally, we return the best individual stored in the `ShareData` object, as follows:

```
for (int i=0; i<numTasks; i++) {
    threads[i]=new Thread(tasks[i]);
            threads[i].start();
        }

        for (int i=0; i<numTasks; i++) {
            try {
                threads[i].join();
            } catch (InterruptedException e) {
                e.printStackTrace();
            }
        }

        return data.getBest();
    }
}
```

The ConcurrentMain class

This class executes the genetic algorithm for the two datasets used in this section: the `lau15` with 15 cities and the `kn57` with 57 cities. Its code is analogous to the `SerialMain` class, but it uses the `ConcurrentGeneticAlgorithm` instead of `SerialGeneticAlgorithm`.

Comparing the two solutions

Now it's time to test both solutions and see which has the better performance. As we mentioned before, we have used two datasets from the **City Distance Datasets** (http://people.sc.fsu.edu/~jburkardt/datasets/cities/cities.html) - the `lau15` with 15 cities and the `kn57` with 57 cities. We have also tested different sizes for the population (100, 1,000, and 10,000) individuals and different numbers of generations (10, 100, and 1,000).

We have executed the examples using the **JMH framework**
(http://openjdk.java.net/projects/code-tools/jmh/), which allows you to implement micro benchmarks in Java. Using a framework for benchmarking is a better solution that simply measures time using methods such as currentTimeMillis() or nanoTime(). We have executed them 10 times in two different architectures:

- A computer with an Intel Core i5-5300 CPU with Windows 7 and 16 GB of RAM. This processor has two cores and each core can execute two threads, so we will have four parallel threads
- A computer with an AMD A8-640 APU with Windows 10 and 8 GB of RAM. This processor has four cores

Lau15 dataset

These are the execution times (in milliseconds) for the first dataset:

AMD Architecture	Population					
	100		1000		10000	
Generations	Serial	Concurrent	Serial	Concurrent	Serial	Concurrent
10	11.59	27.15	53.98	54.40	208.67	121.10
100	42.80	58.61	180.24	96.54	1849.15	904.76
1000	148.01	117.93	1412.81	517.14	15040.81	5660.30

Intel Architecture	Population					
	100		1000		10000	
Generations	Serial	Concurrent	Serial	Concurrent	Serial	Concurrent
10	9.27	15.79	28.67	29.12	117.01	93.29
100	45.53	25,08	115.41	87.38	1041.76	756.16
1000	94.92	74.70	724.77	440.36	7867.56	4464.52

Kn57 dataset

These are the execution times (in milliseconds) for the second dataset:

AMD Architecture	Population					
	100		1000		10000	
Generations	Serial	Concurrent	Serial	Concurrent	Serial	Concurrent
10	25.29	31.33	104.72	124.88	889.07	347.62
100	95.21	76.80	795.64	280.20	8479.72	3052.44
1000	778.21	267.67	7913.98	2524.28	83131.09	29417.48

Intel Architecture	Population					
	100		1000		10000	
Generations	Serial	Concurrent	Serial	Concurrent	Serial	Concurrent
10	20.51	32.04	69.27	86.12	449.80	274.99
100	57.46	56.54	418.39	224.93	4423.52	2183.10
1000	417.38	221.47	4069.09	2161.46	41714.95	21858.51

Conclusions

The behavior of the algorithms is similar for both datasets with both architectures. You can see, as we have a low number of individuals and generations, the serial version of the algorithm has a better execution time, but when the number of individuals or the number of generations grows, the concurrent version has better throughput. For example, for the kn57 data set with 1,000 generations and 10,000 individuals, the speed-up is:

$$S_{AMD} = \frac{T_{serial}}{T_{concurrent}} = \frac{83131.09}{29417.48} = 2.82$$

$$S_{Intel} = \frac{T_{serial}}{T_{concurrent}} = \frac{41714.95}{21858.51} = 1.91$$

Summary

In this chapter, we explained one of the most powerful synchronization mechanisms provided by the Java concurrency API: the phaser. Its main objective is to provide synchronization between tasks that execute algorithms divided into phases. None of the tasks can begin the execution of a phase before the rest of the tasks have finished the previous one.

The phaser has to know how many tasks have to be synchronized. You have to register your tasks in the phaser using the constructor, the `bulkRegister()` method, or the `register()` method.

Tasks can synchronize with the phaser in different ways. The most common task is indicating to the phaser that it has finished the execution of one phase and wants to continue with the next one with the `arriveAndAwaitAdvance()`. This method will sleep the thread until the rest of the tasks have finished the actual phase. But there are other methods you can use to synchronize your tasks. The `arrive()` method is used to notify the phaser that you have finished the current phase, but you won't wait for the rest of the tasks (be very careful using this method). The `arriveAndDeregister()` method is used to notify the phaser that you have finished the current phase and you don't want to continue in the phaser (normally, because you have finished your job). Finally, the `awaitAdvance()` method can be used to wait for the finalization of the current phase.

You can control the phase change and execute code after all the tasks have finished the current phase and before they start the new one using the `onAdvance()` method. This method is called between the executions of two phases and receives as parameters the number of the phase and the number of participants in the phaser. You can extend the `Phaser` class and override this method to execute code between two phases.

A phaser can be in two states: active, when it is synchronizing tasks, and in the termination state, when it has finished its job. A phaser will enter into the termination state when all the participants call the `arriveAndDeregister()` method or when the `onAdvance()` method returns the true value (by default, it always returns `false`). When a `Phaser` class is in the termination state, it won't accept new participants and the synchronization methods will always return immediately.

We used the `Phaser` class to implement two algorithms: a keyword extraction algorithm and a genetic algorithm. In both cases, we got an important increase of throughput against the serial version of those algorithms.

In the next chapter, you will learn how to use another Java concurrency framework to solve special kinds of problems. It's the fork/join framework, which has been developed to execute in a concurrent way those problems that can be solved using the divide and conquer algorithm. It's based in an executor, with a special work-stealing algorithm that maximizes the performance of the executor.

7
Optimizing Divide and Conquer Solutions - The Fork/Join Framework

In Chapter 3, *Managing Lots of Threads - Executors*, Chapter 4, *Getting the Most from Executors*, and Chapter 5, *Getting Data from Tasks - The Callable and Future Interfaces*, you learned how to work with executors as a mechanism to improve the performance of concurrent applications that execute lots of concurrent tasks. The Java 7 Concurrency API introduced a special kind of executor through the fork/join framework. This framework is designed to implement optimal concurrent solutions to those problems that can be solved using the divide and conquer design paradigm. In this chapter, we will cover the following topics:

- An introduction to the fork/join framework
- The first example - the k-means clustering algorithm
- The second example - a data filtering algorithm
- The third example - the merge sort algorithm

An introduction to the fork/join framework

The executor framework, introduced in Java 5, provides a mechanism to execute concurrent tasks without creating, starting, and finishing threads. This framework uses a pool of threads that executes the tasks you send to the executor, reusing them for multiple tasks. This mechanism provides the following advantages to programmers:

- It's easier to program concurrent applications because you don't have to worry about creating threads.
- It's easier to control the resources used by the executor and your application. You can create an executor that only uses a predefined number of threads. If you send more threads, the executor stores them in a queue until a thread is available.
- Executors reduce the overhead introduced by thread creation by reusing the threads. Internally, it manages a pool of threads that reuses threads to execute multiple tasks.

The divide and conquer algorithm is a very popular design technique. To solve a problem using this technique, you divide it into smaller problems. You repeat the process in a recursive way until the problems you have to solve are small enough to be solved directly. You have to be very careful selecting the base case that is resolved directly. A bad choice of the size of that problem can give you poor performance. This kind of problem can be solved using the executor, but to solve them in a more efficient way, the Java 7 Concurrency API introduced the fork/join framework.

This framework is based on the `ForkJoinPool` class, which is a special kind of executor, two operations, the `fork()` and `join()` methods (and their different variants), and an internal algorithm named the **work-stealing** algorithm. In this chapter, you will learn the basic characteristics, limitations, and components of the fork/join framework in implementing the following three examples:

- The k-means clustering algorithm applied to the clustering of a set of documents
- A data filter algorithm to get the data that meets certain criteria
- The merge sort algorithm to sort big groups of data in an efficient way

Basic characteristics of the fork/join framework

As we mentioned before, the fork/join framework must be used to implement solutions to problems based on the divide and conquer technique. You have to divide the original problem into smaller problems until they are small enough to be solved directly. With this framework, you will implement tasks whose main method will be something like this:

```
if ( problem.size() > DEFAULT_SIZE) {
  divideTasks();
  executeTask();
  taskResults=joinTasksResult();
  return taskResults;
} else {
  taskResults=solveBasicProblem();
  return taskResults;
}
```

The most important benefit of this method is that it allows you to divide and execute the child tasks in an efficient way and to get the results of those child tasks to calculate the results of the parent tasks. This functionality is supported by two methods provided by the `ForkJoinTask` class:

- **The fork() method**: This method allows you to send a child task to the fork/join executor
- **The join() method**: This method allows you to wait for the finalization of a child task and returns its result

These methods have different variants, as you will see in the examples. The fork/join framework has another critical feature: the work-stealing algorithm, which determines which tasks are to be executed. When a task is waiting for the finalization of a child task using the `join()` method, the thread that is executing that task takes another task from the pool of tasks that are waiting and starts its execution. In this way, the threads of the fork/join executor are always executing a task by improving the performance of the application.

Java 8 included a new feature in the fork/join framework. Now, every Java application has a default `ForkJoinPool` named `common pool`. You can obtain it by calling the `ForkJoinPool.commonPool()` static method. You don't need to create one explicitly (although you can). This default fork/join executor will automatically use the number of threads determined by the available processors of your computer. You can change this default behavior by changing the value of the system property `java.util.concurrent.ForkJoinPool.common.parallelism`.

Some features of the Java API use the fork/join framework to implement concurrent operations. For example, the parallelSort() method of the Arrays class, which sorts arrays in a parallel fashion, and the parallel streams introduced in Java 8 (described later, in Chapter 8, *Processing Massive Datasets with Parallel Streams - The Map and Reduce Model* and Chapter 9, *Processing Massive Datasets with Parallel Streams - The Map and Collect Model*) both use this framework.

Limitations of the fork/join framework

As the fork/join framework is used to solve a certain kind of problem, it has some limitations that you have to take into account when you use it to address your problem. These limitations are as follows:

- The basic problems that you're not going to subdivide have to be not very large, but also not very small. According to the Java API documentation, it should have between 100 and 10,000 basic computational steps.
- You should not use blocking I/O operations, such as reading user input or data from a network socket that is waiting until the data is available. Such operations will cause your CPU cores to idle, thereby reducing the level of parallelism, so you will not achieve full performance.
- You can't throw checked exceptions inside a task. You have to include the code to handle them (for example, wrapping into unchecked RuntimeException). Unchecked exceptions have special treatment, as you will see in the examples.

Components of the fork/join framework

There are five basic classes in the fork/join framework:

- **The ForkJoinPool class**: This class implements the Executor and ExecutorService interfaces, and it is the Executor interface you're going to use to execute your fork/join tasks. Java provides you with a default ForkJoinPool object (named common pool), but you have some constructors to create one if you want. You can specify the level of parallelism (the maximum number of running parallel threads). By default, it uses the number of available processors as the concurrency level.

- **The ForkJoinTask class**: This is the base abstract class of all of the fork/join tasks. It's an abstract class, and it provides the `fork()` and `join()` methods and some variants of them. It also implements the `Future` interface and provides methods to know whether the task finished in a normal way, whether it was cancelled, or if it threw an unchecked exception. The `RecursiveTask`, `RecursiveAction`, and `CountedCompleter` classes provide a `compute()` abstract method, which should be implemented in subclasses to perform actual computations.
- **The RecursiveTask class**: This class extends the `ForkJoinTask` class. It's also an abstract class, and it should be your starting point to implement fork/join tasks that return results.
- **The RecursiveAction class**: This class extends the `ForkJoinTask` class. It's also an abstract class, and it should be your starting point to implement fork/join tasks that don't return results.
- **The CountedCompleter class**: This class extends the `ForkJoinTask` class. It should be your starting point to implement tasks that trigger other tasks when they're completed.

The first example - the k-means clustering algorithm

The **k-means clustering** algorithm is a clustering algorithm that groups a set of items not previously classified into a predefined number of clusters, K. It's very popular within the data mining and machine learning world, and is used in these fields to organize and classify data in an unsupervised way.

Each item is normally defined by a vector of characteristics or attributes (we use vector as a math concept, not as a data structure). All the items have the same number of attributes. Each cluster is also defined by a vector with the same number of attributes that represent all the items classified into that cluster. This vector is named the `centroid`. For example, if the items are defined by numeric vectors, the clusters are defined by the mean of the items classified into that cluster.

Basically, the algorithm has four steps:

- **Initialization**: In the first step, you have to create the initial vectors that represent the *K* clusters. Normally, you will initialize those vectors randomly.
- **Assignment**: Then, you classify each item into a cluster. To select the cluster, you calculate the distance between the item and every cluster. You will use a distance measure, such as the **Euclidean distance**, to calculate the distance between the vector that represents the item and the vector that represents the cluster. You will assign the item to the cluster with the shortest distance.
- **Update**: Once all the items have been classified, you have to recalculate the vectors that define each cluster. As we mentioned earlier, you normally calculate the mean of all the vectors of the items classified into the cluster.
- **End**: Finally, you check whether any item has changed its assignment cluster. If there has been a change, you go to the assignment step again. Otherwise, the algorithm ends, and you have your items classified.

This algorithm has the following two main limitations:

- If you make a random initialization of the initial vectors of the clusters, as we suggested earlier, two executions that are used to classify the same item set may give you different results.
- The number of clusters is previously predefined. A bad choice of this attribute will give you poor results in terms of classification.

Despite all this, this algorithm is a very popular method of clustering different kinds of items. To test our algorithm, you are going to implement an application to cluster a set of documents. As a document collection, we have taken a reduced version of the Wikipedia pages containing information about the movies corpus we introduced in Chapter 5, *Getting Data from Tasks - The Callable and Future Interfaces*. We have only taken 1,000 documents. To represent each document, we have to use the vector space model representation. With this representation, each document is represented as a numeric vector where each dimension of the vector represents a word or a term, and its value is a metric that defines the importance of that word or term in the document.

When you represent a document collection using the vector space model, the vectors will have as many dimensions as the number of different words of the whole collection, so the vectors will have a lot of zero values because each document doesn't have all the words. You can use a more optimized representation in memory to avoid all those zero values and save memory, increasing the performance of your application.

In our case, we have chosen **term frequency-inverse document frequency (TF-IDF)** as the metric that defines the importance of each word, and the 50 words with higher TF-IDF as the terms that represent each document.

We use two files: the `movies.words` file stores a list of all the words used in the vectors, and the `movies.data` file stores the representation of each document. The `movies.data` file has the following format:

```
10000202,rabona:23.039285705435507,1979:8.09314752937111,argentina:7.953798
614698405,la:5.440565539075689,argentine:4.058577338363469,editor:3.0401515
284855267,spanish:2.9692083275217134,image_size:1.3701158713905104,narrator
:1.1799670194306195,budget:0.286193223652206,starring:0.25519156764102785,c
ast:0.2540127604060545,writer:0.23904044207902764,distributor:0.20430284744
786784,cinematography:0.182583823735518,music:0.1675671228903468,caption:0.
14545085918028047,runtime:0.127767002869991,country:0.12493801913495534,pro
ducer:0.12321749670640451,director:0.11592975672109682,links:0.079255823038
12376,image:0.07786973207561361,external:0.07764427108746134,released:0.074
47174080087617,name:0.07214163435745059,infobox:0.06151153983466272,film:0.
035415118094854446
```

Here, `10000202` is the identifier of the document, and the rest of the file follows the formant `word:tfxidf`.

As with other examples, we are going to implement the serial and concurrent versions and execute both versions to verify that the fork/join framework gives us an improvement of the performance of this algorithm.

The common classes

There are some features that are shared between the serial and concurrent versions. These features include:

- `VocabularyLoader`: This is a class that loads the list of words that forms the vocabulary of our corpus.
- `Word`, `Document`, and `DocumentLoader`: These three classes load the information about the documents. These classes have little difference between the serial and concurrent versions of the algorithm.
- `DistanceMeasure`: This is a class that is used to calculate the **Euclidean** distance between two vectors.
- `DocumentCluster`: This is a class that is used to store the information about the clusters.

Let's look at these classes in detail.

The VocabularyLoader class

As we mentioned before, our data is stored in two files. One of those files is the `movies.words` file. This file stores a list with all the words used in the documents. The `VocabularyLoader` class will transform that file into `HashMap`. The key of `HashMap` is the whole word, and the value is an integer value with the index of that word in the list. We use that index to determine the position of the word in the vector space model that represents each document.

The class has only one method, named `load()`, which receives the path of the file as a parameter and returns the `HashMap`:

```
public class VocabularyLoader {

  public static Map<String, Integer> load (Path path) throws
                                            IOException {
    int index=0;
    HashMap<String, Integer> vocIndex=new HashMap<String,
                                           Integer>();
    try(BufferedReader reader = Files.newBufferedReader(path)){
      String line = null;
      while ((line = reader.readLine()) != null) {
        vocIndex.put(line,index );
        index++;
      }
    }
    return vocIndex;

  }
}
```

The word, document, and DocumentLoader classes

These classes store all the information about the documents we will use in our algorithm. First, the `Word` class stores information about a word in a document. It includes the index of the word and the TF-IDF of that word in the document. This class only includes those attributes (`int` and `double`, respectively), and implements the `Comparable` interface to sort two words using their TF-IDF value, so we don't include the source code of this class.

The Document class stores all the relevant information about the document. First, it stores an array of Word objects with the words in the document. This is our representation of the vector space model. We only store the words used in the document in order to save a lot of memory space. Then, we store a String with the name of the file that stores the document, and finally a DocumentCluster object to know the cluster associated with the document. It also includes a constructor to initialize those attributes and methods to get and set their value. We only include the code of the setCluster() method. In this case, this method will return a Boolean value to indicate whether the new value of this attribute is the same as the old value or a new one. We will use that value to determine whether or not we should stop the algorithm:

```java
public boolean setCluster(DocumentCluster cluster) {
  if (this.cluster == cluster) {
    return false;
  } else {
    this.cluster = cluster;
    return true;
  }
}
```

Finally, the DocumentLoader class loads the information about the document. It includes a static method, load(), which receives the path of the file, and the HashMap with the vocabulary, and returns an Array of Document objects. It loads the file line by line and converts each line to a Document object. We have the following code:

```java
public static Document[] load(Path path, Map<String, Integer>
                              vocIndex) throws IOException{
  List<Document> list = new ArrayList<Document>();
  try(BufferedReader reader = Files.newBufferedReader(path)) {
    String line = null;
    while ((line = reader.readLine()) != null) {
      Document item = processItem(line, vocIndex);
      list.add(item);
    }
  }
  Document[] ret = new Document[list.size()];
  return list.toArray(ret);

}
```

To convert a line of the text file to a `Document` object, we use the `processItem()` method:

```
private static Document processItem(String line,Map<String,
                                     Integer> vocIndex) {

    String[] tokens = line.split(",");
    int size = tokens.length - 1;

    Document document = new Document(tokens[0], size);
    Word[] data = document.getData();

    for (int i = 1; i < tokens.length; i++) {
        String[] wordInfo = tokens[i].split(":");
        Word word = new Word();
        word.setIndex(vocIndex.get(wordInfo[0]));
        word.setTfidf(Double.parseDouble(wordInfo[1]));
        data[i - 1] = word;
    }
    Arrays.sort(data);
    return document;
}
```

As we mentioned earlier, the first item in the line is the identifier of the document. We obtain it from `tokens[0]`, and we pass it to the `Document` class constructor. Then, for the rest of the tokens, we split them again to obtain the information of every word that includes the whole word and the TF-IDF value.

The DistanceMeasurer class

This class calculates the Euclidean distance between a document and a cluster (represented as a vector). The words in our word arrays (after sorting) are placed in the same order as they would be in a centroid array, but some words might be absent. For such words, we assume that TF-IDF is zero, so the distance is just the square of the corresponding value from the centroid array:

```
public class DistanceMeasurer {

    public static double euclideanDistance(Word[] words, double[]
                                             centroid) {
        double distance = 0;

        int wordIndex = 0;
        for (int i = 0; i < centroid.length; i++) {
            if ((wordIndex < words.length) (words[wordIndex].getIndex()
                                            == i)) {
                distance += Math.pow( (words[wordIndex].getTfidf() -
```

```
                              centroid[i]), 2);
        wordIndex++;
      } else {
        distance += centroid[i] * centroid[i];
      }
    }

    return Math.sqrt(distance);
  }
}
```

The DocumentCluster class

This class stores the information about each cluster generated by the algorithm. This information includes a list of all the documents associated with this cluster and the centroid of the vector that represents the cluster. In this case, this vector has as many dimensions as there are words in the documents' vocabulary. The class has the two attributes, a constructor to initialize them, and methods to get and set their value. It also includes two very important methods. First, it has the calculateCentroid() method. This method calculates the centroid of the cluster as the mean of the vectors that represent the documents associated with this cluster:

```
public void calculateCentroid() {

  Arrays.fill(centroid, 0);

  for (Document document : documents) {
    Word vector[] = document.getData();

    for (Word word : vector) {
      centroid[word.getIndex()] += word.getTfidf();
    }
  }

  for (int i = 0; i < centroid.length; i++) {
    centroid[i] /= documents.size();
  }
}
```

The second method is the `initialize()` method, which receives a `Random` object and initializes the centroid vector of the cluster with random numbers, as follows:

```
public void initialize(Random random) {
  for (int i = 0; i < centroid.length; i++) {
    centroid[i] = random.nextDouble();
  }
}
```

The serial version

Now that we have described the common features of the application, let's see how to implement the serial version of the k-means clustering algorithm. We are going to use two classes: `SerialKMeans`, which implements the algorithm, and `SerialMain`, which implements the `main()` method to execute the algorithm.

The SerialKMeans class

The `SerialKMeans` class implements the serial version of the k-means clustering algorithm. The main method of the class is the `calculate()` method. It receives the following as parameters:

- The array of `Document` objects with information about the documents
- The number of clusters you want to generate
- The size of the vocabulary
- A seed for the random number generator

The method returns an `Array` of the `DocumentCluster` objects. Each cluster will have a list of documents associated with it. First, the document creates the `Array` of clusters determined by the `numberClusters` parameter and initializes them using the `initialize()` method and a `Random` object, as follows:

```
public class SerialKMeans {

  public static DocumentCluster[] calculate(Document[] documents,
                int clusterCount, int vocSize, int seed) {
    DocumentCluster[] clusters = new DocumentCluster[clusterCount];

    Random random = new Random(seed);
    for (int i = 0; i < clusterCount; i++) {
```

```
    clusters[i] = new DocumentCluster(vocSize);
    clusters[i].initialize(random);
}
```

Then, we repeat the assignment and update phases until all the documents stay in the same cluster. Finally, we return the array of clusters with the final organization of the documents, as follows:

```
boolean change = true;

int numSteps = 0;
while (change) {
    change = assignment(clusters, documents);
    update(clusters);
    numSteps++;
}
System.out.println("Number of steps: "+numSteps);
return clusters;
}
```

The assignment phase is implemented in the `assignment()` method. This method receives the array of `Document` and `DocumentCluster` objects. For each document, it calculates the Euclidean distance between the document and all the clusters, and assigns the document to the cluster with the lowest distance. It returns a Boolean value to indicate whether one or more of the documents has changed their assigned cluster from one position to the next one, as shown in the following code:

```
private static boolean assignment(DocumentCluster[] clusters, Document[]
documents) {

    boolean change = false;

    for (DocumentCluster cluster : clusters) {
        cluster.clearClusters();
    }

    int numChanges = 0;
    for (Document document : documents) {
        double distance = Double.MAX_VALUE;
        DocumentCluster selectedCluster = null;
        for (DocumentCluster cluster : clusters) {
            double curDistance = DistanceMeasurer.euclideanDistance
                            (document.getData(), cluster.getCentroid());
            if (curDistance < distance) {
                distance = curDistance;
                selectedCluster = cluster;
            }
```

```
    }
    selectedCluster.addDocument(document);
    boolean result = document.setCluster(selectedCluster);
    if (result)
      numChanges++;
    }
    System.out.println("Number of Changes: " + numChanges);
    return numChanges > 0;
  }
```

The update step is implemented in the `update()` method. It receives the array of `DocumentCluster` with the information of the clusters, and it simply recalculates the centroid of each cluster:

```
  private static void update(DocumentCluster[] clusters) {
    for (DocumentCluster cluster : clusters) {
      cluster.calculateCentroid();
    }
  }
}
```

The SerialMain class

The `SerialMain` class includes the `main()` method, which launches the tests of the k-means algorithm. First, it loads the data (words and documents) from the files:

```
public class SerialMain {

  public static void main(String[] args) {
    Path pathVoc = Paths.get("data", "movies.words");

    Map<String, Integer> vocIndex=VocabularyLoader.load(pathVoc);
    System.out.println("Voc Size: "+vocIndex.size());

    Path pathDocs = Paths.get("data", "movies.data");
    Document[] documents = DocumentLoader.load(pathDocs,
                                               vocIndex);
    System.out.println("Document Size: "+documents.length);
```

Then, it initializes the number of clusters we want to generate and the seed for the random number generator. If they don't come as parameters of the `main()` method, we use a set of default values, as follows:

```
    if (args.length != 2) {
      System.err.println("Please specify K and SEED");
      return;
```

```
    }
    int K = Integer.valueOf(args[0]);
    int SEED = Integer.valueOf(args[1]);
}
```

Finally, we launch the algorithm, measuring its execution time, and write the number of documents per cluster.

```
Date start, end;
start=new Date();
DocumentCluster[] clusters = SerialKMeans.calculate(documents,
                            K ,vocIndex.size(), SEED);
end=new Date();
System.out.println("K: "+K+"; SEED: "+SEED);
System.out.println("Execution Time: "+(end.getTime()-
                    start.getTime()));
System.out.println(Arrays.stream(clusters)
                        .map (DocumentCluster::getDocumentCount)
                        .sorted (Comparator.reverseOrder())
    .map(Object::toString)
    .collect( Collectors.joining(", ", "Cluster sizes: ", "")));
    }
}
```

The concurrent version

To implement the concurrent version of the algorithm, we have used the fork/join framework. We have implemented two different tasks based on the RecursiveAction class. As we mentioned earlier, the RecursiveAction task is used when you want to use the fork/join framework with tasks that do not return a result. We have implemented the assignment and the update phases as tasks to be executed in a fork/join framework.

To implement the concurrent version of the k-means algorithm, we are going to modify some of the common classes to use concurrent data structures. Then, we are going to implement the two tasks, and finally, we are going to implement, first, the ConcurrentKMeans class, which implements the concurrent version of the algorithm, and then the ConcurrentMain class to test it.

Two tasks for the fork/join framework - AssignmentTask and UpdateTask

As we mentioned earlier, we have implemented the assignment and update phases as tasks to be implemented in the fork/join framework.

The assignment phase assigns a document to the cluster that has the lowest Euclidean distance from the document, so we have to process all the documents and calculate the Euclidean distances of all the documents and all the clusters. We are going to use the number of documents that a task has to decide whether we have to split the task or not. We start with the tasks that have to process all the documents, and we are going to split them until we have tasks that have to process a number of documents lower than a predefined size.

The `AssignmentTask` class has the following attributes:

- The array of `ConcurrentDocumentCluster` objects with the data of the clusters
- The array of `ConcurrentDocument` objects with the data of the documents
- Two integer attributes, `start` and `end`, which determine the number of documents the task has to process
- An `AtomicInteger` attribute, `numChanges`, which stores the number of documents that have changed their assigned cluster from the last execution to the current one
- An integer attribute, `maxSize`, which stores the maximum number of documents a task can process

We have implemented a constructor to initialize all these attributes, as well as methods to get and set its values.

The main method of this task is (as with every task) the `compute()` method. First, we check the number of documents the task has to process. If it's less than or equal to the `maxSize` attribute, then we process those documents. We calculate the Euclidean distance between each document and each of the clusters, and select the cluster with the lowest distance. If it's necessary, we increment the `numChanges` atomic variable using the `incrementAndGet()` method. The atomic variable can be updated by more than one thread at the same time without using synchronization mechanisms and without causing any memory inconsistencies. Refer to the following code:

```
protected void compute() {
  if (end - start <= maxSize) {
    for (int i = start; i < end; i++) {
      ConcurrentDocument document = documents[i];
```

```
            double distance = Double.MAX_VALUE;
            ConcurrentDocumentCluster selectedCluster = null;
            for (ConcurrentDocumentCluster cluster : clusters) {
              double curDistance = DistanceMeasurer.euclideanDistance
                            (document.getData(), cluster.getCentroid());
              if (curDistance < distance) {
                distance = curDistance;
                selectedCluster = cluster;
              }
            }
            selectedCluster.addDocument(document);
            boolean result = document.setCluster(selectedCluster);
            if (result) {
              numChanges.incrementAndGet();
            }

        }
```

If the number of documents the task has to process is too big, we split that set into two parts and create two new tasks to process each of those parts, as follows:

```
      } else {
        int mid = (start + end) / 2;
        AssignmentTask task1 = new AssignmentTask(clusters, documents,
                                  start, mid, numChanges, maxSize);
        AssignmentTask task2 = new AssignmentTask(clusters, documents,
                                  mid, end, numChanges, maxSize);

        invokeAll(task1, task2);
      }
    }
```

To execute those tasks in the fork/join pool, we have used the `invokeAll()` method. This method will return when the tasks have finished their execution.

The update phase recalculates the centroid of each cluster as the mean of all the documents, so we have to process all the clusters. We are going to use the number of clusters a task has to process as the measure to decide whether we have to split the task or not. We start with a task that has to process all the clusters, and we are going to split it until we have tasks that have to process a number of clusters lower than a predefined size.

The `UpdateTask` class has the following attributes:

- The array of `ConcurrentDocumentCluster` objects with the data of the clusters
- Two integer attributes, `start` and `end`, which determine the number of clusters the task has to process
- An integer attribute, `maxSize`, which stores the maximum number of clusters a task can process

We have implemented a constructor to initialize all these attributes, as well as methods to get and set its values.

The `compute()` method first checks the number of clusters the task has to process. If that number is less than or equal to the `maxSize` attribute, it processes those clusters and updates their centroid:

```
@Override
protected void compute() {
  if (end - start <= maxSize) {
    for (int i = start; i < end; i++) {
      ConcurrentDocumentCluster cluster = clusters[i];
      cluster.calculateCentroid();
    }
```

If the number of clusters the task has to process is too big, we will divide the set of clusters the task has to process in two and create two tasks to process each half of that set, as follows:

```
  } else {
    int mid = (start + end) / 2;
    UpdateTask task1 = new UpdateTask(clusters, start, mid,
                                      maxSize);
    UpdateTask task2 = new UpdateTask(clusters, mid, end,
                                      maxSize);

    invokeAll(task1, task2);
  }
}
```

The ConcurrentKMeans class

The ConcurrentKMeans class implements the concurrent version of the k-means clustering algorithm. As the serial version, the main method of the class is the calculate() method. It receives the following as parameters:

- The array of ConcurrentDocument objects with the information about the documents
- The number of clusters you want to generate
- The size of the vocabulary
- A seed for the random number generator
- The maximum number of items a fork/join task will process without splitting the task into other tasks

The calculate() method returns an array of the ConcurrentDocumentCluster objects with the information of the clusters. Each cluster has the list of documents associated with it. First, the document creates the array of clusters determined by the numberClusters parameter and initializes them using the initialize() method and a Random object:

```
public class ConcurrentKMeans {

    public static ConcurrentDocumentCluster[] calculate
                    (ConcurrentDocument[] documents int numberCluster
                     int vocSize, int seed, int maxSize) {
        ConcurrentDocumentCluster[] clusters = new
                        ConcurrentDocumentCluster[numberClusters];

        Random random = new Random(seed);
        for (int i = 0; i < numberClusters; i++) {
            clusters[i] = new ConcurrentDocumentCluster(vocSize);
            clusters[i].initialize(random);
        }
```

Then, we repeat the assignment and update phases until all the documents stay in the same cluster. Before the loop, we create ForkJoinPool, which is going to execute that task and all of its subtasks. Once the loop has finished, as with other Executor objects, we have to use the shutdown() method with a fork/join pool to finish its executions. Finally, we return the array of clusters with the final organization of the documents:

```
        boolean change = true;
        ForkJoinPool pool = new ForkJoinPool();

        int numSteps = 0;
        while (change) {
```

```
      change = assignment(clusters, documents, maxSize, pool);
      update(clusters, maxSize, pool);
      numSteps++;
  }
  pool.shutdown();
  System.out.println("Number of steps: "+numSteps);
  return clusters;
}
```

The assignment phase is implemented in the `assignment()` method. This method receives the array of clusters, the array of documents, and the `maxSize` attribute. First, we delete the list of associated documents to all the clusters:

```
private static boolean assignment(ConcurrentDocumentCluster[]
                 clusters, ConcurrentDocument[] documents,
                 int maxSize, ForkJoinPool pool) {

  boolean change = false;

  for (ConcurrentDocumentCluster cluster : clusters) {
    cluster.clearDocuments();
  }
```

Then, we initialize the necessary objects: an `AtomicInteger` to store the number of documents whose assigned cluster has changed and the `AssignmentTask`, which will begin the process. The `AtomicInteger` class supports atomic operations--that is to say, no other threads will see the operation in an intermediate state. To the rest of the threads, the operation is executed or not executed. They also establish a happens-before relation between the `set()` operations and the subsequent `get()` operations. We use an `AtomicInteger` object to guarantee that all the threads can update their value in a thread-safe way.

```
AtomicInteger numChanges = new AtomicInteger(0);
AssignmentTask task = new AssignmentTask(clusters, documents, 0,
                          documents.length, numChanges, maxSize);
ForkJoinPool pool = new ForkJoinPool();
```

Then, we execute the tasks in the pool in an asynchronous way using the `execute()` method of `ForkJoinPool` and wait for finalization with the `join()` method of the `AssignmentTask` object, as follows:

```
pool.execute(task);
task.join();
```

Finally, we check the number of documents that have changed their assigned cluster. If there have been changes, we return the `true` value. Otherwise, we return the `false` value. We have the following code:

```
System.out.println("Number of Changes: " + numChanges);
return numChanges.get() > 0;
}
```

The update phase is implemented in the `update()` method. It receives the array of clusters and the `maxSize` parameters. First, we create an `UpdateTask` object to update all the clusters. Then, we execute that task in the `ForkJoinPool` object that the method receives as a parameter, as follows:

```
private static void update(ConcurrentDocumentCluster[] clusters,
                           int maxSize, ForkJoinPool pool) {
    UpdateTask task = new UpdateTask(clusters, 0, clusters.length,
                                     maxSize, ForkJoinPool pool);
    pool.execute(task);
    task.join();
}
}
```

The ConcurrentMain class

The `ConcurrentMain` class includes the `main()` method to launch the tests of the k-means algorithm. Its code is equal to the `SerialMain` class, but the serial classes are changed for the concurrent ones.

Comparing the solutions

To compare the two solutions, we executed different experiments that changed the values of three different parameters:

- The k-parameter will establish the number of clusters we want to generate. We tested the algorithms with the values 5, 10, 15, and 20.
- The seed for the `Random` number generator determines how the initial centroid is positioned. We tested the algorithms with the values 1 and 13.
- For the concurrent algorithm, the `maxSize` parameter determines the maximum number of items (documents or clusters) a task can process without being split into other tasks. We tested the algorithms with the values 1, 20, and 400.

We executed the examples using the JMH framework (http://openjdk.java.net/project s/code-tools/jmh/), which allows you to implement microbenchmarks in Java. Using a framework for benchmarking is a better solution, which simply measures time using methods such as currentTimeMillis() or nanoTime(). We executed them ten times in two different architectures:

1. **A computer with an Intel Core i5-5300 CPU with Windows 7 and 16 GB of RAM**: This processor has two cores and each core can execute two threads, so we will have four parallel threads
2. **A computer with an AMD A8-640 APU with Windows 10 and 8 GB of RAM**: This processor has four cores

These are the execution times that we obtained in milliseconds. First, we show the results for the AMD architecture:

AMD Architecture					
		Serial	**Concurrent**		
K	**Seed**		**MaxSize=1**	**MaxSize=20**	**maxSize=400**
5	1	8647.129	4919.924	3795.23	3754.424
10	1	9419.145	3665.896	3474.182	3456.362
15	1	16324.931	6320.174	5477.755	5543.474
20	1	25707.589	8360.485	9280.459	8362.34
5	13	5122.681	2754.947	2262.426	2254.837
10	13	12629.098	4919.314	4593.705	4579.875
15	13	16261.68	6838.753	5606.074	5474.2
20	13	23626.983	7605.616	8114.582	6694.77

Here are the results for the Intel architecture:

Intel Architecture					
		Serial	Concurrent		
K	Seed		MaxSize=1	MaxSize=20	maxSize=400
5	1	4049.579	5112.728	4111.275	4141.222
10	1	4290.91	4617.793	3966.848	3957.214
15	1	7155.934	4211.487	6358.552	6493.285
20	1	11444.903	10405.531	5949.083	10009.849
5	13	2437.533	2893.485	2444.874	2489.087
10	13	5702.272	5637.996	5165.333	5206.648
15	13	7110.732	4115.091	6348.288	6445.648
20	13	10495.405	9509.217	5995.638	5371.75

We can draw the following conclusions:

- The seed has an important and unpredictable impact on the execution time. Sometimes, the execution times are lower with seed 13, but other times they are lower with seed 1.
- When you increment the number of clusters, the execution time increments too.
- The maxSize parameter doesn't have much influence on the execution time. The parameter *K*, or seed, has a higher influence on the execution time. If you increase the value of the parameter, you will obtain better performance. The difference between 1 and 20 is bigger than it is between 20 and 400.
- In all the cases, the concurrent version of the algorithm has better performance than the serial one. Only in the Intel architecture with a low number of clusters does the serial version have better results than the concurrent one.

For example, if we compare the serial algorithm with parameters $K = 20$ and *seed = 13* with the concurrent version with parameters $K = 20$, *seed = 13*, and *maxSize = 400* using the speed-up, we obtain the following result:

$$S_{AMD} = \frac{T_{serial}}{T_{concurrent}} = \frac{23626.983}{6694.77} = 3.529$$

$$S_{Intel} = \frac{T_{serial}}{T_{concurrent}} = \frac{10495.405}{5371.75} = 1.95$$

The second example - a data filtering algorithm

Suppose that you have a lot of data that describes a list of items. For example, say that you have a lot of attributes (name, surname, address, phone number, and so on) of a lot of people. It's a common need to obtain the data that meets certain criteria. For example, you might want to obtain the details of people who live in a certain street or with a certain name.

In this section, you will implement one of those filtering programs. We have used the **Census-Income KDD** dataset from the UCI (you can download it from `https://archive.ics.uci.edu/ml/datasets/Census-Income+%28KDD%29`), which contains weighted census data extracted from the 1994 and 1995 current population surveys conducted by the U.S. Census Bureau.

In the concurrent version of this example, you will learn how to cancel tasks that are running in the fork/join pool and how to manage unchecked exceptions that can be thrown in a task.

Common features

We have implemented some classes to read the data from a file and to filter the data. These classes are used by the serial and concurrent versions of the algorithm. The following are the classes:

- **The CensusData class**: This class stores the 39 attributes that define every person. It defines the attributes and methods to get and set their value. We are going to identify each attribute by a number. The `evaluateFilter()` method of this class contains the association between the number and the name of the attribute. You can visit `https://archive.ics.uci.edu/ml/machine-learning-databases/census-income-mld/census-income.names` to get the details of every attribute.
- **The CensusDataLoader class**: This class loads the census data from a file. It has the `load()` method that receives the path to the file as an input parameter and returns an array of `CensusData` with the information of all the people in the file.
- **The FilterData class**: This class defines a filter of data. A filter includes the number of an attribute and the value of that attribute.
- **The Filter class**: This class implements the methods that determine whether a `CensusData` object meets the conditions of a list of filters.

We don't include the source code of these classes. They are very simple, and you can check the source code of the example for details.

The serial version

We have implemented the serial version of the filter algorithm in two classes. The `SerialSearch` class organizes the filtering of the data. It provides two methods:

- **The findAny() method**: This receives the array of the `CensusData` object as a parameter with all the data from the file and a list of filters and returns a `CensusData` object with the first person it finds that meets all the criteria from the filters
- **The findAll() method**: This receives the array of the `CensusData` object as a parameter with all the data from the file and a list of filters and returns an array of `CensusData` objects with all the people that meet all the criteria from the filter

The `SerialMain` class implements the `main()` method of this version and tests it to measure the execution time of this algorithm in some circumstances.

The SerialSearch class

As we mentioned before, this class implements the filtering of data. It provides two methods. The first one, the `findAny()` method, looks for the first data object that meets the filter's criteria. When it finds the first data object, it finishes its execution. Refer to the following code:

```java
public class SerialSearch {

    public static CensusData findAny (CensusData[] data, List<FilterData>
                                      filters) {
        int index=0;
        for (CensusData censusData : data) {
            if (Filter.filter(censusData, filters)) {
                System.out.println("Found: "+index);
                return censusData;
            }
            index++;
        }

        return null;
    }
```

The second one, the `findAll()` method, returns an array of `CensusData` objects with all the objects that meet the filter's criteria, as follows:

```java
    public static List<CensusData> findAll (CensusData[] data,
                                            List<FilterData> filters) {
        List<CensusData> results=new ArrayList<CensusData>();

        for (CensusData censusData : data) {
            if (Filter.filter(censusData, filters)) {
                results.add(censusData);
            }
        }
        return results;
    }
}
```

The SerialMain class

You're going to use this class to test the filtering algorithm in different circumstances. First, we load the data from the file, as follows:

```
public class SerialMain {
  public static void main(String[] args) {
    Path path = Paths.get("data","census-income.data");

    CensusData data[]=CensusDataLoader.load(path);
    System.out.println("Number of items: "+data.length);

    Date start, end;
```

The first thing we are going to do is to use the `findAny()` method to find an object that exists in the first place of the array. You construct a list of filters and then call the `findAny()` method with the data of the file and the list of filters:

```
List<FilterData> filters=new ArrayList<>();
FilterData filter=new FilterData();
filter.setIdField(32);
filter.setValue("Dominican-Republic");
filters.add(filter);
filter=new FilterData();
filter.setIdField(31);
filter.setValue("Dominican-Republic");
filters.add(filter);
filter=new FilterData();
filter.setIdField(1);
filter.setValue("Not in universe");
filters.add(filter);
filter=new FilterData();
filter.setIdField(14);
filter.setValue("Not in universe");
filters.add(filter);
start=new Date();
CensusData result=SerialSearch.findAny(data, filters);
System.out.println("Test 1 - Result: "+result
                    .getReasonForUnemployment());
end=new Date();
System.out.println("Test 1- Execution Time: "+(end.getTime()-
                    start.getTime())));
```

Our filters look for the following attributes:

- `32`: This is the country of the birth father attribute
- `31`: This is the country of the birth mother attribute
- `1`: This is the class of the worker attributes; `Not in universe` is one of their possible values
- `14`: This is the reason for unemployment attribute; `Not in universe` is one of their possible values

We are also going to test other cases, as follows:

- Use the `findAny()` method to find an object that exists in the last position of the array
- Use the `findAny()` method to try to find an object that doesn't exist
- Use the `findAny()` method in an error situation
- Use the `findAll()` method to obtain all the objects that meet a list of filters
- Use the `findAll()` method in an error situation

The concurrent version

We are going to include more elements in our concurrent version:

- **A task manager**: When you use the fork/join framework, you start with one task and you split that task into two (or more) child tasks that you split again and again until your problem has the desired size. There can be situations where you want to finish the execution of all those tasks. For example, when you implement the `findAny()` method and you find an object that meets all the criteria, you don't need to continue with the execution of the rest of the tasks.
- **A RecursiveTask class to implement the findAny() method**: It's the `IndividualTask` class, which extends `RecursiveTask`.
- **A RecursiveTask class to implement the findAll() method**: It's the `ListTask` class, which extends `RecursiveTask`.

Let's look at the details of all these classes.

The TaskManager class

We are going to use this class to control the cancellation of tasks. We are going to cancel the execution of tasks in the following two situations:

- You're executing the findAny() operation and you find an object that meets the requirements
- You're executing the findAny() or findAll() operations and there's an unchecked exception in one of the tasks

The class declares two attributes: ConcurrentLinkedDeque to store all the tasks we need to cancel and an AtomicBoolean variable to guarantee that only one task executes the cancelTasks() method. We use an AtomicBoolean variable to guarantee that all the tasks access their value in a thread-safe way:

```
public class TaskManager {

    private Set<RecursiveTask> tasks;
    private AtomicBoolean cancelled;

    public TaskManager() {
        tasks = ConcurrentHashMap.newKeySet();
        cancelled = new AtomicBoolean(false);
    }
```

It defines methods to add a task to ConcurrentLinkedDeque, delete a task from ConcurrentLinkedDeque, and cancel all the tasks stored in it. To cancel the tasks, we use the cancel() method defined in the ForkJoinTask class. The true parameter forces the interruption of the task if it is running, as follows:

```
public void addTask(RecursiveTask task) {
    tasks.add(task);
}

public void cancelTasks(RecursiveTask sourceTask) {

    if (cancelled.compareAndSet(false, true)) {
        for (RecursiveTask task : tasks) {
            if (task != sourceTask) {
                if(cancelled.get()) {
                    task.cancel(true);
                }
                else {
                    tasks.add(task);
                }
            }
```

```
      }
    }
  }

  public void deleteTask(RecursiveTask task) {
    tasks.remove(task);
  }
```

The `cancelTasks()` method receives a `RecursiveTask` object as a parameter. We're going to cancel all the tasks except the one that is calling this method. We don't want to cancel the tasks that have found the result. The `compareAndSet(false, true)` method sets the `AtomicBoolean` variable to `true` and returns `true` only if the current value is `false`. If the `AtomicBoolean` variable already has a `true` value, then `false` is returned. The whole operation is performed atomically, so it's guaranteed that the body of the `if` statement will be executed once at the most, even if the `cancelTasks()` method is concurrently called several times from different threads.

The IndividualTask class

The `IndividualTask` class extends the `RecursiveTask` class parameterized with the `CensusData` task and implements the `findAny()` operation. It defines the following attributes:

- An array with all the `CensusData` objects
- The `start` and `end` attributes, which determine the elements it has to process
- The `size` attribute, which determines the maximum number of elements the task will process without splitting the task
- A `TaskManager` class to cancel the tasks if necessary
- The following code, which gives a list of filters to apply:

```
private CensusData[] data;
private int start, end, size;
private TaskManager manager;
private List<FilterData> filters;

public IndividualTask(CensusData[] data, int start,
                      int end, TaskManager manager,
                      int size, List<FilterData> filters) {
  this.data = data;
  this.start = start;
  this.end = end;
  this.manager = manager;
  this.size = size;
```

```
        this.filters = filters;
    }
```

The main method of the class is the `compute()` method. It returns a `CensusData` object. If the number of elements the task has to process is less than the size attribute, it looks for the object directly. If the method finds the desired object, it returns the object and uses the `cancelTasks()` method to cancel the execution of the rest of the tasks. If the method doesn't find the desired object, it returns `null`, as shown in the following code:

```
if (end - start <= size) {
    for (int i = start; i < end && ! Thread.currentThread()
            .isInterrupted(); i++) {
        CensusData censusData = data[i];
        if (Filter.filter(censusData, filters)) {
            System.out.println("Found: " + i);
            manager.cancelTasks(this);
            return censusData;
        }
    }
    return null;
}
```

If the number of items it has to process is more than the size attribute, we create two child tasks to process half of the elements:

```
} else {
    int mid = (start + end) / 2;
    IndividualTask task1 = new IndividualTask(data, start, mid, manager,
                                            size, filters);
    IndividualTask task2 = new IndividualTask(data, mid, end, manager,
                                            size, filters);
```

Then, we add the newly created tasks to the task manager and delete the actual tasks. If we want to cancel the tasks, then we want to cancel only the tasks that are running:

```
manager.addTask(task1);
manager.addTask(task2);
manager.deleteTask(this);
```

Then, we send the tasks to `ForkJoinPool` with the `fork()` method, which sends them asynchronously, and wait for its finalization with the `quietlyJoin()` method.

The difference between the `join()` and `quietlyJoin()` methods is that the `join()` method launches an exception if the task is canceled or an unchecked exception is thrown inside the method, whereas the `quietlyJoin()` method doesn't throw any exception.

```
task1.fork();
task2.fork();
task1.quietlyJoin();
task2.quietlyJoin();
```

Then, we delete the child tasks from the `TaskManager` class, as follows:

```
manager.deleteTask(task1);
manager.deleteTask(task2);
```

Now, we obtain the results of the tasks using the `join()` method. If a task throws an unchecked exception, it will be propagated without special handling and the cancellation will just be ignored, as follows:

```
try {
  CensusData res = task1.join();
  if (res != null)
    return res;
    manager.deleteTask(task1);
  } catch (CancellationException ex) {
}
try {
  CensusData res = task2.join();
  if (res != null)
    return res;
    manager.deleteTask(task2);
  } catch (CancellationException ex) {
}
  return null;
}
}
```

The ListTask class

The `ListTask` class extends the `RecursiveTask` class, parameterized with a `List` of `CensusData`. We are going to use this task to implement the `findAll()` operation. It's very similar to the `IndividualTask` task. Both use the same attributes, but they have differences in the `compute()` method.

First, we initialize a `List` object to return the results and check the number of elements the task has to process. If the number of elements the task has to process is less than the size attribute, add all the objects that meet the criteria specified in the filters to the list of results:

```
@Override
protected List<CensusData> compute() {
  List<CensusData> ret = new ArrayList<CensusData>();
  List<CensusData> tmp;

  if (end - start <= size) {
    for (int i = start; i < end; i++) {
      CensusData censusData = data[i];
      if (Filter.filter(censusData, filters)) {
        ret.add(censusData);
      }
    }
  }
```

If the number of items it has to process is more than the size attribute, we will create two child tasks to process half of the elements:

```
int mid = (start + end) / 2;
ListTask task1 = new ListTask(data, start, mid, manager, size,
                              filters);
ListTask task2 = new ListTask(data, mid, end, manager, size, filters);
```

Then, we will add the newly created tasks to the task manager and delete the actual tasks. The actual task won't be canceled--its child tasks will be canceled, as follows:

```
manager.addTask(task1);
manager.addTask(task2);
manager.deleteTask(this);
```

Then, we will send the tasks to `ForkJoinPool` with the `fork()` method, which sends them asynchronously, and wait for its finalization with the `quietlyJoin()` method:

```
task1.fork();
task2.fork();
task2.quietlyJoin();
task1.quietlyJoin();
```

Then, we will delete the child tasks from `TaskManager`:

```
manager.deleteTask(task1);
manager.deleteTask(task2);
```

Now, we obtain the results of the tasks using the `join()` method. If a task throws an unchecked exception, it will be propagated without special handling and the cancellation will just be ignored:

```
    try {
      tmp = task1.join();
      if (tmp != null)
        ret.addAll(tmp);
        manager.deleteTask(task1);
      } catch (CancellationException ex) {
    }
    try {
      tmp = task2.join();
      if (tmp != null)
        ret.addAll(tmp);
        manager.deleteTask(task2);
      } catch (CancellationException ex) {
    }
  }
}
```

The ConcurrentSearch class

The `ConcurrentSearch` class implements the `findAny()` and `findAll()` methods. They have the same interface as the methods of the serial version of the process. Internally, they initialize the `TaskManager` object and the first task, and send them to default `ForkJoinPool` using the execute method. They then wait for the finalization of the task and write the results. This is the code of the `findAny()` method:

```
public class ConcurrentSearch {

  public static CensusData findAny (CensusData[] data,
                        List<FilterData> filters, int size) {
    TaskManager manager=new TaskManager();
    IndividualTask task=new IndividualTask(data, 0, data.length,
                                      manager, size, filters);
    ForkJoinPool.commonPool().execute(task);
    try {
      CensusData result=task.join();
      if (result!=null) {
        System.out.println("Find Any Result: "+result.getCitizenship());
        return result;
      } catch (Exception e) {
      System.err.println("findAny has finished with an error: "+
                      task.getException().getMessage());
    }
```

```
      return null;
   }
```

This is the code of the `findAll()` method:

```
public static CensusData[] findAll (CensusData[] data,
   List<FilterData> filters, int size) {
     List<CensusData> results;
     TaskManager manager=new TaskManager();
     ListTask task=new ListTask(data,0,data.length,manager,
                                 size,filters);
     ForkJoinPool.commonPool().execute(task);
     try {
       results=task.join();

       return results;
     } catch (Exception e) {
     System.err.println("findAny has finished with an
                        error: " + task.getException().getMessage());
   }
   return null;
}
```

The ConcurrentMain class

The `ConcurrentMain` class is used to test the concurrent version of our object filter. It is identical to the `SerialMain` class, but uses the concurrent version of the operations.

Comparing the two versions

To compare the serial and concurrent versions of the filtering algorithm, we test them in six different situations:

- **Test 1**: We test the `findAny()` method by looking for an object, which exists in the first position of the `CensusData` array
- **Test 2**: We test the `findAny()` method by looking for an object, which exists in the last position of the `CensusData` array
- **Test 3**: We test the `findAny()` method by looking for an object, which doesn't exist
- **Test 4**: We test the `findAny()` method in an error situation
- **Test 5**: We test the `findAll()` method in a normal situation
- **Test 6**: We test the `findAll()` method in an error situation

For the concurrent version of the algorithm, we have tested three different values of the size parameter that determines the maximum number of elements a task can process without forking into two child tasks. We have tested this with a maximum threshold of 10, 200, 2000 and 4000 elements.

We have executed the examples using the JMH framework (http://openjdk.java.net/projects/code-tools/jmh/), which allows you to implement microbenchmarks in Java. Using a framework for benchmarking is a better solution, which simply measures time using methods such as currentTimeMillis() or nanoTime(). We have executed them ten times in two different architectures:

1. **A computer with an Intel Core i5-5300 CPU with Windows 7 and 16 GB of RAM**: This processor has two cores and each core can execute two threads, so we will have four parallel threads
2. **A computer with an AMD A8-640 APU with Windows 10 and 8 GB of RAM**: This processor has four cores

As with the other examples, we have measured the execution time in milliseconds. First, we show the results of the AMD architecture:

AMD Architecture					
Test case	Serial	Concurrent size = 10	Concurrent size = 200	Concurrent size = 2000	Concurrent size = 4000	Best
Test 1	2.374	8.041	5.434	4.802	9.339	Serial
Test 2	86.049	75.872	57.954	32.56	32.876	Concurrent
Test 3	58.322	70.562	22.947	30.831	27.033	Concurrent
Test 4	0.65	15090.17	259.597	8.585	5.987	Serial
Test 5	60.129	42.979	44.81	22.741	21.287	Concurrent
Test 6	0.697	14279.35	256.271	9.365	4.842	Serial

Here are the results of the Intel architecture:

Intel Architecture					
Test case	Serial	Concurrent size = 10	Concurrent size = 200	Concurrent size = 2000	Concurrent size = 4000	Best
Test 1	0.796	8.896	3.253	2.08	2.422	Serial
Test 2	31,006	41.312	32.974	14.407	14.55	Concurrent
Test 3	15.076	25.068	9.55	10.729	9.77	Concurrent
Test 4	0.378	10664.607	106.349	4.699	2.898	Serial
Test 5	13.291	18.037	25.061	10.262	8.937	Concurrent
Test 6	0.352	10901.387	91.998	5.246	2.24	Serial

From these tables, we can draw the following conclusions:

- The serial version of the algorithm has better performance when we have to process a smaller number of elements.
- The concurrent version of the algorithm has better performance when we have to process all the elements or some of them.
- In error situations, the serial version of the algorithm has better performance than the concurrent version. The concurrent version has a very poor performance in this situation when the value of the size parameter is small.

In this case, concurrency does not always give us an improvement in performance.

The third example - the merge sort algorithm

The merge sort algorithm is a very popular sorting algorithm, which is often implemented using the divide and conquer technique, so it's a very good candidate to test the fork/join framework.

To implement the merge sort algorithm, we divide the unsorted lists into sublists of one element. Then, we merge those unsorted sublists to produce ordered sublists until we have processed all the sublists, and we have only the original list, but with all the elements sorted.

To make the concurrent version of our algorithm, we have used the `CountedCompleter` tasks, introduced in Java 8. The most important characteristic of these tasks is that they include a method to be executed when all their child tasks have finished their execution.

To test out implementations, we have used the **Amazon product co-purchasing network metadata** (you can download it from `https://snap.stanford.edu/data/amazon-meta.html`). In particular, we have created a list with the salesrank of 542,184 products. We are going to test our version of the algorithm, sorting this list of products and comparing the execution time with the `sort()` and `parallelSort()` methods of the `Arrays` class.

Shared classes

As we mentioned earlier, we have built a list of 542,184 Amazon products with information about those products, including their ID, title, group, salesrank, the number of reviews, number of similar products, and number of categories each product belongs to. We have implemented the `AmazonMetaData` class to store the information of a product. This class declares the necessary attributes and the methods to get and set their values. This class implements the `Comparable` interface to compare two instances of this class. We want to sort the elements by salesrank in ascending order. To implement the `compare()` method, we use the `compare()` method of the `Long` class to compare the salesrank of both objects, as follows:

```
public int compareTo(AmazonMetaData other) {
  return Long.compare(this.getSalesrank(),
    other.getSalesrank());
}
```

We have also implemented `AmazonMetaDataLoader`, which provides the `load()` method. This method receives a route to the file with the data as a parameter and returns an array of `AmazonMetaData` objects with the information of all the products.

We don't include the source code of these classes to focus on the characteristics of the fork/join framework.

The serial version

We have implemented the serial version of the merge sort algorithm in the SerialMergeSort class, which implements the algorithm and the SerialMetaData class and provides the main() method to test the algorithm.

The SerialMergeSort class

The SerialMergeSort class implements the serial version of the merge sort algorithm. It provides the mergeSort() method, which receives the following parameters:

- The array with all the data we want to sort
- The first element the method has to process (included)
- The last element the method has to process (not included)

If the method has to process only one element, it returns; otherwise, it makes two recursive calls to the mergeSort() method. The first call will process the first half of elements, and the second call will process the second half of elements. Finally, we make a call to the merge() method to merge the two halves of the elements and get a sorted list of elements:

```
public void mergeSort (Comparable data[], int start, int end) {
   if (end-start < 2) {
      return;
   }
   int middle = (end+start)>>>1;
   mergeSort(data,start,middle);
   mergeSort(data,middle,end);
   merge(data,start,middle,end);
}
```

We used the (end+start)>>>1 operator to obtain the mid-element to split the array. If you have, for example, 1.5 billion elements (which is not that impossible with modern memory chips), it still fits in the Java array. However, (end+start)/2 will overflow, resulting in a negative number array. You can find a detailed explanation of this problem at http://googleresearch.blogspot.ru/2006/06/extra-extra-read-all-about-it-nearly.html.

The `merge()` method merges two lists of elements to obtain a sorted list. It receives the following parameters:

- The array with all the data we want to sort
- The three elements (`start`, `mid`, and `end`) that determine the two parts of the array (start-mid, mid-end) that we want to merge and sort

We create a temporary array to sort the elements. Then, we sort the elements in the array that is processing both parts of the list, and store the sorted list in the same position as the original array, as shown in the following code:

```
private void merge(Comparable[] data, int start, int middle,
                   int end) {
  int length=end-start+1;
  Comparable[] tmp=new Comparable[length];
  int i, j, index;
  i=start;
  j=middle;
  index=0;
  while ((i<middle) && (j<end)) {
    if (data[i].compareTo(data[j])<=0) {
      tmp[index]=data[i];
      i++;
    } else {
      tmp[index]=data[j];
      j++;
    }
    index++;
  }

  while (i<middle) {
    tmp[index]=data[i];
    i++;
    index++;
  }

  while (j<end) {
    tmp[index]=data[j];
    j++;
    index++;
  }

  for (index=0; index < (end-start); index++) {
    data[index+start]=tmp[index];
  }
 }
}
```

The SerialMetaData class

The `SerialMetaData` class provides the `main()` method to test the algorithm. We're going to execute every sort algorithm 10 times to calculate the average execution time. First, we load the data from the file and create a copy of the array:

```
public class SerialMetaData {

    public static void main(String[] args) {
        for (int j=0; j<10; j++) {
            Path path = Paths.get("data","amazon-meta.csv");

            AmazonMetaData[] data = AmazonMetaDataLoader.load(path);
            AmazonMetaData data2[] = data.clone();
```

Then, we sort the first array using the `sort()` method of the `Arrays` class:

```
Date start, end;

start = new Date();
Arrays.sort(data);
end = new Date();
System.out.println("Execution Time Java Arrays.sort(): " +
                    (end.getTime() - start.getTime()));
```

Then, we sort the second array using our implementation of the merge sort algorithm:

```
SerialMergeSort mySorter = new SerialMergeSort();
start = new Date();
mySorter.mergeSort(data2, 0, data2.length);
end = new Date();
System.out.println("Execution Time Java SerialMergeSort: " +
                    (end.getTime() - start.getTime()));
```

Finally, we check that the sorted arrays are identical:

```
        for (int i = 0; i < data.length; i++) {
            if (data[i].compareTo(data2[i]) != 0) {
                System.err.println("There's a difference is position " +
                                    i);
                System.exit(-1);
            }
        }
        System.out.println("Both arrays are equal");
    }
  }
}
```

The concurrent version

As we mentioned before, we are going to use the Java 8 `CountedCompleter` class as the base class for our fork/join tasks. This class provides a mechanism to execute a method when all its child tasks have finished their execution. This mechanism is the `onCompletion()` method, so we will use the `compute()` method to divide the array and the `onCompletion()` method to merge the sublists into an ordered list.

The concurrent solution you are going to implement has three classes:

- The `MergeSortTask` class, which extends the `CountedCompleter` class and implements the task that executes the merge sort algorithm
- The `ConcurrentMergeSort` task, which launches the first task
- The `ConcurrentMetaData` class, which provides the `main()` method to test the concurrent version of the merge sort algorithm

The MergeSortTask class

As we mentioned earlier, this class implements the tasks that are going to execute the merge sort algorithm. This class uses the following attributes:

- The array of data we want to sort
- The start and end position of the array that the task has to sort

The class also has a constructor to initialize its parameters:

```
public class MergeSortTask extends CountedCompleter<Void> {

  private Comparable[] data;
  private int start, end;
  private int middle;

  public MergeSortTask(Comparable[] data, int start, int end,
                    MergeSortTask parent) {
    super(parent);

    this.data = data;
    this.start = start;
    this.end = end;
  }
```

If the difference between the start and end indexes is greater than or equal to 1024, then the `compute()` method splits the task into two child tasks to process two subsets of the original set. Both tasks use the `fork()` method to send a task to the `ForkJoinPool` asynchronously. Otherwise, we execute `SerialMergeSorg.mergeSort()` to sort the part of the array (which has 1024 or fewer elements) and then we call the `tryComplete()` method. This method will internally call the `onCompletion()` method when the child task has finished its execution, as shown in the following code:

```
@Override
public void compute() {
  if (end - start >= 1024) {
    middle = (end+start)>>>1;
    MergeSortTask task1 = new MergeSortTask(data, start, middle,
                                            this);
    MergeSortTask task2 = new MergeSortTask(data, middle, end,
                                            this);
    addToPendingCount(1);
    task1.fork();
    task2.fork();
  } else {
    new SerialMergeSort().mergeSort(data, start, end);
    tryComplete();
  }
}
```

In our case, we will use the `onCompletion()` method to make the merge and sort operations obtain the sorted list. Once a task finishes the execution of the `onCompletion()` method, it calls `tryComplete()` over its parent to try to complete that task. The source code of the `onCompletion()` method is very similar to the `merge()` method of the serial version of the algorithm, as shown in the following code:

```
@Override
public void onCompletion(CountedCompleter<?> caller) {
  if (middle==0) {
    return;
  }
  int length = end - start + 1;
  Comparable tmp[] = new Comparable[length];
  int i, j, index;
  i = start;
  j = middle;
  index = 0;
  while ((i < middle) && (j < end)) {
    if (data[i].compareTo(data[j]) <= 0) {
      tmp[index] = data[i];
      i++;
    } else {
```

```
            tmp[index] = data[j];
            j++;
        }
        index++;
    }
    while (i < middle) {
      tmp[index] = data[i];
      i++;
      index++;
    }
    while (j < end) {
      tmp[index] = data[j];
      j++;
      index++;
    }
    for (index = 0; index < (end - start); index++) {
      data[index + start] = tmp[index];
    }

  }
```

The ConcurrentMergeSort class

In the concurrent version, this class is very simple. It implements the mergeSort() method, which receives the array of data to sort , as well as the start index (which will always be 0) and the end index (which will always be the length of the array) to sort the array as parameters. We have chosen to maintain the same interface as the serial version.

The method creates a new MergeSortTask and sends it to the default ForkJoinPool using the invoke() method, which returns when the task has finished its execution and the array is sorted:

```
    public class ConcurrentMergeSort {

      public void mergeSort (Comparable data[], int start, int end) {

        MergeSortTask task=new MergeSortTask(data, start, end,null);
        ForkJoinPool.commonPool().invoke(task);

      }
    }
```

The ConcurrentMetaData class

The `ConcurrentMetaData` class provides the `main()` method to test the concurrent version of the merge sort algorithm. In our case, the code is equal to the code of the `SerialMetaData` class, but it uses the concurrent versions of the classes and the `Arrays.parallelSort()` method instead of the `Arrays.sort()` method, so we don't include the source code of the class.

Comparing the two versions

We executed our serial and concurrent versions of the merge sort algorithm and compared its execution times with both them and the `Arrays.sort()` and `Arrays.parallelSort()` methods.

We executed the examples using the JMH framework (`http://openjdk.java.net/projects/code-tools/jmh/`), which allows you to implement microbenchmarks in Java. Using a framework for benchmarking is a better solution, which simply measures time using methods such as `currentTimeMillis()` or `nanoTime()`. We executed them ten times in two different architectures:

1. **A computer with an Intel Core i5-5300 CPU with Windows 7 and 16 GB of RAM**: This processor has two cores and each core can execute two threads, so we will have four parallel threads
2. **A computer with an AMD A8-640 APU with Windows 10 and 8 GB of RAM**: This processor has four cores

These are the execution times in milliseconds that we obtained when we sorted our dataset with 542,184 objects:

	Arrays.sort()	Serial merge sort	Arrays.parallelSort()	Concurrent merge sort
AMD Architecture	858.1	1268.3	392.6	705.1
Intel Architecture	327.608	454.84	209.653	209.732

We can draw the following conclusions:

- The `Arrays.parallelSort()` method obtains the best result. For serial algorithms, the `Arrays.sort()` method obtains better execution time than our implementations.
- For our implementations, the concurrent version of the algorithm has better performance than the serial one.

We can compare our serial and concurrent versions of the merge sort algorithm using the speed-up:

$$S_{AMD} = \frac{T_{serial}}{T_{concurrent}} = \frac{1268.3}{705.33} = 1.80$$

$$S_{Intel} = \frac{T_{serial}}{T_{concurrent}} = \frac{454.84}{298.732} = 1.522$$

Other methods of the fork/join framework

In the three examples shown in this chapter, we have used a lot of methods of the classes that forms the fork/join framework, but there are other interesting methods you have to know.

We have used the methods `execute()` and `invoke()` from the `ForkJoinPool` class to send tasks to the pool. We can use another method, named `submit()`. The main difference between them is that the `execute()` method sends the task to the `ForkJoinPool` and immediately returns a void value, the `invoke()` method sends the task to the `ForkJoinPool` and returns when the task has finished its execution, and the `submit()` method sends the task to the `ForkJoinPool` and immediately returns a `Future` object to control the status of the task and obtain its result.

In all the examples of this chapter, we have used classes based on the `ForkJoinTask` class, but you can use the `ForkJoinPool` tasks based on the `Runnable` and `Callable` interfaces. To do this, you can use the `submit()` method, which has versions that accept a `Runnable` object, a `Runnable` object with a result, and a `Callable` object.

The ForkJoinTask class provides the get(long timeout, TimeUnit unit) method to obtain the results returned by a task. This method waits for the period of time specified in the parameters for the result of the task. If the task finishes its execution before that period of time, the method returns the result. Otherwise, it throws a TimeoutException exception.

The ForkJoinTask class provides an alternative to the invoke() method, namely the quietlyInvoke() method. The main difference between the two versions is that the invoke() method returns the result of the execution of the task or throws an exception if necessary. The quietlyInvoke() method doesn't return the result of the task and doesn't throw any exception. It's similar to the quietlyJoin() method used in the examples.

Summary

The divide and conquer design technique is a very popular approach to solve different kinds of problems. You divide the original problem into smaller problems and those problems into smaller ones until you have enough simple problems to solve them directly. In version 7, the Java Concurrency API introduced a special kind of Executor optimized for this kind of problem, namely the fork/join framework. It's based on the fork operations, that allows you to create a new child task, and the join operation, that allows you to wait for the finalization of a child task before getting its results.

Using those operations, your fork/join tasks will have the following appearance:

```
if ( problem.size() > DEFAULT_SIZE) {
  childTask1=new Task();
  childTask2=new Task();
  childTask1.fork();
  childTask2.fork();
  childTaskResults1=childTask1.join();
  childTaskResults2=childTask2.join();
  taskResults=makeResults(childTaskResults1, childTaskResults2);
  return taskResults;
} else {
  taskResults=solveBasicProblem();
  return taskResults;
}
```

In this chapter, you solved three different problems using the fork/join framework: the k-means clustering algorithm, the data filtering algorithm, and the merge sort algorithm.

You used the default `ForkJoinPool` provided by the API, and created a new `ForkJoinPool` object. You also used the three types of `ForkJoinTasks`. The `RecursiveAction` class, used as the base class for those `ForkJoinTasks` that don't return a result, the `RecursiveTask` class, used as the base class for those tasks that return a result, and finally the `CountedCompleter` class, used as the base class for those tasks that need to execute a method or launch another task when all their child subtasks finish their execution

In the next chapter, you will learn how to use the `MapReduce` programming technique using **parallel streams** to get the best performance when processing very big datasets.

8
Processing Massive Datasets with Parallel Streams - The Map and Reduce Model

Undoubtedly, the most important innovations introduced in Java 8 are **lambda expressions** and the **stream** API. A stream is a sequence of elements that can be processed in a sequential or parallel way. We can transform the stream applying the intermediate operations and then perform a final computation to get the desired result (a list, an array, a number, and so on). In this chapter, we will cover the following topics:

- An introduction to streams
- The first example - a numerical summarization application
- The second example - an information retrieval search tool

An introduction to streams

A stream is a sequence of data (is not a data structure) that allows you to apply a sequence of operations in a sequential or concurrent way to filter, convert, sort, reduce, or organize those elements to obtain a final object. For example, if you have a stream with the data of your employees, you can use a stream to:

- Count the total number of employees (this is an expensive terminal operation)
- Calculate the average salary of all employees who live in a particular place
- Obtain a list of the employees who haven't met their objectives
- Any operation that implies work with all or some of the employees

Streams are greatly influenced by functional programming (the **Scala** programming language provides a very similar mechanism), and work with lambda expressions. Stream API resembles **LINQ** (short for **Language-Integrated Query**) queries available in C# language and, to some extent, could be compared with SQL queries.

In the following sections, we will explain the basic characteristics of streams and the parts you will find in a stream.

Basic characteristics of streams

The main characteristics of a stream are as follows:

- A stream does not store its elements. A stream takes the elements from its source and sends them across all the operations that form the pipeline.
- You can work with streams in parallel without any extra work. When you create a stream, you can use the `stream()` method to create a sequential stream or `parallelStream()` to create a concurrent one. The `BaseStream` interface defines the `sequential()` methods to obtain a sequential version of the stream and `parallel()` to obtain a concurrent version of the stream. You can convert a sequential stream to parallel and a parallel to sequential as many times as you want. Take into account that when the terminal stream operation is performed, all the stream operations will be processed according to the last setting. You cannot instruct a stream to perform some operations sequentially and other operations concurrently. Internally, parallel streams in Oracle JDK 9 and Open JDK 9 use an implementation of the fork/join framework to execute concurrent operations.
- Streams are greatly influenced by functional programming and the Scala programming language. You can use the new lambda expressions as a way to define the algorithm to be executed in an operation over a stream.
- Streams can't be reused. When you obtain a stream, for example, from a list of values, you can use that stream only once. If you want to perform another operation on the same data, you have to create another stream.
- Streams make for lazy processing of data. They don't obtain the data until it's necessary. As you will learn later, a stream has an origin, some intermediate operations, and a terminal operation. The data isn't processed until the terminal operation needs it, so stream processing doesn't begin until the terminal operation is executed.

- You can't access the elements of a stream in a different way. When you have a data structure, you can access one determined element stored in it, for example, indicating its position or its key. Stream operations usually process the elements uniformly, so the only thing you have is the element itself. You don't know the position of the element in the stream and the neighbor elements. In the case of parallel streams, the elements can be processed in any order.
- Stream operations don't allow you to modify the stream source. For example, if you use a list as the stream source, you can store the processing result into the new list, but you cannot add, remove, or replace the elements of the original list. Although this sounds restrictive, it's a very useful feature, as you can return the stream created from your internal collection without a fear that the list will be modified by the caller.

Sections of a stream

A stream has three different sections:

- A **source** which generates the data consumed by the stream.
- Zero or more **intermediate** operations, which generate another stream as an output.
- One **terminal** operation which generates an object, which can be a simple object or a collection as an array, a list, or a hash table. There can also be terminal operations that don't produce any explicit result.

Sources of a stream

The source of the stream generates the data that will be processed by the `Stream` object. You can create a stream from different data sources. For example, the `Collection` interface included the `stream()` methods in Java 8 to generate a sequential stream and `parallelStream()` to generate a parallel one. This allows you to generate a stream to process all the data from almost all the data structures implemented in Java as lists (`ArrayList`, `LinkedList`, and so on), sets (`HashSet`, `EnumSet`), or concurrent data structures (`LinkedBloFmackingDeque`, `PriorityBlockingQueue`, and so on). Another data structure that can generate streams is arrays. The `Array` classes includes four versions of the `stream()` method to generate a stream from the array. If you pass an array of `int` numbers to the method, it will generate `IntStream`. This is a special kind of stream, implemented to work with integer numbers (you can still use `Stream<Integer>` instead of `IntStream`, but performance might be significantly worse).

Similarly, you can create `LongStream` or `DoubleStream` from the `long[]` or `double[]` arrays. Of course, if you pass an array of object to the `stream()` method, you will obtain a generic stream of the same type. In this case, there is no `parallelStream()` method, but once you have obtained the stream, you can call the `parallel()` method defined in the `BaseStream` interface to convert the sequential stream into a concurrent one.

Other interesting functionality provided by the `Stream` API is that you can generate a stream to process the contents of directory or a file. The `Files` class provides different methods to work with files using streams. For example, the `find()` method returns a stream with the `Path` objects of the files in a file tree that meet certain conditions. The `list()` method returns a stream of the `Path` objects with the contents of a directory. The `walk()` method returns a stream of the `Path` objects processing all the objects in a directory tree using a depth-first algorithm. But the most interesting method is the `lines()` method, which creates a stream of `String` objects with the lines of a file, so you can process its contents using a stream. Unfortunately, all of the methods mentioned here parallelize badly unless you have many thousands of elements (files or lines).

Also, you can create a stream using two methods provided by the `Stream` interface: the `generate()` and `iterate()` methods. The `generate()` method receives a `Supplier` parameterized with an object type as a parameter and generates an infinite sequential stream of objects of that type. The `Supplier` interface has the `get()` method. Every time the stream needs a new object, it will call this method to obtain the next value of the stream. As we mentioned earlier, streams process the data in a lazy way, so there is no problem with the infinite nature of the stream. You will use other methods that will convert that infinite stream. The `iterate()` method is similar, but in this case, the method receives a seed and a `UnaryOperator`. The first value is the result of applying the `UnaryOperator` to the seed; the second value is the result of applying the `UnaryOperator` to the first result, and so on. This method should be avoided as much as possible in concurrent applications because of their performance.

There are also more stream sources, as follows:

- `String.chars()`: This returns an `IntStream` with the `char` values of the `String`.
- `Random.ints()`, `Random.doubles()`, or `Random.longs()`: This returns an `IntStream`, `DoubleStream`, and `LongStream`, respectively with pseudorandom values. You can specify the range of numbers between the random numbers or the number of random values that you want to obtain. For example, you can generate pseudorandom numbers between 10 and 20 using new `Random.ints(10,20)`.

- `SplittableRandom`: This class provides the same methods as the `Random` class to generate pseudorandom `int`, `double`, and `long` values, but is more suitable for parallel processing. You can check the Java API documentation to get the details of this class.
- `Stream.concat()`: This receives two streams as parameters and creates a new stream with the elements of the first stream followed by the elements of the second stream.

You can generate streams from other sources, but we think they are not significant.

Intermediate operations

The most important characteristic of intermediate operations is that they return another stream as their result. The objects of the input and output stream can be of a different type, but an intermediate operation will always generate a new stream. You can have zero or more intermediate operations in a stream. The most important intermediate operations provided by the `Stream` interface are:

- `distinct()`: This method returns a stream with unique values. All the repeated elements will be eliminated.
- `filter()`: This method returns a stream with the elements that meet certain criteria.
- `flatMap()`: This method is used to convert a stream of streams (for example, a stream of list, sets, and so on) in a single stream.
- `limit()`: This method returns a stream that contains, at the most, the specified number of the original elements in the encounter order, starting from the first element.
- `map()`: This method is used to transform the elements of a stream from one type to another.
- `peek()`: This method returns the same stream, but it executes some code; normally, it is used to write log messages.
- `skip()`: This method ignores the first elements (the concrete number is passed as a parameter) of the stream.
- `sorted()`: This method sorts the elements of the stream.

Terminal operations

A terminal operation returns an object as a result. It never returns a stream. In general, all streams will end with a terminal operation that returns the final result of the sequence of operations. The most important terminal operations are:

- `collect()`: This method provides a way to reduce the number of elements of the source stream, organizing the elements of the stream in a data structure. For example, if you want to group the elements of your stream by a criterion.
- `count()`: This returns the number of elements of the stream.
- `max()`: This returns the maximum element of the stream.
- `min()`: This returns the minimum element of the stream.
- `reduce()`: This method transforms the elements of the stream into a unique object that represents the stream.
- `forEach()`/`forEachOrdered()`: This methods apply an action to every element in the stream. The second method uses the order of the elements of the stream if the stream has a defined order.
- `findFirst()`/`findAny()`: This returns 1 or the first element of the stream, respectively, if they exist.
- `anyMatch()`/`allMatch()`/`noneMatch()`: They receive a predicate as a parameter and return a Boolean value to indicate if any, all, or none of the elements of the stream match the predicate.
- `toArray()`: This method returns an array with the elements of the stream.

MapReduce versus MapCollect

MapReduce is a programming model to process very large datasets in distributed environments with a lot of machines working in a cluster. It has two steps, generally implemented by two methods:

- **Map**: This filters and transforms the data
- **Reduce**: This applies a summary operation in the data

To make this operation in a distributed environment, we have to split the data and then distribute it over the machines of the cluster. This programming model has been used for a long time in the functional programming world. Google recently developed a framework based on this principle, and in the **Apache Foundation**, the **Hadoop** project is very popular as an open source implementation of this model.

Java 9 with streams allows programmers to implement something very similar to this. The `Stream` interface defines intermediate operations (`map()`, `filter()`, `sorted()`, `skip()`, and so on) that can be considered as `map()` functions, and it provides the `reduce()` method as a terminal operation whose main objective is to make a reduction of the elements of the stream as the reduction of the MapReduce model.

The main idea of the reduce operation is to create a new intermediate result based on a previous intermediate result and a stream element. An alternative method of reduction (also called mutable reduction) is to incorporate the new resulting item into the mutable container (for example, adding it into `ArrayList`). Such reduction is performed by the `collect()` operation, and we will call it as a **MapCollect** model.

We will look at how to work with the MapReduce model in this chapter and how to work with the MapCollect model in `Chapter 9`, *Processing Massive Datasets with Parallel Streams - The Map and Collect Model*.

The first example - a numerical summarization application

One of the most common needs when you have a big set of data is to process its elements to measure certain characteristics. For example, if you have a set with the products purchased in a shop, you can count the number of products you have sold, the number of units per product you have sold, or the average amount that each customer spent. We have named that process **numerical summarization**.

In this chapter, we are going to use streams to obtain some measures of the **Online Retail** dataset of the **UCI Machine Learning Repository**, which you can download from `http://archive.ics.uci.edu/ml/datasets/Online+Retail`. This dataset stores all the transactions occurring between 01/12/2010 and 09/12/2011 for a UK-based and registered non-store online retail.

Unlike other chapters, in this case, we explain the concurrent version using streams and then how to implement a serial equivalent version to verify that concurrency improves performance with streams too. Take into account that concurrency is transparent for the programmer, as we mentioned in the introduction of the chapter.

The concurrent version

Our numerical summarization application is very simple. It has the following components:

- Record: This class defines the internal structure of every record of the file. It defines the 8 attributes of every record and the corresponding get() and set() method to establish their values. Its code is very simple, so it won't be included in the book.
- ConcurrentDataLoader: This class will load the Online_Retail.csv file with the data and convert it to a list of Record objects. We will use streams to load the data and make the conversion.
- ConcurrentStatistics: This class implements the operations that we will use to make the calculations over the data.
- ConcurrentMain: This class implements the main() method to call the operations of the ConcurrentStatistics class and measure its execution time.

Let's describe the last three classes in detail.

The ConcurrentDataLoader class

The ConcurrentDataLoader class implements the load() method which loads the file with the Online Retail dataset and converts it to a list of Record objects. First, we use the method readAllLines() of the Files method to load the file and convert its contents into a list of strings. Every line of the file will be converted in an element of the list:

```
public class ConcurrentDataLoader {

  public static List<Record> load(Path path) throws IOException {
    System.out.println("Loading data");

    List<String> lines = Files.readAllLines(path);
```

Then, we apply the necessary operations to the stream to get the list of Record objects:

```
List<Record> records = lines.parallelStream()
                    .skip(1).map(l -> l.split(";"))
                    .map(t -> new Record(t))
                    .collect(Collectors.toList());
```

The operations we use are:

- `parallelStream()`: We create a parallel stream to process all the lines of the file.
- `skip(1)`: We ignore the first item of the stream; in this case, the first line of the file, which contains the headers of the file.
- `map (l → l.split(";"))`: We convert each string in a `String[]` array dividing the line by the `;` character. We use a lambda expression, where `l` represents the input parameter and `l.split()` will generate the array of strings. We call this method in a stream of strings, and it will generate a stream of `String[]`.
- `map(t → new Record(t))`: We convert each array of strings in a `Record` object using the constructor of the `Record` class. We use a lambda expression, where `t` represents the array of strings. We call this method in a stream of `String[]`, and we generate a stream of `Record` objects.
- `collect(Collectors.toList())`: This method converts the stream into a list. We will work with the collect method in more detail in Chapter 9, *Processing Massive Datasets with Parallel Streams - The Map and Collect Model*.

As you can see, we have made the transformation in a compact, elegant, and concurrent way without the utilization of any thread, task, or framework. Finally, we return the list of `Record` objects, as follows:

```
        return records;
    }
}
```

The ConcurrentStatistics class

The `ConcurrentStatistics` class implements the methods that make the calculus over the data. We have seven different operations to obtain information about the dataset. Let's describe each of them.

Customers from the United Kingdom

The main objective of this method is to obtain the number of products ordered by each customer from the the United Kingdom.

This is the source code of this method:

```
public static void customersFromUnitedKingdom(List<Record> records) {
   System.out.println("*************************************");
   System.out.println("Customers from UnitedKingdom");
   Map<String, List<Record>> map = records.parallelStream().filter(r ->
r.getCountry().equals("the United
Kingdom")).collect(Collectors.groupingBy(Record::getCustomer));

   map.forEach((k, l) -> System.out.println(k + ": " + l.size()));
   System.out.println("*************************************");
}
```

The method receives the list of `Record` objects as input parameters. First, we use a stream to obtain a `ConcurrentMap<String, List<Record>>` object where there are different customer IDs and the list includes the records of each customer. This stream starts with the `parallelStream()` method to create a parallel stream. Then, we use the `filter()` method to select those `Record` objects with the country attribute equals to `'the United Kingdom'`. Finally, we use the `collect()` method passing the `Collectors.groupingByConcurrent()` method to group the actual elements of the stream by the values of the job attribute. Take into account that the `groupingByConcurrent()` method is an unordered collector. The records collected into the list can be in an arbitrary order, not in the original order (unlike the simple `groupingBy()` collector).

Once we have the `ConcurrentMap` object, we use the `forEach()` method to write the information on the screen.

Quantity from the United Kingdom

The main objective of this method is to obtain statistical information (maximum, minimum, and average values) on the number of products in the orders from the the United Kingdom. This is the source code of the method:

```
public static void quantityFromUnitedKingdom(List<Record> records) {

   System.out.println("*************************************");
   System.out.println("Quantity from the United Kingdom");
   DoubleSummaryStatistics statistics = records.parallelStream()
           .filter(r -> r.getCountry().equals("the United Kingdom"))
           .collect(Collectors.summarizingDouble(Record::getQuantity));

   System.out.println("Min: " + statistics.getMin());
   System.out.println("Max: " + statistics.getMax());
   System.out.println("Average: " + statistics.getAverage());
```

```
        System.out.println("*******************************************");
    }
```

This method receives the list of `Record` objects as input parameters and uses a stream to get a `DoubleSummaryStatistics` object with the statistical information. First, we use the `parallelStream()` method to get a parallel stream. Then, we use the `filter()` method to obtain the records from the the United Kingdom. Finally, we use the `collect()` method with the `Collectors.summarizingDouble()` parameter to obtain the `DoubleSummaryStatistics` object. This class implements the `DoubleConsumer` interface and collects statistical data of the values it receives in the `accept()` method. This `accept()` method is called internally by the `collect()` method of the stream. Java also provides the `IntSummaryStatistics` and `LongSummaryStatistics` classes also to obtain statistical data from the `int` and `long` values.

In this case, we use the `max()`, `min()`, and `average()` methods to obtain the maximum, minimum, and average values, respectively.

Countries for product

The main objective of this method is to obtain the `list` of countries that have ordered the product with the ID `85123A`.

This is the source code of the method:

```
    public static void countriesForProduct(List<Record> records) {

    System.out.println("*******************************************");
    System.out.println("Countries for product 85123A");

    records.parallelStream().filter(r -> r.getStockCode()
                        .equals("85123A")).map(r -> r
                        .getCountry()).distinct().sorted()
                        .forEachOrdered(System.out::println);
    System.out.println("*******************************************");
    }
```

The method receives the list of `Record` objects as input parameters and uses the `parallelStream()` method to get a parallel stream. Then, we use the `filter()` method to only get the records associated with that product. Then, we use the `map()` method to obtain a stream of `String` objects with the country name associated with the record. With the distinct method, we take only the unique values, and with the `sorted()` method, we sort those values alphabetically.

Finally, we use `forEachOrdered()` to print the result. Be careful not to use `forEach()` here, as it will print the results in no particular order, which would make the `sorted()` step useless. The `forEach()` operation is useful when the elements, order is not important and may work much faster for parallel streams than `forEachOrdered()`.

Quantity for product

One of the most common mistakes we make when we use streams is to try to reuse a stream. We will show you the consequences of this mistake with this method, whose main objective is to obtain the maximum and minimum number of products associated with a record of the product with the ID `85123A`.

The first version of the method is to try to reuse a stream. This is its source code:

```
public static void quantityForProduct(List<Record> records) {

    System.out.println("****************************************");
    System.out.println("Quantity for Product");

    IntStream stream = records.parallelStream().filter(r ->  r
                            .getStockCode().equals("85123A"))
                        .mapToInt(r -> r.getQuantity());

    System.out.println("Max quantity: " + stream.max().getAsInt());
    System.out.println("Min quantity: " + stream.min().getAsInt());
    System.out.println("****************************************");
}
```

The method receives the list of `Record` objects as an input parameter. First, we create an `IntStream` object using that list. With the `parallelStream()` method, we create a parallel stream. Then, we use the `filter()` method to get records associated with the product and the `mapToInt()` method to convert the `Stream` of the `Record` object in an `IntStream` object, replacing each object by the value of the `getQuantity()` method.

We try to use that stream to get the maximum value, with the `max()` method, and the minimum value, with the `min()` method. If we execute this method, we will obtain `IllegalStateException` in the second call with the message **the stream has already been operated upon or closed**.

We can solve this problem by creating two different streams, one to obtain the maximum, and the other to obtain the minimum. This is the source code of this option:

```
public static void quantityForProductOk(List<Record> records) {

    System.out.println("*****************************************");
    System.out.println("Quantity for Product Ok");
    int value = records.parallelStream().filter(r ->
r.getStockCode().equals("85123A")).mapToInt(r -> r.getQuantity()).max()
.getAsInt();

    System.out.println("Max quantity: " + value);

    value = records.parallelStream().filter(r ->  r.getStockCode()
                .equals("85123A")).mapToInt(r -> r
                .getQuantity()).min().getAsInt();

    System.out.println("Min quantity: " + value);
    System.out.println("*****************************************");
}
```

Another option is to use the `summaryStatistics()` method to obtain an `IntSummaryStatistics` object, as shown in a previous method.

Multiple data filter

The main objective of this method is to obtain the number of records that meet at least one of the following conditions:

- The `quantity` attribute has a value bigger than 50
- The `unitPrice` attribute has a value bigger than 10

One solution to implement this method is to implement a filter that checks whether the elements meet one of these conditions. You can implement another solution with the `concat()` method provided by the Stream interface. This is the source code:

```
public static void multipleFilterData(List<Record> records) {

    System.out.println("*****************************************");
    System.out.println("Multiple Filter");

    Stream<Record> stream1 = records.parallelStream()
                            .filter(r -> r.getQuantity() > 50);
    Stream<Record> stream2 = records.parallelStream()
                            .filter(r -> r.getUnitPrice() > 10);
```

```
Stream<Record> complete = Stream.concat(stream1, stream2);

Long value = complete.parallel().unordered().map(r -> r
                                 .getStockCode()).distinct().count();

System.out.println("Number of products: " + value);
System.out.println("****************************************");
```

This method receives the list of `Record` objects as input parameters. First, we create two streams with the elements that meet each of the conditions and then we use the `concat()` method to generate a single stream. The `concat()` method only creates a stream with the elements of the first stream followed by the elements of the second stream. For this reason, with the final stream, we use the `parallel()` method to convert the final stream into a parallel once, the `unordered()` method to get an unordered stream that will give us better performance in the `distinct()` method with parallel streams, the `map()` method to convert each record into a `String` value with the `stockCode` of the product, the `distinct()` method to get only unique values, and the `count()` method to obtain the number of elements in the stream.

This is not the most optimal solution. We have used it to show you how the `concat()` and `distinct()` methods work. You can implement the same in a more optimal way using the following code:

```
public static void multipleFilterDataPredicate (List<Record> records) {

    System.out.println("****************************************");
    System.out.println("Multiple filter with Predicate");

    Predicate<Record> p1 = r -> r.getQuantity() > 50;
    Predicate<Record> p2 = r -> r.getUnitPrice() > 10;

    Predicate<Record> pred = Stream.of(p1, p2)
                                  .reduce(Predicate::or).get();

    long value = records.parallelStream().filter(pred).count();

    System.out.println("Number of products: " + value);
    System.out.println("****************************************");
}
```

We create a stream of two predicates and reduce them via the `Predicate::or` operation to create the compound predicate, which is `true` when either of the input predicates is `true`. You can also use the `Predicate::and` reduction operation to create a predicate, which is `true` when all the input predicates are `true`.

Highest invoice amounts

The main objective of this method is to obtain the 10 highest amounts of full invoices'.

First, we build a map where the keys are the IDs of the invoices and the values are a list to all the records related with an invoice.

```
public static void getBiggestInvoiceAmmounts(List<Record> records) {

    System.out.println("*****************************************");
    System.out.println("Biggest Invoice Ammounts");

    Map<String, List<Record>> map = records.stream().unordered()
                    .parallel().collect(Collectors
                            .groupingByConcurrent(r -> r.getId()));
```

We use the `unordered()` method to delete the encounter order associated with a list a get a good performance with parallel operations. Then, we convert the stream into a parallel one using the `parallel()` method, and finally we use the `collect()` method with the `groupingByConcurrent()` collector to get the final map.

In the second step, we build a `ConcurrentLinkedDeque` data structure of `Invoice` objects. This is the source code of this block:

```
ConcurrentLinkedDeque<Invoice> invoices= new ConcurrentLinkedDeque();
map.values().parallelStream().forEach( list -> {
    Invoice invoice = new Invoice();
    invoice.setId(list.get(0).getId());
    double ammount=list.stream().mapToDouble(r -> r.getUnitPrice()* r
                                        .getQuantity()).sum();
    invoice.setAmmount(ammount);
    invoice.setCustomerId(list.get(0).getCustomer());

    invoices.add(invoice);
});
```

We have two streams here. First, we have a parallel stream to process all the values of the previous map. For each list with the records of an invoice, we create an `Invoice` object with the id of the invoice, the ID of the customer, and its total amount. To calculate the total amount of every invoice, we use another stream and the `mapToDouble()` method to change each record as per the quantity of the product and `unitPrice` attributes and the `sum()` method to sum all the values of the final `Stream`. We use a `ConcucrrentLinkedDeque` data structure because it allows us to make concurrent inserts on it without data-race conditions, and that property is very important for us in this situation.

Finally, we obtain the 10 invoices with a biggest amount. This is the source code of this part:

```
System.out.println("Invoices: "+invoices.size()+": "+map.getClass());
invoices.stream().sorted(Comparator.comparingDouble
        (Invoice::getAmmount).reversed()).limit(10).forEach(i ->
                System.out.println("Customer:"+i.getCustomerId() +
                                "; Ammount: "+ i.getAmmount())));
System.out.println("*******************************************");
}
```

We use the `ConcurrentLinkedDeque` data structure to create a `Stream`, sort them using the `sorted()` method to first get the invoices with the highest amount and in the last positions the ones with a lower amount, take the first 10 invoices using the `limit()` method and print them in the console with the `forEach()` method. We work with a sorted stream in this block, so we use a sequential stream. A parallel one wouldn't give us better performance.

Products with a unit price between 1 and 10

The main objective of this method is to obtain the number of products in the file with a unit price between 1 and 10.

This is the source code of this:

```
public static void productsBetween1and10(List<Record> records) {

    System.out.println("*******************************************");
    System.out.println("Products between 1 and 10");
    int count=records.stream().unordered().parallel().filter(r -> (r
                    .getUnitPrice() >=1 ) && (r.getUnitPrice() <=10))
                    .map(i -> i.getStockCode()).distinct()
                    .mapToInt(a -> 1).reduce(0, Integer::sum);
    System.out.println("Products between 1 and 10: "+count);
    System.out.println("*******************************************");
}
```

The method receives the list of `Record` objects as input parameters and uses the `stream()`, `unordered()` and `parallel()` methods to get a parallel stream without the encounter order restriction in the stream. Then, we use the `filter()` method to get only the records with a `unitPrice` between 1 and 10. Then, we use the `map()` method to replace each record by the value of the `stockCode` attribute. Then, the `distinct()` method deletes the duplicates and the `map()` method transforms each value in the value 1. Finally, the `reduce()` method sums all the 1 values and returns the final result.

The first parameter of the reduce() method is the identity value, and the second parameter is the operation that is used to obtain a single value from all the elements of the stream.

In this case, we use the Integer::sum operation. The first sum is between the initial and the first value of the stream, the second sum is between the result of the first sum and the second value of the stream, and so on.

The ConcurrentMain class

The ConcurrentMain class implements the main() method to test the ConcurrentStatistic class. First, we implement the measure() method, which measures the execution time of a task:

```
public class ConcurrentMain {
    static Map<String, List<Double>> totalTimes = new LinkedHashMap<>();
    static List<Record> records;

    private static void measure(String name, Runnable r) {
        long start = System.nanoTime();
        r.run();
        long end = System.nanoTime();
        totalTimes.computeIfAbsent(name, k -> new ArrayList<>())
                .add((end - start) / 1_000_000.0);
    }
}
```

We use a map to store all the execution times of every method. We are going to execute each method 10 times to see how the execution time decreases after the first execution. Then, we include the main() method code. It uses the measure() method to measure the execution time of every method and repeats this process 10 times:

```
public static void main(String[] args) throws IOException {
    Path path = Paths.get("data\\Online_Retail.csv");

    for (int i = 0; i < 10; i++) {
        measure("Customers from UnitedKingdom", () -> ConcurrentStatistics
                .customersFromUnitedKingdom(records));
        measure("Quantity from UnitedKingdom", () -> ConcurrentStatistics
                .quantityFromUnitedKingdom(records));
        measure("Countries for Product", () -> ConcurrentStatistics
                .countriesForProduct(records));
        measure("Quantity for Product", () -> ConcurrentStatistics
                .quantityForProductOk(records));
        measure("Multiple Filter for Products", () -> ConcurrentStatistics
                .multipleFilterData(records));
        measure("Multiple Filter for Products with Predicate", () ->
```

```
            ConcurrentStatistics.multipleFilterDataPredicate(records));
    measure("Biggest Invoice Ammount", () -> ConcurrentStatistics
            .getBiggestInvoiceAmmounts(records));
    measure("Products Between 1 and 10", () -> ConcurrentStatistics
            .productsBetween1and10(records));
}
```

Finally, we write in the console all the execution times and the average execution time, as follows:

```
    times.stream().map(t -> String.format("%6.2f", t))
        .collect(Collectors.joining(" ")),
        times.stream().mapToDouble(Double::doubleValue)
        .average().getAsDouble()));
    }
}
```

The serial version

In this case, the serial version is almost equal to the concurrent one. We only replace all the calls to the `parallelStream()` method by calls to the `stream()` method to obtain a sequential stream instead of a parallel stream. We also have to delete the call to the `parallel()` method we used in one of the samples and changed the call to the `groupingByConcurrent()` method to `groupingBy()`.

Comparing the two versions

We executed both versions of the operations to test whether the use of parallel streams provides us with better performance.

We executed the examples using the JMH framework (`http://openjdk.java.net/projects/code-tools/jmh/`), which allows you to implement micro benchmarks in Java. Using a framework for benchmarking is a better solution which simply measures time using methods such as `currentTimeMillis()` and `nanoTime()`. We executed them 10 times in two different architectures:

- **A computer with an Intel Core i5-5300 CPU with Windows 7 and 16 GB of RAM**: This processor has two cores and each core can execute two threads, so we will have four parallel threads.
- **A computer with an AMD A8-640 APU with Windows 10 and 8 GB of RAM**: This processor has four cores.

These are the results in milliseconds:

Operation	Intel Architecture		AMD Architecture	
	Sequential Streams	Parallel Streams	Sequential Streams	Parallel Streams
Countries for product	19.146	15.517	80.994	45.833
Customers from United Kingdom	242.593	240.003	783.044	750.199
Biggest invoice amounts	81.612	70.853	358.488	174.395
Multiple filter data	24.371	20.026	101.658	60.098
Multiple filter data with predicates	11.338	9.462	56.81	34.715
Products between 1 and 10	45.065	27.394	187.91	85.299
Quantity for Products	24.614	22.675	126.088	65.897
Quantity from United Kingdom	24.488	14.722	132.161	55.278

We can see how parallel streams always achieve better performance than serial streams. This is the speed-up for all the examples:

Operation	Speed-up - Intel	Speed-up - AMD
Countries for product	1.23	1.77
Customers from the United Kingdom	1.01	1.04
Biggest invoice amounts	1.15	2.06
Multiple filter data	1.21	1.69
Multiple filter data with predicates	1.19	1.64
Products between 1 and 10	1.64	2.20
Quantity for product	1.08	1.91
Quantity from the United Kingdom	1.66	2.39

The second example - an information retrieval search tool

According to Wikipedia (`https://en.wikipedia.org/wiki/Information_retrieval`), information retrieval is:

> *"The activity obtaining information resources relevant to an information need from a collection of information resources"*

Usually, the information resources are a collection of documents and the information needed is a set of words, which summarizes our need. To do a quick search over the document collection, we use a data structure named **inverted index**. It stores all the words of the document collection, and for each word, a list of the documents that contains that word. In `Chapter 5`, *Getting Data From the Tasks - The Callable and Future Interfaces*, you constructed an inverted index of a document collection constructed with the Wikipedia pages with information about movies to construct a set of 100,673 documents. We have converted each Wikipedia page into a text file. This inverted index is stored in a text file where each line contains the word, its document frequency, and all the documents in which the word appears with the `tfxidf` attribute of the word in the document. The documents are sorted by the value of the `tfxidf` attribute. For example, a line of the file looks like this:

```
velankanni:4,18005302.txt:10.13,20681361.txt:10.13,45672176.txt:10
13,6592085.txt:10.13
```

This line contains the `velankanni` word with a DF of `4`. It appears in the `18005302.txt` document with a `tfxidf` value of `10.13`, in the `20681361.txt` document with a `tfxidf` value of `10.13`, in the document `45672176.txt` with a `tfxidf` value of `10.13`, and in the `6592085.txt` document with a `tfxidf` value of `10.13`.

In this chapter, we will use the stream API to implement different versions of our search tool and obtain information about the inverted index.

An introduction to the reduction operation

As we mentioned earlier in this chapter, the reduce operation applies a summary operation to the elements of a stream to generate a single summary result. This single result can be of the same type as the elements of the stream or of another type. A simple example of a `reduce()` operation is to calculate the sum of a stream of numbers.

The stream API provides the `reduce()` method to implement reduction operations. This method has the following three different versions:

- `reduce(accumulator)`: This version applies the `accumulator` function to all the elements of the stream. There is no initial value in this case. It returns an `Optional` object with the final result of the `accumulator` function or an empty `Optional` object if the stream is empty. This `accumulator` function must be an `associative` function. It implements the `BinaryOperator` interface. Both parameters could be either the stream elements or the partial results returned by previous accumulator calls.

- `reduce(identity, accumulator)`: This version must be used when the final result and the elements of the stream have the same type. The identity value must be an identity value for the `accumulator` function. That is to say, if you apply the `accumulator` function to the identity value and any value `V`, it must return the same value `V`: `accumulator(identity,V)=V`. That identity value is used as the first result for the accumulator function and is the returned value if the stream has no elements. As in the other version, the accumulator must be an `associative` function that implements the `BinaryOperator` interface.

- `reduce(identity, accumulator, combiner)`: This version must be used when the final result has a different type than the elements of the stream. The identity value must be an identity for the combiner function, that is to say, `combiner(identity,v)=v`. A combiner function must be compatible with the accumulator function, that is to say, `combiner(u,accumulator(identity,v))=accumulator(u,v)`. The accumulator function takes a partial result and the next element of the stream to generate a partial result, and the combiner takes two partial results to generate another partial result. Both functions must be associative, but in this case, the accumulator function is an implementation of the `BiFunction` interface and the combiner function is an implementation of the `BinaryOperator` interface.

The `reduce()` method has a limitation. As we mentioned before, it must return a single value. You shouldn't use the `reduce()` method to generate a collection or a complex object. The first problem is performance. As the documentation of the stream API specifies, the `accumulator` function returns a new value every time it processes an element. If your `accumulator` function works with collections, it processes an element and creates a new collection every time, which is very inefficient. Another problem is that, if you work with parallel streams, all the threads will share the identity value.

If this value is a mutable object, for example, a collection, all the threads will be working over the same collection. This does not comply with the philosophy of the `reduce()` operation. In addition, the `combiner()` method will receive always two identical collections (all the threads are working over only one collection), which doesn't comply with the philosophy of the `reduce()` operation either.

If you want to make a reduction that generates a collection or a complex object, you have the following two options:

- Apply a mutable reduction with the `collect()` method. Chapter 9, *Processing Massive Datasets with Parallel Streams - The Map and Collect Model*, explains in detail how to use this method in different situations.
- Create the collection and use the `forEach()` method to fill the collection with the required values.

In this example, we will use the `reduce()` method to obtain information about the inverted index, and the `forEach()` method to reduce the index to the list of relevant documents for a query.

The first approach - full document query

In our first approach, we will use all the documents associated with a word. The steps of this implementation of our search process are:

- We select in the inverted index the lines corresponding with the words of the query.
- We group all the document lists into a single list. If a document appears that is associated with two or more different words, we sum the `tfxidf` value of those words in the document to obtain the final `tfxidf` value of the document. If a document is only associated with one word, the `tfxidf` value of that word will be the final `tfxidf` value for that document.
- We sort the documents using their `tfxidf` value, from high to low.
- We show the user the 100 documents with the highest value of `tfxidf`.

We have implemented this version in the `basicSearch()` method of the `ConcurrentSearch` class. This is the source code of the method:

```
public static void basicSearch(String query[]) throws IOException {

    Path path = Paths.get("index", "invertedIndex.txt");
    HashSet<String> set = new HashSet<>(Arrays.asList(query));
    QueryResult results = new QueryResult(new ConcurrentHashMap<>());

    try (Stream<String> invertedIndex = Files.lines(path)) {

        invertedIndex.parallel().filter(line -> set
                        .contains(Utils.getWord(line)))
                        .flatMap(ConcurrentSearch::basicMapper)
                        .forEach(results::append);

        results.getAsList().stream().sorted().limit(100)
                .forEach(System.out::println);

        System.out.println("Basic Search Ok");
    }

}
```

We receive an array of string objects with the words of the query. First, we transform that array into a set. Then, we use a try-with-resources stream with the lines of the `invertedIndex.txt` file, which is the file that contains the inverted index. We use a try-with-resources so we don't have to worry about opening or closing the file. The aggregate operations of the stream will generate a `QueryResult` object with the relevant documents. We use the following methods to obtain that list:

- `parallel()`: First, we obtain a parallel stream to improve the performance of the search process.
- `filter()`: We select the lines that associate the word in the set with the words in the query. The `Utils.getWord()` method obtains the word from the line.
- `flatMap()`: We convert the stream of string where each string is a line of the inverted index in a stream of `Token` objects. Each token contains the `tfxidf` value of a word in a file. Of every line, we will generate as many tokens as files that contain that word.
- `forEach()`: We generate the `QueryResult` object, adding every token with the `add()` method of that class.

Once we have created the `QueryResult` object, we create another stream to obtain the final list of results using the following methods:

- `getAsList()`: The `QueryResult` object returns a list with the relevant documents
- `stream()`: Creates a stream to process the list
- `sorted()`: To sort the list of documents by their `tfxidf` values
- `limit()`: To get the first 100 results
- `forEach()`: To process the 100 results and write the information on the screen

Let's describe the auxiliary classes and methods used in the example.

The basicMapper() method

This method converts a stream of strings into a stream of Token objects. As we will describe in detail later, a token stores the `tfxidf` value of a word in a document. This method receives a string with a line of the inverted index. It splits the line into the tokens and generates as many Token objects as documents that contain the word. This method is implemented in the `ConcurrentSearch` class. This is the source code:

```
public static Stream<Token> basicMapper(String input) {
    ConcurrentLinkedDeque<Token> list = new ConcurrentLinkedDeque();
    String word = Utils.getWord(input);
    Arrays.stream(input.split(",")).skip(1).parallel()
            .forEach(token -> list.add(new Token(word, token)));

    return list.stream();
}
```

First, we create a `ConcurrentLinkedDeque` object to store the Token objects. Then, we split the string using the `split()` method and use the `stream()` method of the `Arrays` class to generate a stream. Skip the first element (containing the information of the word) and process the rest of the tokens in parallel. For each element, we create a new Token object (we pass to the constructor the word and the token that has the `file:tfxidf` format) and add it to the stream. Finally, we return a stream using the `stream()` method of the `ConcurrenLinkedDeque` object.

The Token class

As we mentioned earlier, this class stores the tfxidf value of a word in a document. So, it has three attributes to store this information, as follows:

```
public class Token {

    private final String word;
    private final double tfxidf;
    private final String file;
```

The constructor receives two strings. The first one contains the word, and the second one contains the file and the tfxidf attribute in the file:tfxidf format, so we have to process it as follows:

```
public Token(String word, String token) {
    this.word=word;
    String[] parts=token.split(":");
    this.file=parts[0];
    this.tfxidf=Double.parseDouble(parts[1]);
}
```

Finally, we have added methods to obtain (not to set) the values of the three attributes and to convert an object to a string, as follows:

```
@Override
public String toString() {
    return word+":"+file+":"+tfxidf;
}
```

The QueryResult class

This class stores the list of documents relevant to a query. Internally, it uses a map to store the information of the relevant documents. The key is the name of the file that stores the document, and the value is a Document object that also contains the name of the file and the total tfxidf value of that document to the query, as follows:

```
public class QueryResult {

    private Map<String, Document> results;
```

We use the constructor of the class to indicate the concrete implementation of the map interface we will use. We use a `ConcurrentHashMap` to the concurrent version and a `HashMap` in the serial version:

```
public QueryResult(Map<String, Document> results) {
   this.results=results;
}
```

The class includes the append method, which inserts a token in the map, as follows:

```
public void append(Token token) {
   results.computeIfAbsent(token.getFile(), s -> new
Document(s)).addTfxidf(token.getTfxidf());
}
```

We use the `computeIfAbsent()` method to create a new `Document` object if there is no `Document` object associated with the file, or to obtain the corresponding one if it already exists, and add the `tfxidf` value of the token to the total `tfxidf` value of the document using the `addTfxidf()` method.

Finally, we have included a method to obtain the map as a list, as follows:

```
public List<Document> getAsList() {
   return new ArrayList<>(results.values());
}
```

The `Document` class stores the name of the file as a string and the total `tfxidf` value as `DoubleAdder`. This class is a new feature of Java 8 and allows us to sum values to the variable from different threads without worrying about synchronization. It implements the `Comparable` interface to sort the documents by their `tfxidf` value, so the documents with the highest `tfxidf` will be first. Its source code is very simple, so it is not included.

The second approach - reduced document query

The first approach creates a new `Token` object per word and file. We have noted that common words, for example, `the`, take a lot of documents associated and a lot of them have low values of `tfxidf`. We have changed our mapper method to take into account only 100 files per word, so the number of `Token` objects generated will be smaller.

We have implemented this version in the `reducedSearch()` method of the `ConcurrentSearch` class. This method is very similar to the `basicSearch()` method. It only changes the stream operations that generates the `QueryResult` object, as follows:

```
invertedIndex.parallel().filter(line -> set
            .contains(Utils.getWord(line)))
            .flatMap(ConcurrentSearch::limitedMapper)
            .forEach(results::append);
```

Now, we use the `limitedMapper()` method as function in the `flatMap()` method.

The limitedMapper() method

This method is similar to the `basicMapper()` method, but, as we mentioned earlier, we only take into account the first 100 documents associated with every word. As the documents are sorted by their `tfxidf` values, we are using the 100 documents in which the word is more important, as follows:

```
public static Stream<Token> limitedMapper(String input) {
  ConcurrentLinkedDeque<Token> list = new ConcurrentLinkedDeque();
  String word = Utils.getWord(input);

Arrays.stream(input.split(",")).skip(1).limit(100).parallel().forEach(token
  -> {
     list.add(new Token(word, token));
  });

  return list.stream();
}
```

The only difference with the `basicMapper()` method is the `limit(100)` call, which takes the first 100 elements of the stream.

The third approach - generating an HTML file with the results

While working with a search tool using a web search engine (for example, Google), when you make a search, it returns the results of your search (the 10 most important) and for every result the title of the document and a fragment of the document where the words you searched for appear.

Our third approach to the search tool is based on the second approach, but by adding a third stream to generate an HTML file with the results of the search. For every result, we will show the title of the document and three lines where one of the words introduced in the query appears. To implement this, you need access to the files that appears in the inverted index. We have stored them in a folder named docs.

This third approach is implemented in the `htmlSearch()` method of the `ConcurrentSearch` class. The first part of the method to construct the `QueryResult` object with the 100 results is equal to the `reducedSearch()` method, as follows:

```
public static void htmlSearch(String query[], String fileName) throws
                            IOException {
  Path path = Paths.get("index", "invertedIndex.txt");
  HashSet<String> set = new HashSet<>(Arrays.asList(query));
  QueryResult results = new QueryResult(new ConcurrentHashMap<>());

  try (Stream<String> invertedIndex = Files.lines(path)) {

    invertedIndex.parallel().filter(line -> set
                    .contains(Utils.getWord(line)))
                  .flatMap(ConcurrentSearch::limitedMapper)
                  .forEach(results::append);
```

Then, we create the file to write the output and the HTML headers in it:

```
path = Paths.get("output", fileName + "_results.html");
try (BufferedWriter fileWriter = Files.newBufferedWriter(path,
      StandardOpenOption.CREATE)) {

  fileWriter.write("<HTML>");
  fileWriter.write("<HEAD>");
  fileWriter.write("<TITLE>");
  fileWriter.write("Search Results with Streams");
  fileWriter.write("</TITLE>");
  fileWriter.write("</HEAD>");
  fileWriter.write("<BODY>");
  fileWriter.newLine();
```

Then, we include the stream that generates the results in the HTML file:

```
results.getAsList().stream().sorted().limit(100).map(new
ContentMapper(query)).forEach(l -> {
    try {
      fileWriter.write(l);
      fileWriter.newLine();
    } catch (IOException e) {
      e.printStackTrace();
```

```
    }
  });

  fileWriter.write("</BODY>");
  fileWriter.write("</HTML>");

}
```

We have used the following methods:

- `getAsList()` to get the list of relevant documents for the query.
- `stream()` to generate a sequential stream. We can't parallelize this stream. If we try to do so, it results in the final file not being sorted by the `tfxidf` value of the documents.
- `sorted()` to sort the results by its `tfxidf` attribute.
- `map()` to convert a `Result` object into a string with the HTML code for each result using the `ContentMapper` class. We will explain the details of this class later.
- `forEach()` to write the `String` objects returned by the `map()` method in the file. The methods of the `Stream` object can't throw a checked exception, so we have to include the `try...catch` block which be thrown.

Let's look at the details of the `ContentMapper` class.

The ContentMapper class

The `ContentMapper` class is an implementation of the `Function` interface that converts a `Result` object in an HTML block with the title of the document and three lines that include one or more words of the query.

The class uses an internal attribute to store the query and implements a constructor to initialize that attribute, as follows:

```
public class ContentMapper implements Function<Document, String> {
  private String query[];

  public ContentMapper(String query[]) {
    this.query = query;
  }
```

The title of the document is stored in the first line of the file. We use a try-with-resources instruction and the `lines()` method of the `Files` class to create and stream of `String` objects with the lines of the file and take the first one with the `findFirst()` to obtain the line as a string:

```
public String apply(Document d) {
  String result = "";
  try (Stream<String> content = Files.lines(Paths.get("docs",d
                                  .getDocumentName())))) {
    result = "<h2>" + d.getDocumentName() + ": " +
              content.findFirst().get() + ": " +
              d.getTfxidf() + "</h2>";
  } catch (IOException e) {
    e.printStackTrace();
    throw new UncheckedIOException(e);
  }
```

Then, we use a similar structure, but in this case, we use the `filter()` method to get only the lines that contain one or more words of the query, and the `limit()` method to take three of those lines. Then, we use the `map()` method to add the HTML tags for a paragraph (<p>) and the `reduce()` method to complete the HTML code with the selected lines:

```
  try (Stream<String> content = Files.lines(Paths.get ("docs",
                                  d.getDocumentName())))) {
    result += content.filter(l -> Arrays.stream(query)
                  .anyMatch (l.toLowerCase()::contains))
                  .limit(3).map(l -> "<p>"+l+"</p>")
                  .reduce("",String::concat);
    return result;
  } catch (IOException e) {
    e.printStackTrace();
    throw new UncheckedIOException(e);
  }
}
```

The fourth approach - preloading the inverted index

The three previous solutions have a problem when they are executed in parallel. As we mentioned earlier, parallel streams are executed using the common fork/join pool provided by the Java concurrency API. In Chapter 7, *Optimizing Divide and Conquer Solutions - The Fork/Join Framework*, you learned that you shouldn't use I/O operations as read or write data in a file inside the tasks. This's because when a thread is blocked reading or writing data from or to a file, the framework doesn't use the work-stealing algorithm. As we use a file as the source of our streams, we are penalizing our concurrent solution.

One solution to this problem is to read the data to a data structure and then create our streams from that data structure. Obviously, the execution time of this approach will be less when we compare it with the other approaches, but we want to compare the serial and concurrent versions to see (as we expect) whether the concurrent version gives us better performance than the serial version. The bad part of this approach is that you need to have your data structure in memory, so you will need a large amount of memory.

This fourth approach is implemented in the preloadSearch() method of the ConcurrentSearch class. This method receives the query as an Array of String and an object of the ConcurrentInvertedIndex class (we will look at the details of this class later) with the data of the inverted index as parameters. This is the source code of this version:

```
public static void preloadSearch(String[] query,
                  ConcurrentInvertedIndex invertedIndex) {

    HashSet<String> set = new HashSet<>(Arrays.asList(query));
    QueryResult results = new QueryResult(new ConcurrentHashMap<>());

    invertedIndex.getIndex().parallelStream()
            .filter(token -> set.contains(token.getWord()))
            .forEach(results::append);

    results.getAsList().stream().sorted().limit(100)
            .forEach(document -> System.out.println(document));

    System.out.println("Preload Search Ok.");
}
```

The ConcurrentInvertedIndex class has List<Token> to store all the Token objects read from the file. It has two methods, get() and set() for this list of elements.

As in other approaches, we use two streams: the first one to get a
ConcurrentLinkedDeque of Result objects with the whole list of results, and the second
one to write the results in the console. The second one doesn't change over other versions,
but the first one changes. We use the following methods in this stream:

- getIndex(): First, we obtain the list of Token objects
- parallelStream(): Then, we create a parallel stream to process all the elements
  of the list
- filter(): We select the token associated with the words in the query
- forEach(): We process the list of tokens, adding them to the QueryResult
  object using the append() method

The ConcurrentFileLoader class

The ConcurrentFileLoader class loads into memory the contents of the
invertedIndex.txt file with the information of the inverted index. It provides a static
method named load(), which receives a path with the route of the file where the inverted
index is stored and returns a ConcurrentInvertedIndex object. We have the following
code:

```
public class ConcurrentFileLoader {

    public ConcurrentInvertedIndex load(Path path) throws IOException {
        ConcurrentInvertedIndex invertedIndex = new ConcurrentInvertedIndex();
        ConcurrentLinkedDeque<Token> results=new ConcurrentLinkedDeque<>();
```

We open the file using a try-with-resources structure and create a stream to process all the
lines:

```
        try (Stream<String> fileStream = Files.lines(path)) {
          fileStream.parallel().flatMap(ConcurrentSearch::limitedMapper)
                  .forEach(results::add);
        }

        invertedIndex.setIndex(new ArrayList<>(results));
        return invertedIndex;
    }
}
```

We use the following methods in the stream:

- `parallel()`: We convert the stream into a parallel one
- `flatMap()`: We convert the line into a stream of `Token` objects using the `limitedMapper()` method of the `ConcurrentSearch` class
- `forEach()`: We process the list of `Token` objects, adding them to a `ConcurrentLinkedDeque` object using the `add()` method

Finally, we convert the `ConcurrentLinkedDeque` object into `ArrayList` and set it in the `InvertedIndex` object using the `setIndex()` method.

The fifth approach - using our own executor

To go further with this example, we're going to test another concurrent version. As we mentioned in the introduction of this chapter, parallel streams use the common fork/join pool introduced in Java 8. However, we can use a trick to use our own pool. If we execute our method as a task of the fork/join pool, all the operations of the stream will be executed in the same fork/join pool. To test this functionality, we have added the `executorSearch()` method to the `ConcurrentSearch` class. This method receives the query as an array of `String` objects as a parameter, the `InvertedIndex` object, and a `ForkJoinPool` object. This is the source code of this method:

```
public static void executorSearch(String[] query,
        ConcurrentInvertedIndex invertedIndex, ForkJoinPool pool) {
    HashSet<String> set = new HashSet<>(Arrays.asList(query));
    QueryResult results = new QueryResult(new ConcurrentHashMap<>());

    pool.submit(() -> {
        invertedIndex.getIndex().parallelStream()
                    .filter(token -> set.contains(token.getWord()))
                    .forEach(results::append);

        results.getAsList().stream().sorted().limit(100)
                .forEach(document -> System.out.println(document));
    }).join();

    System.out.println("Executor Search Ok.");

}
```

We execute the content of the method, with its two streams, as a task in the fork/join pool using the `submit()` method, and waits for its finalization using the `join()` method.

Getting data from the inverted index - the ConcurrentData class

We have implemented some methods to get information about the inverted index using the `reduce()` method in the `ConcurrentData` class.

Getting the number of words in a file

The first method calculates the number of words in a file. As we mentioned earlier in this chapter, the inverted index stores the files in which a word appears. If we want to know the words that appear in a file, we have to process all the inverted indices. We have implemented two versions of this method. The first one is implemented in `getWordsInFile1()`. It receives the name of the file and the `InvertedIndex` object as parameters, as follows:

```
public static void getWordsInFile1(String fileName, ConcurrentInvertedIndex
index) {
  long value = index.getIndex().parallelStream()
                          .filter(token -> fileName
                          .equals(token.getFile())).count();
  System.out.println("Words in File "+fileName+": "+value);
}
```

In this case, we get the list of Token objects using the `getIndex()` method and create a parallel stream using the `parallelStream()` method. Then, we filter the tokens associated with the file using the `filter()` method, and finally, we count the number of words associated with that file using the `count()` method.

We have implemented another version of this method using the `reduce()` method instead of the `count()` method. It's the `getWordsInFile2()` method:

```
public static void getWordsInFile2(String fileName, ConcurrentInvertedIndex
index) {

  long value = index.getIndex().parallelStream()
                      .filter(token -> fileName.equals(token.getFile()))
                      .mapToLong(token -> 1).reduce(0, Long::sum);
  System.out.println("Words in File "+fileName+": "+value);
}
```

The start of the sequence of operations is the same as the previous one. When we have obtained the stream of Token objects with the words of the file, we use the mapToInt() method to convert that stream into a stream of 1 and then the reduce() method to sum all the 1 numbers.

Getting the average tfxidf value in a file

We have implemented the getAverageTfxidf() method, which calculates the average tfxidf value of the words of a file in the collection. We have used here the reduce() method to show how it works. You can use other methods here with better performance:

```
public static void getAverageTfxidf(String fileName,
            ConcurrentInvertedIndex index) {

    long wordCounter = index.getIndex().parallelStream()
                    .filter(token -> fileName.equals(token.getFile()))
                    .mapToLong(token -> 1).reduce(0, Long::sum);

    double tfxidf = index.getIndex().parallelStream()
                    .filter(token -> fileName.equals(token.getFile()))
                    .reduce(0d, (n,t)-> n+t.getTfxidf(),(n1,n2) -> n1+n2);

    System.out.println("Words in File "+fileName+": "+
                    (tfxidf/wordCounter));
}
```

We use two streams. The first one calculates the number of words in a file and has the same source code as the getWordsInFile2() method. The second one calculates the total tfxidf value of all the words in the file. We use the same methods to get the stream of Token objects with the words in the file and then we use the reduce method to sum the tfxidf value of all the words. We pass the following three parameters to the reduce() method:

- 0: This is passed as the identity value.
- (n,t) -> n+t.getTfxidf(): This is passed as the accumulator function. It receives a double number and a Token object and calculates the sum of the number and the tfxidf attribute of the token.
- (n1,n2) -> n1+n2: This is passed as the combiner function. It receives two numbers and calculates their sum.

Getting the maximum and minimum tfxidf values in the index

We have also used the `reduce()` method to calculate the maximum and minimum `tfxidf` values of the inverted index in the `maxTfxidf()` and `minTfxidf()` methods:

```
public static void maxTfxidf(ConcurrentInvertedIndex index) {
  Token token = index.getIndex().parallelStream()
                        .reduce(new Token("", "xxx:0"), (t1, t2) -> {
    if (t1.getTfxidf()>t2.getTfxidf()) {
      return t1;
    } else {
      return t2;
    }
  });
  System.out.println(token.toString());
}
```

The method receives the `ConcurrentInvertedIndex` as a parameter. We use the `getIndex()` to obtain the list of `Token` objects. Then, we use the `parallelStream()` method to create a parallel stream over the list the `reduce()` method to obtain the `Token` with the highest `tfxidf`. In this case, we use the `reduce()` method with two parameters: an identity value and an `accumulator` function. The identity value is a `Token` object. We don't care about the word and the file name, but we initialize its `tfxidf` attribute with the value 0. Then, the `accumulator` function receives two `Token` objects as parameters. We compare the `tfxidf` attribute of both objects and return the one with the greater value.

The `minTfxidf()` method is very similar, as follows:

```
public static void minTfxidf(ConcurrentInvertedIndex index) {
  Token token = index.getIndex().parallelStream()
                        .reduce(new Token("", "xxx:1000000"),(t1, t2) -> {
    if (t1.getTfxidf()<t2.getTfxidf()) {
      return t1;
    } else {
      return t2;
    }
  });
  System.out.println(token.toString());
}
```

The main difference is that, in this case, the identity value is initialized with a very high value for the `tfxidf` attribute.

The ConcurrentMain class

To test all the methods explained in the previous sections, we have implemented the `ConcurrentMain` class, which implements the `main()` method to launch our tests. In these tests, we have used the following three queries:

- query1, with the words `james` and `bond`
- query2, with the words `gone`, `with`, `the`, and `wind`
- query3, with the words `rocky`

We have tested the three queries with the three versions of our search process measuring the execution time of each test. All the tests have a code similar to this:

```
public class ConcurrentMain {

  public static void main(String[] args) {

    String query1[]={"james","bond"};
    String query2[]={"gone","with","the","wind"};
    String query3[]={"rocky"};

    Date start, end;

    bufferResults.append("Version 1, query 1, concurrent\n");
    start = new Date();
    ConcurrentSearch.basicSearch(query1);
    end = new Date();
    bufferResults.append("Execution Time: " + (end.getTime() -
                    start.getTime()) + "\n");
```

To load the inverted index from the file to an `InvertedIndex` object, you can use the following code:

```
ConcurrentInvertedIndex invertedIndex = new
                    ConcurrentInvertedIndex();
ConcurrentFileLoader loader = new ConcurrentFileLoader();
invertedIndex = loader.load(Paths.get("index",
                    "invertedIndex.txt"));
```

To create the `Executor` to use in the `executorSearch()` method, you can use the following code:

```
ForkJoinPool pool = new ForkJoinPool();
```

The serial version

We have implemented a serial version of this example with the `SerialSearch`, `SerialData`, `SerialInvertendIndex`, `SerialFileLoader`, and `SerialMain` classes. To implement that version, we have made the following changes:

- Use sequential streams instead of parallel ones. You have to delete the use of the `parallel()` method to convert the streams into parallel ones or replace the method `parallelStream()` to create a parallel stream for the `stream()` method to create a sequential one.
- In the `SerialFileLoader` class, use `ArrayList` instead of `ConcurrentLinkedDeque`.

Comparing the solutions

Let's compare the solutions of the serial and concurrent versions of all the methods we have implemented.

We executed the examples using the JMH framework (http://openjdk.java.net/projects/code-tools/jmh/), which allows you to implement micro benchmarks in Java. Using a framework for benchmarking is a better solution which simply measures time using methods such as `currentTimeMillis()` and `nanoTime()`. We have executed them 10 times in two different architectures:

- **A computer with an Intel Core i5-5300 CPU with Windows 7 and 16 GB of RAM**: This processor has two cores and each core can execute two threads, so we will have four parallel threads.
- **A computer with an AMD A8-640 APU with Windows 10 and 8 GB of RAM**: This processor has four cores.

For the first query, with the words `james` and `bond`, these are the execution times obtained in milliseconds:

	Intel Architecture		AMD Architecture	
	Serial	Concurrent	Serial	Concurrent
Basic search	1310.845	650.83	3286.336	1732.431
Reduced search	1179.955	645.184	3172.025	1521.285
HTML search	1457.035	785.553	3351.34	2089.5
Preload search	84.174	43.716	152.663	104.394
Executor search	90.714	47.865	144.375	111.829

For the second query, with the words `gone`, `with`, `the`, and `wind`, these are the execution times obtained in milliseconds:

	Intel Architecture		AMD Architecture	
	Serial	Concurrent	Serial	Concurrent
Basic search	1425.664	853.543	3822.322	1787.31
Reduced search	1159.872	644.429	3236.021	1540.008
HTML search	1428.503	807.955	3358.694	2330.248
Preload search	75.803	49.417	161.131	120.313
Executor search	89.737	44.969	149.358	109.485

For the third query, with the words `rocky`, these are the execution times obtained in milliseconds:

	Intel Architecture		AMD Architecture	
	Serial	Concurrent	Serial	Concurrent
Basic search	1274.524	706.979	3163.459	1446.918
Reduced search	1165.619	767.027	3167.887	1586.318
HTML search	1167.504	677.001	3196.033	2224.549
Preload search	74.287	45.014	140.17	101.741
Executor search	81.929	47.868	142.389	107.507

Finally, these are the average execution times in milliseconds for the methods that return information about the inverted index:

	Intel Architecture		AMD Architecture	
	Serial	Concurrent	Serial	Concurrent
`getWordsInFile1`	80.112	37.111	121.379	79.084
`getWordsInFile2`	68.627	30.371	121.452	75.397
`getAverageTfxidf`	127.382	62.966	259.749	145.967
`maxTfxidf`	31.64	28.207	89.013	76.604
`minTfxidf`	40.256	30.228	91.784	82.566

We can draw the following conclusions:

- When we read the inverted index to obtain the list of relevant documents, concurrent versions of the algorithms give us better performance.
- When we work with a preload version of the inverted index, concurrent versions of the algorithms give us better performance in all cases too.
- For the methods that give us information about the inverted index, concurrent versions of the algorithms always give us better performance.

We can compare the parallel and sequential streams for the three queries in this end using the speed-up, for example, for the 'James Bond' query pre-loading the inverted index:

$$S_{AMD} = \frac{T_{serial}}{T_{concurrent}} = \frac{152.663}{104.304} = 1.46$$

$$S_{Intel} = \frac{T_{serial}}{T_{concurrent}} = \frac{84.174}{43.716} = 1.92$$

Finally, in our third approach, we generate an HTML web page with the results of the queries. These are the first results with the query `james bond`:

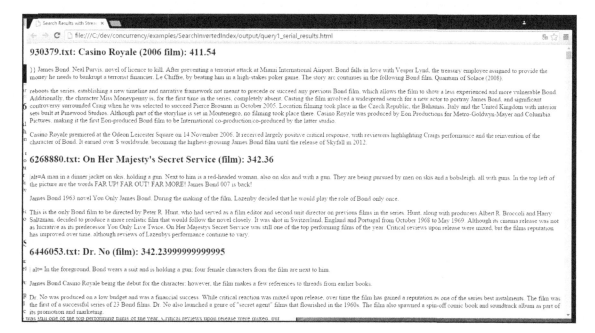

For the query `gone with the wind`, these are the first results:

Finally, these are the first results for the query `rocky`:

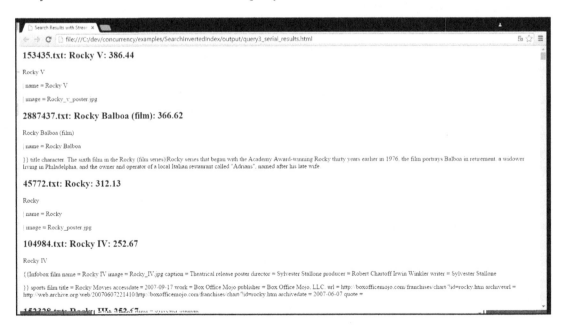

Summary

In this chapter, we were introduced to streams, a new feature introduced in Java 8 inspired by functional programming, and got ready to work with the new lambda expressions. A stream is a sequence of data (is not a data structure), which allows you to apply a sequence of operations in a sequential or concurrent way to filter, convert, sort, reduce, or organize those elements to obtain a final object.

You also learned the main characteristics of the streams that we have to take into account when we use streams in our sequential or concurrent applications.

Finally, we used streams in two samples. In the first sample, we used almost all the methods provided by the `Stream` interface to calculate the statistical data of a large Dataset. We used the Bank Marketing dataset of the UCI Machine Learning Repository with its 45,211 records. In the second sample, we implemented different approaches to a search application in an inverted index to obtain the most relevant documents to a query. This is one of the most common tasks in the information retrieval field. For this purpose, we used the `reduce()` method as the terminal operation of our streams.

In the next chapter, we will continue working with streams, but with more focus on the `collect()` terminal operation.

9
Processing Massive Datasets with Parallel Streams - The Map and Collect Model

In `Chapter 8`, *Processing Massive Datasets with Parallel Streams - The Map and Reduce Model*, we introduced the concept of streams . A `Stream` is a sequence of elements that can be processed in a parallel or sequential way. In this chapter, you will learn how to work with streams with the following topics:

- The collect() method
- The first example - searching data without indexing
- The second example - a recommendation system
- The third example - common contacts in a social network

Using streams to collect data

In `Chapter 8`, *Processing Massive Datasets with Parallel Streams - The Map and Reduce Model*, we made an introduction to streams. Let's remember their most important characteristics:

- Streams don't store their elements. They only process the elements stored on a data source (a data structure, a file, and so on)
- Streams can't be reusable
- Streams make a lazy processing of data

- The stream operation cannot modify the stream source
- Streams allow you to chain operations so the output of one operation is the input of the next one

A stream is formed by the following three main elements:

- A source that generates stream elements
- Zero or more intermediate operations that generate output as another stream
- One terminal operation that generates a result that could be either a simple object, array, collection, map, or anything else

The `Stream` API provides different terminal operations, but there are two more significant operations for their flexibility and power. In `Chapter 8`, *Processing Massive Datasets with Parallel Streams - The Map and Reduce Model*, you learned how to use the `reduce()` method, and in this chapter, you will learn how to use the `collect()` method. Let's make an introduction to this method.

The collect() method

The `collect()` method allows you to transform and group the elements of the stream generating a new data structure with the final results of the stream. You can use up to three different data types: an input data type, the data type of the input elements that come from the stream, an intermediate data type used to store the elements while the `collect()` method is running, and an output data type returned by the `collect()` method.

There are two different versions of the `collect()` method. The first version accepts the following three functional parameters:

- **Supplier**: This is a function that creates an object of the intermediate data type. If you use a sequential stream, this method will be called once. If you use a parallel stream, this method may be called many times and must produce a fresh object every time.
- **Accumulator**: This function is called to process an input element and store it in the intermediate data structure.
- **Combiner**: This function is called to merge two intermediate data structures into one. This function will be only called with parallel streams.

This version of the `collect()` method works with two different data types: the input data type of the elements that comes from the stream and the intermediate data type that will be used to store the intermediate elements and to return the final result.

The second version of the `collect()` method accepts an object that implements the `Collector` interface. You can implement this interface by yourself, but it's easier to use the `Collector.of()` static method. The arguments of this method are as follows:

- **Supplier**: This function creates an object of the intermediate data type, and it works as seen earlier
- **Accumulator**: This function is called to process an input element, transform it if necessary, and store it in the intermediate data structure
- **Combiner**: This function is called to merge two intermediate data structures into one, and it works as seen earlier
- **Finisher**: This function is called to transform the intermediate data structure into a final data structure if you need to make a final transformation or computation
- **Characteristics**: You can use this final variable argument to indicate some characteristics of the collector you are creating

Actually, there's a slight difference between the two versions. The three-param collector accepts a combiner, that is `BiConsumer`, and it must merge the second intermediate result into the first one. Unlike that, this combiner is `BinaryOperator` and should return the combiner. Therefore, it has the freedom to merge either the second inside the first or the first inside the second, or create a new intermediate result. There is another version of the `of()` method, which accepts the same arguments except the finisher; in this case, the finishing transformation is not performed.

Java provides you with some predefined collectors in the `Collectors` factory class. You can get those collectors using one of its static methods. Some of those methods are:

- `averagingDouble()`, `averagingInt()`, and `averagingLong()`: This returns a collector that allows you to calculate the arithmetic mean of a `double`, `int`, or `long` function.
- `groupingBy()`: This returns a collector that allows you to group the elements of a stream by an attribute of its objects, generating a map where the keys are the values of the selected attribute and the values are a list of the objects that have a determined value.
- `groupingByConcurrent()`: This is similar to the previous one except there are two important differences. The first one is that it may work faster in the parallel but slower in the sequential mode than the `groupingBy()` method. The second and most important difference is that the `groupingByConcurrent()` function is an unordered collector. The items in the lists are not guaranteed to be in the same order as in the stream. The `groupingBy()` collector, on the other hand, guarantees the ordering.

- `joining()`: This returns a `Collector` factory class that concatenates the input elements into a string.
- `partitioningBy()`: This returns a `Collector` factory class that makes a partition of the input elements based on the results of a predicate.
- `summarizingDouble()`, `summarizingInt()`, and `summarizingLong()`: These return a `Collector` factory class that calculates summary statistics of the input elements.
- `toMap()`: This returns a `Collector` factory class that allows you to transform input elements into a map based on two mapping functions.
- `toConcurrentMap()`: This is similar to the previous one, but in a concurrent way. Without a custom merger, `toConcurrentMap()` is just faster for parallel streams. As occurs with `groupingByConcurrent()`, this is an unordered collector too, whereas `toMap()` uses the encounter order to make the conversion.
- `toList()`:This returns a `Collector` factory class that stores the input elements into a list.
- `toCollection()`: This method allows you to accumulate the input elements into a new `Collection` factory class (`TreeSet`, `LinkedHashSet`, and so on) in the encounter order. The method receives an implementation of the `Supplier` interface that creates the collection as a parameter.
- `maxBy()` and `minBy()`: These return a `Collector` factory class that produces the maximal and minimal element according to the comparator passed as a parameter.
- `toSet()`: This returns a `Collector` that stores the input elements into a set.

The first example - searching data without an index

In `Chapter 8`, *Processing Massive Datasets with Parallel Streams - The Map and Reduce Model*, you learned how to implement a search tool to look for the documents similar to an input query using an inverted index. This data structure makes the search operation easier and faster, but there will be situations where you will have to make a search operation over a big set of data and you won't have an inverted index to help you. In these cases, you have to process all the elements of the dataset to get the correct results. In this example, you will see one of these situations and how the `reduce()` method of the `Stream` API can help you.

To implement this example, you will use a subset of the **Amazon product co-purchasing network metadata** that includes information about 548,552 products sold by Amazon, which includes title, salesrank, and the lists of similar products, categories, and reviews. You can download this dataset from `https://snap.stanford.edu/data/amazon-meta.html`. We have taken the first 20,000 products and stored each product record in a separate file. We have changed the format of some of the fields to ease the data processing. All the fields have the `property:value` format.

Basic classes

We have some classes that are shared between the concurrent and serial versions. Let's see the details of each one.

The Product class

The `Product` class stores the information about a product. The following are the `Product` classes:

- `id`: This is a unique identifier of the product.
- `asin`: This is the Amazon standard identification number.
- `title`: This is the title of the product.
- `group`: This is the group of the product. This attribute can take the values `Baby Product`, `Book`, `CD`, `DVD`, `Music`, `Software`, `Sports`, `Toy`, `Video`, or `Video Games`.
- `salesrank`: This indicates the Amazon salesrank.
- `similar`: This is the number of similar items included in the file.
- `categories`: This is a list of `String` objects with the categories assigned to the product.
- `reviews`: This is a list of `Review` objects with the reviews (user and value) assigned to the product.

This class includes only the definition of the attributes and the corresponding `getXXX()` and `setXXX()` methods, so its source code is not included.

The Review class

As we mentioned earlier, the Product class includes a list of Review objects with the information of the reviews made by the users to a product. This class stores the information of each review in the following two attributes:

- user: The internal code of the user that made the review
- value: The score given by the user to the product

This class includes only the definition of the attributes and the corresponding getXXX() and setXXX() methods, so its source code is not included.

The ProductLoader class

The ProductLoader class allows you to load the information of a product from a file to a Product object. It implements the load() method that receives a Path object with the path to the file with the information of the product and returns a Product object. This is its source code:

```
public class ProductLoader {
    public static Product load(Path path) {
        try (BufferedReader reader = Files.newBufferedReader(path)) {
            Product product=new Product();
            String line=reader.readLine();
            product.setId(line.split(":")[1]);
            line=reader.readLine();
            product.setAsin(line.split(":")[1]);
            line=reader.readLine();
            product.setTitle(line.substring (line.indexOf(':')+1));
            line=reader.readLine();
            product.setGroup(line.split(":")[1]);
            line=reader.readLine();
            product.setSalesrank(Long.parseLong (line.split(":")[1]));
            line=reader.readLine();
            product.setSimilar(line.split(":")[1]);
            line=reader.readLine();

            int numItems=Integer.parseInt(line.split(":")[1]);

            for (int i=0; i<numItems; i++) {
                line=reader.readLine();
                product.addCategory(line.split(":")[1]);
            }

            line=reader.readLine();
```

```
        numItems=Integer.parseInt(line.split(":")[1]);
        for (int i=0; i<numItems; i++) {
          line=reader.readLine();
          String tokens[]=line.split(":");
          Review review=new Review();
          review.setUser(tokens[1]);
          review.setValue(Short.parseShort(tokens[2]));
          product.addReview(review);
        }
        return product;
      } catch (IOException x) {
        throw newe UncheckedIOException(x);
      }


    }
  }
```

The first approach - basic search

The first approach receives a word as the input query and searches all the files that store the information of the products, whether that word is included in one of the fields that define the product, no matter which. It will only show the name of the file that includes the word.

To implement this basic approach, we have implemented the ConcurrentMainBasicSearch class that implements the main() method. First, we initialize the query and the base path that stores all the files:

```
public class ConcurrentMainBasicSearch {

  public static void main(String args[]) {
    String query = args[0];
    Path file = Paths.get("data");
```

We need only one stream to generate a list of strings with the results as follows:

```
try {
  Date start, end;
  start = new Date();
  ConcurrentLinkedDeque<String> results = Files.walk(file,
          FileVisitOption.FOLLOW_LINKS).parallel().filter(f ->
          f.toString().endsWith(".txt"))
          .collect(ArrayList<String>::new,
          new ConcurrentStringAccumulator (query), List::addAll);
  end = new Date();
```

Our stream contains the following elements:

1. We start the stream with the `walk()` method of the `Files` class passing the base `Path` object of our collection of files as a parameter. This method will return all the files as a stream and directories stored under that route.
2. Then, we convert the stream into a concurrent one using the `parallel()` method.
3. We are only interested in the files that end with the `.txt` extension, so we filter them using the `filter()` method.
4. Finally, we use the `collect()` method to convert the stream of `Path` objects into `ConcurrentLinkedDeque` of `String` objects with the names of the files.

We use the three parameters version of the `collect()` method using the following functional parameters:

- **Supplier**: We use the `new` method reference of the `ArrayList` class to create a new data structure per thread to store the corresponding results.
- **Accumulator**: We have implemented our own accumulator in the `ConcurrentStringAccumulator` class. We will describe the details of this class later.
- **Combiner**: We use the `addAll()` method of the `ConcurrentLinkedDeque` class to join two data structures. In this case, all the elements from the second collection will be added to the first one. The first collection will be used for further combining or as a final result.

Finally, we write the results obtained with the stream in the console:

```
System.out.println("Results for Query: "+query);
System.out.println("*************");
results.forEach(System.out::println);
System.out.println("Execution Time: "+(end.getTime()-
                    start.getTime()));
} catch (IOException e) {
    e.printStackTrace();
}
}
}
```

The accumulator functional parameter will be executed each time we want to process a path of the stream to evaluate whether we have to include its name into the result list. To implement this functionality, we have implemented the `ConcurrentStringAccumulator` class. Let's see the details of this class.

The ConcurrentStringAccumulator class

The `ConcurrentStringAccumulator` class loads a file with the information of a product to determine whether it contains the term of the query. It implements the `BiConsumer` interface because we want to use it as a parameter of the `collect()` method. We have parameterized that interface with the `List<String>` and `Path` classes:

```
public class ConcurrentStringAccumulator implements BiConsumer
                    <List<String>, Path> {
```

It defines the query as an internal attribute that is initialized in the constructor as follows:

```
private String word;

public ConcurrentStringAccumulator (String word) {
  this.word=word.toLowerCase();
}
```

Then, we implement the `accept()` method defined in the `BiConsumer` interface. This method receives two parameters: one of the `ConcurrentLinkedDeque<String>` classes and one of the `Path` classes.

To load the file and determine whether it contains the query, we use the following stream:

```
@Override
public void accept(List<String> list, Path path) {

  long counter;

  try  {
    counter = Files.lines(path).map(l -> l.split(":")[1].toLowerCase())
              .filter(l -> l.contains(word.toLowerCase())).count();
```

Our stream contains the following elements:

1. First, we load the lines of the file into a `Stream` using the `lines()` method of the `Files` class. Every line of the file has the format `property:value`.
2. Then, we take the value of every property using the `map()` method.
3. Then, we take only the lines that contains the word we're searching for with the `filter()` method.
4. Finally, we count the number of elements that remain in the `Stream` with the `count()` method.

If the counter variable has a value bigger than 0, the file contains the query term, and we include the name of the file in the `ConcurrentLinkedDeque` class with the results:

```
      if (counter>0) {
        list.add(path.toString());
      }
    } catch (Exception e) {
      System.out.println(path);
      e.printStackTrace();
    }
  }
}
```

The second approach - advanced search

Our basic search has some drawbacks:

- We look for the query term in all the properties, but maybe we only want to look for it in some of them; for example, in the title
- We only show the name of the file, but it would be more informative if we show additional information as the title of the product

To solve these problems, we are going to implement the `ConcurrentMainSearch` class that implements the `main()` method. First, we initialize the query and the base `Path` object that stores all the files:

```
public class ConcurrentMainSearch {
  public static void main(String args[]) {
    String query = args[0];
    Path file = Paths.get("data");
```

Then, we generate a `ConcurrentLinkedDeque` class of `Product` objects using the following stream:

```
try {
  Date start, end;
  start=new Date();
  List<Product> results = Files.walk(file, FileVisitOption
                          .FOLLOW_LINKS).parallel().filter(f -> f
                          .toString().endsWith(".txt"))
                          .collect(ArrayList<Product>::new, new
                          ConcurrentObjectAccumulator(query),
                          List::addAll);
```

This stream has the same elements as the one we implemented in the basic approach with the following two changes:

- In the `collect()` method, we use the `ConcurrentObjectAccumulator` class in the accumulator parameter
- We parameterize the `ConcurrentLinkedDeque` class with the `Product` one

Finally, we write the results in the console, but in this case, we write the title of each product:

```
System.out.println("Results");
System.out.println("*************");
results.forEach(p -> System.out.println(p.getTitle()));
System.out.println("Execution Time: "+(end.getTime()-
                   start.getTime()));

} catch (IOException e) {
    e.printStackTrace();
}
}
}
```

You can change this code to write whatever information about the product you like, such as the salesrank or the categories.

The most important change between this implementation and the previous one is the `ConcurrentObjectAccumulator` class. Let's see the details of this class.

The ConcurrentObjectAccumulator class

The `ConcurrentObjectAccumulator` class implements the `BiConsumer` interface parameterized with the `ConcurrentLinkedDeque<Product>` and `Path` classes because we want to use it in the `collect()` method. It defines an internal attribute named `word` to store the query term. This attribute is initialized in the constructor of the class:

```
public class ConcurrentObjectAccumulator implements BiConsumer
                              <List<Product>, Path> {

    private String word;

    public ConcurrentObjectAccumulator(String word) {
        this.word = word;
    }
```

The implementation of the `accept()` method (defined in the `BiConsumer` interface) is very simple:

```
@Override
public void accept(List<Product> list, Path path) {

  Product product=ProductLoader.load(path);

  if (product.getTitle().toLowerCase().contains(word.toLowerCase())){
    list.add(product);
  }
}

}
```

The method receives the `Path` object that points to the file we are going to process as a parameter and the `ConcurrentLinkedDeque` class to store the results. We load the file in a `Product` object using the `ProductLoader` class and then check whether the title of the product contains the query term. If it contains the query, we add the `Product` object to the `ConcurrentLinkedDeque` class.

A serial implementation of the example

As with the rest of the examples in this book, we have implemented a serial version of both versions of the search operations to verify that the concurrent stream allows us to get an improvement of the performance.

You can implement the serial equivalent of the four classes described earlier by deleting the `parallel()` calls in the `Stream` objects to make the streams concurrent.

With the source code of the book, we have included the `SerialMainBasicSearch`, `SerialMainSearch`, `SerialStringAccumulator`, and `SerialObjectAccumulator` classes, which are the serial equivalent ones with the changes commented earlier.

Comparing the implementations

We have tested our implementations (the two approaches: serial and concurrent versions) to compare their execution times. To test them, we have used three different queries:

- Patterns
- Java
- Tree

We have executed the examples using the JMH framework (`http://openjdk.java.net/projects/code-tools/jmh/`) that allows you to implement micro benchmarks in Java. Using a framework for benchmarking is a better solution that simply measures time using methods such as `currentTimeMillis()` or `nanoTime()`. We have executed them 10 times in two different architectures:

- A computer with an Intel Core i5-5300 CPU with Windows 7 and 16 GB of RAM: This processor has two cores and each core can execute two threads, so we will have four parallel threads.
- A computer with an AMD A8-640 APU with Windows 10 and 8 GB of RAM: This processor has four cores.

These are the results in milliseconds. First, we show you the results of the string search operation:

String Search						
	Intel Architecture			AMD Architecture		
	Java	Patterns	Tree	Java	Patterns	Tree
Serial	735.569	709.484	700.929	2245.603	2243.152	2207.034
Concurrent	401.276	524.252	395.022	1058.712	1045.201	1057.155

Now, the results of the object search operation:

Object search						
	Intel Architecture			AMD Architecture		
	Java	Patterns	Tree	Java	Patterns	Tree
Serial	867.534	840.082	854.299	2723.535	2634.614	2640.329
Concurrent	460.29	463.201	476.244	1218.425	1232.45	1204.245

We can draw the following conclusions:

- The results obtained with different queries are very similar. There's only a few milliseconds of difference between them.
- The execution time of the string search is always better than the execution time of the object search.
- Concurrent streams get better performance than serial ones in all cases.

If we compare the concurrent and serial versions, for example, for the string search with the query patterns using the speed-up, we obtain the following result:

$$S_{AMD} = \frac{T_{serial}}{T_{concurrent}} = \frac{2243.152}{1045.201} = 2.15$$

$$S_{Intel} = \frac{T_{serial}}{T_{concurrent}} = \frac{709.484}{524.252} = 1.35$$

The second example - a recommendation system

A **recommendation system** recommends a product or a service to a customer based on the products/services he has bought/used and in the products/services bought/used by the users that have bought/used the same services as him.

We have used the example explained in the previous section to implement a recommendation system. Each description of a product includes the reviews of a number of customers to a product. This review includes the score the customer gives to the product.

In this example, you will use these reviews to get a list of the products that may be interesting to a customer. We will obtain the list of the products purchased by a customer. In order to get that list, a list of the users who have purchased those products and the list of products purchased by those users are sorted using the average score given in the reviews. That will be the suggested products for the user.

Common classes

We have added two new classes to the ones used in the previous section. These classes are:

- ProductReview: This class extends the product class with two new attributes
- ProductRecommendation: This class stores the information of the recommendation of a product

Let's see the details of both classes.

The ProductReview class

The ProductReview class extends the Product class, adding two new attributes:

- buyer: This attribute stores the name of a customer of the product
- value: This attribute stores the value given by this customer to the product in his review

The class includes the definition of the attributes: the corresponding getXXX() and setXXX() methods, a constructor to create a ProductReview object from a Product object, and the values for the new attributes. It's very simple, so its source code is not included.

The ProductRecommendation class

The `ProductRecommendation` class stores the necessary information for a product recommendation that includes the following:

- `title`: The title of the product we are recommending
- `value`: The score of that recommendation, which is calculated as the average score of all the reviews for that product

This class includes the definition of the attributes, the corresponding `getXXX()` and `setXXX()` methods, and the implementation of the `compareTo()` methods (the class implements the `Comparable` interface) that will allow us to sort the recommendations in descending order by its value. It's very simple, so its source code is not included.

Recommendation system - the main class

We have implemented our algorithm in the `ConcurrentMainRecommendation` class to obtain the list of recommended products to a customer. This class implements the `main()` method that receives as a parameter the ID of the customer whose recommended products we want to obtain. We have the following code:

```
public static void main(String[] args) {
   String user = args[0];
   Path file = Paths.get("data");
   try {
     Date start, end;
     start=new Date();
```

We have used different streams to transform the data in the final solution. The first one loads the whole list of the `Product` objects from its files:

```
List<Product> productList = Files.walk(file, FileVisitOption
                        .FOLLOW_LINKS).parallel().filter(f-> f
                        .toString().endsWith(".txt"))
                        .collect(ArrayList<Product>::new, new
                        ConcurrentLoaderAccumulator(),
                        List::addAll);
```

This stream has the following elements:

1. We start the stream with the `walk()` method of the `Files` class. This method will create a stream to process all the files and directories under the data directory.
2. Then, we use the `parallel()` method to convert the stream into a concurrent one.
3. Then, we get the files with the extension `.txt` only.
4. Finally, we use the `collect()` method to obtain a `ConcurrentLinkedDeque` class of the `Product` objects. It's very similar to the one used in the previous section with the difference that we use another accumulator object. In this case, we use the `ConcurrentLoaderAccumulator` class, which we will describe later.

Once we have the list of products, we are going to organize those products in a map using the identifier of the customer as the key for that map. We use the `ProductReview` class to store the information of the customers of the products. We need a `ProductReview` object for each review of a `Product`. We use the following stream to make the transformation:

```
Map<String, List<ProductReview>> productsByBuyer=
            productList.parallelStream()
            .<ProductReview>flatMap(p -> p.getReviews()
            .stream().map(r -> new ProductReview(p, r.getUser(),
            r.getValue())))).collect(Collectors
            .groupingByConcurrent( p -> p.getBuyer()));
```

This stream has the following elements:

1. We start the stream with the `parallelStream()` method of the `productList` object, so we create a concurrent stream.
2. Then, we use the `flatMap()` method to convert the stream of `Product` objects we have into a unique stream of `ProductReview` objects.
3. Finally, we use the `collect()` method to generate the final map. In this case, we have used the predefined collector generated by the `groupingByConcurrent()` method of the `Collectors` class. The returned collector will generate a map where the keys will be the different values of the buyer attribute and the values of a list of `ProductReview` objects with the information of the products purchased by that user. This transformation will be done, as the method name indicates, in a concurrent way.

The next stream is the most important stream of this example. We take the products purchased by a customer and generate the recommendations to that customer. It's a two-phase process made by one stream. In the first phase, we obtain the users that purchased the products purchased by the original customer. In the second phase, we generate a map with the products purchased by those customers with all the reviews of those products made by those customers. This is the code for that stream:

```
Map<String,List<ProductReview>> recommendedProducts= productsByBuyer
                        .get(user).parallelStream().map(p -> p
                        .getReviews()).flatMap(Collection::stream)
                        .map(r -> r.getUser()).distinct()
                        .map(productsByBuyer::get)
                        .flatMap(Collection::stream)
                        .collect(Collectors.groupingByConcurrent
                                    (p -> p.getTitle()));
```

We have the following elements in that stream:

1. First, we get the list of products purchased by the user and generate a concurrent stream using the `parallelStream()` method.
2. Then, we get all the reviews for those products using the `map()` method.
3. At this moment, we have a stream of `List<Review>`. We convert that stream into a stream of `Review` objects. Now we have a stream with all the reviews of the products purchased by the user.
4. Then, we transform that stream into a stream of `String` objects with the names of the users who made the reviews.
5. Then, we get the unique names of the users with the `distinct()` method. Now we have a stream of `String` objects with the names of the users who purchased the same products as the original user.
6. Then, we use the `map()` method to transform each customer into its list of purchased products.
7. At this moment, we have a stream of `List<ProductReview>` objects. We convert that stream into a stream of `ProductReview` objects using the `flatMap()` method.
8. Finally, we generate a map of products using the `collect()` method and the `groupingByConcurrent()` collector. The keys of the map will be the title of the product and the values of the list of `ProductReview` objects with the reviews made by the customers obtained earlier.

To finish our recommendation algorithm, we need to complete one last step. For every product, we want to calculate its average score in the reviews and sort the list in descending order to show the top-rated products at first place. To make that transformation, we use an additional stream:

```
ConcurrentLinkedDeque<ProductRecommendation> recommendations
        = recommendedProducts.entrySet().parallelStream()
            .map(entry -> new ProductRecommendation(entry
            .getKey(), entry.getValue().stream().mapToInt(p->
            p.getValue()).average().getAsDouble()))
            .sorted().collect(Collectors.toCollection
                            (ConcurrentLinkedDeque::new));
    end=new Date();
    recommendations. forEach(pr -> System.out.println (pr.getTitle()
                                    +": "+pr.getValue()));

    System.out.println("Execution Time: "+(end.getTime()-
                    start.getTime())));

} catch (IOException e) {
    e.printStackTrace();
}
}
}
```

We process the map obtained in the previous step. For each product, we process its list of reviews, generating a ProductRecommendation object. The value of this object is calculated as the average value of each review using a stream using the mapToInt() method to transform the stream of ProductReview objects into a stream of integers and the average() method to get the average value of all the numbers in the string.

Finally, in the recommendations ConcurrentLinkedDeque class, we have a list of ProductRecommendation objects. We sort that list using the other stream with the sorted() method. We use that stream to write the final list in the console.

The ConcurrentLoaderAccumulator class

To implement this example, we have used the `ConcurrentLoaderAccumulator` class used as the accumulator function in the `collect()` method that transforms the stream of `Path` objects with the routes of all the files to process into the `ConcurrentLinkedDeque` class of `Product` objects. This is the source code of this class:

```
public class ConcurrentLoaderAccumulator implements
  BiConsumer<List<Product>, Path> {

    @Override
    public void accept(List<Product> list, Path path) {

    Product product=ProductLoader.load(path);
    list.add(product);

    }
}
```

It implements the `BiConsumer` interface. The `accept()` method uses the `ProductLoader` class (explained earlier in this chapter) to load the product information from the file and add the resultant `Product` object in the `List` class received as a parameter.

The serial version

As with other examples in the book, we have implemented a serial version of this example to check that parallel streams improve the performance of the application. To implement this serial version, we have to follow these steps:

1. Replace the `ConcurrentLinkedDeque` data structure by the `List` or `ArrayList` data structures.
2. Change the `parallelStrem()` method by the `stream()` method.
3. Change the `gropingByConcurrent()` method by the `groupingBy()` method.

You can see the serial version of this example in the source code of the book.

Comparing the two versions

To compare the serial and concurrent versions of our recommendation system, we have obtained the recommended products for three users:

- A2JOYUS36FLG4Z
- A2JW67OY8U6HHK
- A2VE83MZF98ITY

We have executed the examples using the JMH framework (http://openjdk.java.net/projects/code-tools/jmh/) that allows you to implement micro benchmarks in Java. Using a framework for benchmarking is a better solution that simply measures time using methods as currentTimeMillis() or nanoTime(). We have executed them 10 times in two different architectures:

- **A computer with an Intel Core i5-5300 CPU with Windows 7 and 16 GB of RAM**: This processor has two cores and each core can execute two threads, so we will have four parallel threads.
- **A computer with an AMD A8-640 APU with Windows 10 and 8 GB of RAM**: This processor has four cores.

These are the results in milliseconds:

	A2JOYUS36FLG4Z	**A2JW67OY8U6HHK**	**A2VE83MZF98ITY**
Intel Architecture			
Serial	1639.685	1542.804	1595.341
Concurrent	1030.635	1061.247	1054.213
AMD Architecture			
Serial	3361.956	3412.680	3351.890
Concurrent	1866.653	1871.919	1999.916

We can draw the following conclusions:

- The results obtained are very similar for the three users
- The execution time of the concurrent streams is always better than the execution time of the sequential ones

If we compare the concurrent and serial versions, for example, for the second user using the speed-up, we obtain the following result:

$$S_{AMD} = \frac{T_{serial}}{T_{concurrent}} = \frac{3412.680}{1871.919} = 1.82$$

$$S_{Intel} = \frac{T_{serial}}{T_{concurrent}} = \frac{1542.804}{1061.247} = 1.45$$

The third example - common contacts in a social network

Social networks are transforming our society and the way people relate to each other. Facebook, LinkedIn, Twitter, and Instagram have millions of users who use these networks to share life moments with their friends, make new professional contacts, promote their professional brand, meet new people, or simply know the latest trends in the world.

We can see a social network as a graph where users are the nodes of the graph and relations between users are the arcs of the graph. As occurs with graphs, there are social networks such as Facebook, where relations between users are undirected or bidirectional. If a user *A* is connected with user *B*, the user *B* is connected with *A* too. On the contrary, there are social networks such as Twitter where relations between users are directed. We say in this case that user *A* follows user *B*, but the contrary is not necessarily true.

In this section, we are going to implement an algorithm to calculate the common contacts for every pair of users in a social network with bidirectional relations between users. We are going to implement the algorithm described in `http://stevekrenzel.com/finding-frien ds-with-mapreduce`. The main steps of that algorithm are as follows:

- Our data source will be a file where we store every user with their contacts:

```
A-B,C,D,
B-A,C,D,E,
C-A,B,D,E,
D-A,B,C,E,
E-B,C,D,
```

- This means that user A has users B, C, and D as contacts. Take into account that the relations are bidirectional, so if B is a contact for A, A will be a contact for B too and both relations have to be represented in the file. So, we have elements with the following two parts:
  - A user identifier
  - The list of contacts for that user

- In the next step, we generate a set of elements with three parts per every element. The three parts are:
  - A user identifier
  - The user identifier of a friend
  - The list of contacts for that user

- Thus, for user A, we will generate the following elements:

```
A-B-B,C,D
A-C-B,C,D
A-D,B,C,D
```

- We follow the same process for all the elements. We are going to store the two user identifiers alphabetically sorted. Thus, for user B, we generate the following elements:

```
A-B-A,C,D,E
B-C-A,C,D,E
B-D-A,C,D,E
B-E-A,C,D,E
```

- Once we have generated all the new elements, we group them for the two user identifiers. For example, for the tuple A-B we will generate the following group:

```
A-B-(B,C,D),(A,C,D,E)
```

- Finally, we calculate the intersection between the two lists. The resultant lists are the common contacts between the two users. For example, what the users A and B have in common with the contacts C and D.

To test our algorithm, we have used two datasets:

- The test sample presented earlier.
- The social circles: the Facebook dataset that you can download from
  `https://snap.stanford.edu/data/egonets-Facebook.html` contains the contact
  information of 4,039 users from Facebook. We have transformed the original data
  into the data format used by our example.

Base classes

As with other examples in the book, we have implemented the serial and concurrent
versions of this example to verify that parallel streams improve the performance of our
application. Both versions share some classes.

The Person class

The `Person` class stores the information about every person in the social network that
includes the following:

- Its user ID, stored in the ID attribute
- The list of contacts of that user, stored as a list of `String` objects in the contacts
  attribute

The class declares both attributes and the corresponding `getXXX()` and `setXXX()`
methods. We also need a constructor to create the list and a method named `addContact()`
to add a single contact to the list of contacts. The source code of this class is very simple, so
it won't be included here.

The PersonPair class

The `PersonPair` class extends the `Person` class, adding the attribute to store the second
user identifier. We called this attribute `otherId`. This class declares the attribute and
implements the corresponding `getXXX()` and `setXXX()` methods. We need an additional
method named `getFullId()` that returns a string with the two user identifiers separated
by a `,` character. The source code of this class is very simple, so it won't be included here.

The DataLoader class

The `DataLoader` class loads the file with the information of the users and their contacts and converts it into a list of `Person` objects. It implements only a static method named `load()` that receives the path of the file as a `String` object as a parameter and returns the list of `Person` objects.

As we mentioned earlier, the file has the following format:

```
User-C1,C2,C3...CN
```

Here, `User` is the identifier of the user, and `C1, C2, C3....CN` are the identifiers of the contacts of that user.

The source code of this class is very simple, so it won't be included here.

The concurrent version

First, let's analyze the concurrent version of this algorithm.

The CommonPersonMapper class

The `CommonPersonMapper` class is an auxiliary class that will be used later. It will generate all the `PersonPair` objects you can generate from a `Person` object. This class implements the `Function` interface parameterized with the `Person` and `List<PersonPair>` classes.

It implements the `apply()` method defined in the `Function` interface. First, we initialize the `List<PersonPair>` object that we're going to return and obtain and sort the list of contacts for the person:

```java
public class CommonPersonMapper implements Function<Person,
                                    List<PersonPair>> {

    @Override
    public List<PersonPair> apply(Person person) {

        List<PersonPair> ret=new ArrayList<>();

        List<String> contacts=person.getContacts();
        Collections.sort(contacts);
```

Then, we process the whole list of contacts creating the `PersonPair` object per contact. As we mentioned earlier, we store the two contacts sorted in alphabetical order. The lesser one in the ID field and the other in the `otherId` field:

```
for (String contact : contacts) {
  PersonPair personExt=new PersonPair();
  if (person.getId().compareTo(contact) < 0) {
    personExt.setId(person.getId());
    personExt.setOtherId(contact);
  } else {
    personExt.setId(contact);
    personExt.setOtherId(person.getId());
  }
```

Finally, we add the list of contacts to the new object and the object to the list of results. Once we have processed all the contacts, we return the list of results:

```
    personExt.setContacts(contacts);
    ret.add(personExt);
  }
  return ret;
  }
}
```

The ConcurrentSocialNetwork class

The `ConcurrentSocialNetwork` is the main class of this example. It implements only a static method named `bidirectionalCommonContacts()`. This method receives the list of persons of the social network with their contacts and returns a list of `PersonPair` objects with the common contacts between every pair of users who are contacts.

Internally, we use two different streams to implement our algorithm. We use the first one to transform the input list of `Person` objects into a map. The keys of this map will be the two identifiers of every pair of users, and the value will be a list of `PersonPair` objects with the contacts of both users. So, these lists will always have two elements. We have the following code:

```
public class ConcurrentSocialNetwork {

  public static List<PersonPair> bidirectionalCommonContacts
                              (List<Person> people) {    Map<String,
  List<PersonPair>> group = people.parallelStream()
```

```
.map(new CommonPersonMapper())
.flatMap(Collection::stream)
.collect(Collectors.groupingByConcurrent
                (PersonPair::getFullId));
```

This stream has the following components:

1. We create the stream using the `parallelStream()` method of the input list.
2. Then, we use the `map()` method and the `CommonPersonMapper` class explained earlier to transform every `Person` object in a list of `PersonPair` objects with all the possibilities for that object.
3. At this moment, we have a stream of `List<PersonPair>` objects. We use the `flatMap()` method to convert that stream into a stream of `PersonPair` objects.
4. Finally, we use the `collect()` method to generate the map using the collector returned by the `groupingByConcurrent()` method using the value returned by the `getFullId()` method as the keys for the map.

Then, we create a new collector using the `of()` method of the `Collectors` class. This collector will receive a `Collection` of strings as input, use an `AtomicReference<Collection<String>>` as an intermediate data structure, and return a `Collection` of strings as the return type:

```
Collector<Collection<String>, AtomicReference<Collection<String>>,
        Collection<String>> intersecting = Collector.of(() ->
            new AtomicReference<>(null), (acc, list) -> {
  (acc, list) -> {
  if (acc.get() == null) {
    acc.updateAndGet(value -> new ConcurrentLinkedQueue<>(list));
  } else {
    acc.get().retainAll(list);
  }
}, (acc1, acc2) -> {
  if (acc1.get() == null) return acc2;
    if (acc2.get() == null)
      return acc1;
    acc1.get().retainAll(acc2.get());
  return acc1;
}, (acc) -> acc.get() == null ? Collections.emptySet() :
            acc.get(), Collector.Characteristics.CONCURRENT,
            Collector.Characteristics.UNORDERED);
```

The first parameter of the `of()` method is the supplier function. This supplier is always called when we need to create an intermediate structure of data. In serial streams, this method is called only once, but in concurrent streams, this method will be called once per thread.

```
() -> new AtomicReference<>(null),
```

In our case, we simply create a new `AtomicReference` to store the `Collection<String>` object.

The second parameter of the `of()` method is the accumulator function. This function receives an intermediate data structure and an input value as parameters:

```
(acc, list) -> {
  if (acc.get() == null) {
    acc.updateAndGet(value -> new ConcurrentLinkedQueue<>(list));
  } else {
    acc.get().retainAll(list);
  }
}
```

In our case, the `acc` parameter is an `AtomicReference` and the `list` parameter is a `ConcurrentLinkedDeque`. If the `acc` reference stores a null value, we use the `updateAndGet()` method of the `AtomicReference`. This method updates the current value and returns the new value. In our case, we create a new `ConcurrentLinkedDeque` with the elements of the list. If the `AtomicReference` is not null, we use the `retainAll()` method to add all the elements of the list.

The third parameter of the `of()` method is the combiner function. This function is only called in parallel streams, and it receives two intermediate data structures as a parameter to generate only one.

```
(acc1, acc2) -> {
  if (acc1.get() == null)
    return acc2;
  if (acc2.get() == null)
    return acc1;
    acc1.get().retainAll(acc2.get());
  return acc1;
},
```

In our case, if one of the parameters is null, we return the other. Otherwise, we use the `retainAll()` method in the `acc1` parameter and return the result.

The fourth parameter of the `of()` method is the finisher function. This function converts the final intermediate data structure in the data structure we want to return. In our case, the intermediate and final data structures are the same, so no conversion is needed.

```
(acc) -> acc.get() == null ? Collections.emptySet() : acc.get(),
```

Finally, we use the last parameter to indicate to the collector that the collector is concurrent: the accumulator function can be called concurrently with the same result container from multiple threads, and unordered; that is to say, this operation will not preserve the original order of the elements.

As we have defined the collector, we now have to convert the map generated with the first stream into a list of `PersonPair` objects with the common contacts of each pair of users. We use the following code:

```
List<PersonPair> peopleCommonContacts = group
        .entrySet().parallelStream().map((entry) -> {
Collection<String> commonContacts =  entry
                .getValue().parallelStream().map(p -> p
                .getContacts()).collect(intersecting);
PersonPair person = new PersonPair();
person.setId(entry.getKey().split(",")[0]);
person.setOtherId(entry.getKey().split (",")[1]);
person.setContacts(new ArrayList<String> (commonContacts));
return person;
}).collect(Collectors.toList());

    return peopleCommonContacts;
  }
}
```

We use the `entySet()` method to process all the elements of the map. We create a `parallelStream()` method to process all the `Entry` objects and then use the `map()` method to convert every list of `PersonPair` objects into a unique `PersonPair` object with the common contacts.

For each entry, the key is the identifier of a pair of users concatenated with a , as a separator, and the values are a list of two `PersonPair` objects. The first one contains the contacts of one user, and the other contains the contacts of the other user.

We create a stream for that list to generate the common contacts of both users with the following elements:

1. We create the stream using the `parallelStream()` method of the list.
2. We use the `map()` method to replace each `PersonPair()` object for the list of contacts stored in it.
3. Finally, we use our collector to generate `ConcurrentLinkedDeque` with the common contacts.

Finally, we create a new `PersonPair` object with the identifier of both users and the list of common contacts. We add that object to the list of results. When all the elements of the map have been processed, we can return the list of results.

The ConcurrentMain class

The `ConcurrentMain` class implements the `main()` method to test our algorithm. As we mentioned earlier, we have tested it with the following two datasets:

- A very simple dataset to test the correctness of the algorithm
- A dataset based on real data from Facebook

This is the source code of this class:

```
public class ConcurrentMain {

  public static void main(String[] args) {

    Date start, end;
    System.out.println("Concurrent Main Bidirectional - Test");
    List<Person> people=DataLoader.load("data","test.txt");
    start=new Date();
    List<PersonPair> peopleCommonContacts= ConcurrentSocialNetwork
                          .bidirectionalCommonContacts (people);
    end=new Date();
    peopleCommonContacts.forEach(p -> System.out.println
            (p.getFullId()+": "+getContacts(p.getContacts())));
    System.out.println("Execution Time: "+(end.getTime()-
                    start.getTime()));
    System.out.println("Concurrent Main Bidirectional -
                    Facebook");
    people=DataLoader.load("data","facebook_contacts.txt");
    start=new Date();
    peopleCommonContacts= ConcurrentSocialNetwork
                          .bidirectionalCommonContacts (people);
```

```
    end=new Date();
    peopleCommonContacts.forEach(p -> System.out.println
                (p.getFullId()+": "+getContacts(p.getContacts())));
    System.out.println("Execution Time: "+(end.getTime()-
                        start.getTime()));

}

private static String formatContacts(List<String> contacts) {
    StringBuffer buffer=new StringBuffer();
    for (String contact: contacts) {
        buffer.append(contact+",");
    }
    return buffer.toString();
}
}
```

The serial version

As with other examples in this book, we have implemented a serial version of this example. This version is equal to the concurrent one but makes the following changes:

- Replace the `parallelStream()` method by the `stream()` method
- Replace the `ConcurrentLinkedDeque` data structure by the `ArrayList` data structure
- Replace the `groupingByConcurrent()` method by the `groupingBy()` method
- Don't use the final parameter in the `of()` method

Comparing the two versions

We have executed the examples using the JMH framework (`http://openjdk.java.net/projects/code-tools/jmh/`) that allows you to implement micro benchmarks in Java. Using a framework for benchmarking is a better solution that simply measures time using methods as `currentTimeMillis()` or `nanoTime()`. We have executed them 10 times in two different architectures:

- **A computer with an Intel Core i5-5300 CPU with Windows 7 and 16 GB of RAM**: This processor has two cores and each core can execute two threads, so we will have four parallel threads.
- **A computer with an AMD A8-640 APU with Windows 10 and 8 GB of RAM**: This processor has four cores.

These are the results in milliseconds:

	Example	Facebook
Intel Architecture		
Serial	0.562	3193.83
Concurrent	2.037	1778.239
AMD Archtiecture		
Serial	3.325	8953.173
Concurrent	2.976	3447.576

We can draw the following conclusions:

- For the example dataset, the serial version obtains a better execution time in the Intel architecture and very similar results in the AMD architecture. The reason for this result is that the example dataset has few elements.
- For the Facebook dataset, the concurrent version obtains better execution time in both architectures.

If we compare the concurrent and serial versions for the Facebook dataset, we obtain the following results:

$$S_{AMD} = \frac{T_{serial}}{T_{concurrent}} = \frac{8953.173}{3447.576} = 2.60$$

$$S_{Intel} = \frac{T_{serial}}{T_{concurrent}} = \frac{3193.83}{1778.239} = 1.80$$

Summary

In this chapter, we used the different versions of the `collect()` method provided by the `Stream` framework to transform and group the elements of a `Stream`. This and `Chapter 8`, *Processing Massive Datasets with Parallel Streams - the Map and Reduce Model*, teach you how to work with the whole stream API.

Basically, the `collect()` method needs a collector that processes the data of the stream and generates a data structure returned by the set of aggregate operations that forms the stream. A collector works with three different data structures-the class of the input elements, an intermediate data structure used while processing the input elements, and a final data structure that is returned.

We used the different versions of the `collect()` method to implement a search tool that must look for a query in a set of files without an inverted index, a recommendation system, and a tool to calculate the common contacts between two users in a social network.

In the next chapter, we will take a deep look at **Reactive Stream** programming, a new feature introduced in Java 9.

10
Asynchronous Stream Processing - Reactive Streams

Reactive streams (http://www.reactive-streams.org/) define a standard for asynchronous stream processing with non-blocking back pressure. The biggest problem with these kinds of systems is resource consumption. A fast producer can overload a slower consumer. The queue of data between those components can increase its size in excess and affects the behavior of the whole system. The back pressure mechanism ensures that the queue which mediates between the producer and a consumer has a limited number of elements.

Reactive streams define a minimal set of interfaces, methods, and protocols that describe the necessary operations and entities. They are based on the following three elements:

- A publisher of information
- One or more subscribers of that information
- A subscription between the publisher and a consumer

The reactive streams specification determines how these classes should interact between them, according to the following rules:

- The publisher will add the subscribers that want to be notified
- The subscriber receives a notification when they're added to a publisher
- The subscribers request one or more elements from the publisher in an asynchronous way, that is to say, the subscriber requests the element and continues with their execution
- When the publisher has an element to publish, it sends it to all its subscribers that have requested an element

As we mentioned before, all this communication is asynchronous, so we can take advantage of all the power of our multi-core processor.

Java 9 has included three interfaces, the `Flow.Publisher`, the `Flow.Subscriber`, and the `Flow.Subscription`, and a utility class, the `SubmissionPublisher` class, to allow us to implement reactive stream applications. In this recipe, you will learn how to use all these elements to implement a basic reactive stream application.

In this chapter, you will learn how to work with reactive streams in the following topics:

- Introduction to reactive streams in Java
- The first example - a centralized system for event notification
- The second example - a news system

Introduction to reactive streams in Java

In the introduction of this chapter, we explained what reactive streams are, which elements form the standard, and how those elements are implemented in Java:

- **The Flow.Publisher interface**: This interface represents a producer of items.
- **The Flow.Subscriber interface**: This interface represents a consumer of items.
- **The Flow.Subscription interface**: This interface represents the connection between a producer and a consumer. The class that implements it manages the item interchange between the producer and the consumer.

In addition to these three interfaces, we have the `SubmissionPublisher` class that implements the `Flow.Publisher` interface. It also uses an implementation of the `Flow.Subscription` interface. It implements the method of the `Flow.Publisher` interface that allows the subscription of consumers and also methods to send items to those consumers, so we only have to implement one or more classes that implement the `Flow.Subscriber` interface.

Let's look at the methods provided by those classes and interfaces in detail.

The Flow.Publisher interface

As we mentioned before, this interface represents a producer of items. It only provides one method:

- subscribe(): This method receives as a parameter an implementation of the Flow.Subscriber interface and adds that subscriber to its internal list of subscribers. This method doesn't return any results. Internally, it uses the methods provided by the Flow.Subscriber interface to send items, errors, and the subscription object to the subscribers.

The Flow.Subscriber interface

As we mentioned earlier, this interface represents a consumer of items. It provides four methods:

- onSubscribe(): This method is invoked by the publisher to complete the subscription of a subscriber. It sends to the subscriber the Flow.Subscription object that manages the communication between the publisher and the subscriber.
- onNext(): This method is invoked by the publisher when it wants to send a new item to the subscriber. In this method, the subscriber has to process that item. It doesn't return any results.
- onError(): This method is invoked by the publisher when an unrecoverable error has occurred and no other methods of the subscriber will be called. It receives as a parameter a Throwable object with the error that has occurred.
- onComplete(): This method is invoked by the publisher when it's not going to send any more items. It doesn't receive parameters and it doesn't return a result.

The Flow.Subscription interface

As we mentioned earlier, this object represents the communication between a publisher and a subscriber. It provides two methods that can be used by the subscriber to tell the publisher how their communication will evolve.

- `cancel()`: This method is invoked by the subscriber to tell the publisher it doesn't want any more items.
- `request()`: This method is invoked by the subscriber to tell the publisher it wants more items. It receives the number of items the subscriber wants as a parameter.

The SubmissionPublisher class

As we mentioned earlier, this class, provided by the Java 9 API, implements the `Flow.Publisher` interface. It also uses the `Flow.Subscription` interface and provides methods to send items to the consumers, to know the number of consumers, the subscription between the publisher and the consumer, and to close the communication between them. These are its more significant methods:

- `subscribe()`: This method is provided by the `Flow.Publisher` interface. It's used to subscribe a `Flow.Subscriber` object to this publisher
- `offer()`: This method publishes an item to each subscriber by asynchronously invoking its `onNext()` method
- `submit()`: This method publishes an item to each subscriber by asynchronously invoking its `onNext()` method, blocking uninterruptedly while resources for any subscriber are unavailable
- `estimateMaximumLag()`: This method estimates the items produced by this publisher but not yet consumed by its subscribed subscribers
- `estimateMinimumDemand()`: This method estimates the number of items requested by the consumers but not yet produced by this publisher
- `getMaxBufferCapacity()`: This method returns the maximum size of the buffer for each subscriber
- `getNumberOfSubscribers()`: This method return the number of subscribers

- `hasSubscribers()`: This method returns a `Boolean` value that indicates whether the publisher has subscribers or not
- `close()`: This method calls the `onComplete()` method of all the subscribers of this publisher
- `isClosed()`: This method returns a `Boolean` value to indicate if this publisher is closed or not

The first example - a centralized system for event notification

In our first example, we are going to implement a system to send items from generators of events to consumers of events. We're going to use the `SubmissionPublisher` class to implement the communication between the producers and the consumers of events.

The Event class

This class stores the information of every item. Each item contains three attributes:

- The `msg` attribute, to store a message in the `Event`
- The `source` attribute, to store the name of the class that produces the `Event`
- The `date` attribute, to store the date when the `Event` was produced

You have to declare the three attributes as private and include the methods to `get()` and `set()` the values of the attributes in the class.

The Producer class

We're going to use this class to implement tasks that generate events that will be sent to the consumers using a `SubmissionPublisher` object. The class implements the `Runnable` interface and stores two attributes:

- The `publisher` attribute, that stores the `SubmissionPublisher` object to send the events to the consumers
- The `name` attribute, to store the name of this producer

We use the constructor of the class to initialize both attributes:

```
public class Producer implements Runnable {

  private SubmissionPublisher<Event> publisher;
  private String name;

  public Producer(SubmissionPublisher<Event> publisher, String name) {
    this.publisher = publisher;
    this.name = name;
  }
```

Then, we implement the `run()` method. On it, we generate 10 events. Between one event and the next one, we wait a random number of seconds between 0 and 10. This is the source code of this method:

```
@Override
public void run() {

  Random random = new Random();

  for (int i=0 ; i < 10; i++) {
    Event event = new Event();
    event.setMsg("Event number "+i);
    event.setSource(this.name);
    event.setDate(new Date());

    publisher.submit(event);

    int number = random.nextInt(10);

    try {
      TimeUnit.SECONDS.sleep(number);
    } catch (InterruptedException e) {
      e.printStackTrace();
    }

  }
}
```

The Consumer class

Now it's time to implement the consumers of events in the `Consumer` class. This class implements the `Flow.Subscriber` interface parameterized with the `Event` class, so we have to implement the four methods provided by that interface.

First, we declare two attributes:

- The `name` attribute, to store the name of the consumer
- The `subscription` attribute, to store the `Flow.Subscription` instance that manages the communication between the consumer and the producer

We use the constructor of the class to initialize the name attribute, as you can see in the following piece of code:

```
public class Consumer implements Subscriber<Event> {

  private String name;
  private Subscription subscription;

  public Consumer (String name) {
    this.name = name;
  }
```

Now it's time to implement the four methods of the `Flow.Subscriber` interface. The `onComplete()` and `onError()` methods will only show information in the console:

```
@Override
public void onComplete() {
  this.showMessage("No more events");
}

@Override
public void onError(Throwable error) {
  this.showMessage("An error has ocurred");
  error.printStackTrace();
}
```

In the `onSubscribe()` method, that will be called by the `SubmissionPublisher` class when the consumer wants to subscribe to its notifications, we store the `Subscription` object passed as a parameter in the subscription attribute and then we request the first message to the publisher using the `request()` method. Finally, we write a message in the console:

```
@Override
public void onSubscribe(Subscription subscription) {
  this.subscription=subscription;
  this.subscription.request(1);
  this.showMessage("Subscription OK");
}
```

Finally, the onNext() method will be called by the SubmissionPublisher class for each event. We show a message in the console with the information of the event, request the next event using the request() method, and we call the auxiliary method proccesEvent():

```
@Override
public void onNext(Event event) {
   this.showMessage("An event has arrived: "+event.getSource()+":
                    "+event.getDate()+": "+event.getMsg());
   this.subscription.request(1);

   processEvent(event);
}
```

We use the processEvent() method to simulate a time while the consumer is processing the event. We implement this behavior waiting a random number of seconds between 0 and 3:

```
private void processEvent(Event event) {
   Random random = new Random();

   int number = random.nextInt(3);

   try {
      TimeUnit.SECONDS.sleep(number);
   } catch (InterruptedException e) {
      e.printStackTrace();
   }

}
```

Finally, we have to implement the auxiliary method showMessage() used in the previous method. It shows the String received as a parameter with the name of the thread that is executing the consumer and the name of the consumer:

```
private void showMessage (String txt) {
   System.out.println(Thread.currentThread().getName()+":"+this
                    .name+":"+txt);
   }
}
```

The Main class

Finally, we implement the Main class with the main() method that creates and runs all the components of this example:

We create the following elements:

- A SubmissionPublisher object called publisher. We're going to use this object to send the events to the consumers.
- Five Consumer objects that will receive all the events created by the publishers. We subscribe the consumers to the publisher using the subscribe() method.
- Two Producer objects that will generate the events and send them to the consumers using the publisher object. We execute the producer objects using the default ForkJoinPool object provided by the JVM. We use the commonPool() method to get the ForkJoinPool object and the submit() method to execute them.

```
public class Main {

  public static void main(String[] args) {

    SubmissionPublisher<Event> publisher = new SubmissionPublisher();

    for (int i = 0; i < 5; i++) {
      Consumer consumer = new Consumer("Consumer "+i);
      publisher.subscribe(consumer);
    }

    Producer system1 = new Producer(publisher, "System 1");
    Producer system2 = new Producer(publisher, "System 2");

    ForkJoinTask<?>task1 = ForkJoinPool.commonPool().submit(system1);
    ForkJoinTask<?>task2 = ForkJoinPool.commonPool().submit(system2);
```

Then, we include a while loop to write information about the tasks and the publisher object every ten seconds with the following block of code:

```
do {
  System.out.println("Main: Task 1: "+task1.isDone());
  System.out.println("Main: Task 2: "+task2.isDone());

  System.out.println("Publisher: MaximunLag:"+
                     publisher.estimateMaximumLag());
  System.out.println("Publisher: Max Buffer Capacity: "+
                     publisher.getMaxBufferCapacity());
```

```
    try {
      TimeUnit.SECONDS.sleep(10);
    } catch (InterruptedException e) {
      e.printStackTrace();
    }

  } while ((!task1.isDone()) || (!task2.isDone()) ||
          (publisher.estimateMaximumLag() > 0));
```

To finish the execution of the loop, we wait for three conditions:

- The task that executes the first producer object has finished its execution.
- The task that executes the second producer object has finished its execution.
- There are no pending events in the SubmissionPublisher object. We use the estimateMaximumLag() method to get that number.

Finally, we use the close() method of the SubmissionPublisher object to notify the subscribers about the end of the execution.

During the execution of the example, the producers send events to the SubmissionPublisher using the submit() method. The SubmissionPublisher sends the events to the different consumers. Each consumer requests the events one by one using the request() method.

The following screenshot shows part of the output of one execution of the program:

```
<terminated> Main [Java Application] C:\Program Files\Java\jdk-9\bin\javaw.exe (2 abr. 2017 23:27:31)
ForkJoinPool.commonPool-worker-1:Consumer 4: An event has arrived: System 1: Sun Apr 02 23:27:49 CEST 2017: Event number 4
ForkJoinPool.commonPool-worker-2:Consumer 3: An event has arrived: System 2: Sun Apr 02 23:27:53 CEST 2017: Event number 6
Main: Task 1: true
Main: Task 2: true
Publisher: MaximunLag: 9
Publisher: Max Buffer Capacity: 256
ForkJoinPool.commonPool-worker-2:Consumer 3: An event has arrived: System 2: Sun Apr 02 23:27:53 CEST 2017: Event number 7
ForkJoinPool.commonPool-worker-1:Consumer 4: An event has arrived: System 1: Sun Apr 02 23:27:53 CEST 2017: Event number 5
ForkJoinPool.commonPool-worker-1:Consumer 4: An event has arrived: System 2: Sun Apr 02 23:27:53 CEST 2017: Event number 6
ForkJoinPool.commonPool-worker-2:Consumer 3: An event has arrived: System 1: Sun Apr 02 23:27:54 CEST 2017: Event number 6
ForkJoinPool.commonPool-worker-2:Consumer 3: An event has arrived: System 2: Sun Apr 02 23:27:55 CEST 2017: Event number 8
ForkJoinPool.commonPool-worker-1:Consumer 4: An event has arrived: System 2: Sun Apr 02 23:27:53 CEST 2017: Event number 7
ForkJoinPool.commonPool-worker-1:Consumer 4: An event has arrived: System 1: Sun Apr 02 23:27:54 CEST 2017: Event number 6
ForkJoinPool.commonPool-worker-1:Consumer 4: An event has arrived: System 2: Sun Apr 02 23:27:55 CEST 2017: Event number 8
ForkJoinPool.commonPool-worker-1:Consumer 4: An event has arrived: System 2: Sun Apr 02 23:27:57 CEST 2017: Event number 9
ForkJoinPool.commonPool-worker-2:Consumer 3: An event has arrived: System 2: Sun Apr 02 23:27:57 CEST 2017: Event number 9
ForkJoinPool.commonPool-worker-1:Consumer 4: An event has arrived: System 1: Sun Apr 02 23:27:58 CEST 2017: Event number 7
ForkJoinPool.commonPool-worker-2:Consumer 3: An event has arrived: System 1: Sun Apr 02 23:27:58 CEST 2017: Event number 7
ForkJoinPool.commonPool-worker-1:Consumer 4: An event has arrived: System 1: Sun Apr 02 23:27:59 CEST 2017: Event number 8
ForkJoinPool.commonPool-worker-1:Consumer 4: An event has arrived: System 1: Sun Apr 02 23:27:59 CEST 2017: Event number 9
ForkJoinPool.commonPool-worker-2:Consumer 3: An event has arrived: System 1: Sun Apr 02 23:27:59 CEST 2017: Event number 8
ForkJoinPool.commonPool-worker-2:Consumer 3: An event has arrived: System 1: Sun Apr 02 23:27:59 CEST 2017: Event number 9
ForkJoinPool.commonPool-worker-1:Consumer 0: No more events
ForkJoinPool.commonPool-worker-1:Consumer 2: No more events
ForkJoinPool.commonPool-worker-1:Consumer 4: No more events
ForkJoinPool.commonPool-worker-3:Consumer 1: No more events
```

You can see how the `main()` method writes information about the tasks and the `publisher` object, how the consumers receive the different events, and finally, how they write the message written by the `onComplete()` method called when the `main()` method calls the `close()` method of the `SubmissionPublisher` object.

The second example - a news system

In the previous example, we used the `SubmissionPublisher` class, so we didn't implement the `Flow.Publisher` and the `Flow.Subscription` interfaces. If the functionality provided by the `SubmissionPublisher` doesn't fit our needs, we will have to implement our own publisher and subscription.

In this section, you will learn how to implement both interfaces to learn the specification of the reactive streams. We are going to implement a news system where each piece of news will be associated with a category. A subscriber will be subscribed to one or more categories and the publisher will only send a piece of news to each subscriber if it's subscribed to its category.

The News class

The first class we're going to implement is the `News` class. This class represents each piece of news we're going to send from the publisher to the consumer. We're going to store three attributes:

- **The category attribute**: An `int` value that stores the category of the news. It can take the values 0, 1, 2, or 3 to represent news from sports, world, economic, and science categories.
- **The txt attribute**: A `String` value that stores the text of the news.
- **The date attribute**: A `Date` value that stores the date of the news.

As usual, declare the attributes as private and implement methods to `get()` and `set()` the values of these attributes.

The publisher classes

We need four classes to implement the Flow.Publisher and the Flow.Subscription interfaces. The first one is the MySubscription class that implements the Flow.Subscription interface. We are going to store three attributes in this class:

1. The canceled attribute: A Boolean value that indicates if the subscription is cancelled or not
2. The requested attribute: An AtomicLong value that stores the number of news items that have been requested by the consumer
3. The categories attribute: A Set of Integer values that stores the categories of the news associated with this subscription

The following code shows the declaration of the attributes:

```
public class MySubscription implements Subscription {
    private boolean cancelled = false;
    private AtomicLong requested = new AtomicLong(0);
    private Set<Integer> categories;
```

Then, we have to implement the two methods provided by the Flow.Subscription interface: the cancel() and request() methods:

```
@Override
public void cancel() {
    cancelled=true;
}

@Override
public void request(long value) {
    requested.addAndGet(value);
}
```

The cancel() method only sets the cancelled attribute to true and the request() method increments the value of the requested attribute. In a real example, you may have to include validations of the values passed as parameters to these methods.

Then, we have implemented other additional methods to get and set the value of the attributes of this class:

- isCancelled(): This method returns the value of the cancelled attribute
- getRequested(): This method returns the value of the requested attribute using the get() method

- `decreaseRequested()`: This method decrements the value of the `requested` attribute using the `decrementAndGet()` method
- `setCategories()`: This method establishes the value of the `categories` attribute
- `hasCategory()`: This method returns a `Boolean` value to indicate if the category (an `int` value) received as a parameter is associated with this subscription

Then we're going to implement the `ConsumerData` class. We will use this class to store the information of a `Subscriber` and the `Subscription` between the `Publisher` and that `Subscriber`. So, this class will have two attributes:

- **The consumer attribute**: A `Subscriber` value parameterized with the `News` class. It will store a reference to a consumer of news.
- **The subscription attribute**: A `MySubscription` value that references the subscription between the publisher and the `Subscriber`.

We have included methods to `get()` and `set()` the values of the attributes.

Then, we´re going to implement the `PublisherTask` class that implements the `Runnable` interface. We will use this task to send an item to a consumer. We declare two attributes to store the data related to the consumer, the subscription between the consumer and the publisher, and the item (in our case, a piece of news) we want to send:

- **The consumerData attribute**: A `ConsumerData` object that, as we explained before, stores the `Subscriber` object and the `MySubscription` object with the consumer of items and the subscription between the publisher and it respectively
- **The news attribute**: A `News` object with the piece of news we want to send to the subscriber

We use the constructor of the class to initialize both attributes:

```
public class PublisherTask implements Runnable {

  private ConsumerDataconsumerData;
  private News news;

  public PublisherTask(ConsumerDataconsumerData, News news) {
    this.consumerData = consumerData;
    this.news = news;
  }
```

Then, we implement the `run()` method. It will check if it has to send the news object to the subscriber. It will check three conditions:

- The subscription is not cancelled: We use the `isCancelled()` method of the `subscription` object.
- The subscriber has requested more items: We use the `getRequested()` method of the `subscription` object.
- The category of the news object is in the categories associated with the subscriber. We use the `hasCategory()` method of the `subscription` object.

If the `news` object passes the three conditions, we send it to the subscriber using the `onNext()` method. We also use the `decreaseRequested()` method of the `subscription` object to decrement the number of items requested by this subscriber. This is the source code of this method:

```
@Override
public void run() {
  MySubscription subscription = consumerData.getSubscription();
  if (!(subscription.isCanceled()) && (subscription.getRequested() > 0)
      && (subscription.hasCategory(news.getCategory()))) {
    consumerData.getConsumer().onNext(news);
    subscription.decreaseRequested();
  }
}
```

Finally, we implement the `MyPublisher` class that is the class that implements the `Flow.Publisher` interface parameterized with the `News` class. We are going to use two attributes to implement the behavior of the class:

- **The consumers attribute**: A `ConcurrentLinkedDeque` object parameterized with the `ConsumerData` class to store the information of all the `Subscribers` subscribed to this publisher
- **The executor attribute**: A `ThreadPoolExecutor` object we're going to use to execute the `PublisherTask` objects

We use the constructor of the class to initialize both attributes.

```
public class MyPublisher implements Publisher<News> {

  private ConcurrentLinkedDeque<ConsumerData> consumers;
  private ThreadPoolExecutor executor;

  public MyPublisher() {
    consumers=new ConcurrentLinkedDeque<>();
```

```
    executor = (ThreadPoolExecutor)Executors.newFixedThreadPool
            (Runtime.getRuntime().availableProcessors());
}
```

Then, we implement the `subscribe()` method provided by the `Flow.Publisher` interface. This method receives the `Subscriber` object that wants to subscribe to this publisher as a parameter. We create a new `MySubscription` object, a new `ConsumerData` object, add the last one to the consumer's data structure, and call the `onSubscribe()` method of the `Subscriber` object passing the `MySubscription` object, as a parameter.

```
@Override
public void subscribe(Subscriber<? super News> subscriber) {

    ConsumerDataconsumerData=new ConsumerData();
    consumerData.setConsumer((Subscriber<News>)subscriber);

    MySubscription subscription=new MySubscription();
    consumerData.setSubscription(subscription);

    subscriber.onSubscribe(subscription);

    consumers.add(consumerData);
}
```

Then, we implement the `publish()` method. This method receives a `News` object as a parameter and tries to send it to all the subscriber's of this publisher. We process all the elements stored in the consumers data structure, create a new `PublisherTask` object, and execute them in the executor using the `execute()` method.

If an error occurs, we use the `onError()` method to the `subscriber` object to notify the error to the subscriber.

```
public void publish(News news) {
    consumers.forEach( consumerData -> {
        try {
            executor.execute(new PublisherTask(consumerData, news));
        } catch (Exception e) {
            consumerData.getConsumer().onError(e);
        }
    });
}
```

Finally, we implement the `shutdown()` method to notify the end of the communication to all subscribers and to finish the execution of the `ThreadPoolExecutor` used internally:

```
public void shutdown() {
  consumers.forEach( consumerData -> {
    consumerData.getConsumer().onComplete();
  });
  executor.shutdown();
  }
}
```

With these four classes, we have implemented the publisher part of the example. Now it's time for the consumer part.

The Consumer class

This class implements the `Flow.Subscriber` interface and implements the consumer of news. Internally, it uses three attributes:

- **The subscription attribute**: A `MySubscription` object that stores the subscription between this subscriber and the publisher
- **The name attribute**: A `String` attribute that stores the name of the subscriber
- **The categories attribute**: A `Set` of `Integer` numbers that stores the categories of the news this subscriber wants to receive

As usual, we use the constructor of the class to initialize these attributes:

```
public class Consumer implements Subscriber<News> {

  private MySubscription subscription;
  private String name;
  private Set<Integer> categories;

  public Consumer(String name, Set<Integer> categories) {
    this.name=name;
    this.categories = categories;
  }
```

Now, we have to implement the methods provided by the `Flow.Subscriber` interface. The `onComplete()` and `onError()` methods only write information in the console:

```
@Override
public void onComplete() {
  System.out.printf("%s - %s: Consumer - Completed\n", name,
```

```
                            Thread.currentThread().getName());
    }

    @Override
    public void onError(Throwable exception) {
        System.out.printf("%s - %s: Consumer - Error: %s\n", name,
                            Thread.currentThread().getName(),
                            exception.getMessage());
    }
```

The onSubscribe() method, that receives the Subscription object as a parameter, stores that object in the subscription attribute, and updates it with the categories associated to this subscriber. Finally, we ask for the first News object with the request() method:

```
    @Override
    public void onSubscribe(Subscription subscription) {
        this.subscription = (MySubscription)subscription;
        this.subscription.setCategories(this.categories);
        this.subscription.request(1);
        System.out.printf("%s: Consumer - Subscription\n",
                            Thread.currentThread().getName());
    }
```

Finally, the onNext() method, that receives a News object as a parameter, writes the information of that object in the console and asks for the next one using the request() method:

```
    @Override
    public void onNext(News item) {
        System.out.printf("%s - %s: Consumer - News\n", name,
                            Thread.currentThread().getName());
        System.out.printf("%s - %s: Text: %s\n", name,
                            Thread.currentThread().getName(),item.getTxt());
        System.out.printf("%s - %s: Category: %s\n", name,
                            Thread.currentThread().getName(),
                            item.getCategory());
        System.out.printf("%s - %s: Date: %s\n", name,
                            Thread.currentThread().getName(),item.getDate());
        subscription.request(1);
    }
```

The Main class

Finally, we implement the `Main` class with the `main()` method to test all the classes we have implemented in this example.

We create a `MyPublisher` object and three `Consumer` objects, which are as follows:

- The `consumer1` object wants to receive only news about sports
- The `consumer2` object wants to receive only news about science
- The `consumer3` object wants to receive news of the four categories

We create the objects and subscribe them to the publisher:

```java
public class Main {

  public static void main(String[] args) {

    MyPublisher publisher=new MyPublisher();

    Subscriber<News>consumer1, consumer2, consumer3;

    Set<Integer> sports = new HashSet();
    sports.add(News.SPORTS);
    consumer1=new Consumer("Sport Consumer",sports);

    Set<Integer> science = new HashSet();
    science.add(News.SCIENCE);
    consumer2=new Consumer("Science Consumer", science);

    Set<Integer> all = new HashSet();
    all.add(News.ECONOMIC);
    all.add(News.SCIENCE);
    all.add(News.SPORTS);
    all.add(News.WORLD);
    consumer3=new Consumer("All Consumer", all);

    publisher.subscribe(consumer1);
    publisher.subscribe(consumer2);
    publisher.subscribe(consumer3);

    System.out.printf("Main: Start\n");
```

Then, we send four pieces of news to the consumers using the `publisher` object, one for each category. We left 1 second between each piece of news:

```
News news=new News();
news.setTxt("Basketball news");
news.setCategory(News.SPORTS);
news.setDate(new Date());

publisher.publish(news);

try {
  TimeUnit.SECONDS.sleep(1);
} catch (InterruptedException e) {
  e.printStackTrace();
}

news=new News();
news.setTxt("Money news");
news.setCategory(News.ECONOMIC);
news.setDate(new Date());
publisher.publish(news);

try {
  TimeUnit.SECONDS.sleep(1);
} catch (InterruptedException e) {
  e.printStackTrace();
}

news=new News();
news.setTxt("Europe news");
news.setCategory(News.WORLD);
news.setDate(new Date());
publisher.publish(news);

try {
  TimeUnit.SECONDS.sleep(1);
} catch (InterruptedException e) {
  e.printStackTrace();
}

news=new News();
news.setTxt("Space news");
news.setCategory(News.SCIENCE);
news.setDate(new Date());
publisher.publish(news);
```

Finally, we use the `shutdown()` method of the `publisher` object to finish the execution of all the elements of the system:

```
publisher.shutdown();
    System.out.printf("Main: End\n");
  }
}
```

The following screenshot shows part of the output of an execution of this example. You can see how the `consumer3` object receives all the news, but the `consumer1` and `consumer2` objects only receive the news of their associated categories:

```
<terminated> Main [Java Application] C:\Program Files\Java\jdk-9\bin\javaw.exe (4 abr. 2017 0:44:
All Consumer - pool-1-thread-3: Category: 0
Sport Consumer - pool-1-thread-1: Category: 0
Sport Consumer - pool-1-thread-1: Date: Tue Apr 04 00:44:25 CEST 2017
All Consumer - pool-1-thread-3: Date: Tue Apr 04 00:44:25 CEST 2017
All Consumer - pool-1-thread-4: Consumer - News
All Consumer - pool-1-thread-4: Text: Money news
All Consumer - pool-1-thread-4: Category: 2
All Consumer - pool-1-thread-4: Date: Tue Apr 04 00:44:26 CEST 2017
All Consumer - pool-1-thread-2: Consumer - News
All Consumer - pool-1-thread-2: Text: Europe news
All Consumer - pool-1-thread-2: Category: 1
All Consumer - pool-1-thread-2: Date: Tue Apr 04 00:44:27 CEST 2017
Science Consumer - pool-1-thread-3: Consumer - News
All Consumer - pool-1-thread-1: Consumer - News
Science Consumer - pool-1-thread-3: Text: Space news
Science Consumer - pool-1-thread-3: Category: 3
All Consumer - pool-1-thread-1: Text: Space news
Science Consumer - pool-1-thread-3: Date: Tue Apr 04 00:44:28 CEST 2017
All Consumer - pool-1-thread-1: Category: 3
All Consumer - pool-1-thread-1: Date: Tue Apr 04 00:44:28 CEST 2017
Sport Consumer - main: Consumer - Completed
Science Consumer - main: Consumer - Completed
All Consumer - main: Consumer - Completed
Main: End
```

Summary

In this chapter, you have learnt how Java 9 implements the reactive streams specification. It defines a standard for asynchronous stream processing with non-blocking back pressure. It's based on the following three elements:

- A publisher of information
- One or more subscribers of that information
- A subscription between the publisher and a consumer

Java provides three interfaces to implement those elements:

- The `Flow.Publisher` interface, to implement the publishers of information
- The `Flow.Subscriber` interface, to implement the subscribers (consumers) of that information
- The `Flow.Subscription` interface, to implement the subscription between publishers and subscribers

Java also provides a utility class, the `SubmissionPublisher` class that implements the `Publisher` interface and can be used if our application has default behavior.

We have implemented two examples with the two implementation variants you can use with reactive streams in Java. We have implemented an event notification system implementing the `Subscriber` class and using the `SubmissionPublisher` class to send the events to the subscribers, and a news system implementing all the necessary elements.

Take into account that the reactive streams specification defines the expected behavior of these kinds of streams but, as Java provides interfaces, we can implement a different behavior. This is not a good idea.

In the next chapter, we are going to explain the data structures and synchronization mechanisms we can use in concurrent applications in detail.

11
Diving into Concurrent Data Structures and Synchronization Utilities

One of the most important elements in every computer program is the **data structures**. Data structures allow us to store the data that our applications read, transform, and write in different ways according to our needs. The selection of an adequate data structure is a critical point to achieve good performance. A bad choice can degrade the performance of an algorithm considerably. Java Concurrency API includes some data structures designed to be used in concurrent applications without provoking data inconsistencies or loss of information.

Another critical point in concurrent applications are **synchronization mechanisms**. You use them to implement mutual exclusion by creating a critical section, that is to say, a piece of code that can only be executed by one thread at a time. But you can also use synchronization mechanisms to implement dependencies between threads when, for example, a concurrent task must wait for the finalization of another task. The Java Concurrency API includes basic synchronization mechanisms, such as the `synchronized` keyword and very high-level utilities, such as the `CyclicBarrier` class or the `Phaser` class you used in `Chapter 6`, *Running Tasks Divided into Phases - The Phaser Class*.

In this chapter, we will cover the following topics:

- Concurrent data structures
- Synchronization mechanisms

Concurrent data structures

Every computer program works with data. They get the data from a database, a file, or another source, transform that data, and then write the transformed data into a database, a file, or another destination. Programs work with data stored in memory and use data structures to store the data in memory.

When you implement a concurrent application, you must be very careful with the utilization of data structures. If different threads can modify the data stored in a unique data structure, you have to use a synchronization mechanism to protect the modifications over that data structure. If you don't do this, you may have a data race condition. Your application may sometimes work correctly, but next time may crash with a random exception, stuck in an infinite loop or silently produce an incorrect result. The outcome will depend on the order of execution.

To avoid data race conditions, you can:

- Use a non-synchronized data structure and add the synchronization mechanisms by yourself
- Use a data structure provided by the Java Concurrency API that implements the synchronization mechanism internally and is optimized to be used in concurrent applications

The second option is the most recommended. Through the pages of this section, you will review the most important concurrent data structures.

Blocking and non-blocking data structures

The Java Concurrency API provides two kinds of concurrent data structures:

- **Blocking data structures**: This kind of data structure provides methods to insert and delete data on it that, when the operation cannot be done immediately (for example, you want to take an element and the data structure is empty), the thread that made the call will be blocked until the operation can be done
- **Non-blocking data structures**: This kind of data structure provides methods to insert and delete data on it that, when the operation cannot be done immediately, returns a special value or throws an exception

Sometimes, we have a non-blocking equivalent for the blocking data structure. For example, the `ConcurrentLinkedDeque` class is a non-blocking data structure and the `LinkedBlockingDeque` is the blocking equivalent. Blocking data structures have methods that have a behavior of non-blocking data structures. For example, the `Deque` interface defines the `pollFirst()` method that does not block and returns `null` if the deque is empty. On the other hand, the `getFirst()` method throws an `Exception` in that circumstance. Every blocking queue implementation implements this method as well.

Concurrent data structures

The **Java Collections Framework (JCF)** provides a set of different data structures that can be used in sequential programming. The Java Concurrency API extends those structures, providing others that can be used in concurrent applications. This includes:

- **Interfaces**: That extends the interfaces provided by the JCF, adding some methods that can be used in concurrent applications
- **Classes**: That implements the previous interfaces to provide the implementations that can be used in the applications

In the following sections, we make an introduction to the interfaces and classes you can use in concurrent applications.

Interfaces

First, let's describe the most important interfaces implemented by the concurrent data structures.

BlockingQueue

A **queue** is a linear data structure that allows you to insert elements at the end of the queue and get elements from the start. It's a **First-In-First-Out (FIFO)** data structure, where the first elements introduced in the queue are the first ones that are processed.

The JCF defines the `Queue` interface that defines the basic operations to be implemented in a queue. This interface provides methods to:

- Insert an element at the end of the queue
- Retrieve and remove an element from the head of the queue
- Retrieve, but not remove, an element from the head of the queue

The interface defines two versions of these methods that have different behavior when the method can be done (for example, if you want to retrieve an element of an empty queue):

- Methods that throw an exception
- Methods that return a special value, for example `false` or `null`

The next table includes the names of the methods for every operation:

Operation	Exception	Special value
Insert	add()	offer()
Retrieve and remove	remove()	poll()
Retrieve but don't remove	element()	peek()

The `BlockingDeque` interface extends the `Queue` interface, adding methods that block the calling thread if the operation can be done. These methods are:

Operation	Blocks
Insert	put()
Retrieve and remove	take()
Retrieve but don't remove	N/A

BlockingDeque

A **deque** is a linear data structure, similar to a queue, but it allows you to insert and delete elements from both sides of the data structure. The JCF defines the `Deque` interface that extends the `Queue` interface. In addition to the methods provided by the `Queue` interface, it provides methods to insert, retrieve and remove, and retrieve but not remove at both ends:

Operation	Exception	Special value
Insert	addFirst(), addLast()	offerFirst(), offerLast()
Retrieve and remove	removeFirst(), removeLast()	pollFirst(), pollLast()
Retrieve but don't remove	getFirst(), getLast()	peekFirst(), peekLast()

The `BlockingDeque` interface extends the `Deque` interface adding the methods that block the calling threads when the operation can't be done:

Operation	Blocks
Insert	`putFirst()`, `putLast()`
Retrieve and remove	`takeFirst()`, `takeLast()`
Retrieve but don't remove	N/A

ConcurrentMap

A `map` (sometimes also called an associative array) is a data structure that allows you to store key-value pairs. The JCF provides the `Map` interface that defines the basic operations to work with the map. This includes methods to:

- `put()`: Insert a key-value pair into the map
- `get()`: Return the value associated with a key
- `remove()`: Remove the key-value pair associated with the specified key
- `containsKey()` and `containsValue()`: Return true if the map contains the specified key of the value

This interface was modified in Java 8 to include the following new methods. You will learn how to work with these methods later in this chapter:

- `forEach()`: This method executes the given function over all the elements of the map.
- `compute()`, `computeIfAbsent()`, and `computeIfPresent()`: These methods allows you to specify a function that calculates the new value associated with a key.
- `merge()`: This method allow you to specify to merge a key-value pair into an existing map. If the key isn't in the map, it's inserted directly. If not, the function specified is executed.

`ConcurrentMap` extends the `Map` interface to provide the same methods to concurrent applications. Notice that in Java 8 and Java 9 (unlike Java 7), the `ConcurrentMap` interface didn't add new methods to the `Map` interface.

TransferQueue

This interface extends the `BlockingQueue` interface and adds methods to transfer elements from producers to consumers, where producers can wait until a consumer takes off its element. The new methods added by this interface are:

- `transfer()`: Transfer an element to a consumer and wait (blocking the calling thread) until the element is consumed.
- `tryTransfer()`: Transfer an element if there is a consumer waiting. If not, this method returns the `false` value and doesn't insert the element in the queue.

Classes

The Java Concurrency API provides different implementations of the interfaces described before. Some of them don't add any new characteristics, but others add new, interesting functionality.

LinkedBlockingQueue

This class implements the `BlockingQueue` interface to provide a queue with blocking methods that optionally can have a limited number of elements. It also implements the `Queue`, `Collection`, and `Iterable` interfaces.

ConcurrentLinkedQueue

This class implements the `Queue` interface to provide a thread-save unlimited queue. Internally, it uses a non-blocking algorithm to guarantee that there won't be a data race in your application.

LinkedBlockingDeque

This class implements the `BlockingDeque` interface to provide a deque with blocking methods that optionally can have a limited number of elements. It has more functionality than `LinkedBlockingQueue`, but may have more overhead, thus `LinkedBlockingQueue` should be used when deque features are unnecessary.

ConcurrentLinkedDeque

This class implements the `Deque` interface to provide a thread-save unlimited deque that allows you to add and delete elements at both ends of the deque. It has more functionality than `ConcurrentLinkedQueue`, but may have more overhead, as occurs with `LinkedBlockingDeque`.

ArrayBlockingQueue

This class implements the `BlockingQueue` interface to provide an implementation of a blocking queue with a limited number of elements based on an array. It also implements the `Queue`, `Collection`, and `Iterable` interfaces. Unlike non-concurrent, array-based data structures (`ArrayList` and `ArrayDeque`), `ArrayBlockingQueue` allocates the array of a fixed size specified in the constructor and never resizes it.

DelayQueue

This class implements the `BlockingDeque` interface to provide an implementation of a queue with blocking methods and an unlimited number of elements. The elements of this queue must implement the `Delayed` interface, so they have to implement the `getDelay()` method. If that method returns a negative or zero value, the delay has expired and the element can be taken off the queue. The head of the queue is the element with the most negative value of delay.

LinkedTransferQueue

This class provides an implementation of the `TransferQueue` interface. It provides a blocking queue with an unlimited number of elements and with the possibility to use them as a communication channel between producers and consumers, where producers can wait for consumers to process their elements.

PriorityBlockingQueue

This class provides an implementation of the `BlockingQueue` interface where the elements can be polled according to their natural order or by a comparator specified in the constructor of the class. The head of this queue is determined by the sorting order of the elements.

ConcurrentHashMap

This class provides an implementation of the `ConcurrentMap` interface. It provides a thread-safe hash table. In addition to the methods added in the `Map` interface in the Java 8 version, this class has added other ones:

- `search()`, `searchEntries()`, `searchKeys()`, and `searchValues()`: These methods allow you to apply a search function over the key-value pairs, over the keys, or over the values. The search function can be a lambda expression and the method ends when the search function returns a not-null value. That is the result of the execution of the method.
- `reduce()`, `reduceEntries()`, `reduceKeys()`, and `reduceValues()`: These methods allows you to apply a `reduce()` operation to transform the key-value pairs, the keys, or the entries, as occurs with streams (refer to Chapter 9, *Processing Massive Datasets with Parallel Streams - The Map and Collect Model* to get more details about the `reduce()` method).

`ConcurrentHashMap` is for programs that rely on its thread safety but not on its synchronization details. Resizing of the map may be a slow operation. More methods have been added (`forEachValue`, `forEachKey`, and so on), but they are not covered here.

Using the new features

In this section, you will learn how to use the new features introduced in Java 8 and Java 9 for the concurrent data structures.

First example with ConcurrentHashMap

In Chapter 9, *Processing Massive Datasets with Parallel Streams - The Map and Collect Model*, you implemented an application to make a search in a dataset from 20,000 Amazon products. We took that information from the Amazon product co-purchasing network metadata that includes information about 548,552 products, including title, salesrank, and similar products. You can download this dataset from https://snap.stanford.edu/data/amazon-meta.html. In that example, you used a `ConcurrentHashMap<String, List<ExtendedProduct>>` named `productsByBuyer` to store information about the products purchased by a user. The keys of this map are the identifier of the user and the values in a list of the products purchased by the user. You're going to use that map to learn how to work with the new methods of the `ConcurrentHashMap` class.

The forEach() method

This method allows you to specify a function that will be executed on every key-value pair of ConcurrentHashMap. There are many versions of this method, but the most basic version has only a BiConsumer function that can be expressed as a lambda expression. For example, you can use this method to print how many products every user has purchased, using the following code:

```
productsByBuyer.forEach( (id, list) -> System.out.println(id+":
                                    "+list.size()));
```

This basic version is a part of the usual Map interface and is always executed sequentially. In this code, we have used a lambda expression where id is the key of the element and list is the value of the element.

In this other example, we have used the forEach() method to calculate the average rating given per user:

```
productsByBuyer.forEach( (id, list) -> {
    double average=list.stream().mapToDouble(item -> item.getValue())
                    .average().getAsDouble();
    System.out.println(id+": "+average);
});
```

In this code, we have also used a lambda expression where id is the key of the element and list is its value. We have used a stream applied to the list of products to calculate the average rating.

Other versions of this method are as follows:

- forEach(parallelismThreshold, action): This is the version of the method you have to use in concurrent applications. If the map has more elements than the number specified in the first parameter, this method will be executed in parallel.
- forEachEntry(parallelismThreshold, action): The same as the previous, but in this case, the action is an implementation of the Consumer interface that receives a Map.Entry object with the key and the value of the element. You can also use a lambda expression in this case.

- `forEachKey(parallelismThreshold, action)`: The same as the previous, but in this case, the action will be applied only over the keys of `ConcurrentHashMap`.
- `forEachValue(parallelismThreshold, action)`: The same as the previous, but in this case, the action will be applied only over the values of `ConcurrentHashMap`.

The current implementation uses the common `ForkJoinPool` instance to execute the parallel tasks.

The search() method

This method applies a search function to all the elements of `ConcurrentHashMap`. This search function can return a null value or a value different from null. The `search()` method will return the first non-null value returned by the search function. This method receives two parameters:

- `parallelismThreshold`: If the map has more elements than the number specified by this parameter, this method will be executed in parallel.
- `searchFunction`: This is an implementation of the `BiFunction` interface that can be expressed as a lambda expression. This function receives the key and the value of each element as parameters and, as we mentioned before, has to return a non-null value if you find what you are searching for and a null value if you don't.

For example, you can use this function to find the first book that contains a word:

```
ExtendedProduct firstProduct=productsByBuyer.search(100,
                                    (id, products) -> {
  for (ExtendedProduct product: products) {
    if (product.getTitle().toLowerCase().contains("java")) {
      return product;
    }
  }
  return null;
});
if (firstProduct!=null) {
  System.out.println(firstProduct.getBuyer()+":"+
                    firstProduct.getTitle());
}
```

In this case, we use 100 as `parallelismThreshold` and a lambda expression to implement the search function. In this function, for every element, we process all the products of the list. If we find a product that contains the word `java`, we return that product. This is the value returned by the `search()` method. Finally, we write the buyer and the title of the product in the console.

There are other versions of this method:

- `searchEntries(parallelismThreshold, searchFunction)`: In this case, the search function is an implementation of the `Function` interface that receives a `Map.Entry` object as a parameter
- `searchKeys(parallelismThreshold, searchFunction)`: In this case, the search function is applied only over the keys of `ConcurrentHashMap`
- `searchValues(parallelismThreshold, searchFunction)`: In this case, the search function is applied only over the values of `ConcurrentHashMap`

The reduce() method

This method is similar to the `reduce()` method provided by the Stream framework, but in this case, you work directly with the elements of `ConcurrentHashMap`. This method receives three parameters:

- `parallelismThreshold`: If `ConcurrentHashMap` has more elements than the number specified in this parameter, this method will be executed in parallel.
- `transformer`: This parameter is an implementation of the `BiFunction` interface that can be expressed as a lambda function. It receives a key and a value as parameters and returns a transformation of these elements.
- `reducer`: This parameter is an implementation of the `BiFunction` interface that can be expressed as a lambda function too. It receives two objects returned by the transformer function as parameters. The objective of this function is to group those two objects into a single one.

As an example of this method, we will obtain a list of products that have a review with a value of 1 (the worst value). We have used two auxiliary variables. The first one is `transformer`. It is a `BiFunction` interface that we will use as the `transformer` element of the `reduce()` method:

```
BiFunction<String, List<ExtendedProduct>, List<ExtendedProduct>>
    transformer = (key, value) ->value.stream().filter(product ->
    product.getValue() == 1).collect(Collectors.toList());
```

This function will receive the key, which is the `id` of a user, and a list of `ExtendedProduct` objects with the products purchased by that user. We process all the products of the list and return the products that have a rating of 1.

The second variable is the reducer `BinaryOperator`. We use it as the reducer function of the `reduce()` method:

```
BinaryOperator<List<ExtendedProduct>> reducer = (list1, list2) ->{
    list1.addAll(list2);
    return list1;
};
```

The `reducer` receives two lists of `ExtendedProduct` and concatenates them into a single one using the `addAll()` method.

Now, we only have to implement the call to the `reduce()` method:

```
List<ExtendedProduct> badReviews=productsByBuyer.reduce(10,
                                        transformer, reducer);
badReviews.forEach(product -> {
    System.out.println(product.getTitle()+":"+
                    product.getBuyer()+":"+product.getValue());
});
```

There are other versions of the `reduce()` method:

- `reduceEntries()`, `reduceEntriesToDouble()`, `reduceEntriesToInt()`, and `reduceEntriesToLong()`: In this case, the transformer and reducer functions work over `Map.Entry` objects. The last three versions return respectively, a `double`, an `int`, and a `long` value.
- `reduceKeys()`, `reduceKeysToDouble()`, and `reduceKeysToInt()`, `reduceKeysToLong()`: In this case, the transformer and reducer functions work over the keys of the map. The last three versions return respectively, a `double`, an `int`. and a `long` value.
- `reduceToInt()`, `reduceToDouble()`, and `reduceToLong()`: In this case, the transformer function works over the keys and values and the reducer method works over `int`, `double`, or `long` number respectively. These methods return an `int`, `double`, and `long` values.
- `reduceValues()`, `reduceValuesToDouble()`, `reduceValuesToInt()`, and `reduceValuesToLong()`: In this case, the transformer and reducer functions work over the values of the map. The last three versions return a `double`, an `int`, and a `long` value respectively.

The compute() method

This method (which is defined in the `Map` interface) receives the key of an element and an implementation of the `BiFunction` interface that can be expressed as a lambda expression as parameters. This function will receive the key and value of the element if the key exists in `ConcurrentHashMap`, or null if the key doesn't exist in `ConcurrentHashMap`. The method will replace the value associated with the key with the value returned by the function, insert them in `ConcurrentHashMap` if it doesn't exist, or remove the item if `null` is returned for a previously existing item. Note that, during the `BiFunction` execution, one or several map entries can be locked. Thus, your `BiFunction` should not work for very long and should not try to update any other entries in the same map, otherwise a deadlock might occur.

For example, we can use this method with the new atomic variable introduced in Java 8, named `LongAdder`, to calculate the number of bad reviews associated with every product. We create a new `ConcurrentHashMap` named counter. The keys will be the title of the products and the value an object of the `LongAdder` class to count how many bad reviews every product has.

```
ConcurrentHashMap<String, LongAdder> counter=new ConcurrentHashMap<>();
```

We process all the elements of `badReviewsConcurrentLinkedDeque` calculated in the previous section and use the `compute()` method to create and update the `LongAdder` associated with every product.

```
badReviews.forEach(product -> {
  counter.computeIfAbsent(product.getTitle(), title -> new
                          LongAdder()).increment();
});
counter.forEach((title, count) -> {
  System.out.println(title+":"+count);
});
```

Finally, we write the results in the console.

Another example with ConcurrentHashMap

There is another method added in the `ConcurrentHashMap` class and defined in the `Map` interface. It's the `merge()` method that allows you to merge a key-value pair into the map. If the key doesn't exist in `ConcurrentHashMap`, it is inserted directly.

If the key exists, you have to define which will be the new value associated with that key from the old one and the new one. This method receives three parameters:

- The key we want to merge.
- The value we want to merge.
- An implementation of `BiFunction` that can be expressed as a lambda expression. This function receives the old value and the new value associated with the key as parameters. The method will associate with the key the value returned by this function. `BiFunction` is executed under a partial lock of the map, so it's guaranteed that it's not concurrently executed for the same key.

For example, we have split the 20,000 products of Amazon used in the previous section in files by the year of the review. For every year, we load `ConcurrentHashMap`, where the products are the keys and a list of reviews are the values. So, we can load the reviews of 1995 and 1996 with the following code:

```
Path path=Paths.get("data\\amazon\\1995.txt");
ConcurrentHashMap<BasicProduct, ConcurrentLinkedDeque<BasicReview>>
            products1995=BasicProductLoader.load(path);
showData(products1995);

path=Paths.get("data\\amazon\\1996.txt");
ConcurrentHashMap<BasicProduct,ConcurrentLinkedDeque<BasicReview>>
            products1996=BasicProductLoader.load(path);
System.out.println(products1996.size());
showData(products1996);
```

If we want to merge both `ConcurrentHashMap` into one, we can use the following code:

```
products1996.forEach(10,(product, reviews) -> {
  products1995.merge(product, reviews, (reviews1, reviews2) -> {
    System.out.println("Merge for: "+product.getAsin());
    reviews1.addAll(reviews2);
    return reviews1;
  });
});
```

We process all the elements of the 1996 `ConcurrentHashMap` and for every key-value pair, we call the `merge()` method over the 1995 `ConcurrentHashMap`. The `merge` function will receive two lists of reviews, so we only have to concatenate them into one.

An example with the ConcurrentLinkedDeque class

The Collection interface has also included new methods in Java 8. Most of the concurrent data structures implement this interface, so we can use these new features with them. Two of them are the stream() and parallelStream() methods used in Chapter 8, *Processing Massive Datasets with Parallel Streams - The Map and Reduce Model* and Chapter 9, *Processing Massive Datasets with Parallel Streams - The Map and Collect Model*. Let's see how to use the other two using ConcurrentLinkedDeque with the 20,000 products we used in the previous sections.

The removeIf() method

This method has a default implementation in the Collection interface that is not concurrent and is not overridden by the ConcurrentLinkedDeque class. This method receives an implementation of the Predicate interface as a parameter that will receive an element of the Collection as a parameter and should return a true or a false value. The method will process all the elements of the Collection and will delete those that obtain a true value with the predicate.

For example, if you want to delete all the products with a salesrank higher than 1,000, you can use the following code:

```
System.out.println("Products: "+productList.size());
productList.removeIf(product -> product.getSalesrank() > 1000);
System.out.println("Products; "+productList.size());
productList.forEach(product -> {
  System.out.println(product.getTitle()+": "+
                     product.getSalesrank());
});
```

The spliterator() method

This method returns an implementation of the Spliterator interface. A **spliterator** defines the data source that can be used by the Stream API. You rarely need to use spliterator directly, but sometimes you may want to create your own spliterator to produce a custom source for the stream (for example, if you implement your own data structure). If you have your own spliterator implementation, you can create a stream on top of it using StreamSupport.stream(mySpliterator, isParallel). Here, isParallel is a Boolean value that determines whether the created stream will be parallel or not. A spliterator is like an iterator in the sense that you can use it to traverse all the elements in the collection, but you can split them to make that traversal in a concurrent way.

A spliterator has eight different characteristics that define its behavior:

- CONCURRENT: The spliterator source may be safely concurrently modified
- DISTINCT: All the elements returned by the spliterator are distinct
- IMMUTABLE: The spliterator source cannot be modified
- NONNULL: The spliterator never returns a null value
- ORDERED: The elements returned by the spliterator are ordered (which means their order matters)
- SIZED: The spliterator is capable of returning an exact number of elements with the estimateSize() method
- SORTED: The spliterator source is sorted
- SUBSIZED: If you use the trySplit() method to divide this spliterator, the resulting spliterators will be SIZED and SUBSIZED

The most useful methods of this interface are:

- estimatedSize(): This method will give you an estimation of the number of elements in the spliterator.
- forEachRemaining(): This method allows you to apply an implementation of the Consumer interface that can be represented with a lambda function to the elements of the spliterator that haven't yet been processed.
- tryAdvance(): This method receives an implementation of the Consumer interface. It takes the next element of the spliterator, process them using the Consumer implementation and returns the true value. If the spliterator has no elements to process, it returns the false value.
- trySplit(): This method tries to split the spliterator into two parts. The caller spliterator will process some elements and the returned spliterator will process the others. If the spliterator is ORDERED, the returned spliterator must process a strict prefix of the elements and the call must process the strict suffix.
- hasCharacteristics(): This method allows you to check the properties of the spliterator.

Let's see an example of this method with the ArrayList data structure with 20,000 products.

First, we need an auxiliary task that will process a set of products to convert their title to lowercase. This task will have a `Spliterator` as an attribute:

```
public class SpliteratorTask implements Runnable {

  private Spliterator<Product> spliterator;

  public SpliteratorTask (Spliterator<Product> spliterator) {
    this.spliterator=spliterator;
  }

  @Override
  public void run() {
    int counter=0;
    while (spliterator.tryAdvance(product -> {
      product.setTitle(product.getTitle().toLowerCase());
    })) {
    counter++;
    };
    System.out.println(Thread.currentThread().getName()
                         +":"+counter);
  }

}
```

As you can see, this task writes the number of products processed when it finishes its execution.

In the main method, once we have loaded `ConcurrentLinkedQueue` with the 20,000 products, we can obtain the spliterator, check some of its properties, and look at its estimated size.

```
Spliterator<Product> split1=productList.spliterator();
System.out.println(split1.hasCharacteristics(Spliterator.CONCURRENT));
System.out.println(split1.hasCharacteristics(Spliterator.SUBSIZED));
System.out.println(split1.estimateSize());
```

Then, we can divide the spliterator using the `trySplit()` method and look at the size of the two spliterators:

```
Spliterator<Product> split2=split1.trySplit();
System.out.println(split1.estimateSize());
System.out.println(split2.estimateSize());
```

Finally, we can execute two tasks in an executor, one for the spliterator, to see that every spliterator has really processed the expected number of elements.

```
ThreadPoolExecutor executor=(ThreadPoolExecutor)
                    Executors.newCachedThreadPool();
executor.execute(new SpliteratorTask(split1));
executor.execute(new SpliteratorTask(split2));
```

In the following screenshot, you can see the results of the execution of this example:

```
<terminated> ConcurrentSpliteratorMain [Java Application] C:\Program Files\Java\jdk-9\b
false
true
20000
10000
10000
pool-1-thread-1:10000
pool-1-thread-2:10000
```

You can see how before splitting the spliterator, the estimatedSize() method returns 20,000 elements. After the execution of the trySplit() method, both spliterators have 10,000 elements. These are the elements processed by each of the tasks.

Atomic variables

Atomic variables were introduced in Java 1.5 to provide atomic operations over integer, long, boolean, reference, and Array objects. They provide some methods to increment, decrement, establish the value, return the value, or establish the value if its current value is equal to a predefined one. Atomic variables offer guarantees similar to the volatile keyword.

In Java 8, four new classes were added. These are DoubleAccumulator, DoubleAdder, LongAccumulator, and LongAdder. In a previous section, we used the LongAdder class to count the number of bad reviews of the products. This class provides similar functionality to AtomicLong, but it has better performance when you frequently update the cumulative sum from different threads and request the result only at the end of the operation. The DoubleAdder function is equal to it but with double values. The main objective of both classes is to have a counter that can be updated by different threads in a consistent way. The most important methods of these classes are:

- add(): Increment the value of the counter with the value specified as a parameter
- increment(): Equivalent to add(1)

- decrement(): Equivalent to add(-1)
- sum(): This method returns the current value of the counter

Take into account that the DoubleAdder class doesn't have the increment() and decrement() methods.

The LongAccumulator and LongAdder classes are similar but they have a very important difference. They have a constructor where you specify two parameters:

- The identity value of the internal counter
- A function to accumulate the new value into the accumulator

Note that the function must not depend on the order of accumulation. In this case, the most important methods are:

- accumulate(): This method receives a long value as a parameter. It applies the function to increment or decrement the counter to the current value and the parameter.
- get(): Returns the current value of the counter.

For example, the following code will write 362,880 in the console in all the executions:

```
LongAccumulator accumulator=new LongAccumulator((x,y) -> x*y, 1);

IntStream.range(1, 10).parallel().forEach(x -> accumulator
                                          .accumulate(x));
System.out.println(accumulator.get());
```

We use a commutative operation inside the accumulator so the result is the same for any input order.

Variable handles

A **variable handle** is a dynamically typed reference to a variable, static field, or element of array that allows you different access modes to that variable. You can, for example, protect access to that variable in a concurrent application allowing an atomic access to the variable. Until now, you could only obtain this behavior with atomic variables, but now you can use variable handles to obtain the same functionality without using any synchronization mechanisms.

This mechanism is a new feature in Java 9 and is provided by the `VarHandle` class. You can get the following access methods to a variable handle:

- **Read access mode**: This mode allows you to read the value of the variable with different memory ordering rules depending on the method. You can use the `get()`, `getVolatile()`, `getAcquire()` and `getOpaque()` methods to read the value of the variable. The first method reads the variable as if it was a non-volatile variable. The second method read the value of the variable as if it was a volatile variable. The third method guarantees that other access to this variable will not be reordered before this sentence for optimization purposes and finally the last method is similar to the previous one, but it only affects to the current thread.

- **Write access mode**: This mode allows you to write the value of the variable with different memory ordering rules depending on the method. You can use the methods `set()`, `setVolatile()`, `setRelease()`, and `setOpaque()`. They are equivalent to the previous ones, but with write access.

- **Atomic update access mode**: To get functionality similar to the one provided by the atomic variables with operations to, for example, compare the values of the variable. You can use the following methods:
    - `compareAndSet()`: Change the value of the variable as it was declared as a volatile variable if the expected value passed as a parameter is equal to the current value of the variable.
    - `weakCompareAndSet()` and `weakCompareAndSetPlain()`: Atomically change the current value of the variable with the new one if the expected value passed as parameter is equals to the current one. The first method works as if the variable was a volatile variable and the second one as if the variable was a non-volatile variable

- **Numeric atomic update access mode** : To modify numerical values in an atomic way. You can use the following methods:
    - `getAndAdd()`: Increase the value of the variable and return the previous value as it was declared as a volatile variable atomically.

- **Bitwise atomic update access mode**: To modify bitwise values in an atomic way. You can use methods such as `getAndBitwiseOr()` or `getAndBitwiseAnd()`.

For example, let's use a class named `VarHandleData` with two double attributes named `safeValue` and `unsafeValue`:

```
public class VarHandleData {
    public double safeValue;
    public double unsafeValue;
}
```

Let's implement an example where we have 10 threads that concurrently update the value of both attributes. We are going to use a `VarHandle` to update the value of the `safeValue` attribute and update the value of the `unsafeValue` attribute directly.

The easiest way to create a `VarHandle` object of a field of an object is by using the static method `lookup()` of the `MethodHandles` class. This method returns a `MethodHandles.Lookup` object that is a factory for creating `MethodHandles`. Then, we use the `in()` method to obtain a `MethodHandles` for the class, in this case for the `VarHandleData`, and finally, we use the `findVarHandle()` method to obtain the `VarHandle` object to access a field of the object.

For example, if we want a `VarHandle` to access the `safeValue` attribute of the `VarHandleData` object, we can use the following instruction:

```
handler = MethodHandles.lookup().in(VarHandleData.class)
                  .findVarHandle(VarHandleData.class,
                                "safeValue", double.class);
```

So, we implement a class named `VarHandleTask` that implements the `Runnable` interface that increments and decrements the value of both attributes of a `VarHandleData` object. As we mentioned before, we use a `VarHandle` object to access the `safeValue` attribute (with the `getAndAdd()` method) and we modify the `unsafeValue` attribute directly:

```
public class VarHandleTask implements Runnable {
    private VarHandleData data;
    public VarHandleTask(VarHandleData data) {
        this.data = data;
    }
    @Override
    public void run() {
        VarHandle handler;
        try {
            handler = MethodHandles.lookup().in(VarHandleData.class)
                          .findVarHandle(VarHandleData.class,
                                        "safeValue", double.class);
            for (int i = 0; i < 10000; i++) {
                handler.getAndAdd(data, +100);
```

```
            data.unsafeValue += 100;
            handler.getAndAdd(data, -100);
            data.unsafeValue -= 100;
        }
    } catch (NoSuchFieldException | IllegalAccessException e) {
        e.printStackTrace();
    }
  }
}
```

Finally, we implement the `VarHandleMain` class that creates a `VarHandleData` object and 10 `VarHandleTasks` that update the same object concurrently:

```
public class VarHandleMain {
  public static void main(String[] args) {
    VarHandleData data = new VarHandleData();
      for (int i=0; i<10; i++) {
        VarHandleTask task=new VarHandleTask(data);
        ForkJoinPool.commonPool().execute(task);
      }
      ForkJoinPool.commonPool().shutdown();
      try {
        ForkJoinPool.commonPool().awaitTermination(1, TimeUnit.DAYS);
      } catch (InterruptedException e) {
        // TODO Auto-generated catch block
        e.printStackTrace();
      }
      System.out.println("Safe Value: "+data.safeValue);
      System.out.println("Unsafe Value: "+data.unsafeValue);
    }
  }
}
```

When you execute this example, you will see how the value of the `safeValue` attribute is always 0 as expected, but the value of the `unsafeValue` attribute varies from one execution to another, as you will get data race conditions.

Synchronization mechanisms

Synchronization of tasks is the coordination between those tasks to get the desired results. In concurrent applications, we can have two kinds of synchronizations:

- **Process synchronization**: We use this kind of synchronization when we want to control the order of execution of tasks. For example, a task must wait for the finalization of other tasks before it starts its execution.

- **Data synchronization**: We use this kind of synchronization when two or more tasks access the same memory object. In this case, you have to protect the access in the write operations to that object. If you don't do this, you could have a data race condition where the final results of a program vary from one execution to another.

The Java Concurrency API provides mechanisms that allow you to implement both types of synchronization. The most basic synchronization mechanism provided by the Java language is the synchronized keyword. This keyword can be applied to a method or to a block of code. In the first case, only one thread can execute the method at a time. In the second case, you have to specify a reference to an object. In this case, only one block of code protected by an object can be executed at the same time.

Java also provides other synchronization mechanisms:

- The Lock interfaces and its implementation classes: This mechanism allows you to implement a critical section to guarantee that only one thread will execute that block of code.
- The Semaphore class that implements the well-known **semaphore** synchronization mechanism introduced by *Edsger Dijkstra*.
- CountDownLatch allows you to implement a situation where one or more threads wait for the finalization of other threads.
- CyclicBarrier allows you to synchronize different tasks in a common point.
- Phaser allows you to implement concurrent tasks divided into phases. We made a detailed description of this mechanism in Chapter 6, *Running Tasks Divided into Phases - The Phaser Class*.
- Exchanger allows you to implement a point of data interchange between two threads.
- CompletableFuture, a new feature of Java 8, extends the Future mechanism of executor tasks to generate the result of a task in an asynchronous way. You can specify tasks to be executed after the result is generated, so you can control the order of the execution of tasks.

In the following section, we will show you how to use these mechanisms, giving special attention to the CompletableFuture mechanism introduced in the Java 8 version.

The CommonTask class

We have implemented a class named the CommonTask class. This class will sleep the calling thread for a random period of time between 0 and 10 seconds. This is its source code:

```
public class CommonTask {

  public static void doTask() {
    long duration = ThreadLocalRandom.current().nextLong(10);
    System.out.printf("%s-%s: Working %d seconds\n",
                      new Date(),Thread.currentThread().getName(),
                      duration);
    try {
      TimeUnit.SECONDS.sleep(duration);
    } catch (InterruptedException e) {
      e.printStackTrace();
    }
  }

}
```

All the tasks we're going to implement in the following sections will use this class to simulate its execution time.

The Lock interface

One of the most basic synchronization mechanisms is the Lock interface and its implementation classes. The basic implementation class is the ReentrantLock class. You can use this class to implement a critical section in an easy way. For example, the following task gets a lock in the first line of its code using the lock() method and releases it in the last line using the unlock() method. You must include the calling to the unlock() method in a finally section to avoid any problems. Otherwise, if an Exception is thrown, the lock won't be released and you will have a deadlock. Only one task can execute the code between these two sentences at the same time.

```
public class LockTask implements Runnable {

  private static ReentrantLock lock = new ReentrantLock();
  private String name;

  public LockTask(String name) {
    this.name=name;
  }
```

```
@Override
public void run() {
  try {
    lock.lock();
    System.out.println("Task: " + name + "; Date: " + new Date()
                          + ": Running the task");
    CommonTask.doTask();
    System.out.println("Task: " + name + "; Date: " + new Date()
                          + ": The execution has finished");
  } finally {
    lock.unlock();
  }

  }
}
```

You can check this if, for example, you execute ten tasks in an executor using the following code:

```
public class LockMain {

  public static void main(String[] args) {
    ThreadPoolExecutor executor=(ThreadPoolExecutor)
                                  Executors.newCachedThreadPool();
    for (int i=0; i<10; i++) {
      executor.execute(new LockTask("Task "+i));
    }
    executor.shutdown();
    try {
      executor.awaitTermination(1, TimeUnit.DAYS);
    } catch (InterruptedException e) {
      e.printStackTrace();
    }
  }
}
```

In the following image, you can see the results of an execution of this example. You can see how only one task was executed at a time:

```
<terminated> LockMain [Java Application] C:\Program Files\Java\jdk-9\bin\javaw.exe (12 abr. 2017 1:00:27)
Task: Task 0; Date: Wed Apr 12 01:00:28 CEST 2017: Running the task
Wed Apr 12 01:00:29 CEST 2017-pool-1-thread-1: Working 3 seconds
Task: Task 0; Date: Wed Apr 12 01:00:32 CEST 2017: The execution has finished
Task: Task 1; Date: Wed Apr 12 01:00:32 CEST 2017: Running the task
Wed Apr 12 01:00:32 CEST 2017-pool-1-thread-2: Working 7 seconds
Task: Task 1; Date: Wed Apr 12 01:00:39 CEST 2017: The execution has finished
Task: Task 2; Date: Wed Apr 12 01:00:39 CEST 2017: Running the task
Wed Apr 12 01:00:39 CEST 2017-pool-1-thread-3: Working 3 seconds
Task: Task 2; Date: Wed Apr 12 01:00:42 CEST 2017: The execution has finished
Task: Task 4; Date: Wed Apr 12 01:00:42 CEST 2017: Running the task
Wed Apr 12 01:00:42 CEST 2017-pool-1-thread-5: Working 1 seconds
Task: Task 4; Date: Wed Apr 12 01:00:43 CEST 2017: The execution has finished
Task: Task 6; Date: Wed Apr 12 01:00:43 CEST 2017: Running the task
```

The Semaphore class

The semaphore mechanism was introduced by Edsger Dijkstra in 1962 and is used to control the access to one or more shared resources. This mechanism is based in an internal counter and two methods named wait() and signal().When a thread calls the wait() method, if the internal counter has a value bigger than 0, then the semaphore decrements the internal counter and the thread gets access to the shared resource. If the internal counter has a value of 0, the thread is blocked until a thread calls the signal() method. When a thread calls the signal() method, the semaphore looks whether there are some threads waiting in the waiting state (they have called the wait() method). If there are no threads waiting, it increments the internal counter. If there are threads waiting for the semaphore, it gets one of those threads that will return for the wait() method and access the shared resource. The other threads that were waiting continue waiting for their turn.

In Java, semaphores are implemented in the Semaphore class. The wait() method is called acquire() and the signal() method is called release(). For example, in this example, we have used this task where a Semaphore class is protecting its code:

```java
public class SemaphoreTask implements Runnable{
  private Semaphore semaphore;
  public SemaphoreTask(Semaphore semaphore) {
    this.semaphore=semaphore;
  }
  @Override
  public void run() {
    try {
      semaphore.acquire();
     CommonTask.doTask();
      } catch (InterruptedException e) {
```

```
            e.printStackTrace();
        } finally {
            semaphore.release();
        }
    }
}
```

In the main program, we execute 10 tasks that share a `Semaphore` class initialized with two shared resources, so we will have two tasks running at the same time:

```
public static void main(String[] args) {

    Semaphore semaphore=new Semaphore(2);
    ThreadPoolExecutor executor=(ThreadPoolExecutor)
                            Executors.newCachedThreadPool();

    for (int i=0; i<10; i++) {
        executor.execute(new SemaphoreTask(semaphore));
    }

    executor.shutdown();
    try {
        executor.awaitTermination(1, TimeUnit.DAYS);
    } catch (InterruptedException e) {
        e.printStackTrace();
    }
}
```

The following screenshot shows the results of an execution of this example. You can see how two tasks are running at the same time:

```
<terminated> SemaphoreMain [Java Application] C:\Program Files\Java\jdk-9\bin\javaw.e
Wed Apr 12 01:03:17 CEST 2017-pool-1-thread-2: Working 9 seconds
Wed Apr 12 01:03:17 CEST 2017-pool-1-thread-1: Working 5 seconds
Wed Apr 12 01:03:23 CEST 2017-pool-1-thread-3: Working 6 seconds
Wed Apr 12 01:03:27 CEST 2017-pool-1-thread-4: Working 3 seconds
Wed Apr 12 01:03:29 CEST 2017-pool-1-thread-5: Working 8 seconds
Wed Apr 12 01:03:30 CEST 2017-pool-1-thread-6: Working 9 seconds
Wed Apr 12 01:03:37 CEST 2017-pool-1-thread-7: Working 2 seconds
Wed Apr 12 01:03:39 CEST 2017-pool-1-thread-8: Working 3 seconds
Wed Apr 12 01:03:39 CEST 2017-pool-1-thread-9: Working 6 seconds
Wed Apr 12 01:03:42 CEST 2017-pool-1-thread-10: Working 9 seconds
```

The CountDownLatch class

This class provides a mechanism to wait for the finalization of one or more concurrent tasks. It has an internal counter that must be initialized with the number of tasks we are going to wait for. Then, the `await()` method sleeps the calling thread until the internal counter arrives at zero and the `countDown()` method decrements that internal counter.

For example, in this task, we use the `countDown()` method to decrement the internal counter of the `CountDownLatch` object it receives as a parameter in its constructor:

```
public class CountDownTask implements Runnable {

  private CountDownLatch countDownLatch;

  public CountDownTask(CountDownLatch countDownLatch) {
    this.countDownLatch=countDownLatch;
  }

  @Override
  public void run() {
    CommonTask.doTask();
    countDownLatch.countDown();

  }
}
```

Then, in the `main()` method, we execute the tasks in an executor and wait for their finalization using the `await()` method of `CountDownLatch`. The object is initialized with the number of tasks we want to wait for.

```
public static void main(String[] args) {

  CountDownLatch countDownLatch=new CountDownLatch(10);

  ThreadPoolExecutor executor=(ThreadPoolExecutor)
                              Executors.newCachedThreadPool();

  System.out.println("Main: Launching tasks");
  for (int i=0; i<10; i++) {
    executor.execute(new CountDownTask(countDownLatch));
  }

  try {
    countDownLatch.await();
  } catch (InterruptedException e) {
    e.printStackTrace();
  }
```

```
    System.out.

    executor.shutdown();
}
```

The following screenshot shows the results of an execution of this example:

```
<terminated> CountDownMain [Java Application] C:\Program Files\Java\jdk-9\bin\java
Main: Launching tasks
Wed Apr 12 01:05:14 CEST 2017-pool-1-thread-6: Working 9 seconds
Wed Apr 12 01:05:14 CEST 2017-pool-1-thread-8: Working 9 seconds
Wed Apr 12 01:05:14 CEST 2017-pool-1-thread-4: Working 5 seconds
Wed Apr 12 01:05:14 CEST 2017-pool-1-thread-2: Working 9 seconds
Wed Apr 12 01:05:14 CEST 2017-pool-1-thread-1: Working 5 seconds
Wed Apr 12 01:05:14 CEST 2017-pool-1-thread-9: Working 4 seconds
Wed Apr 12 01:05:14 CEST 2017-pool-1-thread-5: Working 8 seconds
Wed Apr 12 01:05:14 CEST 2017-pool-1-thread-3: Working 3 seconds
Wed Apr 12 01:05:14 CEST 2017-pool-1-thread-10: Working 2 seconds
Wed Apr 12 01:05:14 CEST 2017-pool-1-thread-7: Working 8 seconds
Main: Tasks finished at Wed Apr 12 01:05:24 CEST 2017
```

The CyclicBarrier class

This class allows you to synchronize some tasks at a common point. All tasks will wait at that point until all have arrived. Internally, it also manages an internal counter with the tasks that haven't arrived at that point yet. When a task arrives at the determined point, it has to execute the await() method to wait for the rest of the tasks. When all the tasks have arrived, the CyclicBarrier object wakes them up so they continue with their execution.

This class allows you to execute another task when all the parties have arrived. To configure this, you have to specify a Runnable object in the constructor of the object.

For example, we have implemented the following Runnable that uses a CyclicBarrier object to wait for other tasks:

```
public class BarrierTask implements Runnable {

    private CyclicBarrier barrier;

    public BarrierTask(CyclicBarrier barrier) {
        this.barrier=barrier;
    }

    @Override
    public void run() {
        System.out.println(Thread.currentThread().getName()+": Phase 1");
        CommonTask.doTask();
```

```
    try {
      barrier.await();
    } catch (InterruptedException e) {
      e.printStackTrace();
    } catch (BrokenBarrierException e) {
      e.printStackTrace();
    }
    System.out.println(Thread.currentThread().getName()+": Phase 2");

  }
}
```

We have also implemented another `Runnable` object that will be executed by `CyclicBarrier` when all the tasks have executed the `await()` method.

```
public class FinishBarrierTask implements Runnable {

  @Override
  public void run() {
    System.out.println("FinishBarrierTask: All the tasks have finished");
  }
}
```

Finally, in the `main()` method, we execute 10 tasks in an executor. You can see how `CyclicBarrier` is initialized with the number of tasks we want to synchronize and with an object of the `FinishBarrierTask` object:

```
public static void main(String[] args) {
  CyclicBarrier barrier=new CyclicBarrier(10,new FinishBarrierTask());

  ThreadPoolExecutor executor=(ThreadPoolExecutor)
Executors.newCachedThreadPool();

  for (int i=0; i<10; i++) {
    executor.execute(new BarrierTask(barrier));
  }

  executor.shutdown();

  try {
    executor.awaitTermination(1, TimeUnit.DAYS);
  } catch (InterruptedException e) {
    e.printStackTrace();
  }
}
```

The following screenshot shows the results of an execution of this example:

```
<terminated> BarrierMain [Java Application] C:\Program Files\Java\jdk-9\bin\javaw.exe
Wed Apr 12 01:07:00 CEST 2017-pool-1-thread-8: Working 7 seconds
FinishBarrierTask: All the tasks have finished
pool-1-thread-8: Phase 2
pool-1-thread-9: Phase 2
pool-1-thread-7: Phase 2
pool-1-thread-3: Phase 2
pool-1-thread-1: Phase 2
pool-1-thread-5: Phase 2
pool-1-thread-6: Phase 2
pool-1-thread-4: Phase 2
pool-1-thread-10: Phase 2
pool-1-thread-2: Phase 2
```

You can see how, when all the tasks arrive at the point where the `await()` method is called, `FinishBarrierTask` is executed and then all the tasks continue with their execution.

The CompletableFuture class

This is a synchronization mechanism introduced in the Java 8 concurrency API that has new methods in Java 9. It extends the `Future` mechanism, giving it more power and flexibility. It allows you to implement an event-driven model, linking tasks that will only be executed when others have finished. As with the `Future` interface, `CompletableFuture` must be parameterized with the type of the result that will be returned by the operation. As with a `Future` object, the `CompletableFuture` class represents a result of an asynchronous computation, but the result of `CompletableFuture` can be established by any thread. It has the `complete()` method to establish the result when the computation ends normally and the method `completeExceptionally()` when the computation ends with an exception. If two or more threads call the `complete()` or `completeExceptionally()` methods over the same `CompletableFuture`, only the first call will take effect.

First, you can create `CompletableFuture` using its constructor. In this case, you have to establish the result of the task using the `complete()` method, as we explained before. But you can also create one using the `runAsync()` or `supplyAsync()` methods. The `runAsync()` method executes a `Runnable` object and returns `CompletableFuture<Void>` so that computation can't return any results. The `supplyAsync()` method executes an implementation of the `Supplier` interface parametrized with the type that will be returned by this computation. The `Supplier` interface provides the `get()` method. In that method, we have to include the code of the task and return the result generated by it. In this case, the result of `CompletableFuture` will be the result of the `Supplier` interface.

This class provides a lot of methods that allow you to organize the order of execution of tasks implementing an event-driven model, where one task doesn't start its execution until the previous one has finished. These are some of those methods:

- `thenApplyAsync()`: This method receives an implementation of the `Function` interface that can be represented as a lambda expression as a parameter. This function will be executed when the calling `CompletableFuture` has been completed. This method will return `CompletableFuture` to get the result of the `Function`.
- `thenComposeAsync()`: This method is analogue to `thenApplyAsync`, but is useful when the supplied function returns `CompletableFuture` too.
- `thenAcceptAsync()`: This method is similar to the previous one, but the parameter is an implementation of the `Consumer` interface that can also be specified as a lambda expression; in this case, the computation won't return a result.
- `thenRunAsync()`: This method is equivalent to the previous one, but in this case receives a `Runnable` object as a parameter.
- `thenCombineAsync()`: This method receives two parameters. The first one is another `CompletableFuture` instance. The other is an implementation of the `BiFunction` interfaces that can be specified as a lambda function. This `BiFunction` will be executed when both `CompletableFuture` (the calling one and the parameter) have been completed. This method will return `CompletableFuture` to get the result of the `BiFunction`.
- `runAfterBothAsync()`: This method receives two parameters. The first one is another `CompletableFuture`. The other one is an implementation of the `Runnable` interface that will be executed when both `CompletableFuture` (the calling one and the parameter) have been completed.
- `runAfterEitherAsync()`: This method is equivalent to the previous one, but the `Runnable` task is executed when one of the `CompletableFuture` objects is completed.
- `allOf()`: This method receives a variable list of `CompletableFuture` objects as a parameter. It will return a `CompletableFuture<Void>` object that will return its result when all the `CompletableFuture` objects have been completed.
- `anyOf()`: This method is equivalent to the previous one, but the returned `CompletableFuture` returns its result when one of the `CompletableFuture` is completed.

Finally, if you want to obtain the result returned by CompletableFuture, you can use the get() or join() methods. Both methods block the calling thread until CompletableFuture has been completed and then returns its result. The main difference between both methods is that get() throws ExecutionException, which is a checked exception, but join() throws RuntimeException (which is an unchecked exception). Thus, it's easier to use join() inside non-throwing lambdas (like Supplier, Consumer, or Runnable).

Most of the methods explained before have the Async suffix. This means that these methods will be executed in a concurrent way using the ForkJoinPool.commonPool instance. Those methods that have versions without the Async suffix will be executed in a serial way (that is to say, in the same thread where CompletableFuture is executed) and with the Async suffix and an executor instance as an additional parameter. In this case, CompletableFuture will be executed asynchronously in the executor passed as a parameter.

Java 9 has added some methods to give more power to the CompletableFuture class.

- defaultExecutor(): This method returns the default Executor used for Async operations that don't receive an Executor as a parameter. Normally, it will be the returned value of the ForkJoinPool.commonPool() method.
- copy(): This method creates a copy of a CompletableFuture object. If the original CompletableFuture completes normally, the copy will also be completed normally with the same value. If the original CompletableFuture completes exceptionally, the copy completes exceptionally with a CompletionException.
- completeAsync(): This method receives a Supplier object as a parameter (and optionally, an Executor). Completes the CompletableFuture with the result of the Supplier.
- orTimeout(): Receives a timeout (a period of time and a TimeUnit). If the CompletableFuture is not completed after that period of time, completes exceptionally with a TimeoutException.
- completeOnTimeout(): This method is similar to the previous one, but it completes normally with the value received as a parameter.
- delayedExecutor(): This method returns an Executor that executes a task after the specified delay.

Using the CompletableFuture class

In this example, you will learn how to use the `CompletableFuture` class to implement the execution of some asynchronous tasks in a concurrent way. We will use our collection of 20,000 products from Amazon to implement the following tree of tasks:

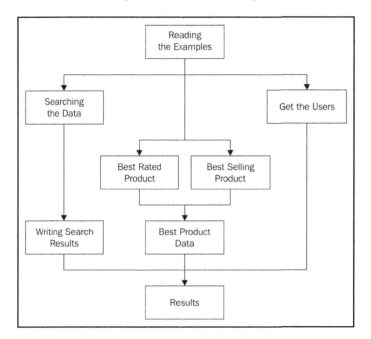

First, we're going to use the examples. Then, we will execute four concurrent tasks. The first one will make a search of products. When the search finishes, we will write the results to a file. The second one will obtain the best-rated product. The third one will obtain the best-selling product. When these both finish, we will concatenate their information using another task. Finally, the fourth task will get a list with the users who have purchased a product. The `main()` program will wait for the finalization of all the tasks and then will write the results.

Let's see the details of the implementation.

Auxiliary tasks

In this example, we will use some auxiliary tasks. The first one is `LoadTask` that will load the product information from the disk and will return a list of `Product` objects:

```java
public class LoadTask implements Supplier<List<Product>> {

    private Path path;

    public LoadTask (Path path) {
        this.path=path;
    }
    @Override
    public List<Product> get() {
        List<Product> productList=null;
        try {
            productList = Files.walk(path, FileVisitOption.FOLLOW_LINKS)
                              .parallel().filter(f -> f.toString()
                              .endsWith(".txt")).map(ProductLoader::load)
                              .collect (Collectors.toList());
        } catch (IOException e) {
            e.printStackTrace();
        }

        return productList;
    }
}
```

It implements the `Supplier` interface to be executed as `CompletableFuture`. Inside, it uses a stream to process and parse all the files obtaining a list of products.

The second task is `SearchTask` that will implement the search in the list of `Product` objects, looking for the ones that contain a word in the title. This task is an implementation of the `Function` interface.

```java
public class SearchTask implements Function<List<Product>,
                                            List<Product>> {

    private String query;

    public SearchTask(String query) {
        this.query=query;
    }

    @Override
    public List<Product> apply(List<Product> products) {
        System.out.println(new Date()+": CompletableTask: start");
        List<Product> ret = products.stream()
```

```
                              .filter(product -> product.getTitle()
                              .toLowerCase().contains(query))
                              .collect(Collectors.toList());
        System.out.println(new Date()+": CompletableTask: end:
                              "+ret.size());
        return ret;
    }

}
```

It receives List<Product> with the information of all the products and returns List<Product> with the products that meet the criteria. Internally, it creates the stream on the input list, filters it, and collects the results in another list.

Finally, the WriteTask is going to write the products obtained in the search task in a File. In our case, we generate a HTML file, but feel free to write this information in the format you want. This task implements the Consumer interface, so its code must be something like the following:

```
public class WriteTask implements Consumer<List<Product>> {

    @Override
    public void accept(List<Product> products) {
        // implementation is omitted
    }
}
```

The main() method

We have organized the execution of the tasks in the main() method. First, we execute the LoadTask using the supplyAsync() method of the CompletableFuture class. We are going to wait three seconds before the start of the LoadTask to show how the delayExecutor() method works.

```
public class CompletableMain {

    public static void main(String[] args) {
        Path file = Paths.get("data","category");
        System.out.println(new Date() + ": Main: Loading products
                         after three seconds....");
        LoadTask loadTask = new LoadTask(file);

        CompletableFuture<List<Product>>loadFuture = CompletableFuture
                         .supplyAsync(loadTask,CompletableFuture
                         .delayedExecutor(3, TimeUnit.SECONDS));
```

Then, with the resultant `CompletableFuture`, we use `thenApplyAsync()` to execute the search task when the load task has been completed:

```
System.out.println(new Date() + ": Main: Then apply for
                    search");

CompletableFuture<List<Product>> completableSearch = loadFuture
                .thenApplyAsync(new SearchTask("love"));
```

Once the search task has been completed, we want to write the results of the execution in a file. As this task won't return a result, we use the `thenAcceptAsync()` method:

```
CompletableFuture<Void> completableWrite = completableSearch
                    .thenAcceptAsync(new WriteTask());

completableWrite.exceptionally(ex -> {
   System.out.println(new Date() + ": Main: Exception "
                    + ex.getMessage());
   return null;
});
```

We have used the `exceptionally()` method to specify what we want to do if the write task throws an exception.

Then, we use the `thenApplyAsync()` method over the `completableFuture` object to execute the task to get the list of users who purchased a product. We specify this task as a lambda expression. Take into account that this task will be executed in parallel with the search task:

```
System.out.println(new Date() + ": Main: Then apply for users");

CompletableFuture<List<String>> completableUsers = loadFuture
                            .thenApplyAsync(resultList -> {

   System.out.println(new Date() + ": Main: Completable users :start");
   List<String> users = resultList.stream()
                    .flatMap(p -> p.getReviews().stream())
                    .map(review -> review.getUser())
                    .distinct()
                    .collect(Collectors.toList());
   System.out.println(new Date() + ": Main: Completable users :end");

   return users;
});
```

In parallel with these tasks, we also executed the tasks using the `thenApplyAsync()` method to find the best-rated product and the best-selling product. We have defined these tasks using a lambda expression too:

```
System.out.println(new Date() + ": Main: Then apply for best
                                rated product....");

CompletableFuture<Product> completableProduct = loadFuture
                          .thenApplyAsync(resultList -> {
  Product maxProduct = null;
  double maxScore = 0.0;

  System.out.println(new Date() + ": Main: Completable product:
                                   start");
  for (Product product : resultList) {
  if (!product.getReviews().isEmpty()) {
    double score = product.getReviews().stream()
                  .mapToDouble(review -> review.getValue())
                  .average().getAsDouble();
    if (score > maxScore) {
      maxProduct = product;
      maxScore = score;
    }
  }
  }
  System.out.println(new Date() + ": Main: Completable product : end");
  return maxProduct;
});

System.out.println(new Date() + ": Main: Then apply for best
                                selling product....");
CompletableFuture<Product> completableBestSellingProduct =
                loadFuture.thenApplyAsync(resultList -> {
  System.out.println(new Date() + ": Main: Completable best
                                selling: start");
  Product bestProduct = resultList.stream()
                      .min(Comparator.comparingLong
                          (Product::getSalesrank))
                      .orElse(null);
  System.out.println(new Date() + ": Main: Completable best
                                selling: end");
  return bestProduct;

});
```

As we mentioned before, we want to concatenate the results of the last two tasks. We can do this using the `thenCombineAsync()` method to specify a task that will be executed after both tasks have been completed:

```
CompletableFuture<String> completableProductResult =
                completableBestSellingProduct
                .thenCombineAsync(
                completableProduct, (bestSellingProduct,
                                     bestRatedProduct) -> {
    System.out.println(new Date() + ": Main: Completable product
                                    result: start");
    String ret = "The best selling product is "
                + bestSellingProduct.getTitle() + "\n";
    ret += "The best rated product is "
          + bestRatedProduct.getTitle();
    System.out.println(new Date() + ": Main: Completable product
                                    result: end");
    return ret;
});
```

Finally, we give one second to the `completableProductResult` task to finish using the `completeOnTimeout()` method. If it doesn't finish before one second, we complete that `CompletableFuture` with the result `"TimeOut"`. Then, we wait for the end of the final tasks using the `allOf()` and `join()` methods and write the results using the `get()` method to obtain them:

```
System.out.println(new Date() + ": Main: Waiting for results");

completableProductResult.completeOnTimeout("TimeOut", 1,
                                    TimeUnit.SECONDS);
CompletableFuture<Void> finalCompletableFuture = CompletableFuture
                .allOf(completableProductResult, completableUsers,
                        completableWrite);
finalCompletableFuture.join();

try {
  System.out.println("Number of loaded products: "
                    + loadFuture.get().size());
  System.out.println("Number of found products: "
                    + completableSearch.get().size());
  System.out.println("Number of users: "
                    + completableUsers.get().size());
  System.out.println("Best rated product: "
                    + completableProduct.get().getTitle());
  System.out.println("Best selling product: "
                    + completableBestSellingProduct.get()
                    .getTitle());
```

```
    System.out.println("Product result: 
                    "+completableProductResult.get());
} catch (InterruptedException | ExecutionException e) {
    e.printStackTrace();
}
```

In the following screenshot, you can see the results of an execution of this example:

```
<terminated> CompletableMain [Java Application] C:\Program Files\Java\jdk-9\bin\javaw.exe (12 abr. 20
Wed Apr 12 01:37:12 CEST 2017: Main: Loading products after three seconds....
Wed Apr 12 01:37:13 CEST 2017: Main: Then apply for search....
Wed Apr 12 01:37:13 CEST 2017: Main: Then apply for users....
Wed Apr 12 01:37:13 CEST 2017: Main: Then apply for best rated product....
Wed Apr 12 01:37:13 CEST 2017: Main: Then apply for best selling product....
Wed Apr 12 01:37:13 CEST 2017: Main: Waiting for results
Wed Apr 12 01:37:16 CEST 2017: LoadTast: starting....
Wed Apr 12 01:38:19 CEST 2017: LoadTast: end
Wed Apr 12 01:38:19 CEST 2017: Main: Completable best selling: start
Wed Apr 12 01:38:19 CEST 2017: CompletableTask: start
Wed Apr 12 01:38:19 CEST 2017: Main: Completable product: start
Wed Apr 12 01:38:19 CEST 2017: Main: Completable best selling: end
Wed Apr 12 01:38:19 CEST 2017: Main: Completable users: start
Wed Apr 12 01:38:19 CEST 2017: CompletableTask: end: 208
Wed Apr 12 01:38:19 CEST 2017: WriteTask: start
Wed Apr 12 01:38:19 CEST 2017: WriteTask: end
Wed Apr 12 01:38:19 CEST 2017: Main: Completable product: end
Wed Apr 12 01:38:19 CEST 2017: Main: Completable users: end
Number of loaded products: 20000
Number of found products: 208
Number of users: 158288
Best rated product: Patterns of Preaching
Best selling product: The Da Vinci Code
Product result: TimeOut
Wed Apr 12 01:38:19 CEST 2017: Main: end
```

First, the `main()` method executes all the configurations and waits for the finalization of the tasks. The execution of the tasks follows the order we have configured. You can see how the `LoadTask` starts after three seconds and how the `completableProductResult` returns the `String "TimeOut"`, as it isn't completed in one second.

Summary

In this chapter, we have reviewed two components of all concurrent applications. The first one is data structures. Every program uses them to store in memory the information it has to process. We have quickly been introduced to concurrent data structures to create a detailed description of the new features introduced in the Java 8 Concurrency API that affects the `ConcurrentHashMap` class and the classes that implement the `Collection` interface.

The second one is the synchronization mechanisms that allow you to protect your data when more than one concurrent task wants to modify them, and to control the order of execution of the tasks if it's necessary. In this case, we have also quickly been introduced to the synchronization mechanisms, giving a detailed description of `CompletableFuture`, a new feature of the Java 8 Concurrency API.

In the next chapter, we will show you how you can implement complete concurrent systems, integrating different parts that can also be concurrent and using different classes to implement concurrency.

—

12
Testing and Monitoring Concurrent Applications

Software testing is a critical task in every development process. Every application has to fulfill end user requirements, and the testing phase is the place to prove this. It has to generate valid results in an acceptable time and with the specified format. The main objective of the testing phase is to detect as many errors as possible in the software to correct them and increase the global quality of the product.

Traditionally, in the waterfall model, the testing phase begins when the development phase is very advanced, but nowadays, more and more development teams are using agile methodologies, where the testing phase is integrated into the development phase. The main objective is to test the software as soon as possible to detect errors earlier in the process.

In Java, there are a lot of tools, such as **JUnit** or **TestNG**, to automatize the execution of tests. Other tools, such as **JMeter**, allow you to test how many users can execute your application at the same time, and there are other tools, such as **Selenium**, that you can use to make integration tests in web applications.

The testing phase is more critical and more difficult in concurrent applications. You have two or more threads running at the same time, but you can't control their order of execution. You can do a lot of tests on an application, but you can't guarantee that there isn't an order of execution of the different threads that provokes a race condition or a deadlock. This circumstance also causes difficulty in the reproduction of errors. You can find an error that only occurs in certain circumstances, so it can be difficult to find its real cause. In this chapter, we will cover the following topics to help you to test concurrent applications:

- Monitoring concurrency objects
- Monitoring concurrency applications
- Testing concurrency applications

Monitoring concurrency objects

Most of the concurrency objects provided by the Java concurrency API include methods to learn their status. This status can include the number of threads that are executing, the number of threads blocked waiting for a condition, the number of tasks executed, and so on. In this section, you will learn the most important methods you can use and the information you can obtain from them. This information can be very useful to detect the cause of an error, especially if it only occurs in very rare conditions.

Monitoring a thread

The thread is the most basic element in the Java concurrency API. It allows you to implement a raw task. You decide what code is going to execute (extending the `Thread` class or implementing the `Runnable` interface), when it starts its execution, and how it synchronizes with other tasks of the application. The `Thread` class provides some methods to obtain information about a thread. These are the most useful methods:

- `getId()`: This method returns the identifier of the thread. It's a `long` positive number and it's unique.
- `getName()`: This method returns the name of the thread. By default, it has the format `Thread-xxx`, but it can be modified in the constructor or using the `setName()` method.
- `getPriority()`: This method returns the priority of the thread. By default, all the threads have a priority of five, but you can change it using the `setPriority()` method. Threads with higher priority may have preference over threads with lower priority.
- `getState()`: This method returns the state of the thread. It returns a value of `Enum Thread.State`, which can take the values: `NEW`, `RUNNABLE`, `BLOCKED`, `WAITING`, `TIMED_WAITING`, and `TERMINATED`. You can check the API documentation to see the real significance of every state.
- `getStackTrace()`: This method returns the stack of calls of this thread as an array of `StackTraceElement` objects. You can print this array to know what calls have made the thread.

For example, you can use a piece of code like this to obtain all the relevant information of a thread:

```
System.out.println("**********************");
System.out.println("Id: " + thread.getId());
System.out.println("Name: " + thread.getName());
System.out.println("Priority: " + thread.getPriority());
System.out.println("Status: " + thread.getState());
System.out.println("Stack Trace");
for(StackTraceElement ste : thread.getStackTrace()) {
  System.out.println(ste);
}

System.out.println("**********************\n");
```

With this block of code, you will obtain an output as follows:

```
<terminated> MainThread [Java Application] C:\Program Files\Java\jdk-9\bin\javaw.exe (17 abr. 2017 22:59:04)

**********************
Id: 13
Name: Thread-0
Priority: 5
Status: TIMED_WAITING
Stack Trace
java.lang.Thread.sleep(java.base@9-ea/Native Method)
java.lang.Thread.sleep(java.base@9-ea/Thread.java:340)
java.util.concurrent.TimeUnit.sleep(java.base@9-ea/TimeUnit.java:401)
com.javferna.packtpub.book.mastering.test.common.CommonTask.run(CommonTask.java:13)
java.lang.Thread.run(java.base@9-ea/Thread.java:843)
**********************

**********************
Id: 13
Name: Thread-0
Priority: 5
Status: TERMINATED
Stack Trace
**********************
```

Monitoring a lock

A **lock** is one of the basic synchronization elements provided by the Java concurrency API. It's defined in the `Lock` interface and in the `ReentrantLock` class. In a basic way, a lock allows you to define a critical section in your code, but the lock mechanism is more flexible than other mechanisms, such as the synchronized keyword (for example, you can have different locks to read and write operations or have non-linear critical sections). The `ReentrantLock` class has some methods that allow you to know the status of a `Lock` object:

- `getOwner()`: This method returns a `Thread` object with the thread that currently has the lock, that is to say, the thread that is executing the critical section.
- `hasQueuedThreads()`: This method returns a `boolean` value to indicate if there are threads waiting to acquire this lock.
- `getQueueLength()`: This method returns an `int` value with the number of threads that are waiting to acquire this lock.
- `getQueuedThreads()`: This method returns a `Collection<Thread>` object with the `Thread` objects that are waiting to acquire this lock.
- `isFair()`: This method returns a `boolean` value to indicate the status of the fairness attribute. The value of this attribute is used to determine which will be the next thread that acquires the lock. You can check the Java API information to get a detailed description of this functionality.
- `isLocked()`: This method returns a `boolean` value to indicate if this lock is owned by a thread or not.
- `getHoldCount()`: This method returns an `int` value with the number of times this thread has acquired the lock. The returned value is zero if this thread does not hold the lock. Otherwise it returns the number of times the `lock()` method was called in the current thread for which the matching `unlock()` method was not called.

The `getOwner()` and the `getQueuedThreads()` methods are protected, so you don't have direct access to them. To solve this problem, you can implement your own `Lock` class and implemented methods that provide you with that information.

For example, you can implement a class named `MyLock`, as follows:

```
public class MyLock extends ReentrantLock {

  private static final long serialVersionUID = 8025713657321635686L;

  public String getOwnerName() {
    if (this.getOwner() == null) {
```

```
      return "None";
    }
    return this.getOwner().getName();
  }

  public Collection<Thread> getThreads() {
    return this.getQueuedThreads();
  }
}
```

So, you can use a fragment of code similar to this to obtain all the relevant information about a lock:

```
System.out.println("************************\n");
System.out.println("Owner : " + lock.getOwnerName());
System.out.println("Queued Threads: " + lock.hasQueuedThreads());
if (lock.hasQueuedThreads()) {
  System.out.println("Queue Length: " + lock.getQueueLength());
  System.out.println("Queued Threads: ");
  Collection<Thread> lockedThreads = lock.getThreads();
  for (Thread lockedThread : lockedThreads) {
    System.out.println(lockedThread.getName());
  }
}
System.out.println("Fairness: " + lock.isFair());
System.out.println("Locked: " + lock.isLocked());
System.out.println("Holds: "+lock.getHoldCount());
System.out.println("***********************\n");
```

With this block of code, you will obtain an output similar to the following:

```
<terminated> MainLock [Java Application] C:\Program Files\Java\jdk-9\bin\

************************

Owner : pool-1-thread-2
Queued Threads: true
Queue Length: 3
Queued Threads:
pool-1-thread-4
pool-1-thread-10
pool-1-thread-7
Fairness: false
Locked: true
Holds: 0
***********************
```

Monitoring an executor

The **executor framework** is a mechanism that allows you to execute concurrent tasks without worrying about the creation and management of threads. You can send the tasks to the executor. It has an internal pool of threads that re-utilize to execute the tasks. The executor also provides a mechanism to control the resources consumed by your tasks so you won't overload the system. The executor framework provides the `Executor` and `ExecutorService` interfaces and some classes that implement those interfaces. The most basic class that implements them is the `ThreadPoolExecutor` class. It provides some methods that allow you to know the status of the executor:

- `getActiveCount()`: This method returns the number of threads of the executor that are executing tasks.
- `getCompletedTaskCount()`: This method returns the number of tasks that have been executed by the executor and have finished its execution.
- `getCorePoolSize()`: This method returns the core number of threads. This number determines the minimum number of threads in the pool. Even if there are no tasks running in the executor, the pool won't have less threads than the number returned by this method.
- `getLargestPoolSize()`: This method returns the maximum number of threads that have been in the pool of the executor at the same time.
- `getMaximumPoolSize()`: This method returns the maximum number of threads that can exist in the pool at the same time.
- `getPoolSize()`: This method returns the current number of threads in the pool.
- `getTaskCount()`: This method returns the number of tasks that have been sent to the executor, including waiting, running, and already completed tasks.
- `isTerminated()`: This method returns true if the `shutdown()` or `shutdownNow()` method has been called and the `Executor` has finished the execution of all its pending tasks. This method returns false otherwise.
- `isTerminating()`: This method returns true if the `shutdown()` or `shutdownNow()` method has been called but the executor is still executing tasks.

You can use a fragment of code similar to this to obtain the relevant information of a
`ThreadPoolExecutor`:

```
System.out.println ("*******************************************");
System.out.println("Active Count: "+executor.getActiveCount());
System.out.println("Completed Task Count: "+
executor.getCompletedTaskCount());
System.out.println("Core Pool Size:"+ executor.getCorePoolSize());
System.out.println("Largest Pool Size: "+ executor.getLargestPoolSize());
System.out.println("Maximum Pool Size: "+ executor.getMaximumPoolSize());
System.out.println("Pool Size: "+executor.getPoolSize());
System.out.println("Task Count: "+executor.getTaskCount());
System.out.println("Terminated: "+executor.isTerminated());
System.out.println("Is Terminating: "+executor.isTerminating());
System.out.println ("*******************************************");
```

With this block of code, you will obtain an output similar to this:

```
<terminated> MainExecutor [Java Application] C:\Program Files\Java\jdk-9\bin\jav
*******************************************
Active Count: 3
Completed Task Count: 7
Core Pool Size: 0
Largest Pool Size: 10
Maximum Pool Size: 2147483647
Pool Size: 10
Task Count: 10
Terminated: false
Is Terminating: false
*******************************************
*******************************************
Active Count: 2
Completed Task Count: 8
Core Pool Size: 0
Largest Pool Size: 10
Maximum Pool Size: 2147483647
Pool Size: 10
Task Count: 10
Terminated: false
Is Terminating: false
*******************************************
```

Monitoring the fork/join framework

The **fork/join** framework provides a special kind of executor for algorithms that can be implemented using the divide and conquer technique. It is based in a work-stealing algorithm. You create an initial task that has to process the whole problem. This task creates other subtasks that process smaller parts of the problem and waits for its finalization. Each task compares the size of the sub-problem it has to process with a predefined size. If the size is smaller than the predefined size, it solves the problem directly. Otherwise, it splits the problem into other subtasks and waits for the results returned by them. The work-stealing algorithm takes advantage of the threads that are executing tasks that are waiting for the results of their child tasks to execute other tasks. The `ForkJoinPool` class provides methods that allow you to obtain its status:

- `getParallelism()`: This method returns the desired level of parallelism established for the pool.
- `getPoolSize()`: This method returns the number of threads in the pool.
- `getActiveThreadCount()`: This method returns the number of threads in the pool that are currently executing tasks.
- `getRunningThreadCount()`: This method returns the number of threads that are not waiting for the finalization of their child tasks.
- `getQueuedSubmissionCount()`: This method returns the number of tasks that have been submitted to a pool that haven't started their execution yet.
- `getQueuedTaskCount()`: This method returns the number of tasks in the work-stealing queues of this pool.
- `hasQueuedSubmissions()`: This method returns true if there are tasks that have been submitted to the pool that haven't started their execution yet. It returns false otherwise.
- `getStealCount()`: This method returns the number of times the fork/join pool has executed the work-stealing algorithm.
- `isTerminated()`: This method returns `true` if the fork/join pool has finished its execution. It returns `false` otherwise.

You can use a fragment of code like this to obtain the relevant information of a `ForkJoinPool` class:

```
System.out.println("**********************");
System.out.println("Parallelism: "+ pool.getParallelism());
System.out.println("Pool Size: "+ pool.getPoolSize());
System.out.println("Active Thread Count: "+ pool.getActiveThreadCount());
System.out.println("Running Thread Count: "+ pool.getRunningThreadCount());
System.out.println("Queued Submission: "+ pool.getQueuedSubmissionCount());
```

```
System.out.println("Queued Tasks: "+pool.getQueuedTaskCount());
System.out.println("Queued Submissions: "+ pool.hasQueuedSubmissions());
System.out.println("Steal Count: "+ pool.getStealCount());
System.out.println("Terminated : "+ pool.isTerminated());
System.out.println("**********************");
```

Where pool is a `ForkJoinPool` object (for example, `ForkJoinPool.commonPool()`). With this block of code, you will obtain an output similar to this:

```
MainFork [Java Application] C:\Program Files\Java\jdk-9\bin\javaw.exe (17 abr. 2017 23:22:58)
**********************
Parallelism: 2
Pool Size: 2
Active Thread Count: 2
Running Thread Count: 0
Queued Submission: 0
Queued Tasks: 9
Queued Submissions: false
Steal Count: 0
Terminated : false
**********************
Mon Apr 17 23:23:32 CEST 2017-ForkJoinPool-1-worker-1: Working 5 seconds
**********************
Parallelism: 2
Pool Size: 2
Active Thread Count: 2
Running Thread Count: 0
Queued Submission: 0
Queued Tasks: 8
Queued Submissions: false
Steal Count: 0
Terminated : false
**********************
```

Monitoring a Phaser

A **Phaser** is a synchronization mechanism that allows you to execute tasks that can be divided into phases. This class also includes some methods to obtain the status of the Phaser:

- `getArrivedParties()`: This method returns the number of registered parties that have finished the current phase.
- `getUnarrivedParties()`: This method returns the number of registered parties that haven't finished the current phase.

- `getPhase()`: This method returns the number of the current phase. The number of the first phase is `0`.
- `getRegisteredParties()`: This method returns the number of registered parties in the Phaser.
- `isTerminated()`: This method returns a `boolean` value to indicate if the Phaser has finished its execution.

You can use a fragment of code like this to obtain the relevant information of a Phaser:

```
System.out.println ("************************************************");
System.out.println("Arrived Parties: "+ phaser.getArrivedParties());
System.out.println("Unarrived Parties: "+ phaser.getUnarrivedParties());
System.out.println("Phase: "+phaser.getPhase());
System.out.println("Registered Parties: "+ phaser.getRegisteredParties());
System.out.println("Terminated: "+phaser.isTerminated());
System.out.println ("************************************************");
```

With this block of code, you will obtain an output similar to this:

```
<terminated> MainPhaser [Java Application] C:\Program Files\Java\jdk-9\bin\javaw.exe
*****************************************
Arrived Parties: 6
Unarrived Parties: 4
Phase: 0
Registered Parties: 10
Terminated: false
*****************************************
*****************************************
Arrived Parties: 8
Unarrived Parties: 2
Phase: 0
Registered Parties: 10
Terminated: false
*****************************************
```

Monitoring the Stream API

The Stream mechanism is one of the most important new features introduced in Java 8. It allows you to process large collections of data in a concurrent way, transforming that data and implementing the map and reduce programming model in an easy way. This class doesn't provide any methods (except the `isParallel()` method that returns if the stream is parallel or not) to know the status of the stream, but includes a method named `peek()` that you can include in the pipeline of methods to write log information about the operations or transformations that you are executing in the stream.

For example, this code calculates the average of the square of the first 999 numbers:

```
double result=IntStream.range(0,1000)
  .parallel()
  .peek(n -> System.out.println (Thread.currentThread()
      .getName()+": Number "+n))
  .map(n -> n*n)
  .peek(n -> System.out.println (Thread.currentThread()
      .getName()+": Transformer "+n))
  .average()
  .getAsDouble();
```

The first `peek()` method writes the numbers that the stream is processing and the second, the square of those numbers. If you execute this code, as you're executing the stream in a concurrent way, you will obtain an output similar to this:

```
<terminated> MainStream [Java Application] C:\Program Files\Java\jdk-9\bin\
ForkJoinPool.commonPool-worker-1: Number 622
ForkJoinPool.commonPool-worker-3: Transformer 186624
ForkJoinPool.commonPool-worker-1: Transformer 386884
ForkJoinPool.commonPool-worker-3: Number 433
ForkJoinPool.commonPool-worker-1: Number 623
ForkJoinPool.commonPool-worker-3: Transformer 187489
ForkJoinPool.commonPool-worker-1: Transformer 388129
ForkJoinPool.commonPool-worker-3: Number 434
ForkJoinPool.commonPool-worker-1: Number 624
ForkJoinPool.commonPool-worker-3: Transformer 188356
ForkJoinPool.commonPool-worker-1: Transformer 389376
ForkJoinPool.commonPool-worker-3: Number 435
ForkJoinPool.commonPool-worker-3: Transformer 189225
ForkJoinPool.commonPool-worker-3: Number 436
ForkJoinPool.commonPool-worker-3: Transformer 190096
Result: 332833.5
```

Monitoring concurrency applications

When you implement Java applications, you normally use an IDE such as Eclipse or NetBeans to create your projects and write your source code. But the **JDK** (short for **Java Development Kit**) includes tools you can use to compile, execute, or generate Javadoc documents. One of those tools is **JConsole**, which is a graphical tool that shows you information about the applications that are executing in a JVM. You can find it in the `bin` directory of your JDK installation (`jconsole.exe`).

If you execute it, you will see a window similar to this:

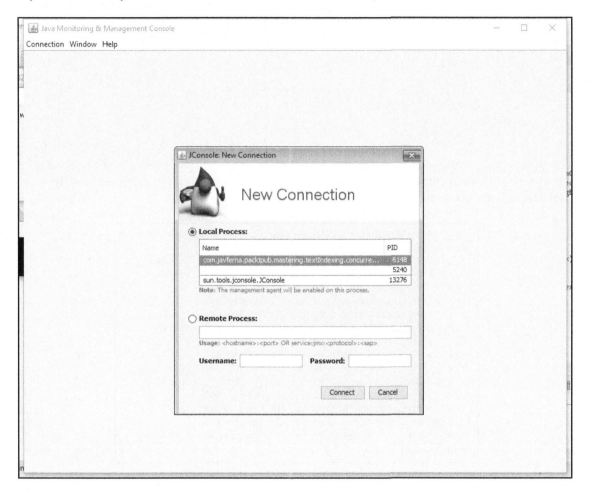

You can monitor processes that are running in your own computer by selecting one of the processes that appear in the **Local Process** section, or a remote process introducing its data in the **Remote Process** section.

Once you have selected or introduced the data of the process you want to monitor, you click the **Connect** button. You may see a window alerting you that you are starting an insecure connection. That window will be similar to this:

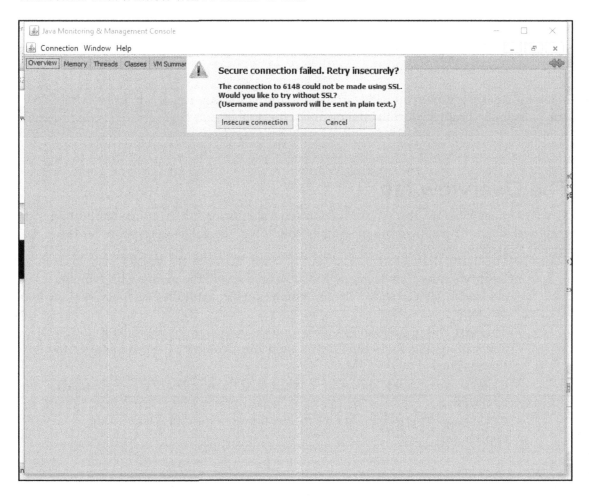

In that case, press the **Insecure connection** button.

You will see a screen with six tabs:

- **Overview**: This tab shows general information about the application.
- **Memory**: This tab shows information about memory use.
- **Threads**: This tab shows the evolution over time of the threads of the application and allows you to see detailed information about a `Thread`.

- **Classes**: This tab shows information about the class loading and the number of classes.
- **VM Summary**: This tab shows information about the Java Virtual Machine that is running the process.
- **MBeans:** This tab shows information about the MBeans of the process. An MBean is a managed Java object that can represent a device, an application, or any resource; and are the base of the JMX API.

In the following sections, you will learn what information you can obtain in every tab. You can consult the complete documentation about this tool at:
`http://docs.oracle.com/javase/7/docs/technotes/guides/management/jconsole.html`.

The Overview tab

As we mentioned before, this tab shows you general information about the application in a graphical way, which allows you to see the evolution of the values across time. This information includes:

- **Heap Memory Use**: This graphic shows the size of the memory used by the application. It also shows the used memory, the committed memory, and the max memory.
- **Threads**: This graphic shows the evolution in the number of threads used by the application. It includes the threads explicitly created by the programmer and the threads created by the JVM.
- **Classes**: This graphic shows the evolution of the number of classes loaded by the application.
- **CPU Usage**: This graphic shows the evolution of the CPU usage of the application.

It has an appearance similar to the following screenshot:

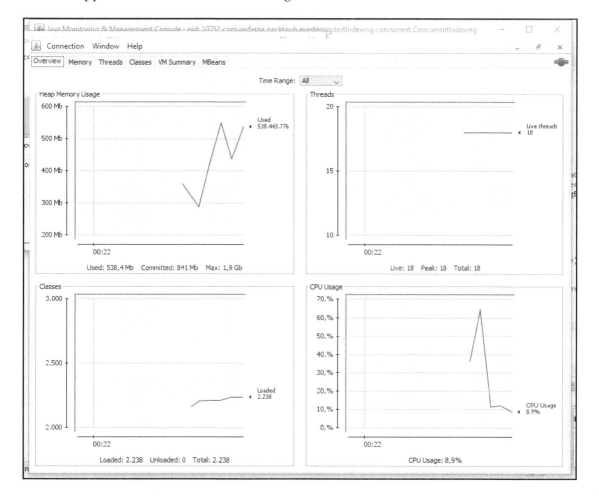

The Memory tab

As we mentioned earlier, this tab shows you graphical information about the memory used by the application. You can see the evolution of these metrics over time. The appearance of this tab is similar to this:

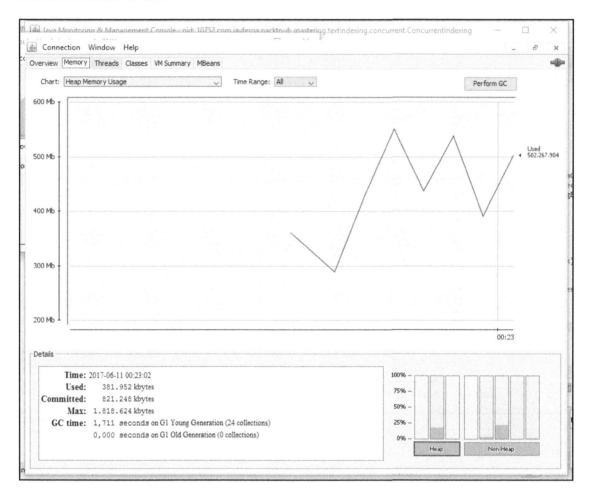

On top of the screen, you have a drop-down menu where you can select the kind of memory. It gives you different options, such as heap memory, non-heap memory, and specific memory tools, such as the **Eden Space**, which shows information about the memory that is initially allocated for most objects, or the **Survivor Space** which shows information about the memory used by objects that survived the garbage collector of the Eden Space.

Then, you have the graphical evolution over time of the selected element. Finally, you have a **Details** section, which shows information about memory consumption:

- **Used**: The current amount of memory use by the application
- **Committed**: The amount of memory that is guaranteed to the JVM
- **Max**: The maximum amount of memory that can be used by the JVM
- **GC time**: The time spent on garbage collection

The Threads tab

As we mentioned earlier, in the **Threads** tab, you can see the evolution of the threads of the application over time. Its appearance is similar to this:

This screen shows the evolution over time of the number of threads. You will see two numbers. The **Live Threads** are the threads that are running and the **Peak** number of threads are the maximum number of threads.

At the bottom, you have a list of all the current threads in the left of the window. If you select one of those threads, on the right-hand side, you will see information about that thread, such as the name, its state, and the current stack trace.

The Classes tab

The **Classes** tab shows you information about class loading. This tab's appearance is similar to this:

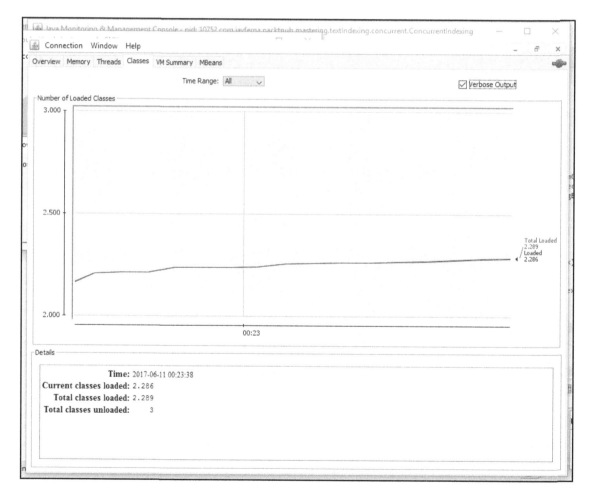

This tab shows a graphic on top with the evolution over time of the number of classes loaded by the application. It shows a red line with the total number of classes loaded by the application and a red line with the current number of classes loaded.

At the bottom of the tab, it shows the details section, which has current information:

- Current classes loaded
- Total classes loaded
- Total classes unloaded

The VM summary tab

The **VM Summary** tab shows you information about the Java Virtual Machine. This tab's appearance is similar to this:

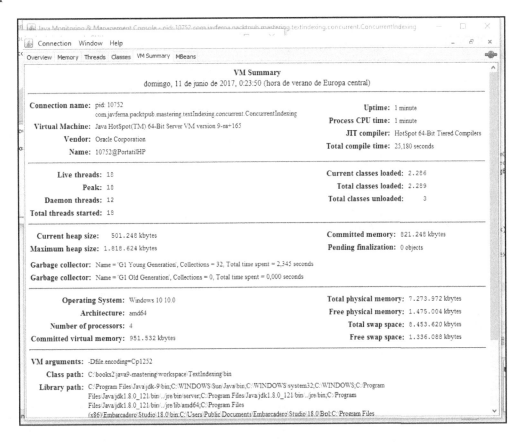

As you can see in the image, this tab shows you the following information:

- **Summary section**: This block shows information about the Java Virtual Machine implementation that is running the process:
    - **Virtual Machine**: Name of the Java Virtual Machine that is executing the process
    - **Vendor**: Name of the organization that has implemented the Java Virtual Machine
    - **Name**: Name of the machine that is running the process
    - **Uptime**: Time since the JVM was started
    - **Process CPU time**: CPU time consumed by the JVM
- **Threads**: This section shows information about the threads of the application:
    - **Live threads**: Total number of threads that are currently running
    - **Peak**: Highest number of threads that have been executing in the JVM
    - **Daemon threads**: Total number of daemon-threads that are currently running
    - **Total threads started**: Total number of threads that have started their execution since the JVM started running
- **Classes**: This section shows information about the number of classes of the application:
    - **Current classes loaded**: Number of classes currently loaded into memory
    - **Total classes loaded**: Number of classes loaded into memory since the JVM started running
    - **Total classes unloaded**: Number of classes unloaded from memory since the JVM started running

- **Memory**: This section shows information about the memory used by the application:
  - **Current heap size**: Size of the heap
  - **Committed memory**: Amount of memory allocated for use by the heap
  - **Maximum heap size**: Maximum size of the heap
  - **Garbage collector**: Information about garbage collection
- **Operating System**: This section shows information about the operating system that is executing the Java Virtual Machine:
  - **Operating System**: Version of the OS that is running the JVM
  - **Number of Processors**: Number of cores and/or CPUs that the computer has
  - **Total physical memory**: Size of the RAM available to the OS
  - **Free physical memory**: Free RAM available to the OS
  - **Committed virtual memory**: Memory guarantee to the current process
- **Other Information**: This section shows additional information about the Java Virtual Machine:
  - **VM arguments**: Arguments passed to the JVM
  - **Class path**: Class path of the JVM
  - **Library path**: Library path of the JVM
  - **Boot class path**: Path where the JVM looks for `java.*` and `javax.*` classes

The MBeans tab

The MBeans tab shows you information about all the MBeans registered in the platform. This tab's appearance is similar to this:

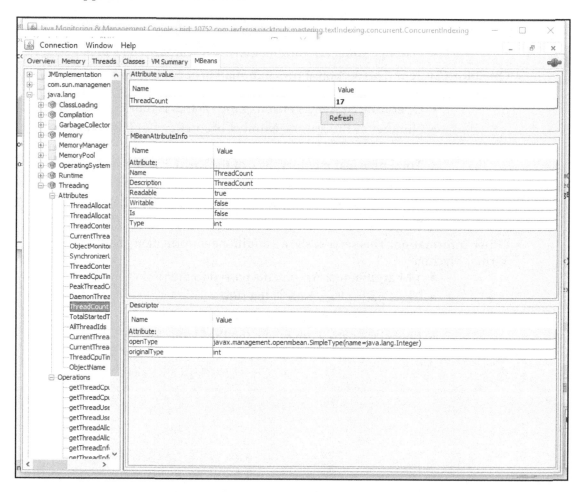

In the left part of the tab, you have all the MBeans that are running, in a tree. When you select one, you will see its MBean Info and its MBean Descriptor in the right-hand side of the tab.

Concurrent applications are represented with the threading MBean, which has two sections. The **Attributes** section with the attributes of the MBean, and the Operations section, that shows all the operations you can run with that MBean.

The About tab

Finally, you can obtain information about the JConsole version you're running with the **About** option in the **Help** menu. You will see a window similar to the following one:

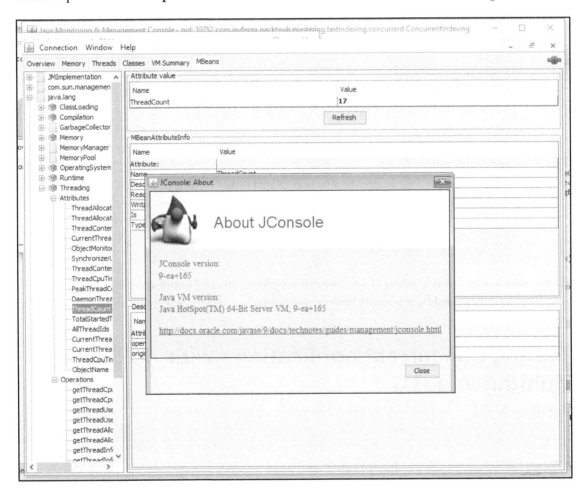

Testing concurrency applications

Testing concurrency applications is a hard task. The threads of your application run on your computer without any guarantee of their execution order (except the synchronization mechanisms that you have included), so it's very difficult (impossible most of the time) to test all the circumstances that can occur. You can have errors impossible to reproduce because it only happens under rare or unique circumstances, or errors that happen on one machine but not on others due to the number of cores within the CPU. To detect and reproduce this situation, you can use different tools:

- **Debug**: You can use a debugger to debug the application. This process will be very tedious if you have only a few threads in the application and you have to go step by step in every thread. You can configure Eclipse or NetBeans to test concurrent applications.
- **MultithreadedTC**: This is an archived project of **Google Code** that can be used to force the order of execution in a concurrent application.
- **Java PathFinder**: This is an execution environment used by NASA for the verification of Java programs. It includes support for validating concurrent applications.
- **Unit testing**: You can create a bunch of unit-tests (using JUnit or TestNG) and launch every test, for example, 1,000 times. If every test succeeds then, even if your application has races, their chances are not very high and probably acceptable for production. You can include assertions in your code to verify that it hasn't any race conditions.

In the following sections, you will see basic examples of testing concurrent applications with the MultithreadedTC and Java PathFinder tools.

Testing concurrent applications with MultithreadedTC

MultithreadedTC is an archived project that you can download from `http://code.google.com/p/multithreadedtc/`. Its latest version is from 2007, but you can still use it to test small concurrent applications or parts of large applications independently. You can't use it to test real tasks or threads, but you can use it to test different orders of execution to check if they provoke race conditions or deadlocks.

It's based on an internal clock that works with ticks, which allows you to control the order of execution of different threads to test if that order of execution could cause any concurrency problems.

First of all, you need to associate two libraries to your project:

- **The MultithreadedTC library**: The latest version is the 1.01 version
- **The JUnit library**: We have tested this example with the 4.12 version

To implement a test using the MultithreadedTC library, you have to extend the `MultithreadedTestCase` class that extends the `Assert` class of the JUnit library. You can implement the following methods:

- `initialize()`: This method will be executed at the beginning of the test execution. You can override it if you need to execute initialization code for the creation of data objects, database connections, and so on.
- `finish()`: This method will be executed at the end of the test execution. You can override it to implement the validations of the test.
- `threadXXX()`: You have to implement a method whose name begins with the thread keyword for every thread you have in your test. For example, if you want to make a test with three threads, you will have three methods in you class.

The `MultithreadedTestCase` provides the `waitForTick()` method. This method receives the number of ticks you wait for as a parameter. This method sleeps the calling thread until the internal clock arrives at that tick.

The first tick is the tick number 0. The MultithreadedTC framework checks the status of the test threads at certain intervals. If all the running threads are waiting in the `waitForTick()` method, it increments the tick number and wakes up all the threads that are waiting for that tick.

Let's look at an example of its use. Suppose you want to test a `Data` object with an internal `int` attribute. You want a thread that increments the value and a thread that decrements the value. You can create a class named `TestClassOk`, extending the `MultithreadedTestCase` class. We use three attributes with the data object: the amount we will use to increment and decrement the data and the initial value of the data:

```
public class TestClassOk extends MultithreadedTestCase {

    private Data data;
    private int amount;
    private int initialData;
```

```
public TestClassOk (Data data, int amount) {
  this.amount=amount;
  this.data=data;
  this.initialData=data.getData();
}
```

We implement two methods to simulate the execution of two threads. The first thread is implemented in the threadAdd() method:

```
public void threadAdd() {
  System.out.println("Add: Getting the data");
  int value=data.getData();
  System.out.println("Add: Increment the data");
  value+=amount;
  System.out.println("Add: Set the data");
  data.setData(value);
}
```

It reads the value of the data, increments its value, and writes the value of the data again. The second thread is implemented in the threadSub() method:

```
public void threadSub() {
  waitForTick(1);
  System.out.println("Sub: Getting the data");
  int value=data.getData();
  System.out.println("Sub: Decrement the data");
  value-=amount;
  System.out.println("Sub: Set the data");
  data.setData(value);
  }
}
```

First, we wait for tick 1. Then, we get the value of the data, decrement its value, and rewrite the value of the data.

To execute the test, we can use the runOnce() method of the TestFramework class:

```
public class MainOk {

  public static void main(String[] args) {

    Data data=new Data();
    data.setData(10);
    TestClassOk ok=new TestClassOk(data,10);

    try {
      TestFramework.runOnce(ok);
    } catch (Throwable e) {
```

```
        e.printStackTrace();
    }


  }
}
```

When the execution of the test begins, the two threads (`threadAdd()` and `threadSub()`) are launched in a concurrent way. `threadAdd()` begins the execution of its code and `threadSub()` waits in the `waitForTick()` method. When `threadAdd()` finishes its execution, the internal clock of the MultithreadedTC detects that the only thread running is waiting in the `waitForTick()` method, so it increments the tick value to 1 and wakes up the thread that executes its code.

In the following screenshot, you can see the output of the execution of this example. In this case, everything goes well:

```
<terminated> MainOk [Java Application] C:\Program Files\Java\jdk-9\bin\javaw.exe (
Add: Getting the data
Add: Increment the data
Add: Set the data
Sub: Getting the data
Sub: Decrement the data
Sub: Set the data
```

But you can change the order of execution of the threads to provoke an error. For example, you can implement the following order, which will provoke a race condition:

```
public void threadAdd() {
  System.out.println("Add: Getting the data");
  int value=data.getData();
  waitForTick(2);
  System.out.println("Add: Increment the data");
  value+=amount;
  System.out.println("Add: Set the data");
  data.setData(value);
}

public void threadSub() {
  waitForTick(1);
  System.out.println("Sub: Getting the data");
  int value=data.getData();
  waitForTick(3);
  System.out.println("Sub: Decrement the data");
  value-=amount;
  System.out.println("Sub: Set the data");
```

```
        data.setData(value);
    }
```

In this case, the order of execution makes sure that both threads first read the value of the data and then makes its operation, so the final result won't be correct.

In the following screenshot, you can see the result of the execution of this example:

```
<terminated> MainKo [Java Application] C:\Program Files\Java\jdk-9\bin\javaw.exe (11 jun. 2017
Add: Getting the data
Sub: Getting the data
Add: Increment the data
Add: Set the data
Sub: Decrement the data
Sub: Set the data
junit.framework.AssertionFailedError: expected:<10> but was:<0>
        at junit.framework.Assert.fail(Assert.java:57)
        at junit.framework.Assert.failNotEquals(Assert.java:329)
        at junit.framework.Assert.assertEquals(Assert.java:78)
        at junit.framework.Assert.assertEquals(Assert.java:234)
        at junit.framework.Assert.assertEquals(Assert.java:241)
        at com.javferna.packtpub.mastering.testing.tc.TestClassKo.finish(
        at edu.umd.cs.mtc.TestFramework.runOnce(TestFramework.java:285)
        at edu.umd.cs.mtc.TestFramework.runOnce(TestFramework.java:235)
```

In this case, the `assertEquals()` method throws an exception because the expected and actual values are not equal.

The main limitation of this library is that it is only useful for testing basic concurrent code and, as you implement the tests, they can't be used to test real thread code.

Testing concurrent applications with Java Pathfinder

Java Pathfinder or JPF is an open source execution environment from NASA that can be used to verify Java applications. It includes its own virtual machine to execute Java bytecode. Internally, it detects the points of the code where it can be more than one execution path and executes all the possibilities. In concurrent applications, this means that it will execute all the possible execution orders between the threads that run in your application. It also includes tools that allow you to detect race conditions and deadlocks.

The main advantage of this tool is that it allows you to completely test your concurrent application to guarantee that it is free of race conditions and deadlocks. The inconvenient features of this tool are:

- You have to install it from its source code
- If your application is complex, you will have thousands of possible paths of execution and the test will be very long (maybe many hours if the application is complex)

In the following sections, we will show you how to test a concurrent application using Java Pathfinder.

Installing Java Pathfinder

As we mentioned earlier, you have to install JPF from its source code. That code is in a Mercurial repository, so the first step is to install Mercurial and, as we will use the Eclipse IDE, the Mercurial plugin for Eclipse.

You can download Mercurial from: `https://www.mercurial-scm.org/wiki/Download`. You download the installation program, which provides an assistant to install Mercurial on your computer. Maybe you will need to restart your system after the installation of Mercurial.

You can download the Mercurial plugin for Eclipse using **Help** | **Install new software** from the Eclipse menu and visiting:
`http://mercurialeclipse.eclipselabs.org.codespot.com/hg.wiki/update_site/stable`
to look for the software. Follow the same steps as with other plugins.

You can also install a JPF plugin for Eclipse. You can download it from:
`http://babelfish.arc.nasa.gov/trac/jpf/raw-attachment/wiki/projects/eclipse-jpf/update`.

Now you can access the Mercurial repository explorer perspective and add the repository of Java Pathfinder. We will use only the core module, which is stored in
`http://babelfish.arc.nasa.gov/hg/jpf/jpf-core`. You don't need a username or password to access the repository. Once you have created the repository, you can right-click the repository and select the **Clone repository** option to download the source code in your computer. The option will open a window to select some options, but you can leave the default values and click on the **Next** button. Then you have to choose the version you want to load. Leave the default value and click on the **Next** button. Finally, click on the **Finish** button to finish the download process. Eclipse will automatically run ant to compile the project. If you have any compilation problems, you have to solve them and relaunch ant.

If everything went well, you will have a project named `jpf-core` in your workspace, as in the following screenshot:

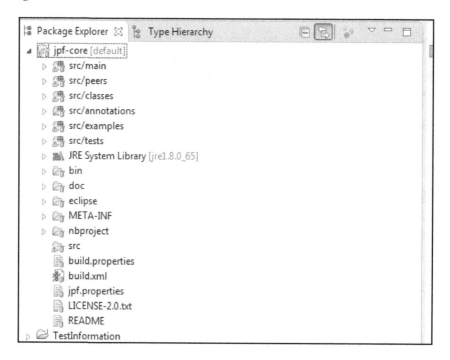

The last configuration step is to create a file named `site.properties` with the configuration of JPF. If you access the configuration window in **Window** | **Preferences** and select the **JPF Preferences** option, you will see the path where the JPF plugin is looking for that file. You can change that path if you want.

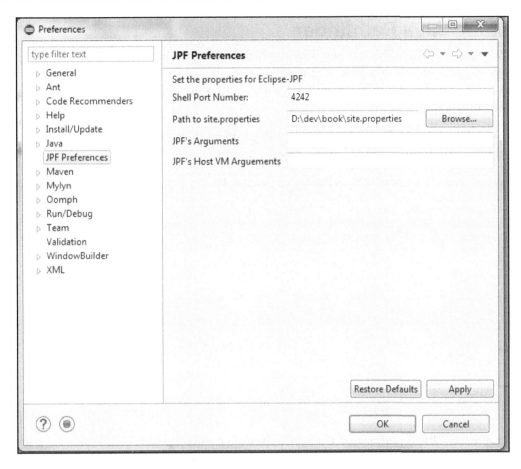

As we will only use the `core` module, the file will only contain the route to the `jpf-core` project:

```
jpf-core = D:/dev/book/projectos/jpf-core
```

Running Java Pathfinder

Once we have installed JPF, let's see how we can use it to test a concurrent application. First, we have to implement a concurrent application. In our case, we will use a Data class with an internal int value. It will be initialized with 0 and will have an increment() method to increment the value.

Then, we will have a task named NumberTask , that implements the Runnable interface that will increment the value of a Data object ten times.

```
public class NumberTask implements Runnable {

  private Data data;

  public NumberTask (Data data) {
    this.data=data;
  }

  @Override
  public void run() {

    for (int i=0; i<10; i++) {
      data.increment(10);
    }
  }

}
```

Finally, we have the MainNumber class, which implements the main() method. We will launch two NumberTasks objects that will modify the same Data object. Finally, we will obtain the final value of the Data object:

```
public class MainNumber {

  public static void main(String[] args) {
    int numTasks=2;
    Data data=new Data();

    Thread threads[]=new Thread[numTasks];
    for (int i=0; i<numTasks; i++) {
      threads[i]=new Thread(new NumberTask(data));
      threads[i].start();
    }

    for (int i=0; i<numTasks; i++) {
      try {
        threads[i].join();
```

```
    } catch (InterruptedException e) {
      e.printStackTrace();
    }
  }

  System.out.println(data.getValue());
}

}
```

If everything goes well and no race conditions occur, the final result will be 200, but our code doesn't use any synchronization mechanisms so it's possible that this circumstance occurs.

If we want to execute this application with JFP, we need to create a configuration file inside the project with the `.jpf` extension. For example, we have created the `NumberJPF.jpf` file with the most basic configuration file we can use:

```
+classpath=${config_path}/bin
target=com.javferna.packtpub.mastering.testing.main.MainNumber
```

We modify the class path of JPF, adding the `bin` directory of our project, and indicate the main class of our application. Now, we're ready to execute the application through JPF. To do this, we right-click the `.jpf` file and select the `Verify` option. We will see a lot of output messages in the console. Every output message comes from a different execution path of the application:

```
Problems  @ Javadoc  Declaration  Search  Console  ᙭
NumberJPF.jpf(run)
Executing command: java -jar D:\dev\book\proyectos\jpf-core\build\RunJPF.jar +site=D:\dev\book\site.proper
JavaPathfinder core system v8.0 (rev 29) - (C) 2005-2014 United States Government. All rights reserved.


======================================================= system under test
com.javferna.packtpub.mastering.testing.main.MainNumber.main()

======================================================= search started: 3/12/15 2:26
200
200
190
190
180
180
```

When JPF ends the execution of all the possible execution paths, it shows statistical information about the execution:

```
70
60
50
40
30
20


======================================================= results
no errors detected

======================================================= statistics
elapsed time:       00:00:16
states:             new=72199,visited=101549,backtracked=173748,end=57
search:             maxDepth=67,constraints=0
choice generators:  thread=72199 (signal=0,lock=2,sharedRef=65612,threadApi=1504,reschedule=5081), data=0
heap:               new=632,released=1301,maxLive=370,gcCycles=173619
instructions:       1721841
max memory:         353MB
loaded code:        classes=64,methods=1476

======================================================= search finished: 3/12/15 2:27
```

The JPF execution says that no errors were detected, but we can see that most of the results are different from 200, so our application has race conditions, as we expected.

In the introduction of this section, we said that JPF provides tools to detect race conditions and deadlocks. JPF implements this as a `Listener` mechanism that implements the `Observer` pattern to respond to certain events that occur in the execution of the code. For example, we can use the following listeners:

- `PreciseRaceDetector`: Use this listener to detect race conditions
- `DeadlockAnalyzer`: Use this listener to detect deadlock situations
- `CoverageAnalyzer`: Use this listener to write coverage information at the end of the execution of JPF

You can configure the listeners you want to use in the `.jpf` file with the configuration of an execution. For example, we have extended the previous test in the `NumberListenerJPF.jpf` file by adding the `PreciseRaceDetector` and the `CoverageAnalyzer` listeners:

```
+classpath=${config_path}/bin
target=com.javferna.packtpub.mastering.testing.main.MainNumber
listener=gov.nasa.jpf.listener.PreciseRaceDetector,gov.nasa.jpf.li
  stener.CoverageAnalyzer
```

If we execute this configuration file through JPF with the `Verify` option, you will see information about this circumstance as the application ends and it detects the first race condition showing in the console:

```
============================================== system under test
com.javferna.packtpub.mastering.testing.main.MainNumber.main()

============================================== search started: 3/12/15 2:43
200
200


============================================== error 1
gov.nasa.jpf.listener.PreciseRaceDetector
race for field com.javferna.packtpub.mastering.testing.common.Data@15e.value
  Thread-1 at com.javferna.packtpub.mastering.testing.common.Data.increment(Data.java:12)
"  WRITE: putfield com.javferna.packtpub.mastering.testing.common.Data.value
  Thread-2 at com.javferna.packtpub.mastering.testing.common.Data.increment(Data.java:12)
"  READ:  getfield com.javferna.packtpub.mastering.testing.common.Data.value


============================================== snapshot #1
thread java.lang.Thread:{id:0,name:main,status:WAITING,priority:5,isDaemon:false,lockCount:0,suspendCount:0}
  waiting on: java.lang.Thread@160
  call stack:
        at java.lang.Thread.join(Thread.java)
        at com.javferna.packtpub.mastering.testing.main.MainNumber.main(MainNumber.java:20)

thread java.lang.Thread:{id:1,name:Thread-1,status:RUNNING,priority:5,isDaemon:false,lockCount:0,suspendCount:0}
  call stack:
        at com.javferna.packtpub.mastering.testing.common.Data.increment(Data.java:13)
        at com.javferna.packtpub.mastering.testing.task.NumberTask.run(NumberTask.java:17)

thread java.lang.Thread:{id:2,name:Thread-2,status:RUNNING,priority:5,isDaemon:false,lockCount:0,suspendCount:0}
  call stack:
        at com.javferna.packtpub.mastering.testing.common.Data.increment(Data.java:12)
        at com.javferna.packtpub.mastering.testing.task.NumberTask.run(NumberTask.java:17)
```

You will also see how the `CoverageAnalyzer` listener writes the information:

```
============================================== coverage statistics

---------------------------------------- class coverage ----------------------------------------
bytecode           line           basic-block        branch             methods            location
----------------------------------------------------------------------------------------------
-                  -              -                  -                  -                  [B
-                  -              -                  -                  -                  [C
-                  -              -                  -                  -                  [D
-                  -              -                  -                  -                  [F
-                  -              -                  -                  -                  [I
-                  -              -                  -                  -                  [J
-                  -              -                  -                  -                  [Ljava.io.ObjectStreamField;
-                  -              -                  -                  -                  [Ljava.lang.String;
-                  -              -                  -                  -                  [Ljava.lang.Thread$State;
-                  -              -                  -                  -                  [Ljava.lang.Thread;
-                  -              -                  -                  -                  [Ljava.util.Hashtable$Entry;
-                  -              -                  -                  -                  [S
-                  -              -                  -                  -                  [Z
-                  -              -                  -                  -                  boolean
-                  -              -                  -                  -                  byte
-                  -              -                  -                  -                  char
0,80 (16/20)       0,75 (6/8)     0,80 (4/5)         -                  0,75 (3/4)         com.javferna.packtpub.mastering.testing.common.Data
0,89 (47/53)       0,77 (10/13)   0,83 (15/18)       1,00 (2/2)         0,50 (1/2)         com.javferna.packtpub.mastering.testing.main.MainNumber
1,00 (18/18)       1,00 (6/6)     1,00 (7/7)         1,00 (1/1)         1,00 (2/2)         com.javferna.packtpub.mastering.testing.task.NumberTask
-                  -              -                  -                  -                  double
-                  -              -                  -                  -                  float
0,00 (0/3)         0,00 (0/1)     0,00 (0/2)         -                  0,00 (0/1)         gov.nasa.jpf.BoxObjectCaches
0,00 (0/31)        0,00 (0/11)    0,00 (0/17)        0,00 (0/2)         0,00 (0/6)         gov.nasa.jpf.ConsoleOutputStream
0,00 (0/36)        0,00 (0/13)    0,00 (0/19)        0,00 (0/3)         0,00 (0/5)         gov.nasa.jpf.FinalizerThread
                                                                                          int
```

JPF is a very powerful application which includes more listeners and more extension mechanisms. You can find its whole documentation at:
`http://babelfish.arc.nasa.gov/trac/jpf/wiki`.

Summary

Testing concurrent applications is a very hard task. There's no guarantee of the order of execution of the threads (unless the synchronization mechanisms have been introduced in your application), so you should test many more different situations than in a serial application. Sometimes, you will have errors in your application that you can reproduce because they only occur in very rare situations, and sometimes you will have errors that only occur on specific machines because of their hardware or software configurations.

In this chapter, you have learned some mechanisms that can help you to test concurrency applications more easily. First, you learned how to obtain information about the status of the most important components of the Java concurrency API as thread, lock, executor, or stream. This information can be very useful if you need to detect the cause of an error. Then, you learned how to use JConsole to monitor Java applications in general and concurrent applications in particular. Finally, you learned to use two different tools to test concurrent applications.

In the next chapter, you will learn how to implement concurrent applications with other languages and libraries that also allow you to implement concurrent applications for the Java Virtual Machine. You will learn the basic principles of concurrent applications with Clojure, Groovy with the GPars library, and Scala.

13

Concurrency in JVM - Clojure and Groovy with the Gpars Library and Scala

Java is the most popular, but not the only programming language we can use to implement programs for the **Java Virtual Machine (JVM)**. In the page `https://en.wikipedia.org/wiki/List_of_JVM_languages` you can find a list of all the programming languages you can use to implement programs for the JVM. Some of them are implementations of existing languages for the JVM, such as **JRuby**, which is an implementation of the Ruby programming language or **Jython**, which is an implementation of the Python programming language. Other languages follow different programming paradigms, such as **Clojure**, which is a functional programming language, and others are scripting and dynamic programming languages, such as **Groovy**. Most of them have good integration with the Java language; in fact you can use elements of Java directly in those programming languages, including concurrency elements such as Threads or Executors. Some of those languages implement their own concurrency models. In this chapter, we will undertake a fast introduction to the concurrency elements provided by three of those languages:

- **Clojure**: Provides reference types such as `Atom` and `Agent` and other elements such as `Future` and `Promise`
- **Groovy**: With the GPars library, provides elements for data parallelization, its own actor model, agents, and dataflow
- **Scala**: Provides two elements, futures and promises

Concurrency in Clojure

Clojure is a dynamic, general-purpose functional programming language based on the Lisp programming language created by Rich Hickey. Via `https://clojure.org/index`, you can download the lastest version of the language (at the time of writing it is the 1.8.0 version) and find documentation and guides about how to program in the Clojure programming language. You can install support for Clojure in the most popular Java IDEs such as Eclipse. Another interesting web page is `http://clojure-doc.org`, where you can find the community-driven documentation site for the Clojure programming language.

In this section, we will show you the most important concurrency elements of the Clojure programming language and how to use them. We are not going to make an introduction to the Clojure programming language. You can review the commented webs to learn how to program in Clojure.

One of the design objectives of the Clojure programming language was to make concurrent programming easier. With this objective in mind, two important decisions were taken:

- Clojure data structures are immutable, so they can be shared between threads without any problem. This does not mean that you can't have mutable values on concurrent applications as you'll see later.
- Clojure separates the concepts of identity and value, almost deleting the need for explicit locks.

Let's describe and work with the most important concurrent structures provided by the Clojure programming language.

Using Java elements

You can use all the Java elements when you're programming in Clojure, including the concurrency ones, so you can create Threads or Executors or use the fork/join framework. This is not good practice, because Clojure makes easier concurrent programming, but you can explicitly create a `Thread`, as you can see in the following block of code:

```
(ns example.example1)

(defn example1 ( [number]
  (println (format "%s : %d" (Thread/currentThread) number))
))

(dotimes [i 10] (.start (Thread. (fn[] (example1 I)))))
```

In this code, first, we define a function called example1 that receives a number as a parameter. Inside the function, we write information about the Thread that is executing the function and the number we have received as a parameter.

Then, we create and execute 10 Thread objects. Each thread will make a call to the function example1.

In the following screenshot, you can see the results of an execution of this code:

```
Thread[Thread-3,5,main] : 0
Thread[Thread-10,5,main] : 7Thread[Thread-9,5,main] : 6

Thread[Thread-11,5,main] : 8
Thread[Thread-12,5,main] : 9
Thread[Thread-4,5,main] : 1
Thread[Thread-5,5,main] : 2
Thread[Thread-8,5,main] : 5
Thread[Thread-6,5,main] : 3
Thread[Thread-7,5,main] : 4
nREPL server started on port 52448 on host 127.0.0.1 - nrepl://127.0.0.1:52448
```

In the previous screenshot, you can see how the name of the Thread is different for all the 10 threads.

Reference types

As we mentioned before, Clojure data structures are immutable, but Clojure provides mechanisms that allow you to work with mutable variables using reference types. We can classify reference types as coordinated or uncoordinated and as synchronous or asynchronous:

- **Coordinated**: When two or more operations cooperate with each other
- **Uncoordinated**: When the operation doesn't affect other operations
- **Synchronous**: When the caller waits for the finalization of the operation
- **Asynchronous**: When the caller doesn't wait for the finalization of the operation

The most important reference types in the Clojure programming language are:

- Atoms
- Agents
- Refs

Let's see in the following sections how to work with these elements.

Atoms

An atom is basically an atomic reference of the Java programming language. Changes in these kinds of variables are visible immediately to all the threads. We're going to use the following functions to work with atoms. They are an uncoordinated and synchronized reference type:

- `atom`: To define a new atom object.
- `swap!`: Atomically changes the value of the atom to a new one based on the result of a function. It follows the format `(swap! atom function)` where `atom` is the name of the atom object, and function is the function that returns the new value of the `atom`.
- `reset!`: Establish the value of the `atom` to a new value. It follows the format `(reset! atom value)` where `atom` is the name of the atom object and `value` the new value.
- `compare-and-set!`: Atomically changes the value of the atom if the actual value is the same as the value passed as a parameter. It follows the format `(compare-and-set! atom old-value new-value)` where `atom` is the name of the atom object, old-value is the expected actual value of the atom, and new value is the new value we want to assign to the `atom`.

Let's see an example of how to work with an `atom` object. First, we declare a function named `company` that receives two parameters named `account` and `salary`. Account will be an `atom` object, as you will see later, and `salary` will be a number. We use the `swap!` function to increment the value of the `account` object. Then, we write in the console information about the `Thread` that is executing the function and the actual value of the `atom` object using the `@` (**dereferencing**) function:

```
(ns example.example2)

(defn company ( [account salary]
  (swap! account + salary)
```

```
    (println (format "%s : %d"(Thread/currentThread) @account))
  ))
```

Then, we create a similar function named `user`. It also receives the `account` atom object as a parameter and another parameter named `money`. We also use the `swap!` function, but in this case, to decrease the value of the Atom object:

```
(defn user ( [account money]
  (swap! account - money)
  (println (format "%s : %d"(Thread/currentThread) @account))
))
```

Then, we create a function named `myTask` that receives an `atom` object named `account` as a parameter and calls the `company` function 1000 times with the value 100 and the `user` function with the value 100, so the final value of the `account` object should be the same:

```
(defn myTask ( [account]
  (dotimes [i 1000]
    (company account 100)
    (user account 100)
    (Thread/sleep 100)
)))
```

Finally, we create the `myAccount` object as an `atom` object with the initial value of 0 and create 10 threads to execute the `myTask` function:

```
(def myAccount (atom 0))

(dotimes [i 10] (.start (Thread. (fn[] (myTask myAccount)))))
```

The following screenshot shows you an execution of this example:

```
Thread[Thread-9,5,main] : 200
Thread[Thread-7,5,main] : 200
Thread[Thread-7,5,main] : 0
Thread[Thread-9,5,main] : 100
Thread[Thread-5,5,main] : 100
Thread[Thread-5,5,main] : 0
Thread[Thread-4,5,main] : 100
Thread[Thread-4,5,main] : 0
Thread[Thread-9,5,main] : 100
Thread[Thread-9,5,main] : 0
```

In this image you can see how there are different threads running the `myTask` function and how the final value of the `myAccount` Atom is 0 as expected.

Agents

An `Agent` is a reference that is updated asynchronously, at some point in the future. It's associated with a single storage location throughout its life and you can only change the value of that location. Agents are an uncoordinated data structure.

You can use the following functions to work with agents:

- `agent`: To create a new `Agent` object.
- `send`: To establish the new value of the agent. It follows the syntax `(send agent function value)` where `agent` is the name of the agent we want to modify, `function` is a function to be executed to calculate the new value of the agent, and `value` is the value that will be passed to the function with the actual value of the agent to calculate the new one.
- `send-of`: You can use this function when you want to use a function to update the value that is a blocking function (for example, reading a file). The `send-of` function will return immediately and the function that updates the value of the agent continues its execution in another thread. It follows the same syntax as the send function.
- `await`: Waits (blocking the current thread) until all the pending operations with the agent have finished. If follows the syntax `(await agent)` where `agent` is the name of the agent we want to wait for.
- `await-for`: You can use this function to wait the number of milliseconds specified as a parameter for the actualization of an `Agent`. It returns a `boolean` value to indicate if the `Agent` has been updated or not. It follows the syntax `(await-for time agent)` where `agent` is the name of the agent and `time` is the number of milliseconds we want to wait.
- `agent-error`: Returns the exception thrown by an `Agent` if the `Agent` fails. It follows the syntax `(agent-error agent)` where `agent` is the name of the agent.
- `shutdown-agents`: To finish the execution of any running agents. It follows the syntax `(shutdown-agents)`.

Let's see with an example, how we can work with agents.

First, we create an `Agent` with an initial value of 300:

```
(ns example.example3)
(def myAgent (agent 300))
```

Then, we implement a function named `myTask`. We repeat a process where we use the send method to first increment the value of the agent 1000 times and then the same method to decrement them, so the final value of the agent should be the same:

```
(defn myTask ( [a]
  (dotimes [i 1000]
    (send a + 100)
    (send a - 100)
    (println (format "%s : %d"(Thread/currentThread) @a))
    (Thread/sleep 100)
)))
```

Finally, we create 10 threads that execute the `myTask` function:

```
(dotimes [i 10] (.start (Thread. (fn[] (myTask myAgent)))))
```

The following screenshot shows an output of the execution of this example:

```
Thread[Thread-7,5,main] : 300
Thread[Thread-5,5,main] : 300
Thread[Thread-8,5,main] : 300
Thread[Thread-3,5,main] : 300
Thread[Thread-12,5,main] : 300
Thread[Thread-6,5,main] : 300
Thread[Thread-10,5,main] : 300
Thread[Thread-8,5,main] : 300
Thread[Thread-3,5,main] : 300
Thread[Thread-6,5,main] : 300
```

In this screenshot, you can see how there are different threads executing the `myTask` function and how the value of the agent is 300 as expected.

Refs

Finally, we come to `Ref` objects. They are the only coordinated reference type in Clojure and are a synchronous data structure. They allow you to modify multiple references concurrently within a transaction, so all the references are modified or none of them are modified.

You will use the following functions to work with refs:

- `ref`: To create a new `Ref` object.
- `alter`: This function modifies the value of the reference value in a safe way. It follows the syntax `(alter ref function)` where ref is the `Ref` name you want to modify and `function` is a function that will be executed to obtain the new value of the reference.

- ref-set: This set establishes the value of a Ref. It follows the syntax (ref-set ref value) where ref is the name of the ref you want to modify and value is the new value of the Ref.

- conmute: This function also changes the value of a Ref. It follows the syntax (conmute ref function) where ref is the name of the Ref you want to modify and function is a function that calculates the new value of the Ref.

- dosync: Executes the expression passed as a parameter in a transaction way. If an exception occurs during the execution of the expression, none of the operations related to Refs will be executed. On the other hand, the functions alter and commuted must be executed inside a dosync function. It follows the syntax (dosync expression) where expression is the expression to execute.

Let's see an example of how to work with Refs.

First, declare two refs named account1 and account2 and initialize them to 0:

```
(ns example.example4)
(def account1 (ref 0))
(def account2 (ref 0))
```

Then, define a function named myTask that will receive two refs objects named source and destination. For 1000 times, we decrement the value of the source and increment the value of the destination, as it were a transaction between two bank accounts. We use the alter function to change the value of the refs, so we have to include both calls inside a dosync function:

```
(defn myTask ( [source, destination]
  (dotimes [i 1000]
    (dosync
      (alter source - 100)
      (alter destination + 100)
    )
    (println (format "%s : %d - %d" (Thread/currentThread)
             @source @destination))
    (Thread/sleep 100)
))))
```

Finally, create 10 threads to call the function myTask where the source is account1 and the destination is account2, and another 10 threads to call the function myTask where the source is account2 and the destination is account1:

```
(dotimes [i 10] (.start (Thread. (fn[] (myTask account1 account2)))))
(dotimes [i 10] (.start (Thread. (fn[] (myTask account2 account1)))))
```

The following screenshot shows the output of an execution of this example:

```
Thread[Thread-12,5,main] : -400 - 400
Thread[Thread-16,5,main] : 300 - -300
Thread[Thread-15,5,main] : 200 - -200
Thread[Thread-3,5,main] : -300 - 300
Thread[Thread-8,5,main] : -300 - 300
Thread[Thread-18,5,main] : 200 - -200
Thread[Thread-19,5,main] : 100 - -100
Thread[Thread-21,5,main] : 0 - 0
Thread[Thread-12,5,main] : -100 - 100
Thread[Thread-15,5,main] : 0 - 0
```

In this screenshot, you can see the different threads that are executing the myTask function and how the final value of both references are 0 as expected.

Delays

A Delay is a data structure that is evaluated the first time it is **dereferenced** to obtain its value. You can use the following functions to work with Delays:

- delay: Use this function to declare a new Delay.
- @: This is the dereferenced function. You can use it to read the value of the Delay. This is the dereferenced function. You can use it to read the value of the Delay.
- realized?: This function will return a boolean value to indicate if the Delay has been initialized or not.

Let's see an example of a Delay.

First, declare three objects named now, otherNow, and later. In this objects we are going to store a String with the current date. The later object will be defined as a Delay:

```
(ns example.example5)

(def now (.toString (java.util.Date.)))
(def otherNow (.toString (java.util.Date.)))
(def later (delay (.toString (java.util.Date.))))
```

Then, define the myTest function. First, write the value of the now variable. Then, sleep the current Thread for five seconds and then write the value of the otherNow and later variables. With the later variable, we have to use the dereference function to obtain its value:

```
(defn myTest ([]
  (println (format "%s" now))
  (Thread/sleep 5000)
  (println (format "%s : %s" otherNow @later))
))
(myTest)
```

The following screenshot shows the output of an execution of this example:

```
Tue May 09 00:57:29 CEST 2017
Tue May 09 00:57:29 CEST 2017 : Tue May 09 00:57:34 CEST 2017
```

In this screenshot, you can see how the values of the Delay are not initialized until the value is obtained using the dereference function.

Futures

A Future is a piece of code that is evaluated in another thread. You can use the following functions to work with futures:

- future: Use this function to create a new Future.
- realized?: Use this function to check if the execution of the future has finished.
- Dereference function (@): Use this function to obtain the value of the Future. Calling the dereference function blocks the current Thread until the Future has finished its execution and returned a value.
- deref: Use this function to block the current Thread with a timeout. If the timeout finish and the Future haven't finished their execution, the function returns.

Let's see an example of the utilization of Futures:

First, declare a function named `initializeEnv` that sleeps its execution thread for a second. It writes information about the `Thread` that is executing the code and finally returns the `"Ok"` value:

```
(ns example.example6)

(def initializeEnv ( future
    (println (format "%s : Initializing environment" (Thread/currentThread)))
    (Thread/sleep 1000)
    (println (format "%s : Environment initialized" (Thread/currentThread)))
    "Ok"
))
```

Then, declare another function called `initilizeApp`. This function is equal to the `initializeEnv` function, but it sleeps its execution `Thread` for three seconds:

```
(def initializeApp ( future
    (println "Initializing app")
    (Thread/sleep 3000)
    (println "Environment app")
    "Ok"
))
```

Finally, include some instructions to call the `realized?` and dereference function:

```
(println (realized? initializeEnv))
(println (realized? initializeApp))
(println @initializeEnv)
(println (realized? initializeEnv))
(println (realized? initializeApp))
(println @initializeApp)
```

When you execute the code, you will see how both futures start their execution at the same time and that first the `initializeEnv` function ends its execution and the `initializeEnv` will return true to the `realized?` function. Then, the `intializeApp` will end its execution.

Promises

A `Promise` is a mechanism similar to a `Future`. The main difference is that it doesn't evaluate a block of code; you have to explicitly establish its value. The functions you can use with a Promise are:

- `promise`: Use this function to create a new `Promise`.
- `realized?`: Use this function to check if the `Promise` has a value or not.
- dereference function (`@`): Use this function to obtain the value of the `Promise`. Calling the dereference function blocks the current `Thread` until the `Promise` has finished its execution and returned a value.
- `deref`: Use this function to block the current `Thread` with a timeout. If the timeout finishes and the `Promise` hasn't finished its execution, the function returns.
- `deliver`: Use this function to establish the return value of a `Promise`.

Let's see an example of how to use a `Promise`. First, define a new `Promise` named myPromise:

```
(ns example.example7)

(def myPromise (promise))
```

Then, create a function named myTest that will receive a `Promise` as a parameter. Wait for five seconds and then verify that the promise has no value yet and establish its value using the deliver function:

```
(defn myTest ([p]
    (def now (java.util.Date.))
    (println (format "Start : %s" now))
    (Thread/sleep 5000)
    (def now (java.util.Date.))
    (println (format "End : %s" now))
    (println (realized? p))
    (deliver p "ok")
))
```

Finally, start a `Thread` to execute the `myTest` function and use the `realized?` and dereference function to check if the `Promise` has value and to write it:

```
(def now (java.util.Date.))
(println (format "Main : %s" now))
(println (realized? myPromise))
(println @myPromise)
(def now (java.util.Date.))
(println (format "Main : %s" now))
(println (realized? myPromise))
```

The following screenshot shows the output of an execution of this example:

```
Main : Tue May 09 01:12:13 CEST 2017
false
Start : Tue May 09 01:12:13 CEST 2017
End : Tue May 09 01:12:18 CEST 2017
false
ok
Main : Tue May 09 01:12:18 CEST 2017
true
```

Concurrency in Groovy with the GPars library

Groovy is a dynamic, object-oriented programming language for the Java platform similar to python, Ruby, or perl. **GPars** is a concurrency and parallelism framework for Groovy and Java. It introduces a lot of classes and elements to make parallel programming easier. The most important are:

- **Data parallelism**: Provides mechanisms that allow you to process data structures in parallel
- **fork/join process**: Allows you to implement concurrent algorithms using the divide and conquer technique
- **Actors**: Implement a message-passing based concurrency model
- **Dataflow**: Allows an alternative concurrency model to process data in a concurrent way
- **Agents**: Inspired by the agents provided in the Clojure programming language explained in the first section of this book

Software transactional memory

Software transactional memory is a mechanism that provides programmers transactional semantic for accessing data in memory. In this section, you will learn how to apply these elements in Groovy. Take into account that we don't make an introduction to the Groovy programming language. You can find a lot of tutorials about the Groovy programming language on the internet. The main page about GPars is `http://gpars.org`. You can download the library and find documentation about how to use them. As we mentioned before, you also can use this library in the Java programming language.

Using Java elements

Groovy is a programming language that generates byte codes for the JVM. You can use all the elements of the Java programming language in a Groovy program, including all those elements related with concurrency.

For example, in the following example you're going to create a `Thread`. First, declare a Groovy class named `Example1` with a `main()` method:

```
class Example1 {
   static main(args) {
```

Then, create and execute a thread using the `start()` method of the `Thread` class. You specify the code executed by the thread. In this case, we will show the current date, sleep the current thread for a second, and then write the current date again:

```
def task = Thread.start {
   println Thread.currentThread().getName()+": Starting the thread:
                                       "+new Date();
   Thread.currentThread().sleep(1000);
   println Thread.currentThread().getName()+": Ending the thread:
                                       "+new Date();
}
```

We can use the `join()` method to wait for the finalization of this `Thread`:

```
task.join();
println Thread.currentThread().getName()+": Main has ended: "
                                    +new Date();
   }
}
```

When you execute this application you will see how the thread shows the first message and a second later the second message. Then, when it has finished its execution, the `main()` method shows its message.

Data parallelism

In this section, we're going to include all the elements provided by the Groovy programming language to process data structures in a concurrent way. The first element we have to consider is the `GParsPool` class. This class is an implementation of the JSR-166y based on the fork/join framework that gives us a very good performance to process data structures in a concurrent way.

Let's see an example of how we can use the `GParsPool` class. First, we have to include the necessary import sentences. Then, create a class name `Example2` with a `main()` method:

```
import groovyx.gpars.GParsPool
import static groovyx.gpars.GParsPool.withPool
class Example2 {
  static main(args) {
```

Then, declare a range of number between one and 1000 and use the `withPool` sentence to process all those numbers in a parallel way. We use the `println` method to write the name of the `Thread` that is processing that number and the number is processing. We can access that number using the it variable:

```
def numbers = 1..1000;
println "Example 2 - Part 1"
withPool {
  numbers.eachParallel {
    println Thread.currentThread().getName() +": "+ it;
  }
}
```

Then we use the `withPool` sentence, but now with a parameter to indicate the maximum number of threads it can use:

```
println "Example 2 - Part 2"
withPool(4){
  List numberList = numbers.collectParallel { it *it}
  List smallNumberList = numberList.findAllParallel{ it < 100 }
  smallNumberList.eachParallel {
    println Thread.currentThread().getName() +": "+ it;
  }
}
```

We use three methods provided by Groovy to process the numbers of the range in a parallel way. With the `collectParallel()` method we calculate the square of each number. With the `findAllParallel()` method we filter the list of numbers to take only those that are smaller than 100 and, finally, with the `eachParallel()` method, we process all the methods of the resultant list.

We can use other methods to process the data of a data structure in a parallel way such as `minParallel()`, `maxParallel()`, or `countParallel()`. Take a look at the GPars API to see the details of all these methods.

The following screenshot shows the output of an execution of this application:

```
Example 2 - Part 2
ForkJoinPool-2-worker-2: 25
ForkJoinPool-2-worker-1: 1
ForkJoinPool-2-worker-2: 36
ForkJoinPool-2-worker-1: 4
ForkJoinPool-2-worker-4: 9
ForkJoinPool-2-worker-3: 16
ForkJoinPool-2-worker-2: 49
ForkJoinPool-2-worker-2: 64
ForkJoinPool-2-worker-2: 81
```

Another option provided by the `GParsPool` class is to call a closure in a different Thread using the `callAsync()` or the `executeAsyncAndWait()` methods. The first method starts the execution of the closure in a different thread and returns immediately while the other waits for the finalization of the closure before it returns. Let's see an example of how we can work with these functions.

First, we include the import sentences and create a new class named `Example3` with the `main()` method. In the `main()` method, we create two closures named `code1` and `code2`:

```
import groovyx.gpars.GParsPool

class Example3 {
  static main(args) {
    Closure code1 = {
      println "Closure 1: "+Thread.currentThread().getName()+": Start:"
                  +new Date();
      Thread.currentThread().sleep(1000)
      println "Closure 1: "+Thread.currentThread().getName()+": End: "
                  +new Date();
    }
    ...
    Closure code2 = {
      println "Closure 2: "+Thread.currentThread().getName()+": Start:"
                  +new Date();
```

```
Thread.currentThread().sleep(2000)
println "Closure 2: "+Thread.currentThread().getName()+": End: "
                +new Date();
}
```

First, we call the two closures in a sequential way, using the normal syntax of Groovy:

```
println "Closure 1 sequential"
code1.call();
println "Closure 2 sequential"
code2.call();
```

Then, we use the `withPool` method of the `GParsPool` class to execute the `code1` closure in a concurrent way using the `callAsync()` method, and then the `code1` and `code2` closures using the `executeAsyncAndWait()` method of the `GParsPool` class:

```
GParsPool.withPool {
  println "Closure 1 async";
  code1.callAsync();
  println "Closure 1 and closure 2 async with wait"
  GParsPool.executeAsyncAndWait(code1,code2);
  println "End"
}
println "Main end"
}
}
```

The following screenshot shows the output of an execution of this example:

```
Closure 1 sequential
Closure 1: main: Start: Tue May 09 01:44:19 CEST 2017
Closure 1: main: End: Tue May 09 01:44:20 CEST 2017
Closure 2 sequential
Closure 2: main: Start: Tue May 09 01:44:20 CEST 2017
Closure 2: main: End: Tue May 09 01:44:22 CEST 2017
Closure 1 async
Closure 1 and closure 2 async with wait
Closure 1: ForkJoinPool-1-worker-1: Start: Tue May 09 01:44:22 CEST 2017
Closure 1: ForkJoinPool-1-worker-2: Start: Tue May 09 01:44:22 CEST 2017
Closure 2: ForkJoinPool-1-worker-3: Start: Tue May 09 01:44:22 CEST 2017
Closure 1: ForkJoinPool-1-worker-1: End: Tue May 09 01:44:23 CEST 2017
Closure 1: ForkJoinPool-1-worker-2: End: Tue May 09 01:44:23 CEST 2017
Closure 2: ForkJoinPool-1-worker-3: End: Tue May 09 01:44:24 CEST 2017
End
Main end
```

You can see how we can easily differentiate the sequential and the concurrent executions of the closures (with the name of the `Thread`).

Another option with the `GParsPool` class is using the **Map/Reduce** programming model to process in parallel any data structure. When you use the Map/Reduce in Groovy, your data structure is converted internally in a parallel array and all the methods you use work over that data structure. It is similar to Stream processing in the Java programming language.

Let's see an example of how to use this functionality. First, introduce the necessary import sentences and create a new class named `Example4` with the `main()` method. In that method, declare a range between 1 and 10000:

```
import groovyx.gpars.GParsPool

class Example4 {

  static main(args) {
    def numbers = 1..10000
```

Then, use the `withPool` sentence and the fork/join functionality to process that range in a parallel way. We use the `parallel` method to convert the range in a parallel data structure, the `map` method to replace each element for its square, the `filter` method to retain only the numbers smaller than 100000, and the `sum` method to sum all the elements of the list:

```
GParsPool.withPool {
  int result = numbers.parallel.map{it*it}.filter{it < 100000}
                   .sum();
  println result;
```

Then, we apply other examples of this functionality. Dynamically create another range between 1 and 1000000 and use the `parallel` method to convert the range in a parallel data structure, the `filter` method to retain only the even numbers, the `map` method to replace every number with its square root, and, finally, the `collection` method to convert the parallel data structure in a list:

```
List numberList = (1..1000000).parallel.filter{it % 2 == 0}
                     .map{Math.sqrt it}.collection
  numberList.forEach{
    println it;
  }
    }
  }
}
```

When you execute this example, you will see the numbers of the output in the console.

Finally, the last aspect we're going to learn about the `GParsPool` class is to use a promise to obtain the value of an asynchronous function. Let's see an example of how to use this functionality. First, create a class named `Example5` with the `main()` method and a closure named `code1`:

```
import static groovyx.gpars.GParsPool.withPool;

class Example5 {

    static main(args) {
        Closure code1 = {
            println "Closure 1: "+Thread.currentThread().getName()+": Start:"
                            +new Date();
            Thread.currentThread().sleep(1000)
            println "Closure 1: "+Thread.currentThread().getName()+": End: "
                            +new Date();
            return new Date().toString();
        }
```

Then, we use the `withPool` sentence to execute in an asynchronous way the `code1` closure with the `asyncFun()` method and then generate a promise with the result of that method. Finally, we use the `get()` method of the promise to obtain the result of the `code1` closure. Take into account that the `get()` method sleeps the calling thread until the closure has finished its execution:

```
        withPool {
            def aCode1 = code1.asyncFun();
            def promise = aCode1();
            println "We have call the closure";
            println "The result is : "+promise.get();
        }
    }
}
```

The following screenshot shows the output of an execution of this example:

```
We have call the closure
Closure 1: ForkJoinPool-1-worker-1: Start: Tue May 09 02:14:50 CEST 2017
Closure 1: ForkJoinPool-1-worker-1: End: Tue May 09 02:14:51 CEST 2017
The result is : Tue May 09 02:14:51 CEST 2017
```

The fork/join processing

The fork/join implementation provided by GPars is similar to the one provided by Java in its concurrency API. The main objective of this functionality is to solve a problem using the divide and conquer technique. The first time you execute the algorithm, with the full problem, you check the size of the problem. If it's smaller than a predefined size, you solve the problem directly. Otherwise, you divide the problem into a predefined number of smaller problems and make asynchronous recursive calls, one for each sub-problem. In each recursive call, the process is the same. You check the size of the problem and if it's smaller than the predefined size, you solve it directly; otherwise, you divide the problem again and make recursive calls again. Once all the recursive calls have ended, the method that started those calls gets the control again to get the results of each call and groups those results. The final result is returned. At the end, we have solved a big problem, by grouping the results of the solution of a lot of small problems.

Take into account that not all the algorithms can be solved using this technique, but if you can use it, it makes an optimized use of the resources and gives very good performance results.

The GPars library provides the following methods to work with the fork/join framework:

- `runForkJoin()`: Create a fork/join execution. You have to specify the parameters of the algorithm and the closure that implements that algorithm. The recursive calls you make have the same parameters.
- `forkOffChild()`: Create a new child task to execute a sub-problem. This task will be executed in the future. The method sends the task to be scheduled in the `ForkJoinPool` that is executing all the tasks, and returns immediately.
- `runChildDirectly()`: Runs a child task within the current thread and returns when it finishes its execution.
- `getChildrenResults()`: Waits for the finalization of all the children tasks and returns a List object with their results. You can use this list to calculate the result that will be returned by the task.

Let's see an example of how to work with the fork/join framework of GPars. We're going to implement a function that counts the number of files that end with the `.log` extension that exists in a directory. First, include the necessary import sentences and create a class named `Example6` with the `main()` method:

```
import static groovyx.gpars.GParsPool.withPool;
import static groovyx.gpars.GParsPool.runForkJoin;

class Example6 {

  static main(args) {
```

Then, in the `withPool` instruction, call the `runForkJoin()` method passing a `File` object as a parameter. This is the path where we are going to start the search of files that end with the `.log` extension. We have to specify the code of the algorithm. For the directory we receive as a parameter, we process all the files and directories that it contains. If the item is a file, we check if its extension is log. If it is, we increment a counter. If the item is a directory, we make a recursive asynchronous call using the `forkOffChild()` method.

When we have processed all the items, we obtain the results of all the children tasks and sum all the results of those tasks with the counter. The final value is the result returned:

```
withPool() {
  def count = runForkJoin(new File("c:\\windows")) {file ->
    long count = 0
    file.eachFile {
      if (it.isDirectory()) {
        println "Forking a child task for $it"
        forkOffChild(it)
      } else {
        if (it.getName().endsWith("log")) {
          count++;
          println it.getName();
        }
      }
    }
    return count + (childrenResults.sum(0))
}
```

Take into account that a children task can have children tasks too and so on. Finally, when the original call ends, we write the final result:

```
        println "Total: "+ count;
      }
    }
  }
}
```

When you execute the example, you will see the total number of files.

Actors

Actors implement a message-passing concurrency model. Each actor is an independent object that sends and receives messages from/to other actors. There's no association between actors and threads. A thread can execute different actors and an actor can be executed by different threads. Actors don't have shared-state and GPars guarantees that the code of the actor will be executed, so no messages will be lost. Memory will also be synchronized each time a thread is assigned to an actor, so no explicit synchronization is needed. There are two types of actors:

- **Stateless actors**: Based on the `DynamicDispatchActor` or the `ReactiveActor` classes. They have no track of what messages have arrived before.
- **Stateful actors**: Based on the `DefaultActor` class. The actor can manage an internal state and each message can change that state and the way it processes the messages.

One of the biggest benefits of actors is the throughput you can obtain in these systems. An actor will be only executed when it has to process a message, so you can have a large number of actors running with a small number of threads.

When you work with actors, you will use the following methods to make the most common actions:

- `send()`: This method sends a message to an actor asynchronously. It returns immediately and doesn't wait for the response.
- `sendAndWait()`: This method sends a message to an actor and waits for the response.
- `sendAndContinue()`: This method sends a message to an actor and returns immediately. It receives as a parameter a closure that will be executed when the response of this message arrives.
- `sendAndPromise()`: This method sends a message to an actor and returns a promise we can use to get the response of the message.
- `react()`: This method will be called to consume the next message. Usually, it will be included in a loop sentence to process all the messages an actor receives.
- `reply()`: This method sends a reply to the sender of a message.
- `forward()`: This method allows us to forward a message received to another actor.
- `join()`: This method waits for the finalization of an actor.

There are different ways to create an `Actor`.

You can use the `actor()` method of the `Actors` class. In this case, you specify the code of the actor using a closure. The actor starts its execution immediately.

You can extend the `DefaultActor` class and implement the `act()` method. In this case, we have to call the `start()` method of the actor to begin its execution.

You can extend the `DynamicDispatchACtor` class and implement one or more versions of the `onMessage()` method (one version for each type of message the actor can receive).

Finally, an actor has a life cycle and has some methods you can implement to execute actions on determined states of that life cycle. These methods are:

- `afterStart()`
- `afterStop()`
- `onTimeOut()`
- `onInterrupt()`
- `onException()`

The name of the method is auto explicative, so no additional description is needed.

Let's see three examples that show how we can work with actors. In the first one, we are only going to create two basic `Actor` objects that will send a message between them.

Create a class named `Example7` with the `main()` method:

```
import groovyx.gpars.actor.Actor
import groovyx.gpars.actor.Actors

class Example7 {

  static main(args) {
```

Then, create an Actor using the `actor()` method of the `Actors` class. In the code of the actor we include the code for the `react()` method. In our case, when a message arrives, we write it in the console and then send a response to that message including the name of the current `Thread` and the text `Ok`:

```
def receiver = Actors.actor {
  println Thread.currentThread().getName()+": Receiver is running"
  react { msg ->
    println Thread.currentThread().getName()+": Recevier:  I've
                                    received a message: "+msg
    reply Thread.currentThread().getName()+": Ok"
  }
```

```
    println Thread.currentThread().getName()+": Receiver has finished"
}
```

Then, we create another `Actor` using the `actors()` method again. In this case, we send a message to the other actor using the `send()` method and we also include the code for the `react()` method that will be executed when the actor receives a message. It will write the message in the console:

```
def sender = Actors.actor {
  println Thread.currentThread().getName()+": Sender is running"
  receiver.send Thread.currentThread().getName()+": From sender to
                                              receiver"
  react { msg ->
    println Thread.currentThread().getName()+": Sender: The response
                                            has arrived: "+msg
  }
  println Thread.currentThread().getName()+": Sender has finished"
}
```

As we explained before, both actors will start execution immediately. Finally, in the `main()` method, we wait for the finalization of both threads using the `join()` method:

```
    sender.join();
    receiver.join();
  }
}
```

The following screenshot shows the output of an execution of this example:

```
Actor Thread 2: Sender is running
Actor Thread 2: Sender has finished
Actor Thread 1: Receiver is running
Actor Thread 1: Receiver has finished
Actor Thread 1: Recevier:  I've received a message: Actor Thread 2: From sender to receiver
Actor Thread 2: Sender: The response has arrived: Actor Thread 1: Ok
```

You can see how the sender sends its message that arrives at the receiver, which sends the response that arrives at the sender.

The second example is an implementation of the producer/consumer problem. First, we are going to implement the consumer class. Create a class named `Consumer` and specify that it implements the `DefaultActor` class:

```
import groovyx.gpars.actor.Actor
import groovyx.gpars.actor.DefaultActor

class Consumer extends DefaultActor {
```

Then, implement the `act()` method that contains the main code of the `Actor`. We use the loop sentence to process all the messages and the `react()` method that will be called for each message received by the `Actor`. We pass the parameter 5000 to the `react()` method. If the actor waits five seconds without receiving a message, it throws a `TimeOut` error and ends its execution. For each message, we only write information about the message and the sender in the console:

```
void act() {
  loop {
    react(5000) { msg ->
      println "*****************************";
      println "Thread Name: "+Thread.currentThread().getName();
      println "Sender: "+sender.remoteClass;
      println "Message: "+msg;
      println "*****************************";
    }
  }
}
```

Then, we implement some of the life cycle methods of the `Actor` to write in the console information about those events:

```
void afterStart() {
  println "Consumer: After Start";
}
void afterStop(List undeliveredMessages) {
  println "Consumer: After Stop";
  println "Undelivered Messages: "+undeliveredMessages.size()
}
void onInterrupt(InterruptedException e) {
  println "Consumer: Interrupted"
  e.printStackTrace()
  terminate()
}
void onTimeout() {
  println "Consumer: Timeout"
  terminate()
}
void onException(Throwable e) {
  println "Consumer: An exception has ocurred"
  e.printStackTrace()
}
}
```

Now is time to implement the `Producer` class. Create a class named `Producer` and specify that it implements the `DefaultActor` class. This class will have two attributes with the name of the `Producer` and the `Consumer` to send the messages and a constructor to initialize them:

```
import java.lang.invoke.AbstractValidatingLambdaMetafactory
import java.util.List

import groovyx.gpars.actor.DefaultActor
import groovyx.gpars.actor.Actor

class Producer extends DefaultActor {

  private Actor consumer;
  private String name;
  def Producer (Actor consumer, String name) {
    this.consumer = consumer
    this.name = name
  }
```

Now, implement the `act()` method with the main code of the `Actor`. It will send 100 messages to the consumer and ends its execution:

```
void act() {
  def i;
  for (i = 0; i<100; i++) {
    def msg = Thread.currentThread().getName()
    msg+= ": "+name
    msg+= ": Message "+i;
    consumer.send msg;
    Thread.currentThread().sleep(500);
  }
}
```

Finally, we write the code of the `afterStop()` method to write a message in the console:

```
void afterStop(List undeliveredMessages) {
  println name+": After Stop";
}
}
```

Now, create a class named `Example8` with the `main()` method:

```
import groovyx.gpars.actor.Actor
import groovyx.gpars.actor.DefaultActor

class Example8 {
```

```
static main(args) {
  Consumer consumer = new Consumer();
  consumer.start();

  Producer producer1 = new Producer(consumer,"Producer 1");
  Producer producer2 = new Producer(consumer, "Producer 2");
  producer1.start();
  Thread.currentThread().sleep(300);
  producer2.start();
  consumer.join();
  println "Main end"
}

}
```

In the `main()` method, we create a consumer and two producers and start the three actors using the `start()` method. We use the `join()` method to wait for the finalization of the consumer actor. That actor will finish five seconds after the finalization of the producers sending a `TimeOut` exception

The following screenshot shows the output of an execution of this example:

```
*****************************
Thread Name: Actor Thread 3
Sender: class groovyx.gpars.actor.impl.MessageStream$RemoteMessageStream
Message: Actor Thread 2: Producer 1: Message 99
*****************************
*****************************
Thread Name: Actor Thread 3
Sender: class groovyx.gpars.actor.impl.MessageStream$RemoteMessageStream
Message: Actor Thread 1: Producer 2: Message 99
*****************************
Producer 1: After Stop
Producer 2: After Stop
Consumer: Timeout
Consumer: After Stop
Undelivered Messages: 0
Main end
```

You can see how the producers end its execution and write the message of the `afterStop()` method. Then, the consumer has a `TimeOut` and executes the methods `onTimeOut()` and `afterStop()`. Then, the main program ends its execution.

The last example about actors will show you how to work with stateless actors. First, create a class named `Event` with two attributes: a `String` attribute named `msg` and a `Date` attribute named `date`:

```
class Event {
  String msg;
  Date date;
  @Override
  public String toString() {
    return "Event: "+msg+": on "+date;
  }
}
```

Now, create a class named `Logger` and specify that it extends the `DynamicDispatchActor`. We implement three versions of the `onMessage()` method that receives respectively an `Event` class, a `String`, and an `Exception`. We only write in the console information about the kind of message it has received:

```
class Logger extends DynamicDispatchActor {

  def onMessage (Event event) {
    println "Logger: "+Thread.currentThread().getName()+": "+event;
    replyIfExists "Logger: Event received";
  }
  def onMessage(String msg) {
    println "Logger: "+Thread.currentThread().getName()+
            ": Direct mgs: "+msg;
    replyIfExists "Logger: Direct msg received";
  }
  def onMessage(Exception e) {
    println "Logger: "+Thread.currentThread().getName()+": Error: 
            "+e.getLocalizedMessage();
    replyIfExists "Logger: Error received"
  }
}
```

Finally, we create a class named `Example9` with the `main()` method. First, we create a `Logger` actor and start its execution with the `start()` method:

```
import groovyx.gpars.actor.Actor
import groovyx.gpars.actor.Actors

class Example9 {
  static main(args) {
    Logger logger = new Logger();
    logger.start();
```

Then, we create another actor with the `actor()` method of the Actors class. In the code, we send three messages to the logger class, one of each type, and include the code to process the three responses:

```
def tester = Actors.actor {
  println "Tester: "+Thread.currentThread().getName()+
          ": is running"
  loop(3) {
    react(1000) { msg ->
      println "Tester: "+Thread.currentThread().getName()+
              ":  I've received a message: "+msg
    }
  }
  Event event = new Event()
  event.msg = "I'm an event"
  event.date = new Date()
  logger.send event
  logger.send "I'm a message"
  Exception e = new Exception("I'm an exception")
  logger.send e;
  println "Tester: "+Thread.currentThread().getName()+
          ": Tester has finished"
}
```

Finally, we wait for the finalization of the tester actor using the `join()` method, stop the `logger` actor using the `stop()` method, and wait for its finalization using the `join()` method:

```
    tester.join();
    logger.stop();
    logger.join();
    println "Main End"
  }
}
```

The following screenshot shows the output of an execution of this example:

```
Tester: Actor Thread 1: is running
Tester: Actor Thread 1: Tester has finished
Logger: Actor Thread 2: Event: I'm an event: on Tue May 09 10:51:21 CEST 2017
Tester: Actor Thread 1:  I've received a message: Logger: Event received
Logger: Actor Thread 2: Direct mgs: I'm a message
Tester: Actor Thread 1:  I've received a message: Logger: Direct msg received
Logger: Actor Thread 2: Error: I'm an exception
Tester: Actor Thread 1:  I've received a message: Logger: Error received
Main End
```

Agent

An **Agent** protects a mutable data object that can be shared between threads in a safe way. The agent accepts messages and processes them asynchronously. Messages are functions or Groovy closures and will be executed inside the agent. The return value of the function or the closure will be the new value/state of the agent. The function or the closure will receive as a parameter the current value/state of the agent.

The commands we send to an agent are stored in order and processed one by one, so no race condition will occur.

To create an agent, you create a new object of the Agent class parameterized with the type of the value stored in the agent.

When you work with agents, you will normally use the following methods:

- send(): This method sends a command to the agent
- addListener(): This method adds a listener that will be notified each time the value of the agent changes
- addValidator(): This method adds a validator that is similar to a listener, but can reject a change in the value of the Agent throwing an Exception

Let's implement an example to see how to work with agents. First, create a class named Account with an internal integer attribute named value, a method named increment() to increment the value of the attribute, a method named decrement() to decrement the value of the attribute, and a method to return the value of the attribute:

```
class Account {
  private int value = 0;
  def void increment (int amount) {
    println "Account.increment: "+Thread.currentThread().getName()+": "
                                 +amount;
    value+=amount
  }
  def void decrement (int amount) {
    println "Account.decrement: "+Thread.currentThread().getName()+": "
                                 +amount;
    value-=amount
  }
  def int getValue() {
    return value;
  }

}
```

Then, create a class named `Example10` with the `main()` method. Create a new `Agent` that will store an `Account` object:

```
class Example10 {

  static main(args) {

    Agent agent = new Agent<Account>(new Account())
```

Then, create an `Actor` that will call 100 times to the `increment()` method of the account object of the agent. You can use the it variable to access the current value of the `Agent`:

```
def incrementer = Actors.actor {
  for (def i=0; i<100; i++) {
    agent.send {it.increment(1000)}
  }
}
```

Now, create another `Actor`. This actor will call 99 times the `decrement()` method of the account object stored in the agent:

```
def decrementer = Actors.actor {
  for (def i=0; i<99; i++) {
    agent.send {it.decrement(1000)}
  }
}
```

Finally, wait for the finalization of both actors and write the final value of the `Agent`:

```
    incrementer.join()
    decrementer.join()
    println "Final value: "+agent.val.getValue()
  }
}
```

If you execute this example, you will see how the result will be 1000 (100 increments and 99 decrements).

Dataflow

Dataflows provide safe channels to share data between producers and consumers. The most basic element of a dataflow is **dataflow variables**. You just create an object of the `Dataflows` class and then we can define variables on it. These variables have two important characteristics:

- You can only set the value once
- When a task tries to use the value of a dataflow's variable, its execution thread is blocked until the variable has a value

The benefits you can obtain with dataflow variables are:

- You don't have race conditions
- You don't need to use locks or other synchronization mechanisms explicitly
- If there's a deadlock provoked by dataflow's variables, you can determine its cause

Let's see an example of how dataflow variables work. First, create a class named `Example1` with a `main()` method:

```
import static groovyx.gpars.dataflow.Dataflow.task;
import java.util.concurrent.TimeUnit
import groovyx.gpars.dataflow.Dataflows;

class Example11 {

  static main(args) {
```

Now, create a `Dataflows` object and a `Date` object with the starting date of the execution of this method:

```
def store = new Dataflows()
def mainStart = new Date();
println "Main: Start "+mainStart
```

Now, we start a logical task that will be executed by another thread using the task function. We sleep its execution thread for one second and then create a variable in our `Dataflows` object and assign to it the value 3:

```
task {
  TimeUnit.SECONDS.sleep(1)
  store.x = 3
}
```

Now, we create another task like the previous one. In this case we sleep its execution thread for two seconds and we assign to it a variable named y, with the value 4:

```
task {
  TimeUnit.SECONDS.sleep(2)
  store.y = 4
}
```

Then, we create a third task that will calculate the sum between the variables x and y and store that value in another dataflow variable called z:

```
task {
  def start = new Date()
  println "Calculus Task: "+start
  store.z = store.x + store.y
  def end = new Date()
  println "Calculus Task: "+end
}
```

Finally, in the main() method, we write the value of the variable z:

```
    println "Main: The final result is: "+store.z
    println "Main: End"
  }
}
```

The following screenshot shows the output of an execution of this example:

```
Main: Start Tue May 09 16:19:49 CEST 2017
Calculus Task: Tue May 09 16:19:50 CEST 2017
Main: The final result is: 7
Main: End
Calculus Task: Tue May 09 16:19:52 CEST 2017
```

We can also create an object of the DataflowVariable class and assign a value to it using the << operator. For example, create a class named Example13 with a main() method and create an object of the DataflowVariable class named data:

```
import static groovyx.gpars.dataflow.Dataflow.task;
import java.util.concurrent.TimeUnit
import groovyx.gpars.dataflow.DataflowVariable;
class Example13 {

  static main(args) {
    def data = new DataflowVariable()
```

Now, create a task that sleeps its execution thread for two seconds and assign the value 2 to the variable using the << operator:

```
task {
  println Thread.currentThread().getName()+": Wait two seconds to
                                             set the value"
  TimeUnit.SECONDS.sleep(2);
  data << 2;
}
```

Finally, in the `main()` method, include a sentence to write the value of the data variable:

```
      println Thread.currentThread().getName()+" : Bind handler : "
                                          +data.val;
   }
 }
```

When you execute this example, you will see the message written by the task and two seconds later the message written by the `main()` method with the value of the `DataflowVariable` object.

Another element provided by dataflows is the **Dataflow Broadcasts**. They allow us to send data between a producer and a consumer as if there were a queue between them. It offers a publish-subscription mechanism to have one or more producers and one or more consumers.

Let's see an example of how this mechanism works. First, create a class name `Producer`. It will have two private attributes: a `DataflowBroadcast` object named broadcast and a `String` object named `name`. Use the constructor of the class to initialize them:

```
import java.util.concurrent.TimeUnit
import groovyx.gpars.dataflow.DataflowBroadcast;

class Producer {

  private DataflowBroadcast broadcast
  private String name
  public Producer (DataflowBroadcast broadcast, String name) {
    this.broadcast = broadcast
    this.name = name
  }
```

Now, implement a method named `execute()`. In this method, write 100 `String` objects into the broadcast object using the << operator. Sleep the execution thread for 500 milliseconds between each message:

```
public void execute() {
  for (int i=0; i<100; i++) {
    def msg = name + " MSG "+i+" : "+new Date();
    broadcast << msg
    TimeUnit.MILLISECONDS.sleep(500);
  }
}
}
```

Now, create a class named `Consumer`. It will have the same attributes as the `Producer` class. Use the constructor of the class to initialize them:

```
import groovyx.gpars.dataflow.DataflowBroadcast
import groovyx.gpars.dataflow.DataflowReadChannel

class Consumer {

  private DataflowBroadcast broadcast
  private String name
  public Consumer (DataflowBroadcast broadcast, String name) {
    this.broadcast = broadcast
    this.name = name
  }
```

Now, implement the `execute()` method. First, create an object of the `DataflowReadChannel` class to read the values from the `DataflowBroadcast`. Then, write 200 messages from it using the `val` function. This function will sleep the current thread until new data is available in the `DataflowBroadcast`:

```
public void execute() {
  DataflowReadChannel stream = broadcast.createReadChannel()
  for (int i=0; i<200; i++) {
    println "Consumer "+name+": "+stream.val
  }
}
}
```

We have the producer and the consumer. Now it's time to put them to work. Create a class named Example12 with a main method. We create a DataflowBroadcast object, two producers, and three consumers. Create a thread to execute each producer and each consumer. Then, wait for their finalization using the join() method:

```
import groovyx.gpars.dataflow.DataflowBroadcast
import static groovyx.gpars.dataflow.Dataflow.task

class Example12 {

  static main(args) {
    DataflowBroadcast dataflow = new DataflowBroadcast()
    def producer1, producer2, consumer1, consumer2, consumer3
    Thread thread1 = Thread.start {
      producer1 = new Producer(dataflow, "Producer 1")
      producer1.execute()
    }
    Thread thread2 = Thread.start {
      producer2 = new Producer(dataflow, "Producer 2")
      producer2.execute()
    }
    Thread thread3 = Thread.start{
      consumer1 = new Consumer(dataflow, "Consumer 1")
      consumer1.execute()
    }
    Thread thread4 = Thread.start {
      consumer2 = new Consumer(dataflow, "Consumer 2")
      consumer2.execute()
    }
    Thread thread5 = Thread.start {
      consumer3 = new Consumer(dataflow, "Consumer 3")
      consumer3.execute()
    }
    thread1.join()
    thread2.join()
    thread3.join()
    thread4.join()
    thread5.join()
    println "Main: end"
  }
}
```

The following screenshot shows the output of an execution of this example:

```
Consumer Consumer 1: Producer 1 MSG 97 : Tue May 09 16:21:34 CEST 2017
Consumer Consumer 3: Producer 1 MSG 97 : Tue May 09 16:21:34 CEST 2017
Consumer Consumer 2: Producer 1 MSG 97 : Tue May 09 16:21:34 CEST 2017
Consumer Consumer 1: Producer 1 MSG 98 : Tue May 09 16:21:34 CEST 2017
Consumer Consumer 2: Producer 1 MSG 98 : Tue May 09 16:21:34 CEST 2017
Consumer Consumer 3: Producer 1 MSG 98 : Tue May 09 16:21:34 CEST 2017
Consumer Consumer 2: Producer 2 MSG 98 : Tue May 09 16:21:34 CEST 2017
Consumer Consumer 1: Producer 2 MSG 98 : Tue May 09 16:21:34 CEST 2017
Consumer Consumer 3: Producer 2 MSG 98 : Tue May 09 16:21:34 CEST 2017
Consumer Consumer 2: Producer 2 MSG 99 : Tue May 09 16:21:35 CEST 2017
Consumer Consumer 2: Producer 1 MSG 99 : Tue May 09 16:21:35 CEST 2017
Consumer Consumer 3: Producer 2 MSG 99 : Tue May 09 16:21:35 CEST 2017
Consumer Consumer 1: Producer 2 MSG 99 : Tue May 09 16:21:35 CEST 2017
Consumer Consumer 3: Producer 1 MSG 99 : Tue May 09 16:21:35 CEST 2017
Consumer Consumer 1: Producer 1 MSG 99 : Tue May 09 16:21:35 CEST 2017
Main: end
```

You can see how each message generated by a producer arrives to the three consumers.

Another functionality provided by dataflows is the option to select a value from multiple channels using the `select()` function. This function receives as parameters a list of channels, and it selects one for all the channels that have a value to read. It returns a `SelectResult` object with the value returned and information about the channel it has selected. This mechanism is very configurable to, for example, prioritize some channels over others.

Let's see an example of how this mechanism works. First, create a class named `Example14` with the `main()` method. Create three `DataflowVariable` objects named `source1`, `source2`, and `source3`:

```
import static groovyx.gpars.dataflow.Dataflow.task
import static groovyx.gpars.dataflow.Dataflow.select
import java.util.concurrent.TimeUnit
import groovyx.gpars.dataflow.DataflowVariable

class Example14 {
  static main(args) {

    def source1 = new DataflowVariable()
    def source2 = new DataflowVariable()
    def source3 = new DataflowVariable()
```

Now, create three tasks to give a value to each data source. Each task will sleep its execution thread for a different time before assigning a value to its `DataflowVariable`:

```
task {
    TimeUnit.SECONDS.sleep(3);
    source1 << "source1"
}

task {
    TimeUnit.SECONDS.sleep(5);
    source2 << "source2"
}

task {
    TimeUnit.SECONDS.sleep(1);
    source3 << "source3"
}
```

Now, use the select function to obtain a value from these data sources and write it in the console:

```
        def result = select([source1, source2, source3])
        println   "Main: "+result.select()
    }

}
```

The following screenshot shows the output of an execution of this example:

```
Main: SelectResult{index=2, value=source3}
```

In this case, the `source3` object is the one that gets the value first, after one second, so it is the one returned by the select function.

Finally, the last mechanism of dataflows we're going to analyze is operators. **Operators** receive values from input channels and generate new values that are written to output channels. All these channels are dataflow's variables. An operator waits for all input channels until it starts its execution.

Let's see an example of how this mechanism works. Create a class named `Example15` with a `main()` method. Create four `DataflowVariable` objects named a, b, c, d:

```
import groovyx.gpars.dataflow.DataflowVariable;
import static groovyx.gpars.dataflow.Dataflow.operator;
import java.util.concurrent.TimeUnit

class Example15 {

  static main(args) {

    def a = new DataflowVariable();
    def b = new DataflowVariable();
    def c = new DataflowVariable();
    def d = new DataflowVariable();
```

Now create a new operator named op using the operator command. It receives three inputs, the dataflows variables a, b, and c, and returns the value for the dataflow variable d. We establish the value of the output using the `bindOutput` function:

```
def op = operator(inputs: [a, b, c], outputs: [d]) {x, y, z ->
  println "Operator"
  bindOutput 0, x + y + z
}
```

Finally, we assign the value for the a, b, and c variables and write the value of the `DataflowVariable` in the console using the val property of the variable d:

```
    a << 3;
    b << 5;
    c << 7;
    println "Main: "+d.val
  }
}
```

When we assign the value to the three `DataflowVariable` objects, the operator executes its code. Once it finishes, the `DataflowVariable` d has its value and is written in the last sentence of the `main()` method.

The following screenshot shows the output of an execution of this example:

```
Operator
Main: 15
```

Concurrency in Scala

Scala is a general purpose multi-paradigm programming language that includes characteristics of object-oriented and functional programming. Its code is compiled to Java byte code. It provides Java interoperability, so you can use elements of Java (including the Java Concurrency API) in Scala code and libraries written in Scala in Java programs.

As we mentioned with Clojure and Groovy, the main purpose of this section is not to provide an introduction to the Scala programming language and its installation and configuration. You can download the tools to work in Scala from `https://www.scala-lang.org/`. You can install a plug-in to get support for Scala in your IDE. Eclipse, for example, has the Scala IDE plug-in that you can install via the Eclipse Marketplace.

The Scala concurrency model is based on **Futures** and **Promises**. A future stores a value that doesn't exist yet and will be calculated by an asynchronous task that will be executed by another thread. A `Future` uses a non-blocking mechanism and makes use of callbacks to process the value when it's available (or when an error occurs). A promise is a mechanism that allows you to complete (gives a value) a `Future`.

A very important element in the Scala concurrency API is the `ExecutionContext` object. It's responsible for executing the `Future` objects started in an application. By default, it is supported by a `ForkJoinPool` of the Java Concurrency API, but you can create a different one. For most of your needs, you can use the default `ExecutionContext`, including the following sentence:

```
import ExecutionContext.Implicits.global
```

This sentence must be included in the import section of your code

Future objects in Scala

As we mentioned before, a `Future` stores a value that doesn't exist yet, but will be available at some point in the future. This value will be calculated by an asynchronous task that will be executed by another thread. Most of the time, you will specify that task when you define the `Future` and the task will be scheduled for its execution that can begin anytime in the future.

Futures don't use a blocking mechanism to get their result. You can associate one or more callback functions that will be executed when the `Future` has a value or an exception occurs during its process.

Futures have two possible return values. If the task ends its execution without errors and returns a value, we say that the Future has been successfully completed and will execute the successful callback. When a Future throws an Exception, we say that the Future failed its execution and the failure callback is executed.

The easiest way to create a Future is using the apply() method of the Future class. This method creates and schedules an asynchronous computation that will execute the code that is specified in the apply() method. This method returns the Future object.

We can associate the different Future callback functions to process its result. These callbacks are:

- onComplete: This function is called when the Future ends its execution, no matter if it ends successfully or with error. Inside the code of this function, you should include code to distinguish if the Future finished with error or not.
- onSuccess: This function is called when the Future ends its execution successfully.
- onFailure: This function is called when the Future ends its execution throwing an exception.

Let's see some examples of how to work with Futures in Scala. Create a class named Task and a method named doAction(). This method will receive a String and an Int as parameters and will return a String. Internally, it writes information about the Thread that is executing the task, sleeps the thread for the number of seconds specified in the parameters, and returns a String object:

```
class Task {
  def doAction(name : String, number: Int) : String = {
    var result : String = "";
    println(Thread.currentThread().getName()+": "+name+": Starting
                                                        execution");
    TimeUnit.SECONDS.sleep(number);
    println(Thread.currentThread().getName()+": "+name+": End
                                                        execution");
    result = name +" has been sleeping for " + number + " seconds ";
    return result;
  }
}
```

Now, let's make some tests with the `Future` class. First, include all the necessary classes for this example and create an object named `TestConcurrency` with the `main()` method:

```
import scala.concurrent.ExecutionContext
import java.util.concurrent.ThreadPoolExecutor
import java.util.concurrent.Executors
import scala.concurrent.Future
import ExecutionContext.Implicits.global
import scala.util.{Success, Failure}
import java.util.concurrent.TimeUnit


object TestConcurrency {
    def main(args: Array[String]) {
```

Then, create 10 `Future` objects using the `Future` class. Each `Future` will create a `Task` object and call the `doAction()` method:

```
for (i  <- 1 to 10 ) {
  val result : Future[String] = Future {
    var task : Task = new Task();
    task.doAction("Task "+i,i);
  }
```

Then, associate the `onComplete` callback to the result `Future` object. If the `Future` finishes with an `Exception` (case `Failure`), we write a message. Otherwise, we write the value returned by the `Future`:

```
    result onComplete {
      case Success(value) => println(value)
      case Failure(e) => println("An error has occured: "
                                 +e.getMessage)
    }
  }
  TimeUnit.SECONDS.sleep(20)
  }
}
```

The following screenshot shows the output of an execution of this example:

```
ForkJoinPool-1-worker-5: Task 9: Starting execution
ForkJoinPool-1-worker-1: Task 6: End execution
Task 6 has been sleeping for 6 seconds
ForkJoinPool-1-worker-1: Task 10: Starting execution
ForkJoinPool-1-worker-3: Task 7: End execution
Task 7 has been sleeping for 7 seconds
ForkJoinPool-1-worker-7: Task 8: End execution
Task 8 has been sleeping for 8 seconds
ForkJoinPool-1-worker-5: Task 9: End execution
Task 9 has been sleeping for 9 seconds
ForkJoinPool-1-worker-1: Task 10: End execution
Task 10 has been sleeping for 10 seconds
```

Now, create a class named `TestConcurrency2`. This class is similar to the `TestConcurrency` class, but with one important difference. In this case, we use two different callback functions. The `onSuccess()` callback function that will be called when the `Future` ends successfully. The `onFailure()` method will be called if the `Future` ends with an `Exception`:

```scala
import scala.concurrent.ExecutionContext
import java.util.concurrent.ThreadPoolExecutor
import java.util.concurrent.Executors
import scala.concurrent.Future
import ExecutionContext.Implicits.global
import scala.util.{Success, Failure}
import java.util.concurrent.TimeUnit

object TestConcurrency2 {
  def main(args: Array[String]) {
    for (i  <- 1 to 10 ) {
      val result : Future[String] = Future {
        var task : Task = new Task();
        task.doAction("Task "+i,i);
      }
      result onSuccess {
        case value => println(value);
      }
      result onFailure {
        case e => println("An error has ocurred: "+e.getMessage);
      }
    }
    TimeUnit.SECONDS.sleep(20)
  }
}
```

Now we're going to implement the same version, but using our `ExecutionContext`.
Create a class named `TestConcurrency3`. To create the `ExecutionContext` object, use the
`fromExecutor()` method of the `ExecutionContext` class. We pass these methods an
`Executor` object that will be used to execute the tasks of the `ExecutionContext`. We use
the `newFixedThreadPool()` method of the `Executors` class to create an `Executor` with
10 execution threads:

```
import scala.concurrent.ExecutionContext
import java.util.concurrent.ThreadPoolExecutor
import java.util.concurrent.Executors
import scala.concurrent.Future
import scala.util.{Success, Failure}
import java.util.concurrent.TimeUnit

object TestConcurrency3 {
  def main(args: Array[String]) {
    implicit val ec : ExecutionContext = ExecutionContext
                     .fromExecutor(Executors.newFixedThreadPool(10));
    for (i   <- 1 to 10 ) {
      val result : Future[String] = Future {
        var task : Task = new Task();
        task.doAction("Task "+i,i);
      }
      result onSuccess {
        case value => println(value);
      }
      result onFailure {
        case e => println("An error has ocurred: "+e.getMessage);
      }
    }
    TimeUnit.SECONDS.sleep(20)
  }
}
```

Now, let's make a test about what happens when a `Future` throws an `Exception`. Create a
class named `Task` and add to it a method named `doAction()` that receives two parameters,
a `String` named name, and an `Int` named number. If number is equal to three, the
`doAction()` method throws an `Exception`. Otherwise, we follow the same behavior of the
`Task` class explained before:

```
class Task {
  def doAction(name : String, number: Int) : String = {
    var result : String = "";
    if (number == 3) {
      throw new Exception("Error");
    }
```

```
    println(Thread.currentThread().getName()+": "+name+": Starting
                                            exeuction");
    TimeUnit.SECONDS.sleep(number);
    println(Thread.currentThread().getName()+": "+name+": End
                                            exeuction");
    result = name +" has been sleeping for " + number + " seconds ";
    return result;
  }
}
```

Then, we create the TestConcurrency class that creates 10 Future objects and associate to them the onComplete() callback:

```
object TestConcurrency {
  def main(args: Array[String]) {
    // First example with error
    for (i   <- 1 to 10 ) {
      val result : Future[String] = Future {
        var task : Task = new Task();
        task.doAction("Task "+i,i);
      }
      result onComplete {
        case Success(value) => println(value)
        case Failure(e) => println("An error has occured: "
                                        +e.getMessage)
      }
    }
    TimeUnit.SECONDS.sleep(20)
  }
}
```

The following screenshot shows the output of an execution of this example:

```
ForkJoinPool-1-worker-5: Task 1: Starting execution
ForkJoinPool-1-worker-1: Task 2: Starting execution
An error has occured: Error
ForkJoinPool-1-worker-3: Task 4: Starting execution
ForkJoinPool-1-worker-7: Task 5: Starting execution
```

When the doAction() method is executed with the parameter 3, the method throws an Exception and the callback associated with that Future executes the Failure case of the onComplete() method, writing the error message you can see in the preceding screenshot.

In the previous examples, we have associated only one callback per event (success or failure), but you can associate more than one callback per event. Let's see an example. You can use one of the previous `Task` objects, but let's create a new `TestConcurrency` class. In this case, we associate the `onComplete()` and `onSuccess()` callback functions to each `Future`. You can even associate more than one callback of the same type (more than one `onComplete()`, `onSuccess()` or `onFailure()`) to one `Future`:

```
object TestConcurrency {
  def main(args: Array[String]) {
    for (i  <- 1 to 10 ) {
      val result : Future[String] = Future {
        var task : Task = new Task();
        task.doAction("Task "+i,i);
      }
      result onComplete {
        case Success(value) => println(value)
        case Failure(e) => println("An error has occured: "
                                +e.getMessage)
      }
      result onSuccess {
        case value => println("Second callback: "+value);
      }
    }
    TimeUnit.SECONDS.sleep(20)
  }
}
```

The following screenshot shows the output of an execution of this example:

```
Task 7 has been sleeping for 7 seconds
ForkJoinPool-1-worker-7: Task 8: End exeuction
Second callback: Task 8 has been sleeping for 8 seconds
Task 8 has been sleeping for 8 seconds
ForkJoinPool-1-worker-5: Task 9: End exeuction
Task 9 has been sleeping for 9 seconds
Second callback: Task 9 has been sleeping for 9 seconds
ForkJoinPool-1-worker-3: Task 10: End exeuction
Task 10 has been sleeping for 10 seconds
Second callback: Task 10 has been sleeping for 10 seconds
```

Another option that `Future` objects give us is to link the execution of two futures; that is to say, they make sure that a `Future` starts its execution after the end of the execution of the other `Future`, and uses the result of the first one as a parameter in the second one. Let's see an example of how to use this functionality.

First, create a class named `Step1` with a method named `doAction()` that receives a `String` and a number as parameters and returns a `String`:

```
class Step1 {
  def doAction(name : String, number: Int) : String = {
    var result : String = "";
    println(Thread.currentThread().getName()+": "+name+": Step 1:
                                Starting execution");
    TimeUnit.SECONDS.sleep(number);
    println(Thread.currentThread().getName()+": "+name+": Step 1: End
                                exeuction");
    result = name +" has been sleeping for " + number + " seconds ";
    return result;
  }
}
```

Then, create a class named `Step2` similar to the previous one:

```
class Step2 {
  def doAction(name: String, msg : String) : String = {
    var result : String = "";
    println(Thread.currentThread().getName()+": "+name+": Step 2:
                                Starting execution");

    result = name +" has executed Step 2: "+msg;
    println(Thread.currentThread().getName()+": "+name+": Step 2: End
                                exeuction");
    return result;
  }
}
```

Finally, create an object named `TestConcurrency` with a `main()` method and a loop that will be executed 10 times:

```
object TestConcurrency {
  def main(args: Array[String]) {

    for (i  <- 1 to 10 ) {
```

Then, create the first `Future` that will create an object of the `Step1` class and call the `doAction()` method:

```
var name : String = "Task "+i;
val result : Future[String] = Future {
  var task : Step1 = new Step1();
  task.doAction(name,i);
}
```

Then, link a `Future` with the result Future object using the `map()` function. This future creates an object of the `Step2` class and calls the `doAction()` method:

```
val result2 = result map { value =>
  var task : Step2 = new Step2();
  task.doAction(name, value);
}
```

The value parameter specified in the body of this `Future` is the result of the first one.

Finally, associate an `onSuccess()` callback with the second `Future` to write the result in the console. The following screenshot shows the output of an execution of this example:

```
ForkJoinPool-1-worker-1: Task 8: Step 2: End exeuction
The output is: Task 8 has executed Step 2: Task 8 has been sleeping for 8 seconds
ForkJoinPool-1-worker-5: Task 9: Step 1: End exeuction
ForkJoinPool-1-worker-7: Task 9: Step 2: Starting execution
ForkJoinPool-1-worker-7: Task 9: Step 2: End exeuction
The output is: Task 9 has executed Step 2: Task 9 has been sleeping for 9 seconds
ForkJoinPool-1-worker-3: Task 10: Step 1: End exeuction
ForkJoinPool-1-worker-3: Task 10: Step 2: Starting execution
ForkJoinPool-1-worker-3: Task 10: Step 2: End exeuction
The output is: Task 10 has executed Step 2: Task 10 has been sleeping for 10 seconds
```

You can see how the second `Future` doesn't start its execution until the first one has finished its execution.

Promises

A **Promise** is a mechanism that can be used to complete a `Future`. First, we create an object of the `Promise` class and then we use that object to create the `Future` this promise will complete. We can associate callback functions with that `Future` so, when we assign a value to the `Promise` using the success or failure methods, the `Future` is completed and the callback functions will be executed.

Let's see an example of how this mechanism works. Create an object named `TestConcurrency` with a `main()` method and create a `Promise` and a `Future` object:

```
object TestConcurrency {

  def main(args: Array[String]) {

    val promise : Promise[String] = Promise[String]()
    val future : Future[String] = promise.future;
```

We use the `Promise` constructor to create the `Promise` object and the `future()` method of the `Promise` object to create the `Future` associated with that `Promise`.

Now, let's associate a callback function to the `future` object:

```
future onSuccess {
  case value => println("The future has been completed: "+value)
}
```

After that, we executed another `Future` to complete the promise. In this case, we use the `success()` method to assign a value to the `Promise` and complete the `Future`:

```
Future {
  promise success "Hola Mundo";
}
```

Finally, we wait for the finalization of the `Future` for 10 seconds using the `ready()` method of the `Await` class:

```
    Await.ready(future, 10 seconds);
  }
}
```

When you execute this example, you will see the message written by the `onSuccess()` function. When you execute the success method of the `Promise`, the future is completed and its `onSuccess()` callback is executed.

Summary

Java is not the only programming language that you can use to make programs to the JVM. There are a lot of different programming languages, of different paradigms, that can be used for that purpose. Most of this has its own mechanism to implement concurrent applications.

In this chapter, we have seen how you can implement concurrent applications using three languages of the JVM. First, Clojure, which is an implementation of the Lisp functional programming language that offers different mechanisms to write concurrency applications as Atoms, agents, references, delays, futures, and promises. Then, Groovy with the GPars library, offers us a lot of different possibilities with its actors, its dataflows, and its concurrent data structures. Finally, we have Scala and its concurrency model based on Futures and Promises.

Index

Made in the USA
Middletown, DE
25 January 2022